365 TECHNICAL SERIES

MODERN IT INFRASTRUCTURE AND OPERATIONS

SYSTEMS, CLOUD, SERVICE MANAGEMENT, AND RESILIENCE

AMMAR AL ALOUSI

MODERN IT INFRASTRUCTURE AND OPERATIONS
FIRST EDITION

management and the foundational disciplines of IT project management, including methodology selection, project planning, and scope and business case development.

Frameworks and standards are referenced throughout where they apply, including ITIL, NIST, ISO, PMI, and SAFe, with attribution to their published sources. The goal is not to reproduce those frameworks, which exist in their authoritative forms elsewhere, but to show how they apply in day-to-day IT management decisions.

This book is the first volume in a two-part series. Volume 1 establishes the foundation: how to build, govern, secure, and operate a stable IT environment, and how to deliver the projects that change it. Volume 2, *IT Project Delivery and Operational Excellence: Governance, Execution, Metrics, and Continuous Improvement*, builds on this foundation with the disciplines that mature IT organizations operate at scale: complex project execution, portfolio management, performance metrics programs, continuous improvement, and IT organizational capability maturity.

If **this** volume answers the question "How do I build and run a stable, well-governed IT environment?", **the second** answers "How do I deliver consistently, improve systematically, and lead an organization that gets measurably better over time?"

The two volumes are designed to be used together. This is the foundation. The second is the operating system you build on top of it.

To my beloved wife, whose unwavering support and love make every journey worthwhile.

To my daughter and my two sons, who inspire me every day with their curiosity, strength, and dreams.

And to my father, Dr. Faiz Al Alousi, whom I lost too soon, but whose wisdom, guidance, and legacy continue to shape my path. Your presence remains a guiding light in my journey, and I remain committed to carrying your values forward.

Acknowledgments

This book was written from years of experience working alongside professionals responsible for building, operating, supporting, and improving modern technology environments. Much of what is covered in these pages comes from real operational challenges, long nights, critical incidents, large-scale projects, and the constant effort required to keep systems reliable and businesses running.

My appreciation goes to the technicians, engineers, project managers, operations teams, and technology leaders whose professionalism and dedication continue to drive the industry forward. The work done behind the scenes in infrastructure, operations, service management, and support is often invisible to most people, yet it remains essential to nearly every organization today.

I would also like to thank the colleagues, mentors, and teams I have worked with throughout my career. The lessons learned through collaboration, accountability, leadership, and problem-solving helped shape both the perspective and practical approach behind this book.

To the professionals and students continuing to grow their knowledge and improve their craft, thank you for helping push the field forward. Curiosity, discipline, and continuous learning remain some of the most valuable qualities in technology.

Finally, thank you to my family and close friends for their patience, encouragement, and support throughout the writing process. Completing a project of this scale would not have been possible without that foundation of support.

Published in the United States of America
10 9 8 7 6 5 4 3 2 1

LIBRARY OF CONGRESS CATALOGING-IN-PUBLICATION DATA
LCCN: 2026912394

Names: Ammar Al Alousi, author.
Title: Modern IT Infrastructure and Operations: Systems, Cloud, Service Management, and Resilience / Ammar Al Alousi.
Description: Virginia: [2026] | Includes bibliographical references and index.

ISBN (Hardcover): 979-8-9922795-6-6
ISBN (Paperback): 979-8-9922795-5-9

CONTENTS

INTRODUCTION

Infrastructure, Operations, and Service Foundations

The IT manager role has expanded faster than the language used to describe it. The job now spans leadership, infrastructure, security, service delivery, project management, governance, and financial accountability, often in environments that change faster than any single person can track.

Most books written for this audience cover one of those areas in depth. The result is technical books that assume leadership is already in place, leadership books that assume the technical foundation is already understood, and project management books that treat the operational environment as a stable backdrop. Practitioners who actually do this work need all of them, integrated.

This book was written to be that integrated reference. It covers what an IT manager needs to understand to lead, design, operate, and improve a modern IT environment, written from operational practice rather than abstract theory. The chapters move from leadership and governance through infrastructure and operations, into security and continuity, and finally into service management and project delivery. Each chapter is grounded in real operational decisions, with case examples that show how the concepts apply when the environment is messy and the deadline is tight.

The book is structured in four layers that build on each other. The first layer addresses the modern IT manager role, IT and business strategy alignment, building high-performing teams, and IT governance. The second covers infrastructure and operational disciplines: servers and storage, networking, data center operations, cloud and virtualization, and monitoring and capacity planning. The third addresses security, compliance, risk, and business continuity. The fourth covers IT service

Part I

IT LEADERSHIP AND STRATEGIC FOUNDATIONS

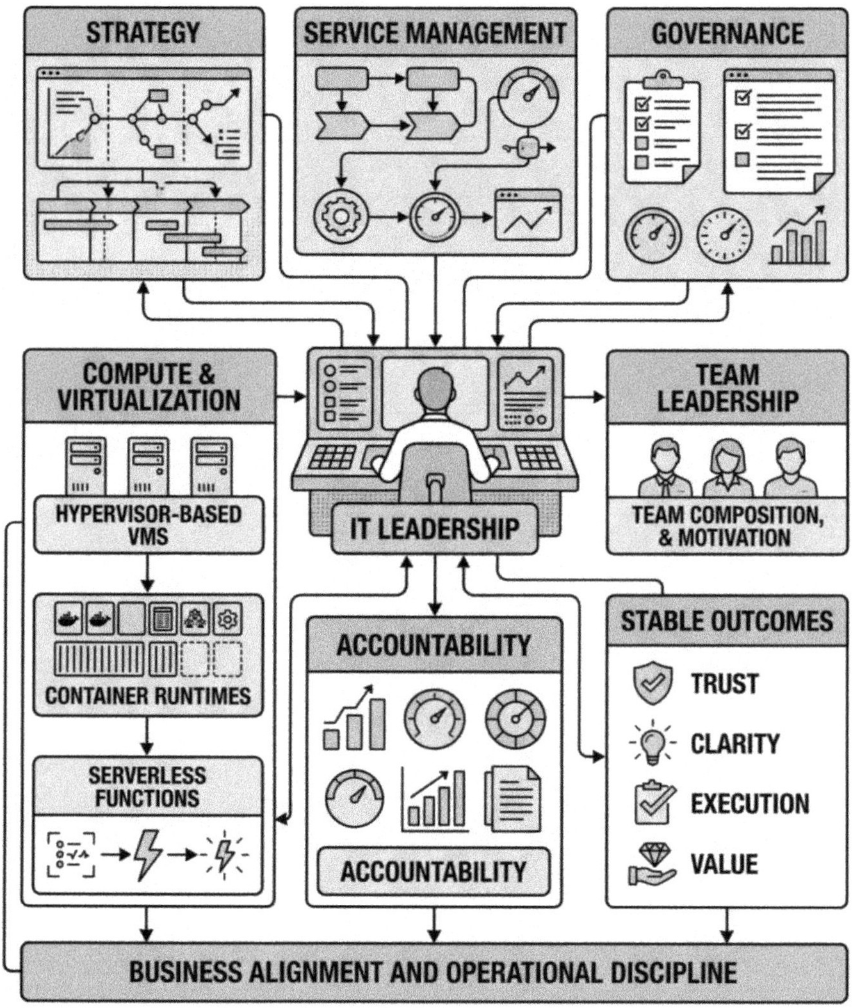
STRATEGY
SERVICE MANAGEMENT
GOVERNANCE
COMPUTE & VIRTUALIZATION
HYPERVISOR-BASED VMS
CONTAINER RUNTIMES
SERVERLESS FUNCTIONS
IT LEADERSHIP
TEAM LEADERSHIP
TEAM COMPOSITION, & MOTIVATION
ACCOUNTABILITY
ACCOUNTABILITY
STABLE OUTCOMES
TRUST
CLARITY
EXECUTION
VALUE
BUSINESS ALIGNMENT AND OPERATIONAL DISCIPLINE

Chapter 1

INTRODUCTION TO IT INFRASTRUCTURE AND SERVICE MANAGEMENT

The IT manager role has changed faster than most job descriptions have kept up with. It used to mean keeping systems running and support queues moving. Today it means managing risk, setting priorities, and making decisions that directly shape how the business operates. Today's IT managers are involved in hiring, budgeting, vendor strategy, security posture, user experience, and modernization decisions.

They operate in environments where failures impact customer satisfaction, revenue, and brand credibility. They must understand software development, cloud architecture, compliance, automation, infrastructure design, and leadership dynamics, often at the same time.

The modern IT manager carries a different weight than the title used to imply. Deep technical knowledge still matters, but the job is fundamentally a business leadership role now, one where technology fluency is the tool, not the product. They must explain technical issues in business terms, build teams capable of navigating change, and design systems that support long-term organizational goals.

This chapter starts from a baseline assumption: the infrastructure is in place, operations are running, and the team has a handle on day-to-day execution. What follows is not a guide to building systems. It is a guide to leading the people and decisions that surround them. The technical foundations get their own treatment elsewhere in this book. Here, the focus is on what the role demands once reliability, scale, and operational maturity stop being purely engineering problems and start showing up on the manager's desk.

Figure 1.1: Evolution of the IT Manager's Role

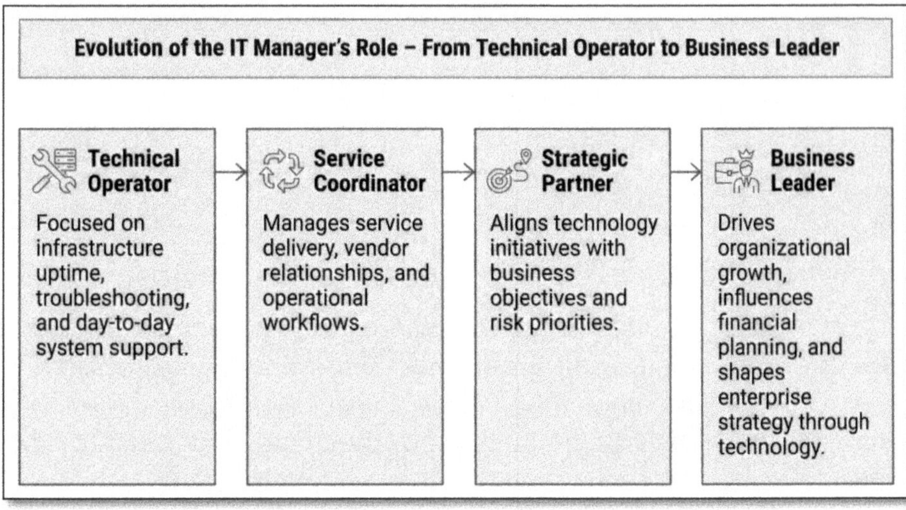

From Technical Operator to Strategic Business Partner

For years, IT managers were evaluated mostly on uptime, ticket resolution, and hardware reliability. The expectations were operational and immediate, keep services stable, restore them quickly when they fail, and keep support queues moving. In that world, the manager's value was proven through execution consistency.

That definition is too narrow for how most organizations run today. Technology is tied directly to revenue capture, customer trust, regulatory posture, and operational continuity. When a critical system slows down, fails, or becomes insecure, the impact rarely stays inside IT. It shows up as missed transactions, delayed fulfillment, chargebacks, compliance findings, or customer churn. The modern IT manager is expected to prevent those outcomes, not just repair them after the fact.

This is what people mean when they call the role a 'strategic business partner.' It is not a title upgrade or a signal to stop getting into the details. It means making decisions that hold up when the business is under pressure. You need to explain why a specific technical choice is the right tradeoff across cost, speed, resilience, and risk, using language leadership can act on. The modern manager still needs technical depth, they just apply it in a broader business context.

Key changes that drive this shift:

1. **Accountability expands beyond technology health:** You are responsible for service outcomes, not just infrastructure status. A healthy server does not matter if the service still fails during peak usage, a change window still creates customer impact, or a vendor dependency still creates outages you cannot control.

2. **Decision-making moves from "can we build it" to "should we build it this way":** Many solutions are technically possible. The modern manager must choose designs that the organization can operate reliably, govern consistently, and sustain financially. The question becomes: What is the long-term operational cost, what are the failure modes, who owns it end to end, and how quickly can the team recover when something breaks?

3. **Communication becomes part of the job, not a side task:** IT managers increasingly brief leadership, finance, audit, and business owners. That requires turning technical realities into clear options. Instead of presenting raw metrics, you explain impact, probability, and tradeoffs, then recommend a direction. If you cannot explain why a technical decision matters to the business, you will lose budget, time, and confidence.

4. **Collaboration extends past IT boundaries:** Modern IT work is cross-functional by default. Security, compliance, procurement, product, facilities, and finance all influence delivery. The manager's effectiveness is often determined by how well they align these groups, set shared expectations, and keep accountability clear.

How the role has shifted

Category	Traditional IT Manager	Modern IT Manager
Primary Focus	System uptime	Business value, risk reduction, innovation
Scope	Infrastructure & support	Cloud, automation, data, product, security
Decision Basis	Technical constraints	Financial, strategic, regulatory, operational
Collaboration	Mostly within IT	Cross-functional, executive-facing
Innovation	Low risk appetite	Required to compete

The table is a practical snapshot. Uptime still matters, but it is not the end objective by itself. What matters is stable delivery of business services under real conditions, growth, constant change, vendor constraints, security requirements, and the limits of teams that have to run and support the environment.

What Modern IT Managers Must Deliver

- Tie technology projects to revenue, efficiency, or customer experience
- Manage risk and compliance with clear reporting
- Influence executive decisions using data
- Lead global, hybrid, or distributed teams
- Drive automation, cloud adoption, and operational maturity

handoff timing) and tied those services to clear operational thresholds. They then pulled a quarter's worth of incidents and changes and categorized each event by impact window, customer-facing symptoms, and recovery driver. The goal was not to overwhelm leadership with detail, but to show repeated patterns: the same failure modes, the same manual steps, the same gaps in detection, and the same delays waiting on the right person.

Next, they translated that pattern into a set of tradeoffs leadership could choose from. Option one was "keep current operations and accept the current risk profile," with the expected downtime trend and support cost left visible. Option two was targeted automation and standardization in the highest-repeat areas, focused on reducing human dependency during incidents and cutting recovery time. Option three included redundancy improvements for the most business-critical paths, with a clear cost increase and a clear reduction in the blast radius of failures. Each option included what would change operationally, what would not, and what success would look like in the next 60 to 90 days.

Finally, they set measurement rules in advance. Leadership agreed that success would be judged using a small set of outcomes, reduction in repeat incidents, lower average impact duration, improved change success rate, and fewer escalations that required senior engineers after hours. That alignment removed the usual debate about whether the investment "worked." When downtime dropped and the same incidents stopped repeating, the automation and governance work was seen as a business win, not an IT upgrade.

Balancing Technology, People, and Process as a Leader

Most strong IT organizations come down to three things working together: technology, people, and process. The modern IT manager has to keep rebalancing those three factors so operations stay stable without turning delivery into molasses. When one area gets all the attention, the other two usually slip quietly until the environment hits a breaking point.

This is why leadership in IT is rarely about finding a perfect system, it is about managing tradeoffs. A team can move fast for a short period by cutting process, but eventually change failures and repeat incidents pile up. A team can run with heavy process for a while, but delivery slows and workarounds spread. A team can buy better tools, but without training and clear operating standards, the tools become another layer of noise.

The practical goal is not to maximize each pillar independently. The goal is to keep the three pillars aligned enough that the organization can deliver work predictably while absorbing incidents, audits, turnover, and growth without constant firefighting.

Technology

The modern technology stack includes hybrid cloud environments, DevOps pipelines, container platforms, observability tools, and AI-driven analytics. IT managers must:

- Evaluate when to modernize vs. maintain legacy systems
- Balance innovation with security and stability
- Standardize architectures to simplify support
- Ensure systems are scalable before growth creates bottlenecks

What changes at the manager level is how technology decisions are framed. The question is not "What is the newest platform," it is "What can this team operate reliably with the talent and time we have." Modernization only pays off if it reduces failure modes, shortens delivery cycles, or lowers operating cost without creating hidden complexity.

A useful way to pressure-test a tech decision is to run it through operational questions:

- Who will own it day to day, and what happens when that person is off?

- What does a failure look like, and how quickly can we detect it?
- What is the rollback plan when a release goes sideways?
- How do we patch it, monitor it, and prove compliance when asked?
- What dependencies are we taking on, vendor, network, identity, or other teams?

Standardization is where managers usually win or lose. A slightly less flexible architecture that is repeatable, well-documented, and easy to monitor often beats a custom design that only one engineer understands. In mature environments, the "best" design is the one that can be supported consistently across shifts, regions, and staff changes.

People

Your team is not a single unit. Cloud engineers, network architects, developers, data analysts, security specialists, and service desk staff each bring different training, different priorities, and different expectations about how work should run. You must:

- Build skill development plans
- Ensure diversity of thought and experience
- Promote psychological safety and transparent communication
- Maintain morale during high-pressure periods
- Reduce silos by rotating responsibilities and fostering knowledge sharing

People is where most IT orgs feel stable or unstable, regardless of tooling. A technically strong team can still underperform if the operating norms are weak, priorities shift daily, or communication breaks down under pressure. The manager's job is to create conditions where good engineers can do good work without spending half their energy on confusion.

That starts with clarity:

- Clear ownership, who owns the service, who owns the change, who owns the incident bridge
- Clear expectations, what "done" means, what quality gates exist, what gets escalated and when
- Clear priorities, what matters this week, what gets deprioritized, what deadlines are real
- Clear communication, how updates are shared, where decisions are recorded, and what channels are used for what purpose so that information does not live in private messages or get lost between shifts

Skill development needs to be tied to what the organization actually runs, not generic training plans. If the environment is hybrid, people need competence in identity, networking boundaries, monitoring, and release workflows across both on-prem and cloud. If the environment is container-heavy, engineers need operational confidence, not just deployment basics, troubleshooting, logging, scaling behavior, and safe rollbacks.

Silo reduction is not a team-building exercise, it is a resilience strategy. When only one person understands a platform, every incident becomes a staffing problem. Rotations, paired work, and shared runbooks reduce that risk. The goal is not to turn everyone into a specialist in everything. The goal is to ensure the organization can function when the usual expert is unavailable.

Process

- Strong people and capable tools still produce unstable outcomes when process is weak or inconsistently applied
- Consistent procedures remove guesswork and produce repeatable results
- Change control disciplines reduce the frequency of self-inflicted outages

- When incidents do happen, a practiced response process shortens the time to resolution and limits customer impact
- Documentation removes dependence on individual memory and keeps the team functional when people rotate out.
- Frameworks like ITIL, COBIT, and ISO give governance structures a common language and tie controls to clear accountability

Process is where stability is built, but it is also where organizations get stuck if they treat process as paperwork instead of operational control. Mature process should reduce load on the team, not increase it. If it adds steps without reducing incidents, confusion, or rework, it is not serving its purpose.

Strong process usually shows up in a few concrete ways:

- Changes are planned, reviewed, and deployed consistently, with rollback ready before the change starts
- Incidents have a clear playbook, roles are known, communication is consistent, and actions are tracked
- Repeated failures lead to fixes, not just postmortems
- Documentation is current enough that a new engineer can execute basic tasks without tribal knowledge
- Metrics are trusted and used to drive decisions, not to punish teams

Governance frameworks only help when they are mapped to daily work. If a control exists, it should be clear where evidence comes from, who owns it, and how it is sustained without last-minute scrambling before audits.

How to keep the triangle balanced in real operations

The "balance" problem usually shows up as recurring symptoms:

- Lots of tools, but slow recovery and poor visibility, technology is ahead of process and training

- Strong engineers, but frequent outages during changes, people are strong but process is weak
- Heavy approval layers, but shadow IT and workarounds, process is too rigid for delivery reality
- Stable operations, but the backlog never shrinks, technology modernization is lagging and debt is compounding

The manager's job is to spot these patterns early and rebalance. Sometimes that means slowing delivery for two sprints to clean up change practices and documentation. Sometimes it means simplifying the toolset and standardizing architectures. Sometimes it means investing in training and rotations to reduce dependency risk.

Figure 1.2: The IT Leadership Triangle

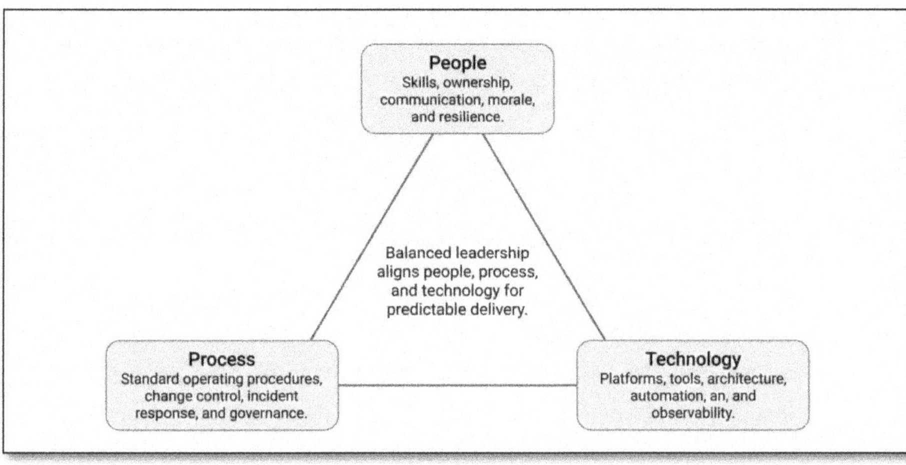

Leadership in a Hybrid IT Environment

Hybrid IT environments are rarely designed on purpose. They accumulate: a data center that predates a cloud migration, SaaS tools adopted outside IT's control, remote teams operating under different security policies, and platforms that were never built to talk to each other. The IT leader's job is to keep that environment governable and its performance visible, even when the architecture was never meant to be coherent.

Challenges of Hybrid Operations

- Fragmented tooling across environments
- Different compliance obligations in each location
- Rapid speed of cloud deployments
- Coordination across time zones and cultures
- Decentralization that makes governance more difficult

Leadership Capabilities Needed

- **Clarity:** Make responsibilities explicit and simplify complex topics for all stakeholders.
- **Coordination:** Ensure teams follow unified standards despite operating in diverse environments.
- **Visibility:** Deploy centralized observability that spans both cloud and on-premise systems.
- **Adaptability:** Switch seamlessly between technical detail and strategic messaging depending on the audience.
- **Cultural Awareness:** Manage teams by recognizing and accommodating different communication norms and expectations."

Case Example

A global e-commerce company running workloads in AWS, Azure, and two regional data centers shifted to a centralized monitoring and governance model. MTTR dropped measurably in the first quarter after rollout, attributed directly to all teams following the same on-call structure and escalation runbook for the first time.

How the operating model was fixed (what the leader actually did)

The leader started by standardizing the incident workflow before touching tools. They defined one severity model tied to customer impact, then created a single on-call and escalation runbook that applied across AWS, Azure, and both data centers. Every major incident used the same roles (incident lead, primary responder, communications owner), the same bridge format, and the same handoff rules for follow-the-sun support.

Next, they cleaned up ownership. Each customer-facing service was mapped to a primary owner and a backup owner, with clear boundaries for when cloud teams vs data center teams were accountable. That eliminated the common hybrid failure pattern where teams debated responsibility while the outage clock kept running.

Only after that did they centralize monitoring. They kept existing tools where needed, but enforced a minimum standard for alert naming, required dashboards, and what signals proved service health. The result was that an outage looked the same regardless of where it happened, and escalations triggered the same way across regions. With confusion removed and handoffs predictable, MTTR dropped by 33%.

Communication and Influence Across the Organization

Modern IT leaders communicate with executives, engineers, vendors, auditors, HR, finance, and external partners. Effective communication is how you build trust, get the budget you need, and keep everyone on the same page.

Upward Communication (Executives)

- Translate technical outcomes into financial or operational impact
- Use concise KPI dashboards
- Present risks in business terms ("impact to customers," not "packet loss")
- Provide options and recommendations, not just data

Operational translation, turning technical work into business-facing outcomes

Technical focus area	What you are really protecting or enabling	What you validate in operations
Availability and resilience	Revenue continuity and customer trust	Service tiering, failover readiness, recovery tests, incident patterns
Change management maturity	Faster delivery with fewer self-inflicted outages	Change success rate, rollback quality, peer review discipline, release guardrails
Security and compliance controls	Reduced exposure, fewer audit surprises	Patch and vulnerability aging, access reviews, control evidence readiness
Observability and response	Faster detection and shorter impact windows	Coverage by critical services, alert quality, MTTR drivers, escalation effectiveness
Automation and standardization	Lower cost, fewer errors, scalable operations	Manual steps removed, runbook completeness, repeatability across environments

Case Example:

A regional IT leader restructured their data center operations around business KPIs instead of technical metrics. By linking system reliability to sales performance outcomes, they built a successful case for automation investment, and within two quarters, repeat incidents and total downtime had dropped significantly.

How the business case was won (what the manager actually did)
To secure funding, the manager stopped leading with technical pain points and instead built a short narrative around business exposure.

First, they selected two or three services that leadership already cared about (order processing, customer portal availability, and warehouse

Downward Communication (Teams)

- Clarify priorities and expectations
- Share the "why" behind decisions (engineers respond well to context)
- Celebrate wins publicly
- Correct problems privately and constructively

Lateral Communication (Partners and Peers)

- Collaborate with HR on staffing and training
- Coordinate with Finance on budgeting and forecasting
- Align with Operations and Product teams on roadmaps and dependencies

Pro Tip

Executives speak the language of risk and capital, not latency and patches. Before you walk into that meeting, swap every technical metric for a dollar sign or a risk level. Don't say, "We need to patch the server to fix a CVE." Say, "We need a 30-minute maintenance window to close a gap that could cost us $50k in compliance fines." If you can't tie the tech to the bottom line, you aren't ready to present it.

Figure 1.3: Cross-Functional Communication Flow for IT Leaders

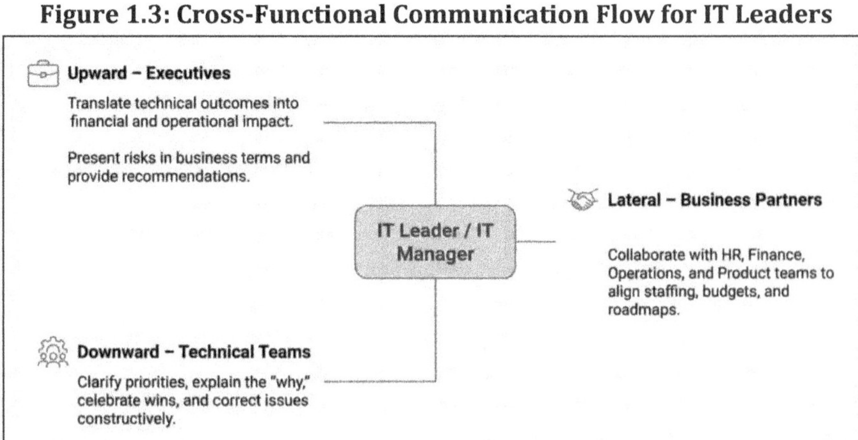

Building Credibility and Trust

Credibility does not come with the role. It has to be earned through consistent delivery, honest reporting, and the willingness to own failures in front of the people who matter. A job title opens the door; it does not keep it open.

Five Practices That Build Trust

1. **Deliver predictable results.** Meet SLAs, finish projects on time, and control operational risk. Reliability is leadership currency.
2. **Communicate accurately.** Share real metrics, even when performance dips. Honest reporting builds executive confidence.
3. **Engage stakeholders early.** Invite operations, finance, and security into planning. Surprises destroy alignment and credibility.
4. **Demonstrate technical and strategic competence.** Stay informed about modernization, security practices, and industry trends.
5. **Own failures and protect the team.** Take responsibility for breakdowns, then guide the team toward corrective action.

Case Example:

A data center manager inherited a team with low confidence from leadership. By creating weekly operational scorecards and sending transparent outage reviews, trust was rebuilt and the team began receiving budget support for long-overdue upgrades.

How credibility was rebuilt (what the manager actually did)
The manager made trust measurable. They defined a small weekly scorecard built around metrics leadership already cared about (availability by tier, incident severity counts, MTTR, change success rate, and backlog aging) and published it on a fixed cadence. The scorecard showed trends and top drivers, without excuses when performance dipped.

They also standardized outage communication. For every customer-impacting incident, they sent a short review within a set window using the same format each time: impact, timeline, cause, containment, and corrective actions with owners and due dates. Corrective actions were tracked like real work items until closed. Over a few weeks, leadership saw consistent reporting and visible follow-through, and budget support for long-delayed upgrades followed.

The IT Manager as a Change Leader

Every system rollout, cloud migration, or process change asks something of the people involved: new workflows, new tools, or different ways of working that conflict with how things have always been done. The manager's job is to reduce the friction in that transition without pretending the friction is not real.

Principles of Effective Change Leadership

- Communicate the purpose of the change
- Include engineers and end users early
- Address resistance calmly and factually
- Provide training and clear documentation
- Measure post-implementation results

Change Leadership Framework Table

Stage	What It Means	IT Example
Communicating the change	People understand what is changing, why it matters, and what the operational impact will be	Announcing a new service desk platform with a clear rationale and timeline

Change Leadership Framework Table (continued)

Stage	What It Means	IT Example
Building readiness	Teams have the training, documentation, and workflow clarity needed to operate in the new environment	Preparing engineers with updated procedures before the cutover date
Going live	The change is executed, the new system or process becomes active, and support is standing by	Migrating the ticketing system with rollback ready and on-call coverage in place
Locking in the new standard	The new behavior becomes the operational default, gaps are tracked and closed, and the old method is fully retired	Monitoring adoption metrics and closing remaining workflow exceptions

The Expanding Skill Set of Modern IT Managers

The modern IT manager needs a balanced portfolio of technical depth, strategic awareness, and leadership maturity.

Technical Skills

- Cloud architecture (AWS, Azure, GCP)
- Infrastructure as code, automation, DevOps
- Networking fundamentals, Zero Trust, segmentation
- Cybersecurity frameworks and compliance
- Observability, monitoring, and SRE principles

Strategic and Business Skills

- Budget ownership and cost analysis
- Vendor and contract management

- Risk assessment and mitigation planning
- Roadmapping and KPI design
- Forecasting future technical capacity needs

Leadership Skills

- Coaching, mentoring, and conflict resolution
- Emotional awareness and interpersonal maturity
- Delegation and accountability setting
- Cross-functional influence
- Succession planning and talent development

Competency Wheel

The competency model for a modern IT manager works like a wheel. Technical knowledge sits at the center, but it is not the whole role. From that core, the manager's effectiveness depends on how well that technical depth is applied across four surrounding domains: business alignment, leadership and communication, governance and risk management, and innovation and modernization. A gap in any one of those areas limits what the technical core can actually deliver.

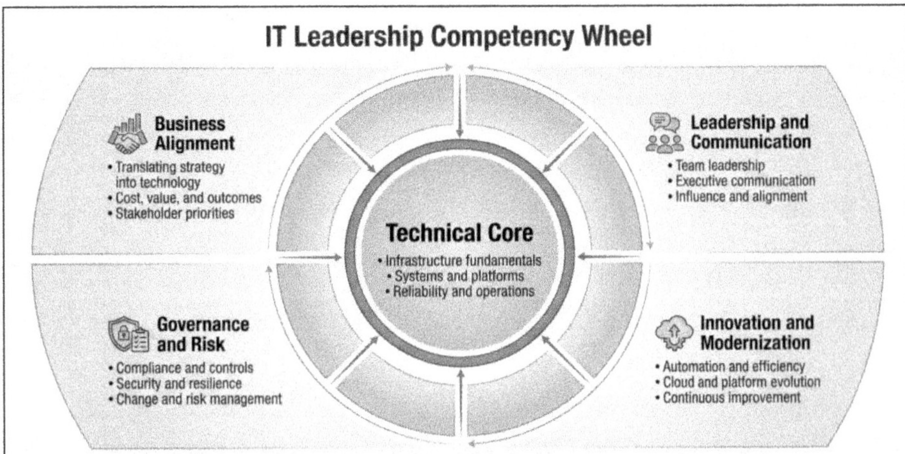

Modern IT leadership extends technical expertise into business alignment, governance, communication, and innovation.

Case Example:

cloud operations manager improved reliability by teaching every team member basic cost optimization techniques. Over the following year, cloud spend dropped noticeably, and engineers began taking broader ownership of service outcomes because they could see the direct connection between their design choices and operational cost.

How the skill shift was built (what the manager actually did)
The manager treated cost as an operational signal, not a finance-only topic. They identified a short list of repeat spend drivers that also created reliability noise (oversized compute, storage sprawl, excessive logging, always-on noncritical services) and ran brief working sessions where engineers learned to read their own service costs and tie them to design choices.

Then they made it routine. New services required a lightweight cost and reliability check before production, and incident reviews included a quick scan for cost side effects (runaway logs, inefficient scaling, failed retry loops). A simple monthly review highlighted the top avoidable patterns and the fixes already shipped. Over time, teams began owning both stability and spend, which is why reliability rose while cloud costs fell.

Building a Culture of Clarity and Accountability

You don't get a strong IT culture by accident. You have to build it on purpose.

Core Cultural Elements

- Clear documentation and knowledge sharing
- Consistent processes and expectations
- Transparency with metrics and performance
- Respect for expertise across all levels
- Shared ownership of results

Indicators of a Healthy IT Culture

- Low turnover
- High engagement in retrospectives
- Predictable on-call rotations
- Few escalations requiring leadership intervention

Conflict Management and Team Dynamics

Conflict is normal in tech. The best teams do not avoid it, they fix the problem fast and move on.

Patterns of Conflict You'll See

- Technical disagreements (architectures, tools, design choices)
- Personal friction (communication style clashes)
- Resource conflicts (time, priority, staffing limits)

Resolution Approach

1. Identify facts clearly
2. Listen to both perspectives
3. Focus on impact, not intention
4. Agree on changes and next steps
5. Document decisions for clarity

Conflict Resolution Matrix

Conflict Type	Signs	Leadership Response
Technical	Long debates on design	Facilitate, ask for data, guide to decision
Personal	Frustration, avoidance	Mediate privately, reset expectations
Process	Work slows down	Update workflow, clarify ownership

Case Example:

Two senior engineers disagreed on storage designs for a cloud migration. By focusing the conversation on business impact, performance, resilience, and cost, the manager turned a conflict into a data-driven decision.

How the conflict was resolved (what the manager actually did)
The manager stopped the debate from turning into a winner-loser argument. They asked both engineers to write a one-page comparison using the same template: target workload assumptions, performance requirements, failure modes, recovery approach, operational overhead, and cost range. Each engineer also had to list the top risks in their own proposal and how those risks would be monitored.

In the next meeting, the manager kept the discussion anchored to agreed constraints, customer impact, recovery expectations, and budget limits. When the engineers disagreed, they were required to point to a measurable factor (latency target, RPO/RTO, throughput, scaling behavior), not preference or past experience. The manager then chose a decision date, assigned an owner to validate the remaining unknowns with a short test plan, and documented the final call with the reasons and the conditions that would trigger a revisit later.

Pro Tip

Technical arguments often drag on because nobody wants to be "wrong." You can break a deadlock by asking both engineers to write a quick "pre-mortem" for their *own* preferred solution, listing exactly how and why it might fail. This forces them to stop defending their ego and start analyzing risk, which usually reveals the stronger option without making anyone feel like they lost the fight.

Managing Remote and Hybrid Teams

Distributed IT teams require structure, clarity, and deliberate communication. Remote work does not break teams by itself. What breaks teams is ambiguity, unclear ownership, and information that lives in private chats or in one person's head. When people are spread across time zones, small gaps turn into delays, duplicate work, or missed escalations.

The manager's job is to build a system where work can move forward even when people are offline. That means shifting from informal coordination to explicit coordination. Teams that operate well remotely are usually not "more connected," they are more predictable. Everyone knows where updates go, how decisions are made, and what "done" means.

Core risks in remote operations

- Silent blockers that sit for hours because nobody sees them
- Uneven workload where one region becomes the default escalation sink
- On-call fatigue when the same people get pulled into every incident
- Decision drift where different regions implement different standards
- Low context for new hires because knowledge is scattered

Best Practices

- **Document everything in shared systems:** Documentation is not a knowledge dump. It is the minimum set of artifacts that allow others to execute work without waiting. At a minimum, distributed teams need current runbooks, escalation paths, service ownership lists, and change procedures that match reality. If the documentation is outdated, people will stop trusting it and revert to private messaging.

- **Schedule overlap hours for live collaboration:** Overlap should be treated like a scarce resource. Use it for decision-making, incident coordination, and unblocking work that cannot move asynchronously. Avoid filling overlap time with status updates that could have been written.

- **Use concise video check-ins to maintain connection:** Short check-ins work when they are structured. The goal is alignment, not social time. Use them to clarify priorities, identify risks, and confirm ownership. If a meeting does not produce a decision, a handoff, or a clear next step, it will eventually be seen as overhead.

- **Rotate on-call fairly:** Rotation fairness is not just a morale question. It is a reliability question. An engineer who has been carrying the on-call load for weeks is not operating at full capacity. They respond more slowly, tolerate more ambiguity, and are more likely to make changes they would otherwise review more carefully. Load needs to be tracked across regions, and if one team is absorbing more incidents than others, that is a process or design problem that needs to be fixed.

- **Encourage asynchronous communication:** Asynchronous does not mean "send messages and hope." It means using defined channels and templates so updates can be consumed quickly. The standard should be: a teammate who wakes up later can understand what happened, what is being done, and what is needed without a live call.

Operating model, what good looks like

- Each service has a clear owner and a backup owner across regions
- Every incident has a single channel, a short timeline, and clear roles
- Decisions are recorded where the team actually works, not buried in chat

- Handoffs include current status, risk, and next action, not just a summary
- Work is prioritized using a visible queue, not informal requests

Workflow Example

A "follow-the-sun" support rotation where each region hands off active issues to the next using a standardized handoff checklist.

How the handoff checklist works (what is included)

- Incident or ticket ID, severity, and customer impact statement
- Current status and what has been ruled out
- Actions already taken and results observed
- Next action with owner expectations (what the next region should do first)
- Time-sensitive risks (change windows, vendor callbacks, SLA deadlines)
- Links to dashboards, logs, bridge notes, and relevant runbooks
- Explicit escalation trigger, what condition requires paging leadership

When this is done consistently, distributed teams stop relying on live coordination to stay aligned. Work progresses across time zones with fewer resets, fewer missed details, and fewer after-hours escalations caused by incomplete context.

Encouraging Innovation and Continuous Improvement

Most operational improvement does not come from large projects or platform replacements. It comes from the team consistently fixing the same class of problem until it stops recurring.

Methods That Work

- Allocate "innovation hours" each week
- Run blameless post-incident reviews
- Allow experimentation in sandboxed environments
- Encourage automation of repetitive tasks
- Build dashboards that highlight improvement opportunities

Case Example

A network operations team dedicated one hour each week to reviewing recurring incidents. Through small, targeted process updates and automation, they steadily reduced the volume of repeat incidents over several months until the pattern had largely stopped recurring.

How the improvement habit was built (what the manager actually did)
The manager treated the hour as a fixed operational commitment. The scope stayed narrow: only recurring incidents, only items the team could influence, and only fixes that could be completed within a week or two.

Each session used the same routine. The team selected one repeat pattern, identified the trigger and the point of failure in detection or response, then shipped one concrete change, a monitoring adjustment, a runbook update, a workflow tweak, or a small automation. Every change had an owner and a due date, and was tracked in the same work queue as production tasks. Over time, small fixes stacked up and repeat incidents dropped.

Succession Planning and Knowledge Retention

Losing a single expert should not destabilize the organization. If one person's departure can stall change windows, slow incident recovery, or block audit evidence, that dependency is not a staffing reality to manage around. It is an operational risk that needs to be treated like one. Succession planning is how you reduce that risk before it turns into an outage, a missed audit, or a long-term delivery slowdown.

This section is not about replacing people. It is about making sure the work can continue predictably when roles change. Promotions, transfers, and resignations are normal. The failure happens when knowledge and authority are concentrated in one individual and the organization treats that concentration as "experience" instead of a single point of failure.

Actions to Strengthen Continuity

- ✓ **Identify critical roles:** Start with roles that carry high blast radius. These usually include infrastructure owners, identity and access administrators, network and firewall authorities, database leads, monitoring owners, and service desk management. A role is critical if it is required to restore service, approve changes, or provide evidence for audits and compliance.

- ✓ **Assign primary and backup owners:** A backup is not a name in a spreadsheet. A backup is someone who can execute the work with minimal help. If the backup cannot run the change, handle the incident, or complete the control evidence, the role is still uncovered.

- ✓ **Maintain current documentation:** Documentation only has value if it reflects reality. For critical services, the minimum requirement is runbooks that include prerequisites, step-by-step actions, validation checks, rollback steps, and escalation triggers. If a runbook cannot be used during an incident, it is not a runbook.

- ✓ **Cross-train regularly:** Cross-training has to include execution. Observation alone creates false confidence. The fastest way to verify knowledge transfer is to have the backup complete real tasks and changes under supervision, then rotate responsibility until the backup can perform independently.

- ✓ **Build internal career pathways:** Succession gets easier when people can grow into roles rather than jump into them. Define progression paths that include technical expectations, operational ownership, and leadership responsibilities. People will prepare for roles when the path is visible.

Succession Template

Role	Primary Owner	Backup	Documentation Status	Next Review
Senior Network Architect	Sarah Jenkins	Michael Ross (Jr. Architect)	Complete (Verified v4.0 Last Month)	Q1 2026
Oracle Database Lead	David Chen	None Identified (Risk)	Partial (Standard Operating Procedures missing)	Immediate
Service Desk Manager	Amanda Lewis	Team Lead (Rotational)	In Progress (Runbooks currently under audit)	Monthly

Use the template as a working control, not a one-time exercise. If a role has no backup, label it as risk. If documentation is partial, label it as risk. The value is in making gaps visible and reviewable on a schedule, not in pretending coverage exists.

Case Example:

A retiring systems engineer worked with two junior staff for six months to transfer knowledge and rebuild server documentation. The transition was smooth and prevented operational gaps.

How the handoff was done (what the manager actually did)
The manager treated knowledge transfer like a project, not informal shadowing. They listed the engineer's core responsibilities and split them into routine tasks, incident tasks, and change tasks, then

assigned each junior staff member ownership of a portion of that scope.

The juniors first observed, then executed tasks with the engineer watching, updating runbooks immediately after each run. In the final phase, they ran changes and recovery tasks end to end while the retiring engineer stayed in a backup role only. Readiness was validated through a few controlled drills (restore, failover, and a standard maintenance window). Documentation was rebuilt in a consistent format (prereqs, steps, validation, rollback, escalation). When the engineer left, ownership and runbooks were already proven in real execution.

Pro Tip

Many new managers hoard knowledge because they think being indispensable makes them safe. This is a trap. If you are the only person who can handle a crisis or approve a change, you are chained to your current role forever. Document your decision-making process and delegate your authority so you are actually free to take a promotion when it comes.

Ethical Leadership and Professional Conduct

Technology leaders influence access, data, user experience, and security. Ethical leadership ensures decisions are transparent, fair, and responsible. In IT, ethics is not a separate topic from operations. It shows up in daily choices: who gets admin access, how incidents are reported, how vendors are handled, and whether promotions and assignments are based on performance or relationships.

Ethical failures in technical environments rarely start as "bad intent." They start as small exceptions that become normal. A shortcut around access controls to move faster. A vague incident update to avoid scrutiny. A vendor relationship that blurs into personal benefit. Over time, these patterns damage trust, increase risk, and create a culture where people assume rules are optional.

Core Ethical Areas

1. **Data privacy and responsible access:** Access should be tied to role and business need, not convenience. Leaders set the tone by enforcing least privilege, pushing for access reviews, and treating customer data as protected by default.

2. **Honest and accurate communication:** Trust collapses when leadership filters facts to protect appearances. Ethical communication means reporting what happened, what impact occurred, and what is known vs unknown, even when the information is uncomfortable.

3. **Secure-by-design principles:** Security cannot be bolted on after deployment. Leaders are responsible for making security a standard part of architecture reviews, change processes, and release criteria, not an afterthought.

4. **Avoiding favoritism in promotions:** Promotions and assignments must follow consistent criteria. When people believe advancement is political, performance drops and retention risk rises. Leaders must be deliberate about transparency and fairness.

5. **Boundaries with vendors:** Vendor relationships can be valuable, but they can also distort decisions. Leaders must keep procurement neutral by separating technical evaluation from personal benefit, and by ensuring decisions are documented and defensible.

6. **Responsible incident handling:** Incidents test ethical leadership. The right behavior is factual reporting, clear accountability, and protection from blame culture. Hiding errors or shifting responsibility only increases long-term risk.

7. **Transparency in decision-making:** When decisions affect cost, security posture, or workload, teams and stakeholders need to understand why choices were made. Transparency does not mean debating every decision. It means documenting rationale and tradeoffs.

Case Example:

A senior IT manager declined a vendor's offer for paid travel to a conference because accepting it would compromise procurement neutrality.

How the situation was handled (what the manager actually did)
The manager responded quickly and kept the boundary clear. They thanked the vendor and declined in writing, then routed the communication to procurement so there was a clean record. Internally, they disclosed the offer to their leadership chain to prevent any later questions about influence or appearance.

They also protected the technical work from being tainted. The vendor remained eligible to compete, but all evaluation was moved into a structured process with documented criteria and multiple reviewers. Any future meetings with the vendor were scheduled with at least two company representatives present, and discussions were limited to technical requirements and contract terms. The message to the team was simple: decisions must stand on technical merit and business value, not personal benefit.

Measuring Leadership Effectiveness and Team Performance

Metrics do two things when used well: they show where the team is delivering and they surface where performance is quietly slipping before it becomes a leadership problem.

Operational KPIs

- MTTR
- SLA compliance
- Number of recurring incidents
- Change success rate

People and Culture KPIs

- Engagement and satisfaction score
- Certification and training activity
- Promotion and internal mobility
- Turnover rate

Figure 1.5: Balanced Leadership Performance Scorecard

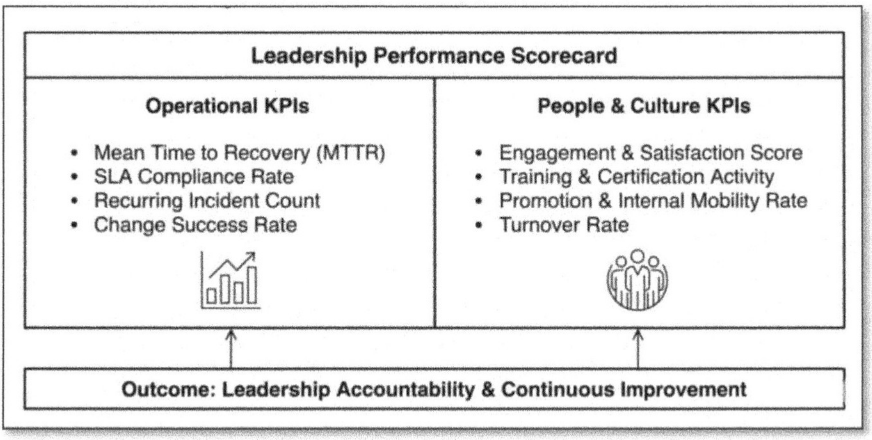

What This Means in Practice

- Modern IT managers are strategic leaders, not just technical experts. Technical depth may help someone reach the role, but strategic judgment, business literacy, and the ability to translate technology decisions into business outcomes are what allow long-term success and growth.
- Success depends on balancing technology, people, and process. Over-investing in any one dimension creates the same result: environments that are technically sound but operationally fragile, teams that are capable but disengaged, or processes that are documented but routinely bypassed.
- Hybrid operations require structure and disciplined communication. Distributed teams, multi-vendor environments, and mixed on-premises and cloud architectures all increase the cost of unclear ownership and informal coordination. Structure is no longer optional. It is what prevents small coordination gaps from becoming visible operational failures.
- Trust is built through transparency, consistency, and competence. Executives extend authority to IT managers they trust to surface bad news early, deliver on commitments, and demonstrate sound judgment under pressure. Trust takes time to build and can be lost quickly through avoidable failures.
- Leadership skills matter as much as technical proficiency. Coaching engineers, managing upward, communicating across functions, and making difficult personnel decisions determine how far the role can scale. Managers who cannot lead eventually reach a ceiling regardless of technical expertise.
- Ethical behavior is foundational to long-term credibility. IT managers often see sensitive data, security weaknesses, and operational risks before anyone else does. How that information is handled, during audits, incident reviews,

vendor negotiations, and private conversations, determines whether the role is trusted or merely tolerated.

- Continuous improvement is part of the role, not a separate initiative. The environment will not remain static. New threats, platforms, business demands, and regulatory requirements arrive continuously. Managers who treat the current state as finished eventually fall behind the operational reality their teams must support.
- Strong teams require deliberate culture, accountability, and development. High-performing IT teams are built intentionally. Clear expectations, consistent feedback, fair workload distribution, and real investment in career growth are what separate organizations that retain strong engineers from those that continually lose them.

Figure 1.6: Modern IT Leadership Framework: Strategy, Execution, and Culture

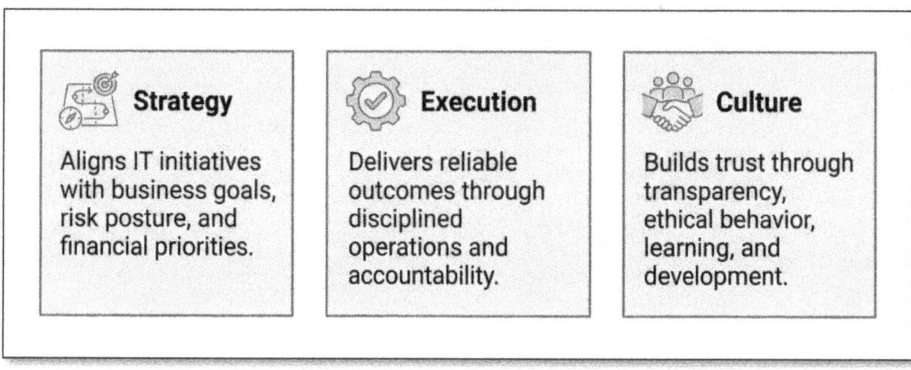

Chapter 2

ALIGNING IT STRATEGY WITH BUSINESS OBJECTIVES

IT creates value when its priorities are tied directly to what the business is trying to achieve. When technology investments connect to measurable outcomes, the dynamic shifts: IT stops being a cost center and starts being the mechanism that improves customer experience, lowers operating cost, enables growth, and builds resilience into the business model.

When IT operates in isolation, the damage is predictable. Decisions get made without business context, systems get duplicated, technical debt accumulates quietly, and at some point executives stop treating IT leadership as a planning partner and start treating it as a cost to manage.

This chapter works through alignment from the ground up, starting with how the business actually runs and finishing with a roadmap that can be funded, governed, and executed without falling apart the first time priorities shift.

This chapter treats strategy as a leadership and decision-making discipline, not a technical implementation guide. The assumption is that infrastructure and operations are already understood. What follows is focused on how IT leaders convert business objectives into priorities, governance structures, funding arguments, and execution models that hold together under real conditions. Operational design details and system-level implementation are covered elsewhere. The focus here is alignment that holds over time, clear accountability, and business impact that can be measured and defended.

Know Your Business Before You Build the Plan

Alignment starts with understanding how the business actually makes money, serves customers, and manages risk. Hardware lists and technical roadmaps come later. They are outputs of business understanding, not substitutes for it.

Questions every IT leader must answer confidently:

1. What are the company's primary strategic goals for the next 12 to 36 months?
2. What financial or market pressures influence how the business invests in technology?
3. Which products, services, or functions depend most heavily on IT?
4. How does the company measure success: profit margin, customer experience, uptime, speed to market, or sustainability?
5. What operational bottlenecks slow down the business today?

Table: Business Goals Connected to IT Solutions

Business Goal	Objective	IT Enabler
Improve customer satisfaction	Faster response and service quality	CRM, analytics, automation
Reduce operational costs	Eliminate manual work and inefficiencies	Process automation, virtualization
Strengthen security posture	Reduce breaches and downtime	IAM, segmentation, compliance tooling
Accelerate innovation	Shorten release cycles	DevOps, cloud-native architecture
Ensure compliance	Pass audits and avoid penalties	GRC systems, automated reporting

Pro Tip

The org chart tells you who has authority, not who has answers. To understand how the business actually works, find the veteran administrative assistants and sales operations staff. They know exactly where the processes break and who bypasses them. Buy them a coffee, and you will learn more about operational reality in twenty minutes than you will in a month of steering committee meetings.

Case Example

A logistics firm aimed to reduce delivery delays by 15 percent. The IT team discovered weak warehouse Wi-Fi was causing inventory scan errors. By implementing a mesh wireless system and updated scanning apps, delays dropped back to target.

How the root cause was found and funded (what the leader actually did)

The IT leader started by translating the goal into a measurable operational chain. They met with dispatch, warehouse supervisors, and a few front-line pickers to map where "delay" was being created, receiving, put-away, picking, staging, loading, and driver departure. Instead of asking for opinions, they asked for timestamps and failure patterns: where rescans happened, where scans failed, and where people stopped trusting the system and used manual workarounds.

Within a few shifts, the pattern was obvious. Scan failures clustered in specific aisles and dock doors, and those failures created two downstream problems: inventory accuracy drift and rework during staging. The leader pulled logs from the scanning system to quantify failure rates by location and time, then validated it with a quick site walk, basic signal tests, and a comparison against access point placement and interference sources.

For funding, they did not pitch "network upgrades." They pitched risk removal from a revenue-critical process. The proposal included three options: low-cost access point repositioning and tuning, a targeted mesh deployment in dead zones, and a full refresh with redundant coverage. Each option listed expected scan success improvement, implementation downtime, and a short payback argument based on reduced rework and fewer delayed departures.

They also kept rollout risk low. The team piloted one warehouse zone first, measured scan success rate and staging rework for two weeks, then expanded site-wide only after the data confirmed improvement. The updated scanning app changes were released with a rollback plan and a short training sheet for floor staff. By the time leadership reviewed results, the team could show a clear link between connectivity, scan accuracy, and on-time departures, which made the investment an operational win rather than an "IT project."

Building Your IT Strategy Step by Step

A clear IT strategy turns business direction into specific work the organization can prioritize, fund, and deliver.

Step 1: Assess the Current State

Start with a clear view of the environment as it exists today. Review infrastructure and applications by lifecycle stage, support status, and technical debt. Identify key risks, including unsupported systems, lack of redundancy, poor documentation, and areas the team is operating without full ownership or depth. Before adding anything new, confirm whether current team capacity and skills are enough to support what is already in place.

Step 2: Define the Future State

Set a practical view of how IT should operate over the next 18 to 36 months. That should include expected automation levels, security maturity, observability, support model, architectural direction, and user experience expectations. The target state needs to reflect business priorities, but it also has to match what the organization can realistically fund, support, and sustain.

Step 3: Build the Strategic Roadmap

Prioritize initiatives based on business value, risk reduction, cost, and available capacity. Do not build the roadmap around what is easiest to deliver or most interesting technically. It should be clear enough for non-technical stakeholders to understand and strong enough to hold up during budget discussions.

Step 4: Establish Measurable Metrics

Define success before execution begins. Every major initiative should have clear measures tied to operational or business outcomes. That may include lower unplanned downtime, stronger SLA performance, more automation in high-volume support work, or meaningful reduction in open audit findings

Examples:

- Unplanned downtime < 0.01% per quarter
- 95% incident SLA compliance
- 50% Tier-1 request automation
- Reduce audit findings by 80%

Step 5: Secure Executive Buy-In

Executive support usually follows business clarity. Each major investment should be presented in terms of the problem being solved, the cost of doing nothing, the options available, and how results will be measured and reported over time.

Communicating IT Value to Executives

Executives focus on outcomes, revenue impact, risk, operational performance, and customer experience. That does not mean the technical detail does not matter. It means they need the information in a form that helps them make a decision. The job is to communicate the reality inside IT in terms they can act on.

Core Practices

- **Focus on business impact, not technical jargon:** Start with what improved, what risk was reduced, or what cost was avoided. Then explain what changed technically in one or two sentences
- **Use clear dashboards with ties to business KPIs:** Dashboards should show service outcomes, not tool outputs. Good dashboards answer: what is the customer feeling, what is the business exposure, and what is trending up or down

- **Translate IT metrics into financial language:** Tie reliability, performance, and delivery speed to measurable effects like lost transactions, support cost, rework hours, or contractual penalties
- **Share risks transparently with mitigation plans:** Executives will accept risk when it is framed clearly, time-bounded, and paired with options. They will not accept "trust us" risk

How to structure an executive update

1. Outcome first, what changed and why it matters
2. Evidence, one chart or a small set of numbers
3. Decision needed, approve, prioritize, accept risk, or fund a change
4. Options, 2 to 3 choices with tradeoffs
5. Next checkpoint, when you will report back and what success looks like

Example

Instead of "latency dropped from 300 ms to 80 ms," say:

"Checkout abandonment dropped 12 percent due to improved performance."

A practical way to build these translations is to maintain a small "metric map" for each critical service:

Table: Translating Technical Metrics into Business Outcomes

Technical signal	Business outcome it influences	What you report
Latency, error rate	Conversion and customer satisfaction	Abandonment rate, failed transactions
Availability	Revenue continuity, SLA exposure	Minutes of impact, credits avoided
MTTR	Duration of customer pain	Impact window reduction trend
Change failure rate	Self-inflicted outages and rework	Delivery risk trend, stability improvements
Capacity headroom	Growth readiness	Time to scale, avoided constraints

The goal is consistency. If you report value the same way every month, leaders stop treating IT as a black box and start treating it like an accountable business function.

How IT Governance Keeps Strategy on Track

Governance is what keeps the plan intact once execution starts. Strategy fails in execution for consistent, predictable reasons: priorities shift without anyone documenting the decision, work begins without clear owners, risk calls get made in hallway conversations, and projects keep running long after the original business case stopped being true.

Governance is what keeps execution from drifting after the plan is approved. When it is done well, it does not slow delivery, it reduces confusion, clarifies decision rights, and makes tradeoffs explicit instead of political.

Key Governance Components

- IT Steering Committee
- Portfolio Management (PPM)
- Change Advisory Board (CAB)

- Quarterly Business Reviews
- Decision and Policy Documentation

Table: Governance Mechanisms and Purposes

Mechanism	Purpose
IT Steering Committee	Align priorities across departments
PPM Dashboard	Track cost, progress, and value
CAB	Control operational risk
Quarterly Business Reviews	Adjust strategy as needed
Policy Repository	Maintain compliance and consistency

What strong governance looks like in practice

- **Clear decision rights:** Everyone knows who can approve spend, accept risk, defer work, and override priorities. When decision rights are unclear, politics fills the gap.
- **One intake path for new work:** Requests come in through a defined pipeline, are sized, risk-rated, and tied to a business objective. This prevents side work from quietly consuming capacity.
- **Visible tradeoffs:** When a new initiative enters the portfolio, something else must move. Governance makes that trade explicit instead of pretending everything is priority one.
- **Risk is managed as a decision, not a surprise:** CAB and security reviews are not there to block progress. They are there to ensure changes are planned, recoverable, and aligned to the organization's risk tolerance.

Simple governance cadence that works

- ✓ Weekly, delivery and blockers review (portfolio view, top risks, decision needs)
- ✓ Biweekly, CAB with strict scope (only changes that can impact production stability)

- ✓ Monthly, scorecard review (value metrics, reliability trends, budget burn)
- ✓ Quarterly, strategy refresh (stop, continue, accelerate decisions)

Governance works when it produces decisions and reduces repeated debate. If the same issue returns every meeting, it means the decision was never actually made, or it was not documented in a way the organization follows.

Aligning Finances and Risk with IT Strategy

Finance and risk are not constraints that show up at the end of planning. They shape what IT can realistically deliver from the start. A technically sound strategy that does not account for budget cycles, cost model preferences, and the organization's actual risk tolerance will not survive the approval process, let alone execution.

Financial Alignment

- **Align budget cycles with business planning:** If the business plans annually, your major investments need to be visible before budget lock. If the business plans quarterly, your roadmap needs modular funding points.
- **Provide consumption reporting: (showback or chargeback)** Visibility changes behavior. When teams see consumption tied to services and owners, waste becomes easier to reduce without arguments.
- **Balance CapEx refreshes with OpEx cloud models:** Hybrid environments often require both. Hardware refresh may be non-negotiable for certain workloads, while cloud may be the right fit for variable demand or faster delivery.
- **Build ROI-driven business cases:** Do not rely on "modernization" as a justification. Tie spend to measurable outcomes: reduced outages, reduced manual labor, reduced audit exposure, or improved speed to deliver.

A business case that leadership can evaluate usually includes:

1. The problem, stated in business terms
2. What the problem is costing today (time, risk, dollars, delays)
3. Practical options, including doing nothing
4. The cost and expected benefit of each option
5. Key dependencies and risks that could change the outcome
6. How success will be measured, and the date you will report results

Risk Alignment

IT risks have to be stated in business terms. A technical label by itself is not a risk statement. A usable risk statement spells out what could happen, how likely it is, and the time window when it matters.

Example:

Instead of saying: "unpatched vulnerability in the customer-facing API"

Say: "If this is not remediated before the next release window, there is a confirmed path to customer account data affecting approximately 800,000 active users, with a two-week window before the next external scan." The first statement describes the technical condition. The second tells the decision-maker what is at risk, how broad the exposure is, and how quickly action is needed.

How to present risk so leaders can act

- Impact: what could happen, to customers, revenue, compliance, or operations
- Likelihood: low, medium, high, and why you believe that
- Time window: when this is most likely to matter
- Mitigation: what you will do, cost, timeline, and residual risk
- Decision: accept, reduce, transfer, or avoid

Risk alignment also means being honest about residual risk. Some risk can only be reduced, not eliminated. Executives will accept that when the tradeoffs are explicit and the plan is credible.

Pro Tip

Be careful assuming that shifting to the cloud (OpEx) is what Finance wants. Many companies actually prefer CapEx because depreciation can favorably impact specific financial metrics like EBITDA. Before you propose a massive shift to SaaS or public cloud, ask your CFO which expense model helps them meet their targets. If you save the company cash but hurt their valuation metrics, you will not get the approval.

Building Partnerships Across Departments

IT cannot align with the business through strategy documents alone. It requires working relationships with every major function, relationships built before a crisis, not during one.

Examples of Cross-Department Alignment

- **Finance:** Budget forecasting, ROI review
- **HR:** Access management, onboarding automation
- **Operations:** Production systems, IoT, logistics
- **Marketing:** Analytics, digital campaign tools
- **Compliance:** Privacy, audit readiness

Case Example

IT and Operations collaborated on predictive maintenance sensors in a manufacturing plant. Downtime dropped significantly and scheduling improved.

How the partnership worked (what the IT leader actually did)
The IT leader began by meeting Operations on their terms, production impact and schedule reliability, not "IoT architecture." They picked one high-pain area, a line with frequent unplanned stops, and agreed on a clear definition of success: fewer unplanned downtime events, faster detection of early failure signals, and less disruption to the production schedule.

They then clarified ownership before deploying anything. Operations owned the maintenance workflow and response actions. IT owned connectivity, data collection, platform stability, and security controls. A simple escalation path was documented so sensor issues did not get treated like equipment failures, and equipment failures did not get bounced back to IT.

To avoid stalled pilots, they ran a small rollout first. Sensors were installed on a limited set of assets, data was collected for a baseline period, and alert thresholds were tuned with the maintenance team so notifications were actionable. Once alerts reliably predicted real issues, Operations baked the work into scheduling, planned maintenance windows, parts staging, and technician dispatch. IT supported reporting dashboards that showed downtime trend, alert accuracy, and response time, which kept both teams aligned and made it easier to justify expansion to other lines.

Tracking and Maintaining Alignment Over Time

Strategy does not stay aligned on its own. Priorities change, markets evolve, and technical debt builds over time. Regular review keeps the roadmap tied to current business needs, not assumptions from when it was first created.

Key Metric Categories

- **Operational:** Uptime, MTTR, SLA compliance
- **Business:** Time-to-market, customer satisfaction
- **Financial:** ROI, IT cost vs. revenue

- **Innovation:** New releases, automation coverage
- **Risk:** Incidents, compliance rate, audit findings

Balanced Scorecard Example

Category	Metric	Business Impact
Reliability	Uptime	Customer trust
Efficiency	Cost variance	Budget accuracy
Innovation	Release cadence	Competitive advantage
Risk	Findings resolved	Audit readiness

Case Study: Alignment That Drove Growth

A global retailer saw rising IT costs and stagnant digital sales. New tools were being added every quarter, but the customer experience was not improving in a way the business could measure. Marketing teams could not get consistent attribution data. Operations could not predict demand shifts accurately. IT was carrying the cost of overlapping platforms, duplicate integrations, and multiple versions of "customer truth."

The root issue was not a lack of effort. It was misalignment. Each function was optimizing its own roadmap, which created duplicated systems and fragmented decision-making.

Actions

- ✓ Unified customer data into a single analytics platform
- ✓ Coordinated roadmaps across IT, marketing, operations
- ✓ Implemented quarterly reviews tied to conversion KPIs
- ✓ Eliminated redundant systems

How the alignment was executed (what the leaders actually did)
The CIO and marketing leader agreed on one shared outcome: conversion rate growth tied to measurable funnel steps, not vanity metrics. They then forced a single definition of customer identity and a single set of conversion events used by every team. That removed the constant debate about whose numbers were "right."

Next, they built a cross-functional roadmap that started from customer journeys, not from team backlogs. Each initiative had one executive sponsor, one delivery owner, and one KPI owner. Projects that could not tie to a funnel metric or cost reduction target were paused or cut.

For governance, they replaced ad hoc steering updates with a quarterly review that used the same scorecard every time. The scorecard linked platform costs and delivery milestones directly to conversion metrics and customer experience indicators. If conversions did not move, the plan had to change, not the narrative.

Finally, they attacked system sprawl. The team ranked redundant tools by cost, integration complexity, and overlap in capability. They migrated in waves, starting with systems that reduced both operating cost and reporting confusion. Integration retirement was treated as real work with timelines, owners, and risk controls, not as cleanup "when there is time."

Results

- Online conversions increased over 30%
- IT spend dropped due to system consolidation
- Leadership began involving IT in all consulting and planning discussions

Why it worked

Alignment became visible and enforceable. Everyone used the same definitions, the same KPIs, and the same review cadence. The business saw IT as a growth lever because IT was no longer reporting activity, it was reporting outcomes tied to conversion and cost.

Aligning IT Architecture with Business Priorities

Architecture is where business alignment either holds or starts to break down. The systems IT builds should support the business, not limit it. When architecture decisions are made without clear connection to business priorities, teams eventually end up working around the tools instead of benefiting from them.

Architecture Alignment Principles

- Standardize platforms to reduce cost and complexity
- Use modular, API-driven designs to support flexibility
- Prioritize security-first architecture for regulated industries
- Choose cloud vs. on-prem based on workload economics and compliance

Case Example

A financial services company modernized its trading platform by decoupling services into an event-driven architecture. Trading latency dropped sharply, directly improving revenue.

How the architecture change was justified and delivered (what the leader actually did)
The architecture lead tied the redesign to business targets, peak latency thresholds, order rejection limits, and recovery expectations, and used those as acceptance criteria. They isolated the latency-critical trade path from latency-tolerant functions like reporting and analytics so noncritical work could not stall execution.

They migrated in stages to control risk: validate events in parallel, move a low-risk workflow first, load-test under market-open conditions, then shift core execution with rollback ready. Latency improved because the trade path no longer depended on synchronous calls and shared resource contention, which translated into faster, more consistent execution and improved revenue.

Portfolio Management as the Connector Between Strategy and Execution

When IT takes on too many projects at once, execution starts to suffer. Capacity gets stretched, sequencing becomes reactive, and the roadmap starts reflecting the latest request instead of the right priorities. Portfolio management keeps budget, capacity, and strategic direction aligned through a clear and governed process.

Portfolio Management Practices

- Categorize projects by value, risk, and urgency
- Eliminate duplicate or low-value initiatives
- Align project scoring with business KPIs
- Maintain real-time visibility across all projects

Table: Sample Project Prioritization Scoring

Criteria	Weight	What It Evaluates
Business Outcome Impact	40%	Direct effect on revenue, operational efficiency, or customer experience
Risk and Compliance Reduction	20%	Security posture improvement, audit exposure, and regulatory standing
Cost and Resource Efficiency	20%	Cost savings, avoidance, and sustainable resource use
Strategic Direction Fit	20%	Alignment with the organization's multi-year technology and business goals

Innovation and Continuous Improvement Alignment

Innovation does not happen by accident or on leftover capacity. If time and budget are not deliberately protected, production work will take over every time. That is how organizations fall behind, not through one big decision, but through repeated failure to make room for improvement.

Innovation Alignment Practices

- Reserve part of the IT budget for experimentation
- Run pilot programs before full deployment
- Use metrics like innovation ROI and adoption rate
- Partner with business teams to co-create solutions

Case Example

An airline used IT-led process automation to reduce gate turnaround time by 8 minutes, a major competitive advantage.

How the automation was scoped and adopted (what the leader actually did)
The IT lead defined "turnaround time" with operations as a shared metric, then mapped the steps that caused most delays and targeted two consistent choke points instead of trying to automate everything.

They piloted in one hub first. The automation pulled updates from existing systems and pushed a single workflow to the gate team with clear owners and escalation triggers. Adoption was handled like an operations change: short role-based training, fast iteration on exceptions, and weekly measurement. Once the pilot consistently saved minutes and reduced missed handoffs, leadership funded expansion based on the results.

Vendor and Partner Alignment

Vendors should support your strategy, not shape it. When vendor influence starts driving priorities, the organization can end up optimizing around the vendor's roadmap instead of its own business goals.

Vendor Alignment Principles

- Tie vendor SLAs directly to business outcomes
- Use scorecards for performance tracking

- Align vendor roadmaps with enterprise strategy
- Involve vendors early in long-term planning

Vendor Scorecard Example

Metric	Target	Actual	Status
SLA Compliance	≥95%	97%	On Track
Delivery Quality	≥4.5/5	4.6	On Track
Cost Variance	≤3%	1.8%	On Track

Pro Tip

Never let the vendor lead the Quarterly Business Review (QBR). If they build the deck, the meeting will just be a sales pitch for their new products. You must own the agenda. Focus entirely on their performance against the contract, outstanding support tickets, and specific roadmap commitments they made to you. If they can't answer those questions, the meeting is over.

Workforce and Skills Alignment

Technology strategy only works when the team can support what it requires. Workforce planning needs to stay aligned with architectural direction, not react after the gap has already become an operational issue.

Workforce Alignment Focus Areas

- Skill mapping to future-state architecture
- Upskilling in automation, cloud, and security
- Clear role definitions and competency models
- Succession planning for critical positions

Case Example

A data center operations team introduced a cross-skilling program that reduced coverage gaps and improved on-call reliability.

How the cross-skilling program was built (what the manager actually did)
The manager reviewed recent incidents and on-call escalations to identify where coverage depended on the same few people and which critical systems had no real backup. That produced a short, service-based skills list tied to operational risk, not a generic training plan.

Each critical area got a primary owner and a trainee. Trainees had to execute real tasks, routine checks, a standard change, and a supervised incident response, while updating runbooks as they learned. On-call was adjusted so trainees started as secondary responders and moved into primary rotation only after a simple readiness checklist. Within a few cycles, escalations spread across more staff and on-call reliability improved because coverage no longer relied on a handful of experts.

Reporting and Transparency as Alignment Mechanisms

Alignment without visibility is just a plan on paper. eporting helps IT turn operational data into business insight, showing trends early, connecting costs to outcomes, and making service performance visible in terms leadership actually cares about.

Reporting Framework Components

- Executive dashboards
- Monthly service reviews
- Quarterly business reports
- Risk and compliance summaries
- Cost and utilization analytics

Reporting Best Practices

- Use simple visuals
- Focus on trends, not raw numbers
- Highlight business impact, not technical detail
- Include recommended actions

The Continuous Alignment Lifecycle

Alignment is not something you achieve once and then keep automatically. Priorities change, budgets shift, technology moves, and the business evolves. Without a deliberate cycle of review and adjustment, strategy documents lose relevance and execution starts drifting toward whatever has the most pull.

Lifecycle Stages

1. **Plan:** Collaborate with business leaders to define direction
2. **Execute:** Deliver projects and services
3. **Measure:** Track operational, financial, and business KPIs
4. **Review:** Adjust roadmap, budget, or governance based on findings
5. **Improve:** Implement lessons learned and process improvements

Figure 2.1: Alignment Lifecycle Loop

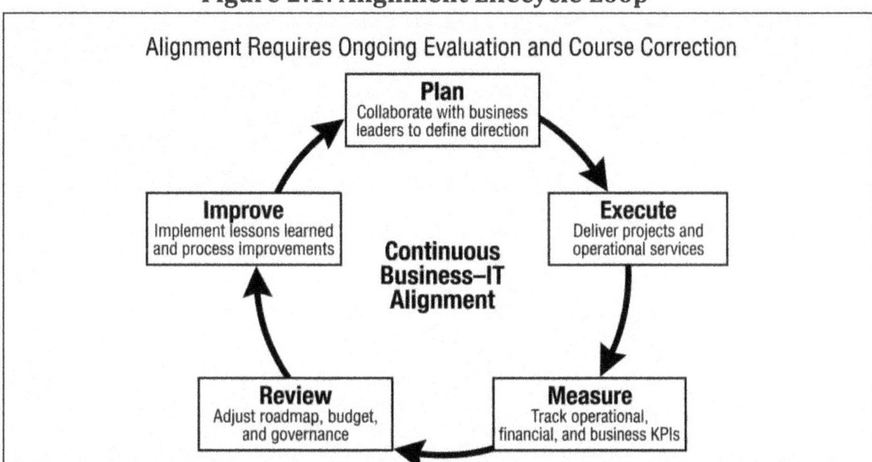

What This Means in Practice

Strong IT teams do not limit alignment to the annual budget cycle. They build it into how work is planned, reviewed, and adjusted all year. When priorities shift, the organization can respond without having to start over:

- **Alignment stops IT from being just a help desk.** When IT roadmaps directly support revenue goals, service quality, customer experience, and operational efficiency, IT becomes inseparable from business performance.
- **Deep business understanding is the starting point.** Technology decisions must be grounded in how the company makes money, what customers expect, and where the organization faces constraints. You cannot align what you do not understand.
- **Communication in business terms builds credibility.** Executives respond to measurable outcomes, financial clarity, and risk reduction. IT earns influence by making the connection between technical decisions and business outcomes visible, repeatedly and consistently, until leadership stops treating IT as a cost center and starts treating it as a planning partner.
- **Governance maintains alignment beyond the planning stage.** Steering committees, portfolio reviews, change control, and transparent reporting keep strategy on track as priorities evolve.
- **Financial and risk alignment are essential.** Roadmaps must reflect budget realities, cost models, and business-oriented risk views. Clear ROI and risk framing improves funding success and leadership trust.
- **Partnerships across departments make alignment sustainable.** IT cannot drive alignment alone. Collaboration with Finance, HR, Operations, Marketing, Compliance, and Security ensures that technology plans support every part of the business.

- **Measurements ensure alignment stays real over time.** Balanced scorecards, operational KPIs, innovation metrics, and business-outcome tracking ensure IT and business leaders share a common understanding of progress.
- **Architecture, vendors, and workforce models must evolve.** Cloud strategy, vendor performance, skills development, and automation roadmaps must all reinforce business goals—not stand apart from them.
- **Innovation must be structured and deliberate.** Intentional experimentation, pilot programs, and innovation KPIs help IT support growth, new capabilities, and competitive advantage.
- **Alignment is a continuous lifecycle.** Priorities shift, markets change, and technology evolves. IT leaders must regularly review, refine, and realign strategy to keep pace with the organization's direction.

Figure 2.2: Continuous IT and Business Alignment Lifecycle

Effective IT organizations continuously align technology strategy, governance, operations, and innovation with evolving business priorities.

Chapter 3

BUILDING AND LEADING HIGH-PERFORMING IT TEAMS

An IT organization can have strong tools, solid architecture, and enough funding, and still underperform if the team is misaligned, unclear on priorities, or lacking trust. Technology changes faster than most organizations can fully plan for. What matters over time is whether the team can solve problems, adapt, and deliver consistently. That is what keeps the environment stable instead of letting risk, technical debt, and operational friction build up.

High-performing IT teams do more than execute technical work. They understand the business outcomes behind the work, take ownership of results, and adjust when priorities shift instead of waiting for direction. As environments become more distributed and automation removes more routine work, the skills that matter most are the ones that are hardest to automate, judgment, communication, adaptability, and composure under pressure. That is where leadership needs to invest mor

This chapter is built around the work IT leaders actually do: hiring strong people, building a culture that holds under pressure, coaching individuals in critical roles, managing conflict in high-stakes environments, and improving team performance without burning people out. The frameworks and examples reflect how enterprise IT actually operates.

Figure 3.1: IT Team Performance Cycle

What Makes an IT Team Truly High-Performing

High-performing teams are built on conditions, not talent alone. Clarity means people know what they own and what decisions they can make. Trust means problems surface early instead of getting managed quietly. Shared accountability means the team measures itself by collective outcomes, not by who was heroic during the last incident. Strong technical skills matter, but without those conditions, even excellent engineers underperform.

Table: Core Characteristics of High-Performance IT Teams

Characteristic	Description
Technical Excellence	Team members develop deep subject-matter expertise and keep their skills current.
Shared Vision	Everyone understands why the work matters and how it connects to the business.
Mutual Accountability	Success is measured collectively; individuals hold each other to high standards.
Psychological Safety	Team members feel safe raising concerns and proposing ideas without getting punished for speaking up.
Process Discipline	Core practices such as documentation, SOP adherence, and incident workflows are followed consistently.

Table: Comparison – Average Team vs. High-Performing Team

Area	Average IT Team	High-Performing IT Team
Collaboration	Reactive, siloed	Cross-functional, transparent
Communication	Inconsistent	Predictable, structured
Incident Handling	Slow escalations	Rapid triage with clear ownership
Knowledge Sharing	Informal	Documented and repeatable
Innovation	Occasional	Continuous and encouraged

Pro Tip

High performance is not just about talent. It comes from how leaders lead, how the team is set up, and what the culture reinforces when pressure is high.

Shifting From Task Management to Coaching and Development

The older model of IT management was mostly transactional, assign work, track status, close tickets. The problem is that approach only works as long as the manager can personally stay on top of everything. Modern IT leadership has to work differently. The manager's role is to build engineers who can make sound decisions, spot problems early, and run their areas with less day-to-day dependence.

Leadership Habits That Elevate Team Performance

1. **Purpose Before Process:** Teams adopt ideas faster when they understand why something matters.
2. **Autonomy With Boundaries:** Offer clear expectations, then trust people to deliver within those parameters.
3. **Continuous Feedback:** Replace once-a-year performance reviews with regular, practical conversations.
4. **Learning Mindset:** Treat mistakes as opportunities to improve systems, not as failures.
5. **Outcome Orientation:** Evaluate success based on impact, not task volume.

Figure 3.2: Leadership Pyramid

Effective leadership develops from foundational trust into clarity, empowerment, and sustained accountability.

Coaching Framework (GROW Model)

A structured coaching conversation usually moves through four stages. It starts with the goal, what the engineer is trying to achieve and why it matters. Next is the current reality, where their skills are today, what is working, and what is getting in the way. From there, the conversation moves into options, possible approaches, the tradeoffs involved, and what seems most realistic given the situation. It ends with commitment, specific actions, clear ownership, and a timeframe the engineer believes is achievable. Often linked to *Sir John Whitmore's coaching model,* this structure helps keep the conversation focused and gives both sides a clear point of reference for follow-up.

Leadership Insight: Coaching changes where a manager adds value. As engineers get better at working through problems and making sound decisions independently, the manager stops being the default escalation path and can focus more on team effectiveness, execution, and long-term development.

Recruiting and Developing Top Talent

Strong IT candidates have options, and they evaluate companies with the same scrutiny companies use on them. They look for meaningful work, capable teammates, and real room to grow. When a job description reads like a certification inventory or a years of experience filter, it often screens out the very people most likely to adapt, learn, and solve problems well.

Effective Talent Acquisition Strategies

- Write job descriptions that explain *expected outcomes*, not endless tool lists
- Use practical simulations such as log review, troubleshooting, and script analysis to evaluate skills
- Involve current engineers in interviews to assess collaboration fit
- Look for adaptability, communication, and learning agility, not just certifications

Retention and Career Development

Development Method	Benefit
Structured career paths	Employees understand how to grow and what skills matter.
Training budgets and certifications	Encourages long-term skill development.
Quarterly development conversations	Keeps progress visible and goals aligned.
Promote from within	Reinforces trust and increases retention.

Figure 3.4: Career Path Example

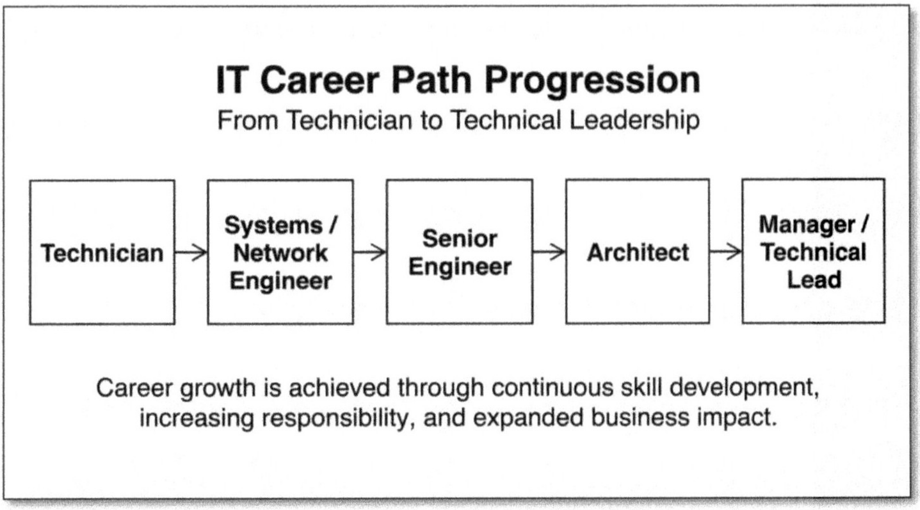

Case Example: Building Internal Talent Pipelines

This case examines how a data center operations team reduced turnover and closed skill gaps by building structured growth paths inside the organization. The focus is on how rotational exposure, documentation discipline, and cross-functional learning helped create more capable engineers while improving retention.

Example

A data center operations group was facing steady turnover and recurring skill gaps across core technical functions. Engineers were often strong in one area but lacked exposure to adjacent disciplines such as networking, systems, monitoring, and facilities operations. This created dependency on a small number of experienced staff and made coverage difficult during incidents, maintenance windows, and shift transitions.

How the program was executed (what the operations manager actually did)

The operations manager built a structured six-month rotation program that moved engineers through networking, systems administration, monitoring operations, and facility support on a defined schedule. Each rotation included core tasks, shadowing periods, required documentation reviews, and hands-on operational work tied to real production activities.

Senior engineers were assigned as mentors for each rotation to standardize knowledge transfer and reduce reliance on informal tribal knowledge. Runbooks and SOPs were updated throughout the program as participants identified gaps, outdated steps, and undocumented recovery actions during daily operations.

The program also introduced cross-functional incident participation. Engineers outside their primary discipline were included in bridges, maintenance reviews, and post-incident discussions so they could better understand operational dependencies and escalation paths across the environment.

Progress was measured through operational readiness checkpoints, technical assessments, and participation in maintenance and incident response activities. Managers used the results to identify future technical leads and target additional training where gaps remained.

Results

- The organization developed a broader pool of engineers capable of supporting multiple operational areas instead of relying on a small number of specialists
- Documentation quality improved substantially as runbooks and operational procedures were reviewed and updated during each rotation cycle
- Cross-team collaboration improved because engineers better understood upstream and downstream operational dependencies

- Turnover decreased significantly within the first year, supported by clearer growth paths, stronger mentorship, and expanded technical development opportunities

Pro Tip

Stop writing "unicorn" job descriptions. If you list twenty "required" technologies, the only candidates who apply are the ones willing to stretch the truth. Honest experts will look at the list, realize they are missing a few, and move on. List the three non-negotiables, then hire for problem-solving ability. A strong engineer can usually learn a new tool quickly, but it is much harder to coach a rigid thinker into calm, structured troubleshooting.

Building and Sustaining a Healthy IT Team Culture

Culture shows up in daily habits, how people escalate issues, whether bad news is raised early, how they treat each other under pressure, and whether they respond to problems with curiosity or defensiveness. It is not defined by what the team says it values. It is defined by how the team actually behaves when pressure is high, especially during a production incident at 2:00 a.m.

In IT, culture becomes visible fastest in two situations: incidents and change. When a production issue hits, do people share facts quickly or protect themselves? Do they escalate early or wait until the problem grows? When changes go wrong, do teams learn and improve or blame and retreat? A healthy culture produces consistent behaviors that reduce chaos and increase trust.

A strong culture also creates reliability. Not because people "feel good," but because communication is clear, ownership is obvious, and problems surface early. Teams with weak culture tend to hide bad news, avoid accountability, and rely on heroics. That works until the org grows, staff changes, or the incident rate increases.

Culture Principles of Effective IT Teams

1. **Transparency:** Share uptime metrics, incident reviews, and root-cause trends openly. Transparency does not mean flooding everyone with data; it means the team has a shared view of reality. The goals are early visibility, fewer surprises, and faster correction. When metrics are hidden or filtered, people fill the gaps with assumptions, and trust breaks down.

2. **Respect for Expertise:** Value operational knowledge, regardless of title. The engineer who knows how systems behave at 3:00 a.m. during peak load often has insights that do not show up in architecture diagrams. Respect shows up in who gets heard during incidents, whose input is used in planning, and whether operational concerns are treated as real constraints.

3. **Collaboration Over Competition:** Reinforce team wins instead of individual heroics. Hero culture creates two problems: it rewards firefighting instead of prevention, and it concentrates knowledge in a few people. Healthy teams reward the work that makes incidents less likely, runbooks clearer, and changes safer. Competition inside the team usually turns into hidden work, guarded information, and avoidance of shared responsibility.

4. **Recognition and Appreciation:** Highlight engineers who improve processes or reduce incidents. Recognition should be specific and tied to outcomes. "Great job" is fine, but "you removed a recurring incident by fixing the alert logic and updating the runbook" is what shapes behavior. Recognition also signals what the organization values: prevention, clarity, and steady execution.

5. **Healthy Workload Management:** Prevent burnout through realistic planning and rotation schedules. Burnout is not a personal weakness; it is a predictable result of overloaded systems and unclear priorities. If the same people are always on-call, always handling escalations, and always cleaning up technical debt, reliability will drop. A healthy culture includes saying no, limiting work in progress, and rotating load fairly.

Common culture failure patterns in IT

- Escalations happen late because people fear blame
- Metrics get massaged to avoid uncomfortable conversations
- One or two "go-to" engineers carry every incident
- Teams avoid documentation because it is not rewarded
- Changes are rushed, and post-incident actions are never closed

Culture work is not flashy, but you can measure the results. When culture improves, you see it in fewer repeat incidents, better handoffs, cleaner on-call rotations, and faster resolution because teams share facts early.

IT Team Engagement Model

- **Communication** creates clarity and reduces ambiguity
- **Autonomy** increases ownership when people understand the boundaries
- **Recognition** reinforces the behaviors you want repeated
- **Purpose** connects daily work to customer impact and business value

This model works as a loop. Communication enables autonomy. Autonomy creates meaningful wins. Recognition reinforces those wins. Purpose keeps the work from turning into ticket churn.

How to build the model into daily operations

- Use a predictable cadence for metrics and incident learnings
- Define ownership clearly, service owners, change owners, and incident roles
- Keep decision logs so debates do not repeat
- Track post-incident actions to closure, not just discussion
- Make process improvement a visible part of performance expectations

Case Example

A weekly internal "demo hour" allowed engineers to share automations, dashboards, or post-incident insights. Collaboration improved, and silos broke down as teams understood each other's workloads and tools.

How the habit was sustained (what the manager actually did)
The manager kept it lightweight and protected it from turning into a meeting. The demo hour had a fixed format: two short demos, one post-incident learning, and a quick list of ideas that deserved follow-up. Demos were required to include three things: the problem being solved, the impact (time saved, incidents reduced, visibility improved), and where the artifact lived (repo, dashboard link, runbook).

Participation rotated to avoid the same confident speakers presenting every week. The manager also made sure the session produced outcomes. If a demo revealed a reusable automation or dashboard, it was tagged and added to a shared library with a named maintainer. If a post-incident insight showed a broader risk, it was converted into a small work item with an owner and due date. Over time, demo hour became a practical exchange of tools and lessons, not a social event, and cross-team trust improved because engineers could see each other's work and constraints.

Managing Conflict and Performance

Conflict in technical teams is not something to eliminate. It is a normal part of smart people working through decisions that carry real operational risk. The real issue is not whether conflict happens. It is whether the team works through it using data and structured discussion, or lets it turn into avoidance, blame, and different versions of the same event.

Four-Step Conflict-Resolution Approach

1. **Identify the Issue Clearly:** Separate symptoms from root causes. "The deployment failed" is a symptom. The issue might be incomplete testing, unclear change ownership, a missing

dependency, or conflicting priorities. Define the problem in a way the team can act on.

2. **Hear Every Perspective:** Avoid assumptions, gather facts. Pull logs, timelines, requirements, and constraints. Give each person space to explain what they saw and what they optimized for. Many technical conflicts are two correct ideas competing under different assumptions.
3. **Discuss Impact Instead of Blame:** Focus on how work was affected, not on intent. Ask: what was the impact to customers, risk posture, on-call load, or delivery timeline? This keeps the conversation productive and reduces defensiveness.
4. **Agree on Specific Next Steps:** Document expectations and follow up. Conflict closes when the team knows what decision was made, who owns the next action, and when results will be reviewed. If you do not document it, you will re-litigate it.

Table: Conflict Resolution Matrix

Conflict Type	Description	Recommended Approach
Technical Disagreement	Differences in design or implementation	Use data, logs, and architecture principles to guide decisions
Process Conflict	SOP gaps or unclear roles	Review documentation and clarify ownership
Personal Conflict	Communication style or trust issues	Facilitate structured mediation and coaching
Workload Conflict	Uneven or unrealistic assignments	Adjust resource allocation and expectations

Performance Management That Supports Growth

Performance management works best when expectations are predictable and tied to outcomes the team can actually influence. In technical teams, performance often degrades when goals are vague, feedback is delayed, or scoring feels inconsistent. The purpose is not to "rate" people, it is to raise execution quality and reduce operational risk over time.

Core practices that keep performance management fair and useful:

- Tie goals to outcomes the business and team can measure (incident reduction, change success rate, automation coverage, backlog health, documentation completeness)
- Provide coaching early, before corrective action becomes necessary
- Use a consistent scoring rubric so expectations do not shift by manager mood or visibility
- Recognize both improvement and excellence, especially work that prevents incidents and reduces rework

Case Example

A service desk introduced a "quality index" combining MTTR, user feedback, and documentation accuracy. Within six months, performance scores improved across the team.

How it was implemented (what the manager actually did)

The manager kept the index simple and transparent. They defined each component with clear rules: MTTR measured by ticket category and severity (to avoid unfair comparisons), user feedback based on a short consistent survey, and documentation accuracy verified through quick monthly audits of a small ticket sample.

They rolled it out as a coaching tool first, not a punishment tool. For the first month, scores were shared privately with each technician along with one specific improvement target. The manager also fixed process gaps that were dragging scores down, like unclear escalation paths and inconsistent ticket categories.

To make it stick, they created weekly micro-habits: a short documentation checklist at ticket close, a standard troubleshooting template for recurring issues, and peer spot-checks for high-impact categories. Within a few cycles, the team improved because expectations were clear, measurement was consistent, and the feedback loop was fast enough to change behavior.

Pro Tip

Beware the "Toxic Rock Star." This is the engineer who closes the most tickets and writes the most complex code but treats the rest of the team with contempt. Keeping them is a net loss. They destroy psychological safety, causing your other quiet, high-performing staff to quit. If you can't coach the arrogance out of them, you must let them go, no matter how technically gifted they are.

Leading Remote and Hybrid IT Teams

Most enterprise IT teams today span at least two time zones, and many span four or more. This is no longer a temporary condition to work around. It is part of the operating model. Leading effectively in that environment means putting enough structure around coordination so the team does not depend on whoever happens to be online to make decisions or keep work moving.

Practical Approaches for Hybrid Teams

- Maintain one authoritative documentation platform (Confluence, SharePoint)
- Create standard overlap hours for real-time collaboration across time zones
- Use video selectively to reinforce connection while avoiding meeting overload.
- Conduct virtual retrospectives after each major incident
- Rotate on-call duties transparently across global regions

Figure 3.6: Hybrid Collaboration Workflow for Remote and Hybrid IT Teams

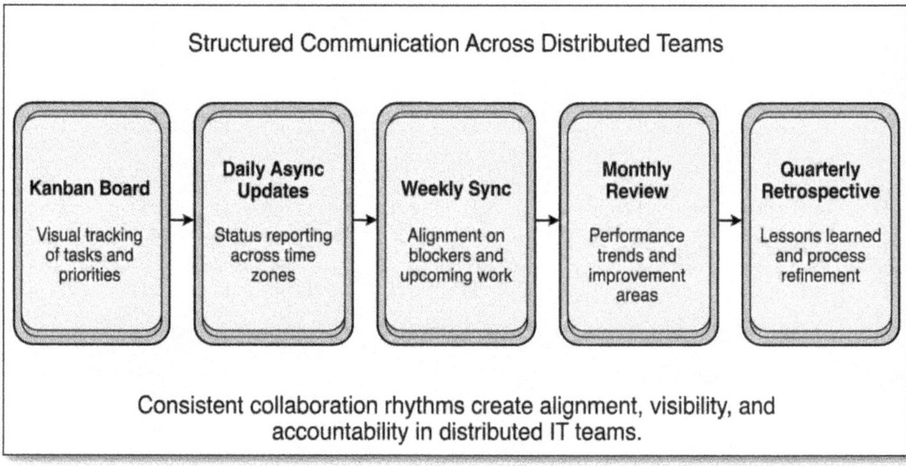

Case Example

A cloud engineering team operating across four continents adopted a follow-the-sun model. Regional handoffs were documented clearly in Jira, reducing MTTR by keeping tickets moving around the clock.

How the follow-the-sun model was made reliable (what the manager actually did)

The manager standardized handoffs so progress did not depend on who was online. Every active incident or priority ticket required a short "handoff block" in Jira: current status, impact, actions taken, next action, and escalation triggers. If it was missing, the ticket could not be handed off.

They also enforced ownership. Each shift assigned a named owner and a receiving owner for the next region, and updates had to be posted in the ticket, not in chat. After major incidents, a short retro reviewed handoff quality, and recurring gaps were turned into runbook or workflow fixes.

Pro Tip

Don't fall into the "Green Dot" trap. If you judge remote employees by how quickly they reply to chat messages or whether their status is set to "Available," you are encouraging them to perform *theater*, not work. Measure output, tickets closed, code committed, documentation written. If you micromanage their online status, they will just buy a mouse jiggler.

Encouraging Innovation and Continuous Improvement

In high-performing teams, improvement does not live on a separate roadmap. It shows up in how engineers debrief incidents, how they respond to recurring alerts, and whether the fix they ship this week prevents the same problem from coming back next month.

The manager's role is to make continuous improvement possible, not just demand it. Teams running at constant full capacity have no room to improve because all available time is already spent maintaining the current environment. Improvement requires protected time to address recurring root causes, automate manual tasks, and test better approaches before they become urgent. When leadership cuts that time first under pressure, teams learn that improvement is optional and revert to firefighting. When leadership protects it, teams understand that reducing future operational work is part of the work, not something separate from it.

Continuous Improvement Loop

- ✓ **Observe** Gather data and user feedback
- ✓ **Analyze** Identify patterns, failure points, inefficiencies
- ✓ **Implement** Run low-risk improvements or small automations
- ✓ **Review** Measure results and refine

Figure 3.7: Continuous Improvement Cycle: Plan, Do, Check, Act (PDCA)[1]

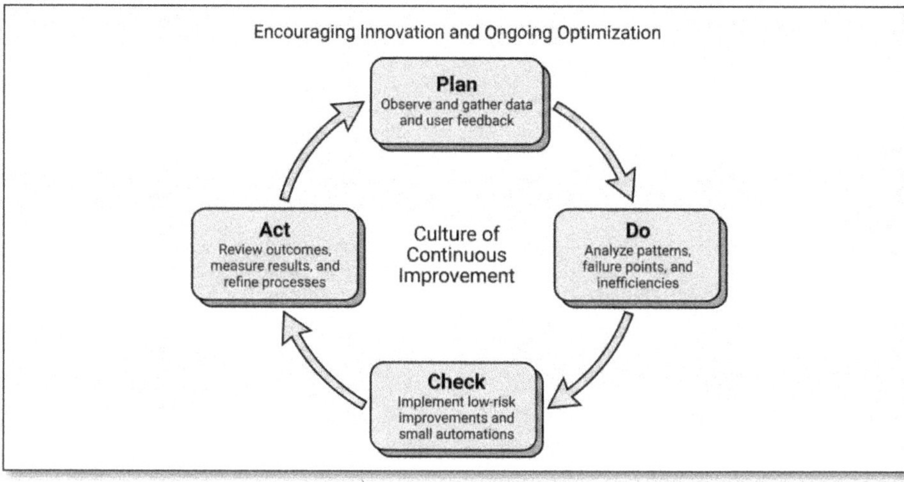

Practical Ways to Foster Innovation

- Allocate protected time for experimentation: even a consistent half-day per sprint is enough to generate meaningful improvements when the scope is focused. Treat it as a fixed commitment, not a reward for finishing production work early.
- Provide sandbox environments for safe testing: engineers need a place to validate ideas without risking production. This does not require dedicated infrastructure in every case; isolated tenants, non-production accounts, or short-lived environments controlled by the team are sufficient.
- Recognize improvements that reduce toil or enhance security: call out specific contributions in team meetings and link them to operational outcomes. Recognition that names the problem solved and the impact achieved shapes behavior more effectively than general praise.
- Encourage cross-team collaboration on scripts, dashboards, and templates: shared tooling reduces duplicated effort and builds the cross-functional relationships that make incident response faster.

[1] The Plan-Do-Check-Act (PDCA) cycle, adapted from W. Edwards Deming's quality management principles, provides a practical loop for continuous improvement in IT operations.

Case Example

A security team adopted a weekly "Threat Hunt Friday." Engineers investigated anomalies beyond standard alerts, discovering potential vulnerabilities months before audits would have detected them.

How "Threat Hunt Friday" was made effective (what the manager actually did)

The manager kept it structured so it did not turn into random exploration. They defined a narrow weekly scope (one environment or one control area at a time) and a standard checklist: identity anomalies, unusual privilege changes, new external exposures, suspicious authentication patterns, and high-risk configuration drift. Each hunt produced a short write-up with evidence links, what was ruled out, and any gaps in detection.

Findings were tracked like real work. Issues were tagged by severity, assigned owners, and given due dates, with quick fixes handled immediately and larger items added to the security backlog. The team also tuned detections based on what they learned, converting common patterns into new alerts, dashboards, or automated checks. Over time, the hunts reduced blind spots and cut the number of "surprises" that typically surface late during audit prep.

Succession Planning and Knowledge Transfer

Every team has knowledge that lives in one person's head, the engineer who knows why a configuration exists, the analyst who understands the exception logic, or the architect who remembers the decision behind the current design. When that person leaves, the gap usually shows up either as slow degradation or as a sudden incident. Succession planning turns that hidden dependency into documented, transferable capability before it becomes an operational problem.

Core Components of Succession Planning

- Identify key roles and skills essential to uptime and security
- Assign primary and backup owners for critical systems

- Maintain updated runbooks and diagrams
- Conduct cross-training and shadowing sessions routinely

Succession Planning Template

The template below is a lightweight starting point. For higher-risk environments, add a Documentation Status column and treat incomplete runbooks as an explicit gap, as discussed in Chapter 1.

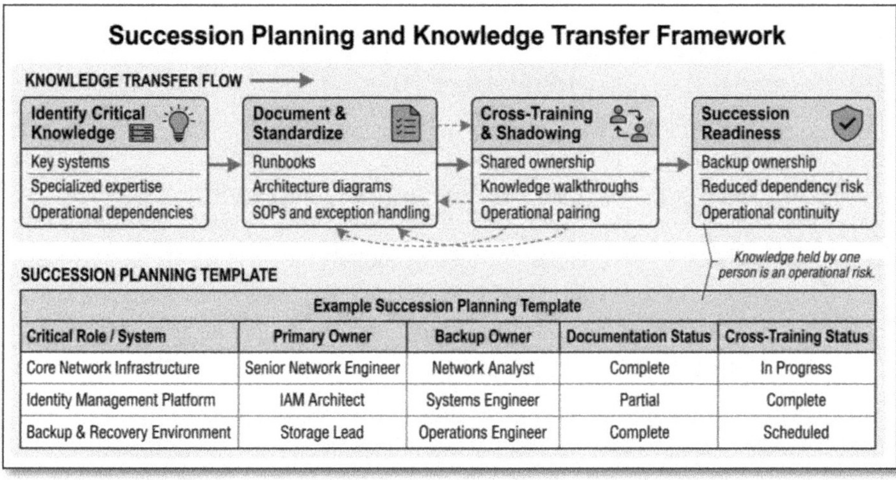

Critical Role / System	Primary Owner	Backup Owner	Documentation Status	Cross-Training Status
Core Network Infrastructure	Senior Network Engineer	Network Analyst	Complete	In Progress
Identity Management Platform	IAM Architect	Systems Engineer	Partial	Complete
Backup & Recovery Environment	Storage Lead	Operations Engineer	Complete	Scheduled

Case Example

When a senior network architect prepared to retire, two engineers shadowed him for six months. They rebuilt documentation, validated diagrams, and refreshed SOPs, ensuring a seamless operational transition.

How the transfer was executed (what the manager actually did)

The manager treated the retirement like a planned risk event. They listed the architect's responsibilities and split them into routine operations, change activities, and incident response. Each shadow engineer owned a portion of that scope and was accountable for being able to run it, not just observe it.

Shadowing progressed in phases: observe and capture steps, execute with supervision, then execute independently with the architect as backup only. Documentation was rebuilt into consistent artifacts, network diagrams with current dependencies, runbooks with validation and rollback steps, and SOPs that matched actual workflows. Readiness was confirmed through a few controlled exercises, a planned change window, a simulated failover, and an on-call handoff drill. By the time the architect left, ownership and documentation had been proven under real execution conditions.

Measuring Team Performance with Fairness and Transparency

Metrics serve two purposes. They show leaders where delivery is strong and where it is slipping, and they give the team a clear, consistent view of what good performance looks like, so expectations are not left to manager judgment or changing priorities.

Operational Performance Indicators

Metric	What It Measures
MTTR	Efficiency in restoring service
SLA Compliance	Consistency of service delivery
Repeat Incidents	Quality of root-cause resolution
Change Success Rate	Stability and process maturity

Engagement and Team Health Indicators

Metric	What It Measures
Employee Engagement Scores	Team morale and satisfaction
Certification Completion Rate	Skill development
Internal Promotion Ratio	Talent pipeline strength
Turnover Rate	Organizational stability

What This Means in Practice

- High-performing IT teams blend technical excellence with trust, accountability, and clear communication
- Leadership today focuses more on coaching, development, and empowerment than task assignment
- Recruitment should prioritize adaptability and problem-solving ability, not just certifications and tool familiarity
- Culture determines how teams behave during incidents, transitions, and major changes
- Conflict, when handled well, strengthens teams and uncovers system gaps
- Remote and hybrid teams require structure, transparency, and predictable communication patterns
- Encouraging innovation and continuous improvement prevents stagnation and reduces operational risk
- Succession planning protects critical knowledge and ensures continuity
- Transparent, fair performance metrics enable stronger leadership decisions and more motivated teams

Figure 3.8: Summary Model – Building and Sustaining High-Performance IT Teams

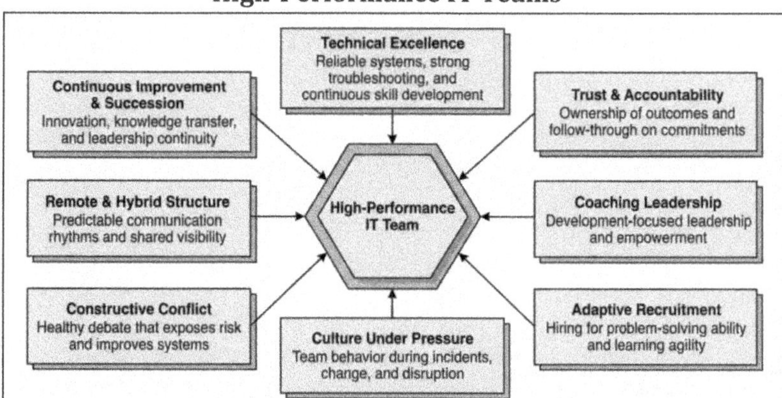

High-performing IT organizations are built through a balanced investment in people, leadership, culture, and execution discipline.

Chapter 4

GOVERNANCE, POLICY, AND ORGANIZATIONAL ACCOUNTABILITY

Strong governance is what separates an IT organization that runs with intention from one that runs reactively. Without it, the technology can be strong and the team capable, but projects still drift, costs rise without clear explanation, and compliance gaps often surface when the organization is least prepared, usually during an audit or an incident.

In most organizations, governance gets reduced to audit preparation and policy documents. That is the baseline, not the purpose. At its best, governance connects strategy, finance, risk, and ethics. It provides the structure needed to keep decisions consistent when the environment is changing, teams are turning over, and pressure is high.

This chapter approaches governance as a leadership discipline, not a compliance checklist. It assumes operational processes are already in place and focuses on the harder question, how leaders structure decisions, distribute responsibility, and enforce policies in a way that holds up under real pressure. The intent is to show how governance connects strategy, risk, finance, and ethics into something the organization can actually follow, not just reference during audit season. The goal is to show how governance links strategy, risk, finance, and ethics into one coherent system that guides IT behavior at scale. Detailed operational procedures are covered separately.

Figure 4.1: IT Governance Framework Overview – Strategy, Policy, Compliance, Accountability

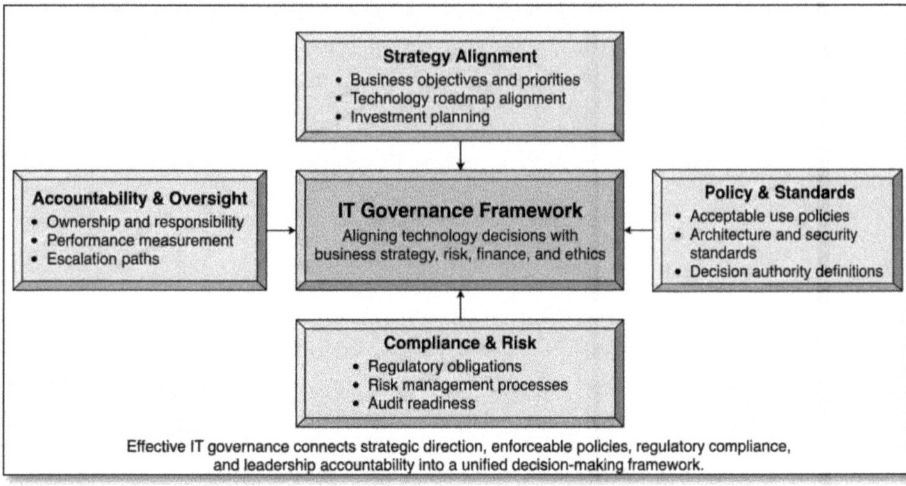

What IT Governance Means in Practice

IT governance is the decision structure that determines how technology investments are prioritized, how risk is accepted or escalated, and how the organization knows whether IT is delivering on its commitments. It is not separate from management. It is the set of rules, forums, and ownership structures within which management operates.

In practice, governance answers a few hard questions that every organization eventually faces:

- Who decides what gets funded and what gets deferred
- How priorities are set when every request is "urgent"
- What level of risk the business is willing to accept, and who can accept it
- How IT proves results, beyond activity and effort
- How the organization stays consistent as teams, vendors, and platforms change

Governance is not the same as management. Management runs the day-to-day, delivers projects, resolves incidents, and keeps services stable. Governance sets the guardrails and decision structure that management operates within. When governance is weak, the organization still delivers work, but delivery becomes chaotic. Projects compete instead of align, risk is handled informally, and priorities shift based on whoever is loudest.

Governance that works is easy to explain to anyone affected by it. The real test is not whether it looks comprehensive on paper. It is whether it helps the right people make better decisions faster and makes it harder to drift from standards without anyone noticing.

Main Goals of IT Governance

Strategic alignment starts with a basic question before any project is funded: which business goal does this support? If the answer is unclear, the project should not be in the portfolio. Value delivery means IT is accountable for outcomes, not just implementation. A system that goes live on schedule but fails to improve the process it was meant to fix has not delivered real value. Risk management requires risks to be surfaced, owned, and addressed through decisions, not carried quietly in the background until something fails. Resource optimization means being deliberate about where people, infrastructure, and budget are focused, and recognizing where they are being consumed by redundancy or low-return work. Performance measurement gives the organization a consistent view of how IT is performing against commitments, using metrics tied to outcomes rather than activity alone.

These five goals reinforce each other, which is why governance fails when it is applied to only one of them. Strategic alignment without performance measurement produces projects that sound aligned but are never checked against results. Risk management without resource optimization leads to controls that cost more than the risk they reduce. The purpose of governance is to keep these goals in balance, so that decisions about what to fund, what to measure, and where to focus effort are made with the same information and the same priorities rather than in isolation.

Table: Relationship Between IT Governance Objectives and Business Impact

Governance Objective	Key Focus	Example Outcome
Strategic Alignment	Linking projects to corporate strategy	Projects prioritized by ROI
Value Delivery	Maximizing investment benefits	Improved cost-to-performance ratio
Risk Management	Reducing vulnerabilities and incidents	Lower audit findings
Resource Optimization	Using assets efficiently	Reduced redundant systems
Performance Measurement	Continuous improvement	Regular KPI-based reviews

What governance looks like on a normal week

Governance becomes real through repeatable habits and decision points, not through documents sitting in a shared drive. In most environments, a practical governance rhythm includes:

- A visible intake process for new work, with basic sizing and priority scoring
- A short decision forum that can approve, defer, or reject work, with reasons recorded
- A method for tracking whether value is being delivered, not just whether milestones are being hit
- A consistent way to document risk decisions, including who accepted the risk and for how long
- A mechanism to stop or re-scope work when assumptions change

If governance exists only during annual planning, it will not protect execution. Most projects drift after kickoff, because constraints and priorities change. Governance is what keeps the plan connected to reality while work is underway.

Decision rights are the core of governance

One of the fastest ways to strengthen governance is to define decision rights clearly:

- Who can approve spend
- Who can accept operational risk
- Who can approve exceptions to standards
- Who can override priorities, and under what conditions
- Who owns each service, system, and major dependency

When these rights are unclear, decisions default to informal influence. That is how you get duplicated tools, inconsistent standards, and projects that continue because stopping them feels politically difficult.

Governance outputs that matter

Governance should produce a small set of outputs that teams actually use:

- A prioritized portfolio list that explains why items are ranked the way they are
- A simple scorecard that ties IT work to business outcomes and risk reduction
- A decision log that captures major calls and prevents repeated debates
- A risk register that is updated, owned, and reviewed, not archived
- Standards and policies that are enforced through workflow, not only through training

The point is not to create more artifacts. The point is to reduce surprises by making priorities, decisions, and risk acceptance visible.

Common governance failure patterns

Governance breaks down in predictable ways:

- Governance becomes a report-out, not a decision forum
- Everyone attends, but nobody owns decisions
- Metrics track activity, not outcomes
- Risk is discussed, but never accepted or funded down
- Exceptions become permanent and are never reviewed
- Projects keep going after the value case is no longer true

If these patterns show up, the answer is usually not more meetings. It is tighter scope, less noise, and a consistent documented path where decisions get made and recorded.

Keep governance practical

Governance should not turn into paperwork. It exists to keep IT consistent, trustworthy, and coordinated across projects and operations. The simplest test is whether it helps teams make better decisions faster; if it does not, it is overhead.

A practical way to scale governance is to start small, define decision rights and a basic intake path, then add only the controls that reduce confusion, prevent repeat debates, and protect production stability.

IT Governance Frameworks and Models

No single governance framework fits every organization out of the box. Most IT environments pull from several, using one for decision and accountability structure, another for service management discipline, and a third for compliance and oversight. The value is not in adopting a framework un full. It is in understanding what each one solves and where the gaps are in the current operating model.

1. **COBIT (Control Objectives for Information and Related Technology):** Developed by ISACA, COBIT is a complete framework for IT governance and management. It focuses on controlling risk, improving process maturity, and maintaining

compliance. It also separates IT responsibilities into governance and management areas to make accountability clear.

2. **ITIL (Information Technology Infrastructure Library)**[2]: ITIL centers on service management and reliable operations. It supports governance by creating consistent ways to handle incidents, problems, and system changes throughout the IT lifecycle.

3. **ISO/IEC 38500:** The ISO/IEC 38500: This standard provides board-level guidance for governing IT. It is commonly summarized around six principles, responsibility, strategy, acquisition, performance, conformance, and human behavior, and it helps boards oversee IT decisions with clear accountability.

4. **NIST Frameworks:** The NIST frameworks focus on cybersecurity and risk management. They offer practical guidance for monitoring systems, managing access, and protecting data.

Figure 4.2: How COBIT, ITIL, and ISO Frameworks Overlap in Governance

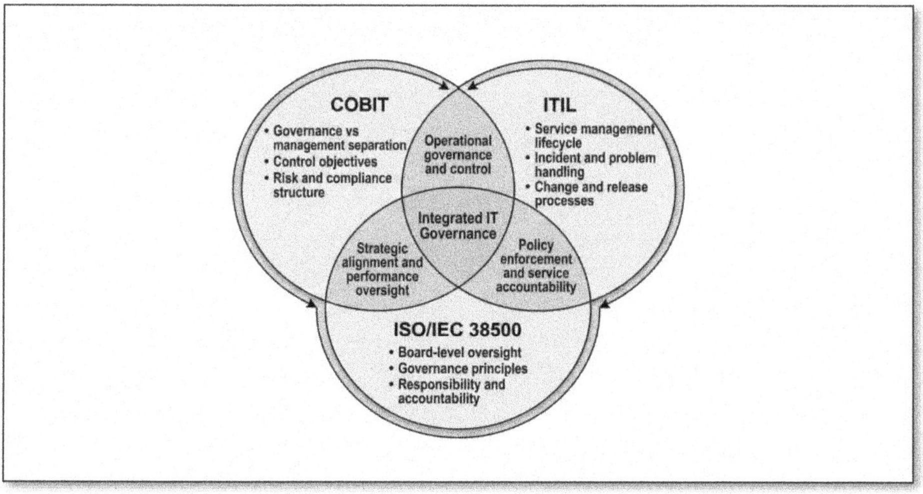

In practice, most organizations layer these frameworks rather than choosing just one. COBIT tends to anchor governance structure and

---

[2] ITIL, formally the Information Technology Infrastructure Library and now maintained by Axelos under the ITIL 4 framework, is the most widely adopted set of practices for IT service management. Organizations pursuing ITIL certification or formal adoption should consult current Axelos publications directly. The framework is summarized here for operational context

accountability. ITIL disciplines service delivery and change management. ISO standards provide the compliance and oversight language auditors and regulators expect. The combination works when each framework is used where it fits best, rather than forced into areas better served by a different model.

Building a Governance Structure

Governance structure answers one foundational question: who decides, and who is accountable when a decision turns out badly? A three-level model, executive, management, and operational, keeps that accountability traceable. Without it, decisions get made in the middle layer but owned by no one, which is where many governance breakdowns start.

1. Executive Governance (Strategic Level):

- Sets overall IT direction
- Approves major investments and projects
- Oversees enterprise risk posture
- Typically includes the CIO, CFO, and business executives

2. Management Governance (Tactical Level):

- Translates executive goals into actionable programs
- Defines policies, budgets, and performance metrics
- Coordinates cross-departmental collaboration

3. Operational Governance (Execution Level):

- Implements controls and processes within daily operations
- Ensures adherence to standards and policies
- Reports progress and issues to management committees

Figure 4.3: IT Governance Hierarchy – Executive, Management, Operational

Effective IT governance relies on clearly defined accountability across executive, management, and operational layers.

Committees Commonly Involved

- **IT Steering Committee** Ensures projects align with business priorities and resources are used wisely
- **Change Advisory Board (CAB)** Evaluates risks associated with configuration or system changes
- **Information Security Council** Leads cybersecurity planning and ensures compliance with internal and external standards
- **Data Governance Board** Oversees data quality, classification, and retention policies

Each committee covers a distinct area of governance. What makes the structure work is how they support one another: the steering committee sets direction, CAB protects production stability, the security council manages risk posture, and the data governance board maintains the integrity of the information the other three depend on. When one committee is missing or inactive, the gap usually appears in the others.

Pro Tip

Don't let the Steering Committee become a "reading club." If you spend the hour reading status slides to executives, you are wasting their time. Use these meetings exclusively for "forcing functions" situations where you need executive authority to kill a zombie project, resolve a stalemate between departments, or approve a budget variance. If you aren't asking for a hard decision, send an email instead.

Policy Development and Enforcement

Policies are how governance becomes day-to-day behavior. A well-written policy that is never checked is not a control. It is just a document. Enforcement is what closes the gap between what the policy says and what the team actually does, and that requires active measurement, not just publication.

The Policy Lifecycle

1. **Creation:** Identify the need (for example a regulation change, an audit gap, or an operational failure).
2. **Review:** Validate technical accuracy and business fit.
3. **Approval:** Obtain formal approval through the governance path.
4. **Communication:** Publish in the official repository and announce changes.
5. **Training:** Confirm people understand the expectations and how the policy affects daily work.
6. **Enforcement:** Measure adherence to the policy through audits, system controls, and operational checks. Apply corrective actions when gaps are identified and track remediation to closure.
7. **Revision or Retirement:** Review policies on a defined cycle. Update them when regulations, systems, or operating conditions change. Retire policies that no longer apply rather than leaving outdated controls in place.

Table: Example Policy Lifecycle Showing Timeline and Responsible Teams

Stage	Purpose in Plain Terms	Primary Owner	Supporting Teams	Typical Duration	Evidence Produced
Need Identification	Detect gaps in current operations, legal exposure, or control weaknesses	IT Governance Lead	Compliance, Audit, Operations	1 to 2 weeks	Risk note, problem statement
Draft Development	Write the first version that explains required behavior and expectations	Policy Author	Technical SMEs, Security	2 to 3 weeks	Draft policy document
Quality Review	Check that the draft is practical, accurate, and usable by staff	IT Management	Legal, HR, Service Owners	1 to 2 weeks	Marked-up draft, review comments
Executive Approval	Confirm leadership agreement and formal sign-off	CIO or Steering Group	Finance, Risk, Legal	1 week	Signed approval record
Organization Release	Make the policy available and easy to locate for all staff	Communications Manager	IT Ops, HR	1 week	Intranet posting, release notice
Workforce Enablement	Teach staff how the policy affects daily tasks	Training Lead	Team Managers	2 to 4 weeks	Training logs, attendance records
Compliance Monitoring	Measure how well teams follow the rules in real work	Audit or QA Team	Operations Managers	Ongoing, quarterly checks	Audit results, compliance metrics
Update or Decommission	Change or remove policies that no longer match reality	IT Governance Lead	Business Owners, Risk	Annual review cycle	Revision history, retirement memo

Pro Tip

Never write a policy you don't intend to audit. An unenforced policy is actually worse than no policy at all because it proves to auditors (and lawyers) that you *knew* the right standard but chose to ignore it. If you can't configure a system to enforce the rule automatically, or if you can't spare the staff to check it manually, leave it out of the official policy document until you can.

Key Policy Categories

- **Security and Access Control Policies:** Define how authentication, authorization, and data handling are managed across the environment. These policies establish who can access what, under which conditions, and with what level of approval. They typically cover password and multi-factor authentication requirements, privileged access controls, role-based permissions, and handling procedures for sensitive or regulated data. Their purpose is to make access decisions consistent, enforceable, and auditable.
- **Change Management Policies:** Standardize how system modifications are reviewed and approved so that change does not become a source of avoidable outages. These policies define what qualifies as a standard, normal, or emergency change, who must approve each type, what testing and rollback planning is required, and how changes are scheduled to avoid conflicts. The goal is to allow the environment to evolve while keeping that evolution controlled and recoverable.
- **Incident Response Policies:** Define how incidents are escalated and how communication flows during operational events. These policies establish severity levels, response-time expectations, escalation paths, role responsibilities, and stakeholder communication requirements. Clear incident response policies allow teams to respond with structure under pressure instead of improvising during the event itself.
- **Vendor Management Policies:** Establish how third-party vendors, contracts, SLAs, and compliance obligations are governed. These policies define onboarding expectations,

required service levels and security commitments, vendor review processes, and the continuity or compliance evidence suppliers must provide. Their purpose is to ensure external dependencies are governed with the same discipline applied internally.

- **Data Retention Policies:** Define how long data is stored and how it is securely deleted when no longer required. These policies align retention periods with legal, regulatory, and business requirements, establish where different classes of data are stored, and define disposal methods for retired information. Well-designed retention policies reduce unnecessary storage costs and limit the risk created by retaining data longer than necessary.

Figure 4.4: Example Policy Architecture Map Covering Corporate, Departmental, and Operational Levels

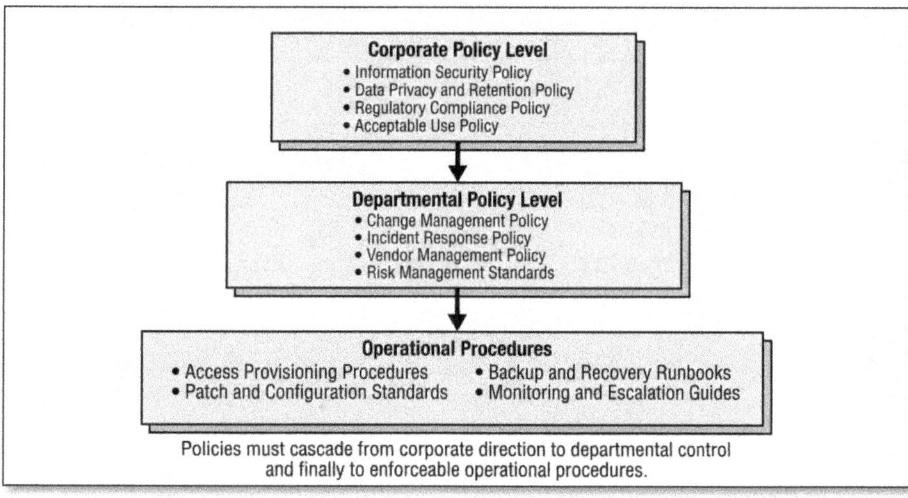

Establishing Accountability and Clear Roles in Governance

Accountability gaps in IT governance are usually traceable to one issue: no one clearly documented who owned the decision. When ownership is left implicit, it often defaults to whoever is most available or most senior in the room, which is not the same as being truly accountable.

Example – Change Management Process RACI

Task	Responsible	Accountable	Consulted	Informed
Submit Change Request	Engineer	Team Lead	CAB	Operations
Assess Risk	Change Manager	CAB	Security Team	CIO
Approve Deployment	CAB	CIO	Vendor	End Users
Implement Change	Systems Engineer	IT Operations	QA	Business Owner
Post-Implementation Review	Change Manager	CIO	Finance	All Stakeholders

Figure 4.5: Example Governance Accountability Chain Showing Roles and Reporting Lines

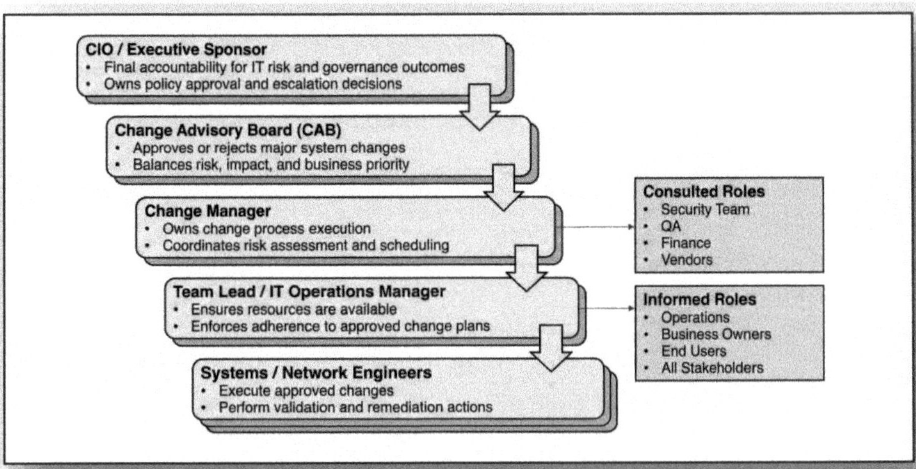

Clear accountability models do not eliminate conflict, but they do remove one of its most common causes: the assumption that someone else owns the decision. When ownership is explicit and traceable, teams spend less time negotiating authority and more time executing.

Pro Tip

Be ruthless with the "Consulted" column in your RACI matrix. Many managers fill this box with everyone they don't want to offend. But in practice, "Consulted" often implies veto power, or at least the right to delay the process while they review. If someone needs to know the outcome but lacks the specific expertise or authority to change the decision, move them to "Informed." You want velocity, not a committee debate.

Managing Governance Across Departments and Global Operations

Governance in multinational environments is not harder because the concepts change. It is harder because the same standard has to hold in a Singapore data center, a Frankfurt office, and a Chicago headquarters at the same time, under different regulations, vendors, labor agreements, and facility designs. The usual failure mode is drift. Regional teams start making local exceptions that never get reviewed, and within a year there is no real global standard left, only a document that says there is. The failure mode in global environments is usually one of two extremes: global rules that ignore local reality, or local exceptions that multiply until there is no longer a standard.

The target is controlled variation, a consistent baseline everywhere, with documented local variants where they are truly required. Core controls stay consistent across regions, while local teams retain flexibility for differences in regulation, infrastructure, labor models, vendors, and facility design. When this is done correctly, leadership can trust the baseline everywhere, and regional teams can still operate efficiently.

Common friction points in global governance:

- Conflicting regulatory requirements across countries and states

- Different facility designs, power topologies, and redundancy tiers
- Vendor and contract differences that change how work is executed
- Inconsistent evidence and reporting formats that slow audits
- Language and time zone gaps that cause policy drift

Best Practices

✓ **Use a federated approach to governance:** Set global standards for what must be true everywhere (safety controls, access principles, change discipline, incident classification, minimum documentation). Then, define a structured path for regional adaptations. Regional flexibility should be documented as an approved variant, not an informal workaround.

✓ **Keep one shared repository for all governance policies:** A single source of truth prevents policy fragmentation. Structure the repository so teams can find what they need quickly: global policies, regional variants, templates, and evidence examples. Include effective dates, owners, and review cycles so people can trust the latest version.

✓ **Schedule quarterly compliance reviews in every region:** Reviews should confirm two things: adherence to global controls and closure of approved exceptions. Keep the agenda focused on gaps, changes, and evidence readiness. Avoid turning these sessions into status meetings that produce no decisions.

✓ **Assign a governance contact person in each department or location:** This person is not a gatekeeper. They are the local owner responsible for policy communication, collecting evidence, tracking exceptions, and feeding local constraints back into the global governance process. Without local ownership, global standards degrade silently.

How to keep global standards consistent without slowing work

- ✓ Define what is mandatory vs adaptable, in plain terms
- ✓ Track exceptions with expiration dates and owners
- ✓ Standardize reporting formats so regions are comparable
- ✓ Require evidence that proves controls are working, not just that a policy exists
- ✓ Maintain a change log for governance updates so sites can adopt changes predictably

Case Example

A global data center operations team unified its maintenance procedures under a shared governance framework. Core safety and EHS rules stayed mandatory across all regions, but each site adjusted local vendor agreements and power designs to match its environment. This approach kept compliance strong while improving operational efficiency.

How the framework was implemented (what the governance lead actually did)
The governance lead first separated maintenance into two layers: a global baseline and a local execution layer. The baseline defined non-negotiables such as safety steps, lockout-tagout requirements, approvals, documentation expectations, and minimum change controls. The local layer covered site-specific details like vendor handoffs, local regulatory steps, and equipment differences.

They then standardized the artifacts that mattered: one maintenance procedure template, one pre-maintenance checklist, one post-maintenance validation checklist, and a consistent evidence package stored in the shared repository. Sites were allowed to add local steps, but they could not remove baseline controls without a documented exception and a review date.

Finally, they made compliance measurable. Each site reported the same small set of indicators quarterly: maintenance completion rate, exception count and age, repeat maintenance-related incidents, and audit evidence readiness. This created comparability across regions without forcing identical site designs, and it reduced operational friction because teams were no longer reinventing procedures at every location.

Figure 4.6: Example Federated Governance Model Showing Global Oversight with Local Flexibility

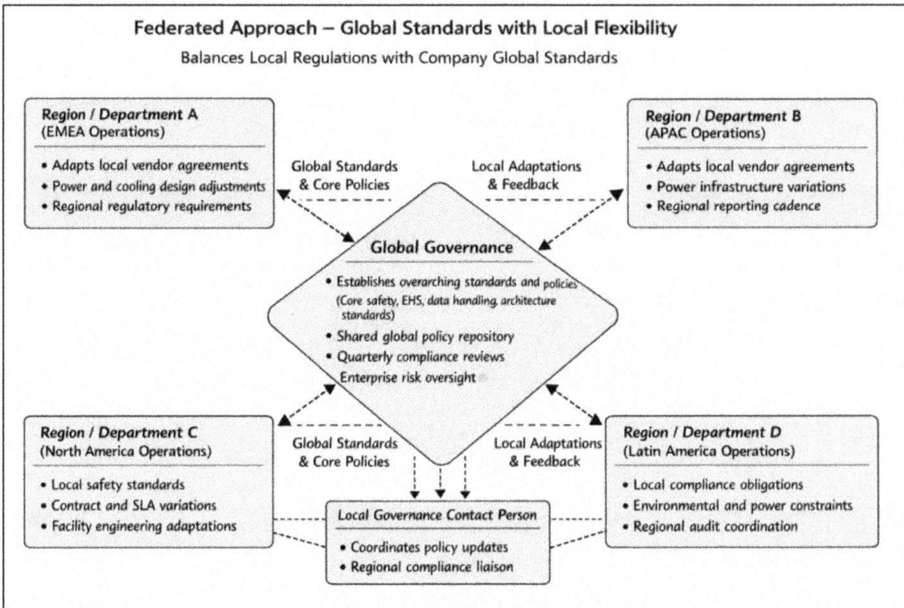

Integrating Governance with Project Management

Most project governance failures do not happen at kickoff. They happen three months later, when the original business case has changed, scope has expanded informally, and the risk register has not been updated since the first steering committee meeting. Building governance into each project stage is not about adding more checkpoints. It is about making sure each major decision is documented, owned, and reviewed against current conditions rather than original assumptions.

How Governance Supports the Project Lifecycle:

1. **Stage-Gate Reviews:** Defined checkpoints where leaders decide whether a project continues, adjusts, or stops.
2. **Project Portfolio Management (PPM):** Consolidated view of all projects to help balance priorities and resources
3. **Change Control Boards:** Review major design or scope changes before approval
4. **Budget Governance:** Regular cost reviews that match spending to key milestones
5. **Post-Implementation Reviews:** Meetings that check if project outcomes match what was originally planned

Figure 4.7: Example Governance Integration Points Across the Project Lifecycle

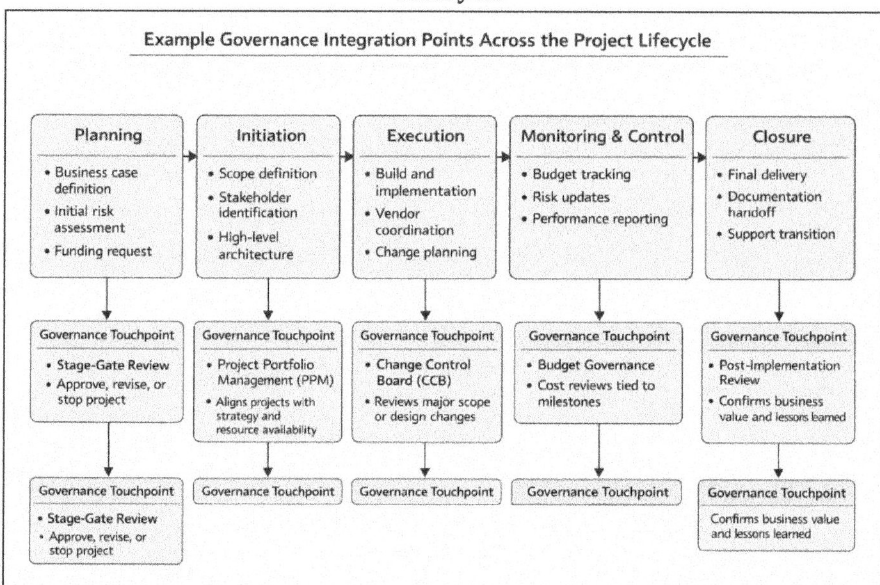

Case Example

A financial institution added governance checkpoints to its software rollout process. At each milestone, the team documented testing results, risk assessments, and rollback plans. Over the following year, no major production failures occurred, proving the value of structured oversight.

How the checkpoints prevented failures (what the program lead actually did)
They used a standard stage-gate template, not ad hoc meetings. Each checkpoint required the same minimum evidence before moving forward: test results against acceptance criteria, a current risk list with owners, operational readiness (monitoring, runbooks, on-call coverage), and a reviewed rollback plan.

Gate outcomes were explicit: proceed, proceed with conditions, or pause. Any conditions became tracked tasks with owners and due dates. High-risk releases also ran a short deployment and rollback rehearsal in a production-like environment. That discipline removed last-minute surprises and kept major failures from reaching production.

Measuring Governance Performance and Driving Improvement

Governance without measurement comes down to opinion backed by authority. Metrics are what make oversight credible. They show whether policies are being followed, whether investments are delivering value, and whether the risk posture is improving or weakening between reviews.

Governance KPIs

- How many IT projects meet their original business objectives
- The rate of policy compliance found during internal audits
- Year-over-year reduction in critical or high-severity incidents
- The percentage of system changes completed successfully without rollback
- Cost savings achieved through consistent standardization
- Vendor performance measured against SLA commitments

Table: Governance Performance Dashboard Example

Governance KPI	Description (Measurement Goal)	Typical Data Source	Industry Standard Reference
Project Success Rate	Percentage of IT projects meeting original business objectives.	Project Management Office (PMO)	PMI / COBIT 2019 (EDM02)
Policy Compliance Rate	Rate of adherence to policies discovered during internal audits.	Internal Audit / GRC Tools	ISACA / COBIT 2019 (MEA03)
Major Incident Reduction	Year-over-year decrease in critical or high-severity incidents.	ITSM / Service Desk Tool	ITIL 4 (Incident Management)
Change Success Rate	Percentage of changes completed successfully without rollback.	Change Advisory Board (CAB) Logs	ITIL 4 (Change Enablement)
Standardization Savings	Cost savings achieved through hardware/software standardization.	IT Finance / Procurement	FinOps / IT Asset Management
Vendor SLA Adherence	Vendor performance measured against Service Level Agreements.	Vendor Management System	ITIL 4 (Supplier Management)

Governance models need to be reviewed on a regular schedule, not only when something breaks. The most useful inputs are audit findings that show where controls failed in practice, post-incident reviews that reveal gaps in decision-making or ownership, and direct feedback from the teams working within the governance structure every day. If the same weaknesses continue to appear, the process is not being improved. It is simply being documented and left unchanged.

Ensuring Ethical and Legal Accountability in IT Governance

The technical controls in IT governance, access policies, change processes, and audit trails, are the visible layer. The ethical layer is less obvious, but just as important. Who approves an access exception and why, how an incident report is written when the manager's own team caused the issue, and whether a vendor relationship influences a procurement decision are all governance questions as well. They are also much harder to manage through tooling alone. Managers must apply policies that protect user privacy, prevent system misuse, and meet regulations such as GDPR, HIPAA, and CCPA.

Core Principles of Ethical Accountability

Integrity means company resources, systems, access, and data are used strictly for business purposes. Administrators should not use privileged access to review information outside a legitimate business need, and purchasing decisions should never be influenced by personal relationships with vendors.

Transparency requires conflicts of interest to be disclosed before decisions are made, not after. That includes vendor relationships, hiring connections, and financial interests tied to procurement. A conflict disclosed early can be managed. One that surfaces later is much harder to contain.

Confidentiality means access to sensitive data is limited to what a role requires for a specific task. Access should be documented, time-bounded where possible, and reviewed on a regular schedule.

Fairness depends on consistent evaluation criteria for both vendors and employees. When scoring methods and evaluation records are documented, decisions are easier to defend and easier to audit.

Auditability requires that every significant governance decision leave a traceable record. That includes risk acceptance, exception approvals, access grants, and policy deviations. If a decision cannot be reconstructed from the record, it was not properly governed.

Figure 4.8: Example Ethical Accountability Model Showing How People, Policy, and Process Work Together

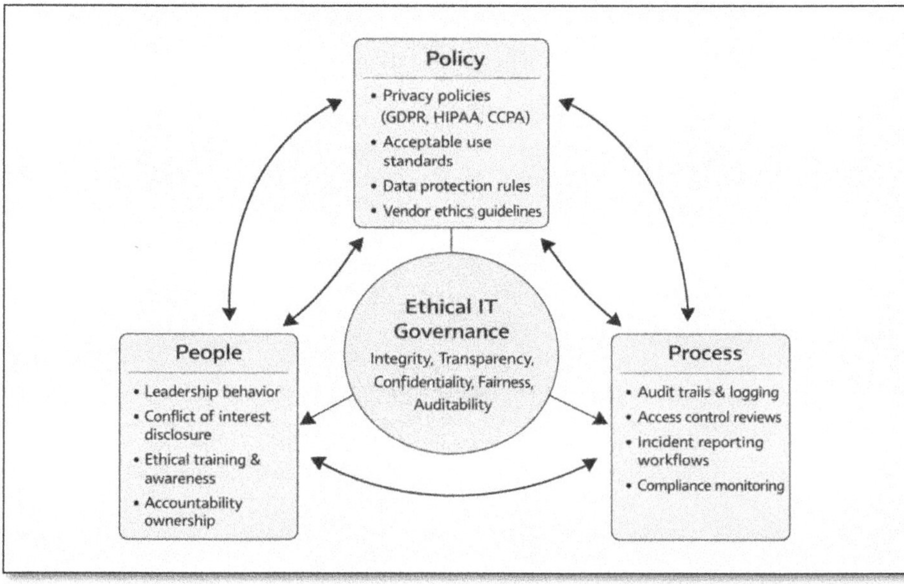

When ethical or policy violations occur, they should be investigated and resolved under HR and legal supervision. Real accountability means that when a policy is violated, the response is consistent and documented regardless of seniority. When a vendor offer creates a conflict of interest, it is disclosed immediately. When an incident is misreported, the correction is made before the review is closed. Governance does not become culture through training alone. It becomes culture when leaders model the standard and the organization sees that the rules apply at every level.

Case Study: Transforming Governance in a Global Technology Company

Background:

A global cloud provider faced audit findings across five regions highlighting inconsistent policy enforcement, missing vendor review records, and weak change management practices.

Actions Taken:

1. Created a central IT governance office that reported directly to the CIO
2. Adopted COBIT controls and standardized accountability charts across teams
3. Launched quarterly compliance reviews that all departments were required to complete
4. Built automated dashboards linking governance data to incident and change systems for real-time reporting

How the transformation was executed (what the governance lead actually did)

The governance lead started with the audit findings rather than a framework rollout. They categorized findings into three buckets: policy gaps (rules that did not exist or were outdated), evidence gaps (rules that existed but could not be proven), and enforcement gaps (rules that existed and were documented but were not being followed). That categorization determined the sequencing.

Policy gaps were closed first. The governance office drafted or updated the ten highest-risk policies using a standard template, ran them through a compressed review cycle with legal and security, and published them with a 30-day adoption window. Evidence gaps came next. The team mapped each control to a specific system or workflow that could generate the evidence automatically rather than relying on manual collection before audits. For enforcement gaps, they built dashboards that showed compliance status in real time so managers could see gaps as they occurred rather than discovering them during a quarterly review.

The centralized governance office removed the coordination problem. Instead of five regional teams interpreting standards independently, one team owned the global baseline, published approved regional variants, and ran quarterly reviews using the same scorecard across all regions. Automated dashboards pulled directly from incident and change systems, which eliminated the manual reporting cycle that had been producing inconsistent data.

Results:

Within a year, audit compliance improved across all five regions, replacing a fragmented baseline with near-full adherence. Policy approvals moved faster once the governance office took ownership of the process end to end, and for the first time, executives had live visibility into IT risk through a connected dashboard.

Figure 4.9: Example Governance Transformation Roadmap Covering Assessment, Implementation, and Optimization Phases

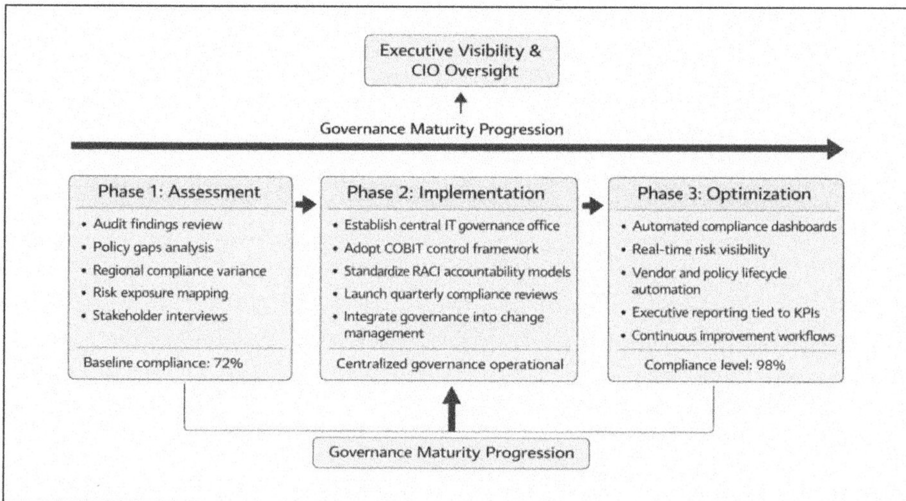

The case illustrates a pattern seen in mature IT organizations: governance structure is not what slows operations down. The real problem is the lack of it. When decision rights are clear, accountability is visible, and metrics are trusted, the organization spends less time debating who owns the problem and more time fixing it.

What This Means in Practice

The themes across this chapter point to one conclusion: governance is most effective when it is not treated as a separate function. When decision rights are clear, policies are enforced through workflow rather than paperwork, and accountability is tied to named owners rather than committees, governance stops being something the organization has to remember and becomes part of how it operates.

- Governance sets the rules for decision-making, ownership, and how success is measured
- Frameworks like COBIT, ITIL, and ISO provide guidance but must be adapted contextually
- Policies give teams a clear framework for how to work and stay consistent
- Accountability keeps ownership visible so that responsibilities are never vague
- Measuring results and using feedback helps governance improve over time
- Ethical and legal compliance protect both the company's integrity and public trust

When governance is embedded in how work gets done rather than added later for audit purposes, the organization gains more than compliance. It gains predictability. Leadership can trust that decisions are being made with the right inputs, that risks are visible and owned, and that when something goes wrong, there is a clear record of what happened, who made the decision, and how the issue was handled. That is what allows the organization to operate consistently under pressure.

Figure 4.10: Summary Model – Governance, Policy, and Accountability Interconnection Map

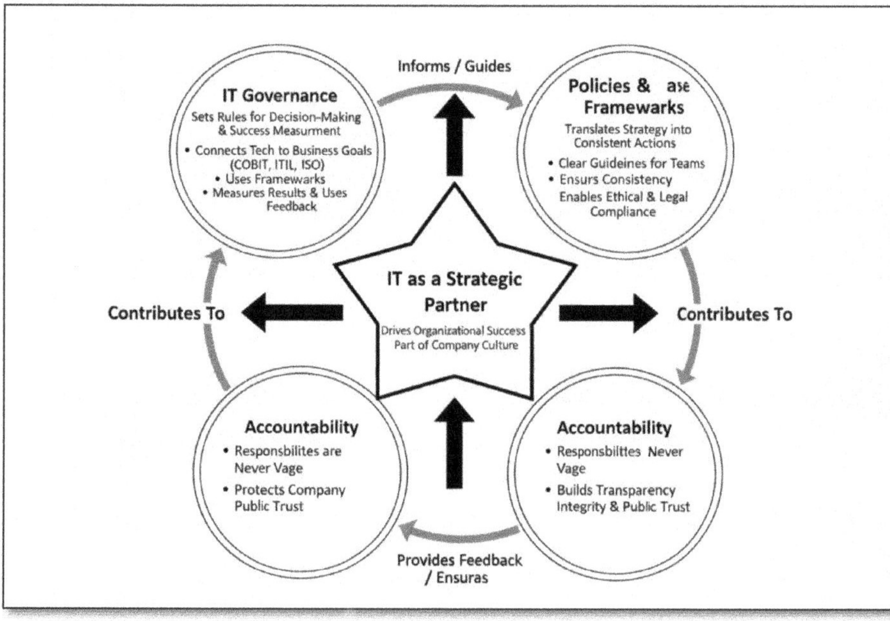

Chapter 5

CORE INFRASTRUCTURE FUNDAMENTALS: SERVERS, STORAGE, AND SYSTEMS

Every IT service runs on something physical: servers that process requests, storage that holds data, and systems that connect them into a working environment. When that foundation is designed well, it stays in the background. When it is not, the weaknesses become highly visible. IT managers are responsible for keeping infrastructure reliable and cost-controlled as the business grows, changes, and becomes more complex.

This chapter covers the infrastructure decisions IT managers are responsible for, how architecture choices affect reliability and cost, how servers and storage are selected and managed across their lifecycle, and how automation and documentation help keep environments stable as they grow. The emphasis is on operational judgment, not step-by-step execution. It also introduces hyperconverged infrastructure (HCI), virtualization, and automation-driven configuration management as they show up in real operations.

Unlike the previous chapters, which focused on leadership, alignment, and governance, this chapter turns to the infrastructure itself. The goal is not to train a server administrator, but to give IT leaders the architectural and operational understanding they need to make sound decisions, evaluate tradeoffs, and hold engineers accountable for the environments they manage. Detailed execution and step-by-step procedures are covered separately.

Figure 5.1: Core Layers of IT Infrastructure – Hardware, Virtualization, Applications, Services

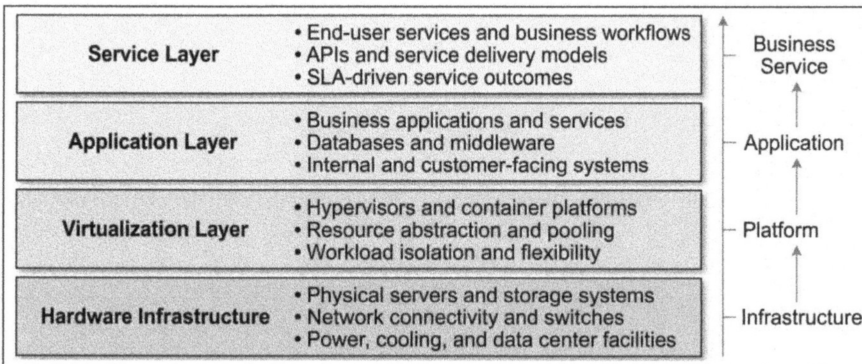

Reliable IT services are built on layered infrastructure, where each level depends on the stability and design of the layer beneath it

How Infrastructure Architecture Shapes IT Systems

Infrastructure architecture is the set of decisions that determines how compute, storage, networking, and supporting systems are assembled to deliver IT services. Those decisions have long-term consequences. A well-designed architecture keeps performance predictable under load, contains the blast radius of failures, and makes the environment easier and less expensive to operate over time. A poorly designed one creates debt that compounds as new workloads are added.

Key Components of Infrastructure Architecture:

1. **Compute (Servers):** The processing engines (physical or virtual) that drive applications and business logic.
2. **Storage:** The data persistence layer, ranging from high-speed flash for databases to archival systems for compliance.
3. **Networking:** The fabric of connectivity and protocols that binds isolated systems into a cohesive service.
4. **Power and Cooling:** The environmental foundation that ensures stability and prevents thermal failure.
5. **Management and Monitoring:** The control plane used to track health, optimize performance, and detect issues before they impact users.

Use a dependency matrix to map each core infrastructure component to what it depends on, what breaks when it fails, and what redundancy strategy removes single points of failure. The goal is to make failure impact and mitigation explicit instead of assumed.

Table: Example Matrix of Core Infrastructure Components and Their Dependencies.

Core Component	Primary Function	Key Dependencies (Upstream/Downstream)	Impact of Failure	Redundancy Strategies
Compute (Servers)	Runs applications and processes business logic.	**Depends on:** Power, Cooling, Network, Storage. **Supports:** Applications, Databases, OS.	Application downtime; inability to process transactions.	**Clustering & Load Balancing:** Grouping servers so if one fails, others take over (e.g., VMware HA).
Storage	Persists data (files, blocks, objects) securely.	**Depends on:** Power, Cooling, Network (SAN/NAS/Cloud). **Supports:** Compute, Backup Systems, Databases.	Data unavailability; potential data corruption or loss.	**RAID & Replication:** Using RAID for disk failure protection and mirroring data across locations.
Networking	Enables communication between systems/users.	**Depends on:** Power, Cabling, ISPs, Routing Hardware. **Supports:** Compute, Storage, Remote Access.	System isolation; loss of connectivity for users and apps.	**Dual Paths & Failover:** Redundant switches, dual NICs in servers, and diverse ISP connections.
Power & Cooling	Maintains environmental operating conditions.	**Depends on:** Utility Grid, UPS, Generators, HVAC. **Supports:** *All* Hardware (Compute, Storage, Network).	Total site outage; hardware damage due to overheating.	**N+1 or 2N Architecture:** Backup generators and UPS systems configured to handle load if primary sources fail.
Management & Monitoring	Tracks performance and controls configuration.	**Depends on:** Network, Compute (to host the tools). **Supports:** IT Operations, Security, Compliance.	Blind spots in operations; delayed incident response.	**Out-of-Band Management:** Separate network paths for management tools to ensure access during outages.

Design Principles for Reliable Infrastructure

- **Scalability:** The ability to add capacity as demand grows without redesigning the entire system
- **Redundancy:** Using back-up components to remove single points of failure
- **Performance:** Maintaining steady response times and throughput under load
- **Maintainability:** Making it easy to upgrade, patch, and isolate issues quickly
- **Security:** Including controls like access segmentation and encryption as part of the architecture itself

Case Example

A financial institution designed its infrastructure around two fully active data centers instead of a primary-and-backup model. Workloads ran across both sites at the same time, supported by diverse power paths, independent network entry points, and real-time storage replication between locations. When a cooling failure hit one facility during peak hours, traffic shifted to the other site with no service interruption and no need for manual intervention.

How the architecture was validated and operated (what the IT manager actually did)

The IT manager treated "active-active" as an operating model, not just a diagram. They started by defining which services were truly required to run in both sites and what "continuous operations" meant in measurable terms (acceptable latency, session behavior, data consistency expectations, and recovery objectives).

Next, they confirmed that redundancy existed end to end, not only in the data centers. Power paths were traced through ATS and UPS dependencies, network diversity was verified across carriers and entrance facilities, and application traffic was tested to ensure it could shift sites without manual intervention. Replication was monitored as a control, with thresholds and alerts for lag, failed writes, and split-brain risk.

Finally, they proved it through routine exercises. Planned maintenance was used as a live test, shifting traffic, draining workloads, validating monitoring and failback steps, and documenting any manual actions that still existed. After each exercise, the team updated runbooks and fixed the weak points that caused slow cutovers. This is what made the design resilient in practice, not just on paper.

Figure 5.2: Example of a Redundant Infrastructure Topology

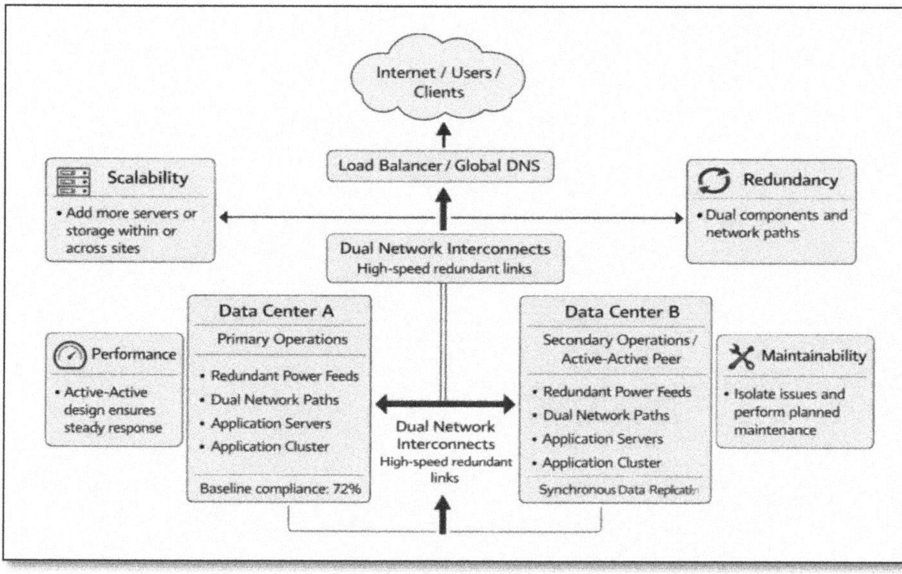

Managing Server Infrastructure Throughout Its Lifecycle

Servers are where workloads run. Whether they are physical hardware in a rack, virtual machines on a hypervisor, or instances rented from a cloud provider, the lifecycle decisions around them, procurement, configuration, patching, and decommissioning, directly affect reliability, cost, and operational complexity. Managing that lifecycle with discipline is what separates environments that stay under control from those that accumulate technical debt and operational risk.

Server Types

- **Rack Servers:** Compact systems mounted in data center racks for efficient use of space and cooling
- **Blade Servers:** Modular units that share power, cooling, and networking inside a single chassis
- **Tower Servers:** Standalone systems used mostly in smaller environments or development labs
- **Virtual Servers:** Software-based machines hosted on hypervisors that share hardware resources
- **Cloud Instances:** Virtual servers rented from cloud providers and scaled on demand

Figure 5.3: Comparison of Server Form Factors

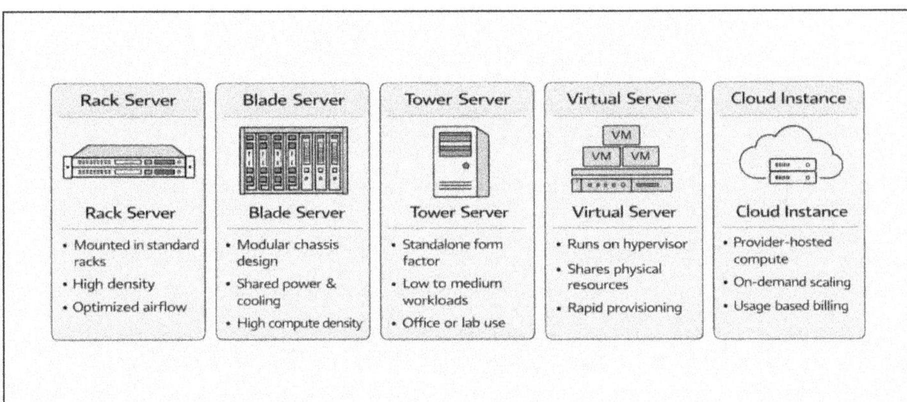

Server Lifecycle Stages

1. **Planning:** Identify business and technical needs, and establish performance and capacity standards.
2. **Procurement:** Purchase hardware or allocate cloud capacity based on approved specifications.
3. **Deployment:** Configure systems, test functionality, and integrate them into production workflows.

4. **Operation:** Continuously monitor server performance, apply updates, and handle issues quickly.
5. **Decommissioning:** Retire outdated hardware safely and ensure all data is properly erased or transferred.

Best Practices

- ✓ Maintain an asset inventory and configuration database (CMDB)
- ✓ Use Infrastructure as Code (IaC) for consistency
- ✓ Perform predictive maintenance based on telemetry data
- ✓ Establish warranty and support contracts with vendors

Case Example

One retail company modernized its data centers by replacing old rack servers with hyperconverged nodes. This upgrade cut power and cooling costs significantly and made new deployments much faster.

How the modernization was executed (what the IT manager actually did)

The IT manager began by building a clean inventory of the server estate and mapping it to workloads, support status, and utilization patterns. They identified the oldest racks with the highest operational drag, frequent hardware faults, high power draw, and slow provisioning due to manual build steps.

They then ran a controlled pilot. A small hyperconverged cluster was deployed to host a defined set of low-to-medium risk workloads, with clear acceptance criteria: performance under peak load, failover behavior, backup and restore time, and compatibility with monitoring and patching workflows. During the pilot, they standardized deployment using templates and automation so new capacity could be brought online consistently.

For rollout, they migrated in waves. Workloads were grouped by dependency and maintenance window constraints, then moved with rollback plans and validation checks. Legacy servers were decommissioned using a documented data handling process, and power and cooling reductions were tracked as measurable outcomes. The biggest speed gain came from repeatable builds, new deployments shifted from "hardware projects" to "adding nodes and applying a standard configuration," which reduced lead time and lowered day-to-day operational effort.

Figure 5.4: Automated Server Provisioning Workflow Diagram

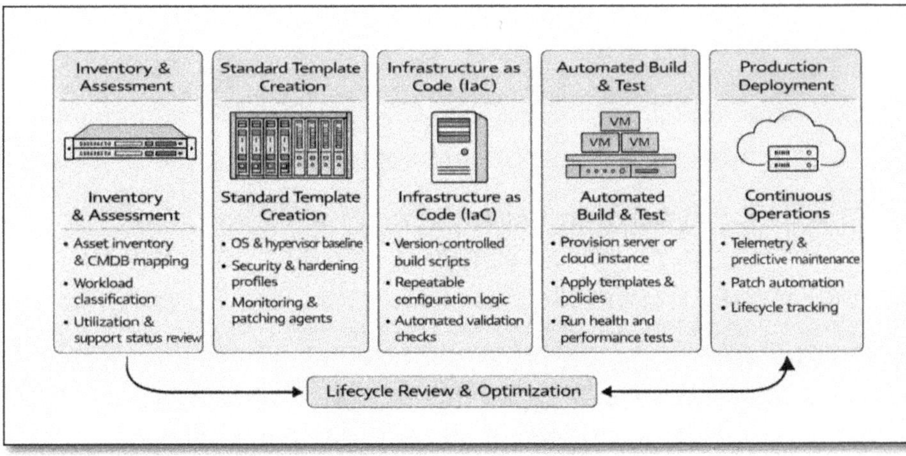

Monitoring platforms such as Nagios, Zabbix, and Azure Monitor track CPU, memory, disk, and service health in real time. Their value is not limited to live dashboards. Trend data on utilization and error rates helps teams plan upgrades and rebalance workloads before performance issues become outages.

Storage Systems and Data Management

Data storage underpins nearly every business process, and the choices you make show up directly in performance, uptime, scalability, and cost. On-prem versus cloud is not a trend decision; it is a workload decision driven by access patterns, compliance constraints, recovery requirements, and economics.

Types of Storage

- **Direct-Attached Storage (DAS):** Local drives attached directly to one server for dedicated performance

- **Network-Attached Storage (NAS):** Shared file storage accessed through the network for collaboration and backups
- **Storage Area Network (SAN):** High-speed block storage connected through Fibre Channel or iSCSI, used for mission-critical systems
- **Object Storage:** A storage architecture that manages data as discrete objects rather than as file hierarchies or blocks. It scales horizontally and handles large volumes of unstructured data well, making it commonly used for backups, media archives, and large datasets. Object storage can be deployed on-premises or consumed as a service from cloud providers

Figure 5.5: Comparison of Storage Architectures – DAS, NAS, SAN, Object

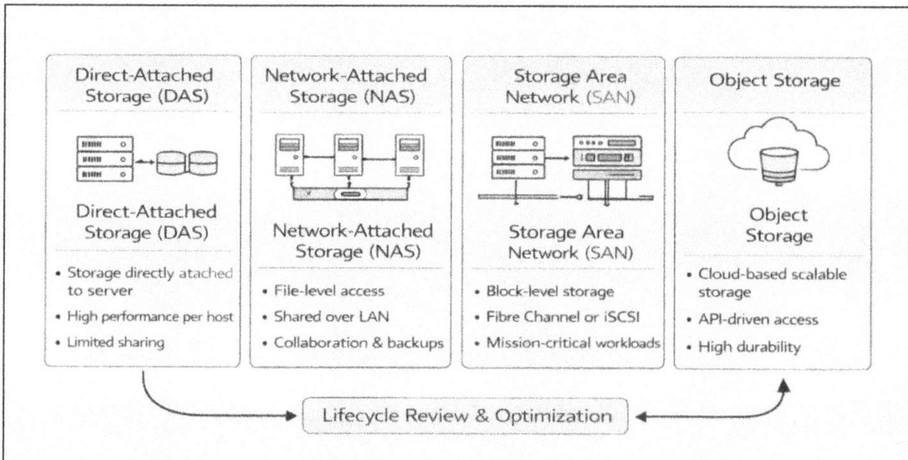

Key Concepts

- **RAID (Redundant Array of Independent Disks):** A disk configuration approach that spreads data, redundancy information, or both across multiple drives so a single drive failure does not immediately cause data loss. The level of protection depends on the RAID type. Some configurations mirror data, while others use parity so data can be reconstructed after a failure. The tradeoff is usually among write performance, storage efficiency, and fault tolerance

- **Snapshots:** Are most effective for short-term operational recovery, typically hours to days. They are not a substitute for backups because they typically live on the same storage platform as the source data, meaning a hardware failure, ransomware event that encrypts the platform, or storage system compromise can affect both the original data and its snapshots simultaneously
- **Replication:** Commits each write to both locations before acknowledging completion, which keeps the two sites consistent but requires a low-latency, high-bandwidth connection to avoid slowing write performance. Asynchronous replication acknowledges the write at the primary site first and then transfers updates to the secondary on an interval or queued basis. That creates replication lag, meaning the secondary copy may not be fully current, but it allows replication across longer distances and lower-bandwidth links
- **Tiering:** Automated tiering systems continuously monitor how often and how recently data is accessed, then move data between tiers based on those patterns without requiring manual intervention. The result is that high-cost, high-performance capacity is used for the data that actually needs it, while lower-cost tiers absorb the data that is accessed infrequently or only for compliance and audit purposes
- **Deduplication:** The tradeoff is processing overhead during data ingestion and backup operations, as the system must hash and compare incoming data blocks before determining whether a duplicate already exists. In environments with high write throughput, this overhead can affect performance, which is why deduplication is more commonly applied at the backup tier or during scheduled processing windows rather than inline on primary production storage

Case Example

A healthcare provider improved efficiency by using tiered storage. Older medical images were moved to cloud archives while active patient records stayed on local SAN arrays. The change cut storage costs significantly and met all compliance standards.

How the tiering decision was made and implemented (what the IT manager actually did)

The IT manager started by classifying data by access pattern and business risk, not by storage technology. They separated "hot" clinical workloads (active patient records, current imaging studies, EHR integrations) from "warm" and "cold" data (older images needed rarely but retained for legal and clinical reasons). They then set clear rules for when data could move: age thresholds, last-access time, and retrieval time requirements for clinicians.

To keep compliance intact, they validated retention, audit logging, encryption, and access controls before moving anything. They also tested retrieval workflows end to end, including how quickly archived images could be pulled back into clinical tools and who could approve expedited retrieval when needed.

Rollout was staged. A limited imaging subset was migrated first, monitoring retrieval latency, user impact, and cost changes. Once the pilot proved stable, the policy was applied broadly, with monthly reviews to adjust tier thresholds and to catch any unexpected access spikes.

Table: Performance vs. Cost Comparison for Common Storage Types

Storage Type	Typical Workloads	Performance Profile	Cost Profile	Scaling Profile	Key Operational Considerations
DAS	Single-server apps, local caching, small databases	High for that host, limited by server	Low per unit, higher operational overhead at scale	Poor, scale is per-server	Harder to share, backup and redundancy must be designed carefully
NAS	File shares, home directories, backups, collaboration	Moderate, depends on network and NAS design	Moderate	Good for capacity growth	Permissions sprawl risk, throughput bottlenecks during peak access
SAN	Databases, virtualization clusters, mission-critical apps	High, low latency, consistent under load	Higher CapEx and support	Good, but design-dependent	Requires careful zoning, multipathing, and change discipline
Object Storage (Cloud or on-prem)	Archives, backups, log retention, large unstructured data	Lower for random access, strong for throughput	Low for cold tiers, variable with retrieval and egress	Excellent	Retrieval time varies by tier, governance needed for lifecycle rules and access controls

Storage Governance

Storage governance connects data classification to technical controls. For each data category, regulated, confidential, internal, or public, governance should define the appropriate storage tier, the required encryption standard, who can access the data and under what conditions, how long it must be retained, and how deletion or disposal will be verified. In regulated environments, storage decisions have a direct impact on audit readiness. HIPAA requires access logging and audit trails for clinical data. GDPR affects where data is stored and who can access it. SOX-relevant data requires controls that can produce evidence of integrity and access history. These decisions should be documented before storage is purchased or provisioned, not worked out later during an audit

Pro Tip

New managers often buy storage based on capacity (terabytes), but many outages and performance incidents are driven by throughput and latency (IOPS, queue depth, response time). You can have 50TB free, but if queue depth is high, databases time out and users feel it immediately. Force application vendors to provide IOPS and latency requirements before you buy hardware, not just capacity.

Virtualization and the Rise of Hyperconverged Infrastructure.

Virtualization reshaped infrastructure by decoupling workloads from specific physical hardware. This allows multiple virtual machines to share a single host while remaining logically isolated, which drastically improves utilization and makes provisioning and mobility easier.

Key Benefits of Virtualization

- Optimized resource utilization
- Simplifies disaster recovery using snapshots and cloning
- Rapid provisioning for development and testing environments
- Reduced hardware footprint and energy costs

Advantages of Hyperconverged Infrastructure

- Scaling is simplified by adding new nodes without redesigning the system
- A single management console lets administrators control all resources
- Software-based redundancy increases fault tolerance and system uptime
- HCI integrates easily with hybrid cloud platforms for flexible deployments

Figure 5.6: Traditional vs. Hyperconverged Architecture Diagram

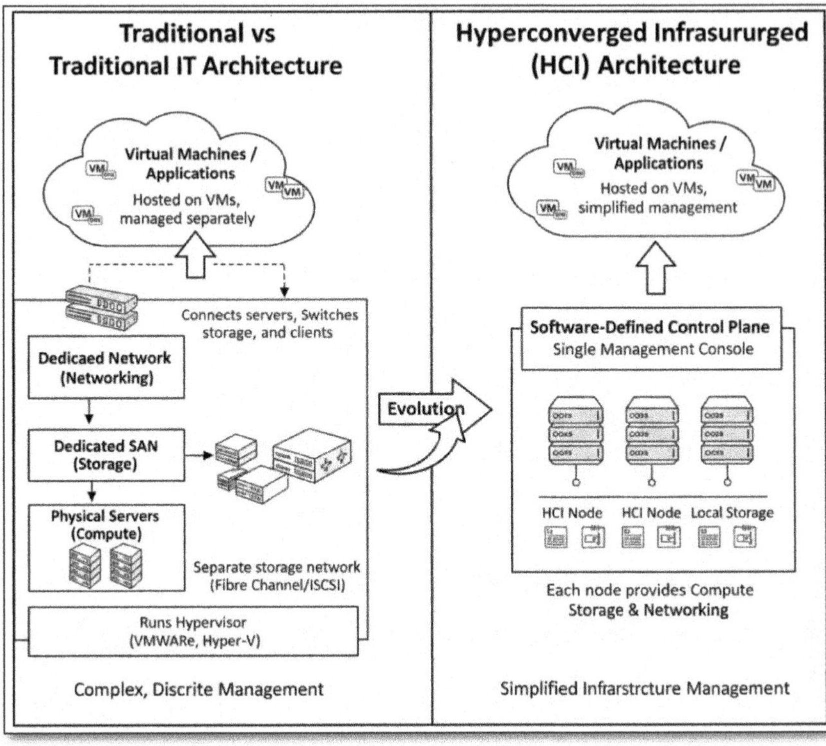

Case Example

A manufacturing company consolidated 200 physical servers into a 12-node HCI cluster running VMware vSAN. The new system used less space, required fewer manual steps to deploy new workloads, and reduced energy consumption significantly.

How the consolidation delivered the benefits (what the infrastructure lead actually did)

The infrastructure lead began by inventorying the 200 servers and grouping workloads by criticality, performance profile, and maintenance window flexibility. Before any migration started, the target cluster was standardized, including firmware baselines, networking, and storage policies, so hosts behaved consistently and failures were easier to contain and recover from. Workloads were then migrated in waves using templates and repeatable provisioning steps, with each wave including validation checks for performance, backup success, and failover behavior. Once most workloads were running stably on the cluster, entire racks of legacy servers were powered down and removed rather than leaving partial capacity stranded. The biggest operational gain came from turning deployments into a consistent workflow: add capacity by node, apply policy, deploy from template, and validate, instead of rebuilding server by server through manual configuration.

Automation and Configuration Management

Manual configuration is not just slow. It is inconsistent by nature, because two engineers following the same verbal instructions will usually produce slightly different systems. At scale, that inconsistency becomes a reliability issue, a compliance issue, and a recurring source of incidents. Automation reduces that variability. When configuration is defined as code, deployed from a known template, and checked against a desired state, the environment behaves more consistently regardless of who built it or when.

Core Principles of Infrastructure Automation

- **Define Once, Deploy Many:** Keep configuration templates as code so they can be reused consistently across systems, eliminating "snowflake" servers
- **Immutable Infrastructure:** Whenever possible, rebuild systems from a known trusted template instead of manually patching a running server
- **Continuous Configuration Monitoring:** Track changes in real time and automatically correct (or alert on) any drift from the approved baseline
- **Self-Healing:** Script automation to detect and resolve known, recurring issues automatically before users notice an impact

Pro Tip

Never automate a process you haven't simplified first. Automation is an accelerator: if you automate a messy, inefficient manual process, you just create a mess at the speed of light. Map the workflow on a whiteboard and remove every unnecessary step before you write a single line of code.

Common Tools

Ansible is commonly used for agent-free configuration and task automation across servers and network devices. It relies on human-readable playbooks and typically does not require software to be installed on target systems, which makes it practical in mixed environments. **Terraform** approaches infrastructure provisioning declaratively. The desired end state is defined in code, and Terraform determines what changes are needed to reach it. Because it works across multiple cloud providers, it is often used in hybrid and multi-cloud environments. **Chef and Puppet** are designed to reduce configuration drift by comparing system state to a defined policy and correcting deviations over time. **PowerShell DSC** serves a similar role in Windows environments, using configuration scripts to define and enforce the desired state of Windows nodes.

Figure 5.7: Infrastructure Automation Lifecycle – Define, Deploy, Monitor, Remediate.

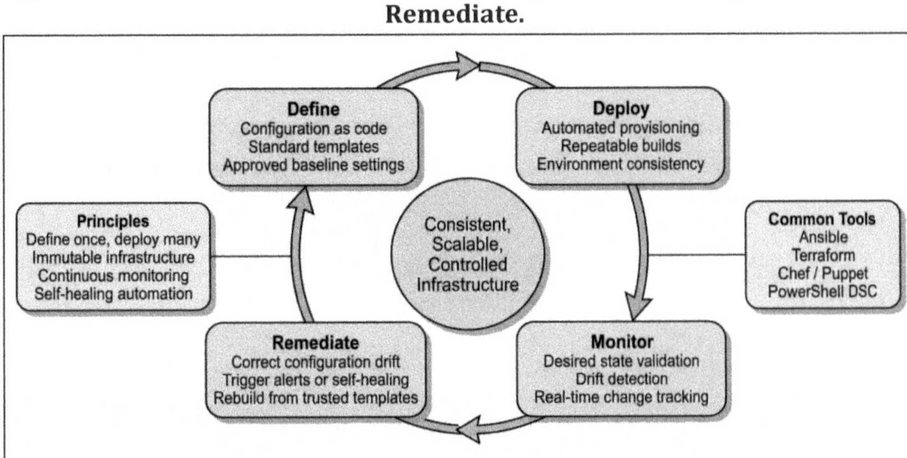

Case Example

A financial data center operations team introduced Ansible playbooks to automate firewall updates and user provisioning. Tasks that once took hours to complete were finished in minutes, and each change included automatic rollback and audit logging for accountability.

How the automation was implemented safely (what the manager actually did)

The team started by fixing the change process, not by writing playbooks. Before any automation was built, they defined which firewall rules and provisioning tasks qualified for automation, what approvals were required before execution (including CAB review for higher-risk rule changes), and how success would be validated after each run. Approval gates were enforced in the pipeline, not left to individual discretion.

Playbooks were built as reusable, parameterized modules with enforced input validation. Engineers submitted structured requests rather than writing raw rule syntax, which prevented unreviewed configurations from entering the pipeline and ensured required fields (ticket ID, approver, scope, and environment) were always present before execution. Every change ran through peer review and produced consistent logs tied to the originating ticket.

Rollback was built in from the start. For firewall changes, the playbook captured the pre-change state, applied updates in small increments, validated connectivity and policy results, and automatically reverted if health checks failed. For provisioning, the playbook enforced role-based access mappings and created a record showing who requested access, who approved it, what was granted, and when it was applied.

Over time, incidents decreased because configuration drift was eliminated from the automated tasks, and audit readiness improved because every change had a traceable record tying the action to an approval, a ticket, and a validation result, rather than relying on engineer memory or informal change logs.

Rollback was built in from the start. For firewall changes, the playbook captured the pre-change state, applied updates in small increments, validated connectivity and policy results, and automatically reverted if health checks failed. For provisioning, the playbook enforced role-based access mappings and created a record showing who requested access, who approved it, what was granted, and when it was applied. Over time, incidents decreased because configuration drift was reduced, and audit readiness improved because changes and approvals were recorded in a consistent, reliable history rather than scattered across manual edits.

Capacity Planning and Resource Optimization

Capacity planning is how IT stays ahead of demand without overbuilding. The goal is predictable headroom, enough runway across compute, storage, and network so growth does not turn into an emergency, but not so much excess that money is tied up in hardware the business does not need.

Practical Steps for Capacity Planning

1. **Collect Baseline Metrics:** Record CPU, memory, IOPS, and network throughput, but do not stop at averages. Include the indicators that expose real contention. In virtualized environments, that includes CPU ready time and memory pressure. For storage, track latency and queue depth. For networks, capture peak utilization, packet loss bursts, and interface errors. Baselines should reflect peak periods and known business cycles, such as month-end close, scheduled batch processing, and seasonal demand.

2. **Forecast Growth:** Use historical trends along with known business drivers such as marketing campaigns, new customer onboarding, product launches, and data retention changes. Forecasting is stronger when it accounts for both steady organic growth and discrete events that create sudden step changes in

demand. Document assumptions clearly so the forecast can be adjusted when business plans shift.

3. **Identify Bottlenecks:** Determine whether the constraint is compute, storage, or network, and whether it is isolated to a specific cluster, datastore, or link, or tied to a shared dependency such as identity services, DNS, databases, or interconnects. Bottlenecks often shift as environments expand, so constraints should be revalidated after each capacity change.

4. **Plan Upgrades Early:** Convert the expected exhaustion date into a decision date. If procurement, approvals, and delivery take three months, and saturation is expected in six months, the real action point is now. Build upgrade plans around maintenance windows, change freezes, testing needs, and validation time, not just hardware delivery dates

5. **Validate ROI:** Capacity increases should be tied to a measurable outcome, not just a general concern that more capacity may be needed. Link each upgrade to a specific result such as lower latency, fewer incidents, stronger transaction success rates, or support for a major business event. When possible, show the cost of inaction, including the risk of degraded performance during revenue-critical periods.

Table: Capacity Planning Example – Metric Thresholds and Alerts

Resource Area	Metric Tracked	Normal Operating Range	Alert Threshold	Critical Threshold	Typical Risk if Exceeded	Recommended Action
Compute	CPU utilization (5-min avg)	30–60%	70% sustained for 30 min	85% sustained for 15 min	Application latency, thread starvation	Add cores, rebalance workloads, review hypervisor oversubscription
Compute	Memory usage	50–65%	75%	90%	OS swapping, service crashes	Increase RAM, tune VM or app memory limits
Storage	IOPS utilization	40–60% of array rating	70%	85%	Write latency, stalled transactions	Add disks, enable tiering, migrate hot data
Storage	Read/write latency	< 5 ms	8 ms sustained	12 ms sustained	User-visible slowness, backup overruns	Add cache, optimize RAID layout
Storage	Capacity consumed	< 65%	75%	85%	Emergency expansions, data growth risk	Expand volumes, archive stale data
Network	Interface throughput	< 50% of link speed	65%	80%	Packet loss, dropped sessions	Upgrade links, add LACP members
Network	Packet error rate	< 0.01%	0.05%	0.1%	Retransmissions, degraded services	Inspect cabling, replace optics
Virtualization	VM density per host	< 70% design limit	80%	90%	Resource contention, HA failures	Add hosts, revise placement policies
Power & Cooling	Rack power draw	< 60% of circuit rating	70%	80%	Breaker trips, thermal shutdowns	Rebalance loads, provision new PDUs
Facilities	Inlet air temperature	18–24°C (64–75°F)	26°C (79°F)	29°C (84°F)	Hardware throttling, shortened lifespan	Improve airflow, adjust CRAC setpoints

Case Example

An e-commerce company used predictive analytics on its VM clusters to forecast demand before major marketing campaigns. Based on those forecasts, the platform team increased compute capacity by 25 percent ahead of peak periods, helping reduce transaction slowdowns during high-traffic events.

How the scaling was made reliable, what the operations lead actually did
They started by aligning forecasting with the business calendar. Marketing shared campaign dates and expected traffic multipliers, and the platform team compared those events with prior peak periods to build a realistic load model. Baselines were drawn from peak-hour telemetry rather than daily averages, and the team identified which services were most sensitive to saturation, such as checkout, payment, and session services, versus those that could tolerate some degradation.

Automation was then limited by clear guardrails. Scaling actions were restricted to pre-approved clusters and defined capacity ranges, and triggers were based on service indicators such as latency, error rate, and queue depth, not CPU alone. Every scale event required validation after execution, including synthetic checkout tests, dashboard checks, and rollback conditions if performance did not improve.

After each campaign, the team treated the event as a learning cycle. Forecasts were compared against actual demand, thresholds were adjusted, and the capacity plan was updated for the next cycle. The 25 percent increase worked because it was planned, bounded, and validated against customer-facing outcomes, not simply because more compute was added.

Infrastructure Documentation and Knowledge Management

Documentation is not something that happens after the real work is done. It is part of the operational control system. Without it, changes become hard to trace, recovery depends on whoever happens to be online, and the environment fills with decisions no one can fully explain. The goal is not to produce records for their own sake. It is to keep the environment understandable and recoverable by anyone qualified to work in it. When it is missing or outdated, two things happen fast: recovery slows down, and decisions become person-dependent. The bigger the environment gets, the more expensive tribal knowledge becomes.

Documentation has to be usable under pressure. If a document cannot be followed during an incident, or it takes ten minutes to find, it will not be used. The standard is that any qualified engineer on shift can understand the system, execute a standard change, and recover a service using the written artifacts, without needing a specific expert online.

Core Documentation Artifacts

- **Network and system topology diagrams with version and date:** Diagrams must show the real operating paths, not just ideal layouts. Include routing boundaries, critical dependencies, management networks, upstream providers, and cross-site links. Every diagram should have: owner, last verified date, version, and where it is sourced from (CMDB export, discovery tool, or manual)
- **Configuration-as-code templates in Git with commit history:** Treat Git as the source of truth for intended state. Templates should include environment variables, validation rules, and guardrails that prevent unsafe changes. Commit messages should describe intent and scope, not just "update." Link changes back to tickets and CAB approvals where applicable
- **Patch logs tied to asset IDs and maintenance windows:** Patch history must map to specific assets, services, and approved windows. Include: patch set, pre-checks, post-checks, success or failure notes, and rollback actions taken. If patching is automated, log output still needs to be summarized and accessible

- **Warranty terms and vendor contacts linked from each asset's CMDB record:** Every asset record should point to: support level, warranty end date, RMA steps, contract identifiers, and escalation contacts. During incidents, engineers should not be searching email threads for vendor details
- **Runbooks with triggers, step-by-step actions, rollback, and named on-call escalations:** A runbook should read like a procedure, not a narrative. Each runbook should include: trigger conditions, prerequisites, decision points, commands or actions, validation checks, rollback steps, and escalation triggers. Include who owns the runbook and when it was last tested

To keep these artifacts healthy, treat them as operational assets with owners and review cycles. A simple rule that works: every critical artifact has a named owner, a last verified date, and a next review date.

Table: Documentation Artifact Ownership and Review Cadence

Artifact	Owner Role	Minimum Review Cadence	Verification Method
Topology diagrams	Network or Systems Lead	Quarterly	Compare to discovery and live configs
IaC templates	Platform Engineering	Each major change plus quarterly	Peer review, pipeline checks
Patch logs	Ops Lead or Patch Owner	Monthly	Spot audit versus CMDB
Vendor and warranty data	Asset Manager	Quarterly	Contract review and CMDB audit
Runbooks	Service Owner	Quarterly plus after incidents	Tabletop or live drill

Figure 5.8: Example of Infrastructure Documentation Hierarchy

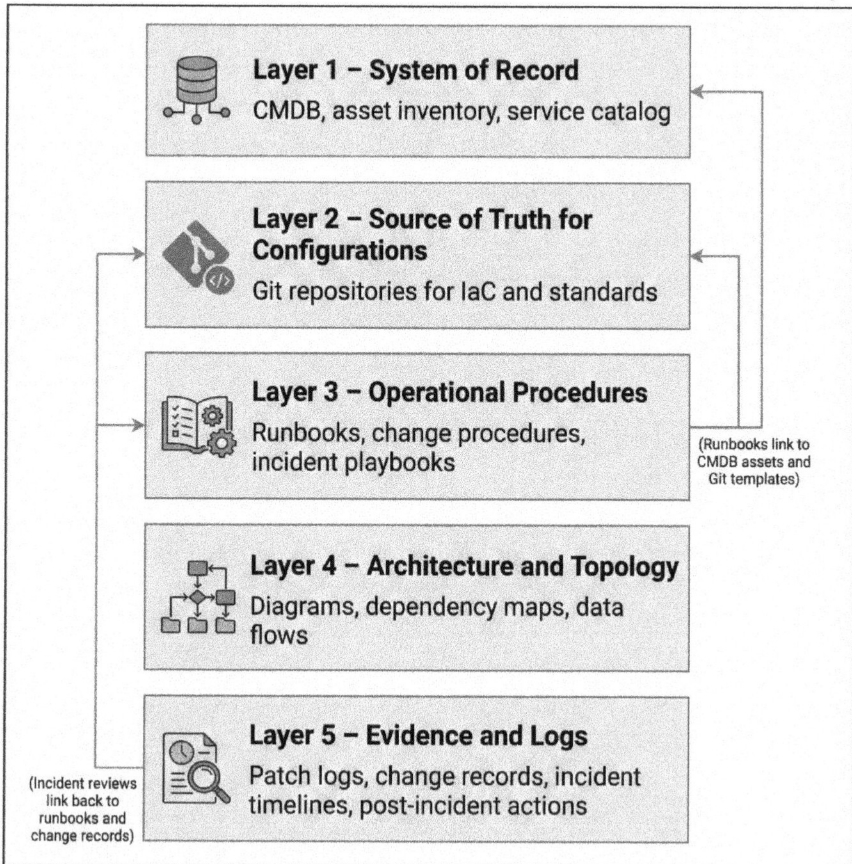

Knowledge Management Best Practices

- **Choose one primary repo and prevent duplicates:** Pick a single home for human-readable documentation (for example Confluence or SharePoint) and enforce it. Do not allow multiple "official" locations. Link out to Git, monitoring dashboards, and the CMDB rather than copying content into multiple places

- **Make documentation a CAB entry criterion:** If the change is not documented, it does not ship. This is one of the few rules that reliably improves documentation quality. Tie documentation updates to the change ticket, and require links to updated runbooks, diagrams, or IaC diffs before approval

- **Review critical docs quarterly against live configs using automated diffs:** Manual reviews miss drift. For critical systems, use automated comparisons where possible: exported configs, discovery data, and IaC intended state. The review should answer: what changed, is it approved, and is documentation updated to match
- **Tag documents so new team members can find "how-to" content fast:** Use a consistent tagging scheme across systems. Keep it simple and predictable, for example: Service, Environment, Component, Task Type (change, incident, maintenance), and Severity (critical, standard). New hires should be able to filter to "service X, incident, recovery" and get the right runbook quickly

Practical standards that prevent documentation decay

- Every document has an owner, last verified date, and next review date
- Every runbook is written to be executed by someone other than the author
- Every critical system has a dependency map linked from the service page
- Every incident produces one update to documentation, either a runbook fix, a diagram correction, or a decision note
- Every recurring issue must point to a specific runbook section or a missing artifact

Case Example

During a database cluster outage, the team restored service in two hours by following a documented dependency map and recovery runbook, instead of losing time to guesswork and dependency misses.

How the recovery happened (what the manager actually did)

The incident lead used the dependency map to confirm what could safely be restarted and in what order, rather than guessing. The map listed upstream and downstream dependencies, storage paths, cluster quorum requirements, and application cutover points. That prevented the common mistake of restoring the database while leaving a broken dependency in place.

The recovery runbook was structured for speed. It started with clear triggers and decision points: whether the cluster was in split-brain risk, whether storage was reachable, and whether the failure was node-level or shared infrastructure. It included validation checks after each action, so the team did not move forward on false assumptions.

While responders executed steps, a second engineer updated the incident timeline and captured any deviations from the runbook. Once service was restored, the manager required a short follow-up: update the runbook with the missing detail that caused hesitation, and update the dependency map where the diagram did not match the live topology. That ensured the documentation improved as a direct result of the outage, instead of the team moving on and forgetting the friction points.

Pro Tip

A reliable way to pressure-test documentation is the "2 AM Test." Hand the disaster recovery runbook to a junior engineer who has never worked that system and ask them to execute a safe read-only task. If they need clarifications, the runbook needs improvement. If they cannot proceed without you, you are not ready for an outage.

Building Sustainable and Energy-Efficient IT Operations

Infrastructure decisions now need to account for environmental impact alongside cost, reliability, and capacity. Smart design and virtualization do more than reduce emissions. They also lower operating cost by reducing power draw, easing cooling demand, and improving utilization of existing equipment. In most data centers, power and cooling are not fixed costs; they scale with how efficiently workloads are placed and how consistently the facility is operated.

Sustainable operations and reliability are tightly linked in practice. The same decisions that improve utilization and reduce waste also improve resilience: fewer stranded servers, fewer unmanaged assets, cleaner capacity planning, and more predictable thermal behavior.

Practical Steps for Greener IT Operations

1. **Consolidate workloads so fewer servers sit idle:** Idle hardware still consumes power and produces heat. Consolidation is about raising utilization safely without creating noisy-neighbor problems or overloading clusters. A practical approach is to consolidate by service tier and workload profile, then enforce placement rules so critical workloads retain adequate headroom.

2. **Choose energy-efficient hardware and modern power supplies to cut consumption:** Older platforms often burn more watts per unit of compute and produce more heat for the same output. When refresh decisions are made, include efficiency metrics alongside performance. For most environments, the cost case is strongest when you target the least efficient hardware first and tie refresh to measurable reductions in power and cooling demand.

3. **Use hot-aisle and cold-aisle layouts to keep cooling predictable and efficient:** Cooling becomes inefficient when supply and exhaust air mix. Consistent airflow design reduces hotspots, avoids overcooling, and increases the usable capacity of

existing cooling systems. In practical terms, it also reduces incident risk caused by thermal alarms and unexpected throttling.

4. **Recycle retired hardware through approved e-waste programs:** Retirement has to be safe and auditable. Data handling must be documented, storage must be sanitized according to policy, and disposal must use approved channels with certificates of destruction where required. This reduces environmental impact and closes compliance gaps.

5. **Enable smart power settings and temperature monitoring to avoid unnecessary energy use:** Power caps, processor power management, and fan curve tuning can reduce consumption without harming service outcomes when done carefully. Temperature monitoring should be treated as an operational signal, not just a facilities metric. If thermal patterns are shifting, it often indicates airflow issues, load concentration problems, or cooling drift.

Figure 5.9: Data Center Energy Efficiency Measures

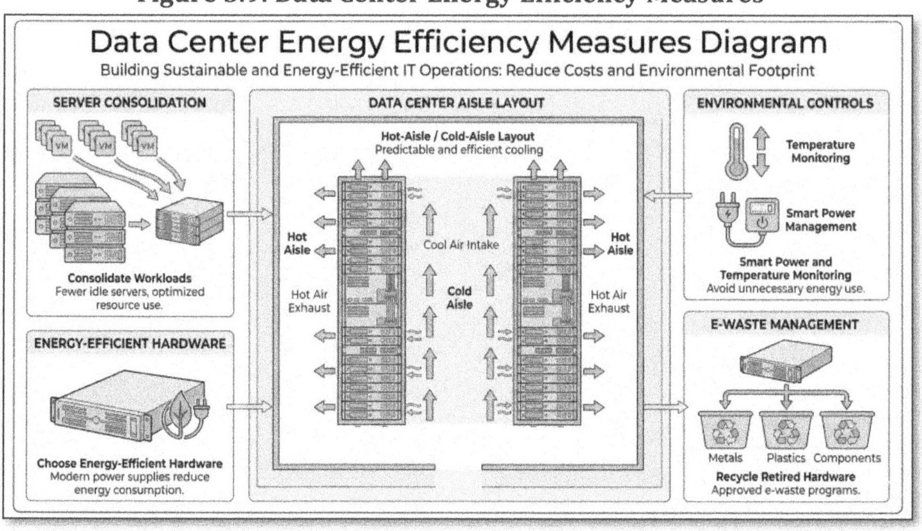

Case Example

A telecommunications provider lowered its environmental impact by replacing aging hardware with energy-efficient blade systems and using workload balancing to avoid idle capacity.

How the savings were achieved (what the manager actually did)
The manager started by establishing a baseline using telemetry, not estimates. They collected per-rack power draw, inlet temperatures, and utilization trends, then identified the least efficient hardware groups where power draw stayed high even when utilization was low. Those racks became the first refresh targets.

They did not replace hardware blindly. Before refresh, the team reduced waste by consolidating workloads onto fewer hosts and enforcing placement rules that kept headroom for peak periods. That allowed entire racks to be powered down, not just lightly loaded. Workload balancing was then used to prevent one cluster from running hot while another sat underused, which reduced both power spikes and cooling strain.

For the hardware refresh, they moved to blade systems in phases and validated impact after each wave: power draw per compute unit, thermal stability, and performance under load. They also adjusted monitoring so energy efficiency did not remain a one-time project. Power and temperature became part of the regular operational scorecard, and exceptions, hotspots, unexpected power drift, and underutilized clusters, triggered follow-up actions the same way reliability issues would.

What This Means in Practice

- Infrastructure reliability does not come from buying the right hardware. It comes from designing for failure, validating redundancy under real conditions, and keeping the environment legible enough to recover quickly when something breaks.
- Architecture decisions carry long consequences. Choices about storage tiers, network paths, and virtualization strategy affect cost, performance, and operational complexity for years. They are worth getting right before workloads are added on top
- Automation is only as good as the process underneath it. Consistent, repeatable configuration management reduces incidents and compliance risk, but it requires clean, simplified workflows before any code is written
- Documentation is a control, not a record. If the environment cannot be operated and recovered by anyone qualified to work in it, the documentation has failed its purpose regardless of how much of it exists
- Energy efficiency and operational discipline overlap more than most teams realize. The same practices that improve utilization, reduce idle hardware, and keep cooling predictable also reduce operating cost and extend the useful life of the environment

Figure 5.10: Infrastructure Excellence Model: Design, Build, Automate, Sustain

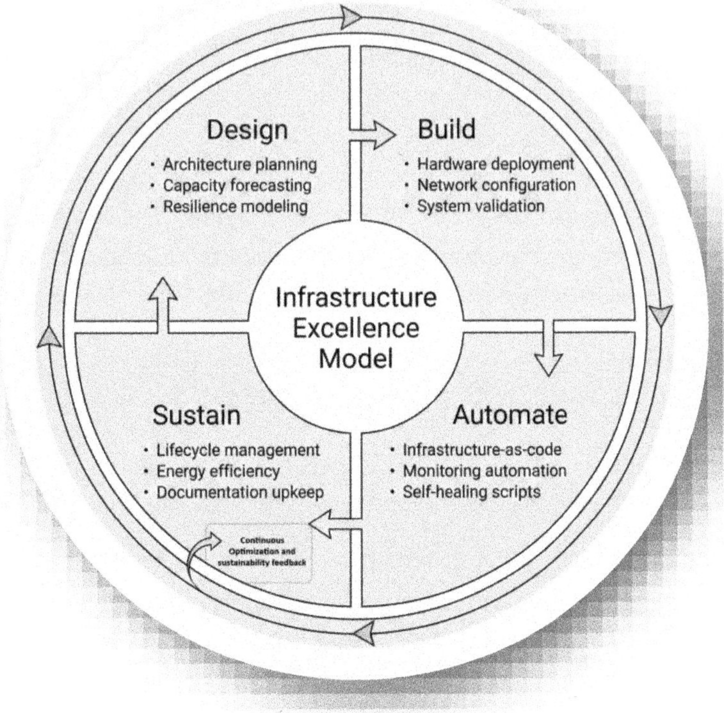

Part II

CORE IT INFRASTRUCTURE AND OPERATIONS

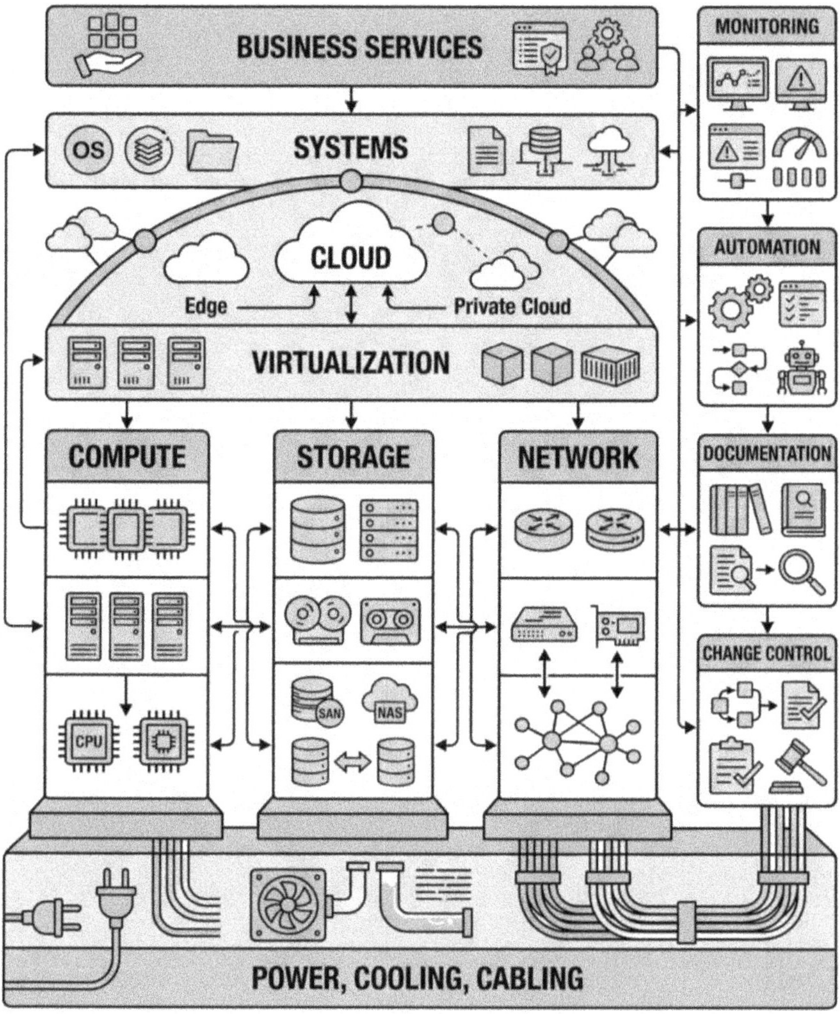
BUSINESS SERVICES
SYSTEMS
OS
CLOUD
Edge
Private Cloud
VIRTUALIZATION
COMPUTE
CPU
STORAGE
SAN
NAS
NETWORK
POWER, COOLING, CABLING
MONITORING
AUTOMATION
DOCUMENTATION
CHANGE CONTROL

Chapter 6

NETWORKING AND CONNECTIVITY MANAGEMENT: LAN, WAN, WIRELESS, AND SD-WAN

Enterprise networks are the infrastructure that makes everything else work. Users depend on them to reach applications. Sites depend on them to connect to data centers and cloud services. Business workflows depend on them to run without interruption. When the network fails, the impact is immediate and visible: transactions stop, collaboration breaks down, and the business starts demanding answers before IT has the full picture.

IT managers who treat networking as purely a technical function tend to underinvest in the operating discipline around it, the policies, monitoring, change controls, and vendor relationships that determine whether the infrastructure performs reliably under real conditions. Architecture usually gets the attention. Governance is what keeps the environment from drifting over time.

This chapter examines enterprise networking from core internal design to broader connectivity and control. It covers LAN design and VLAN strategy, WAN technologies and their tradeoffs, the move to SD-WAN, wireless infrastructure, security segmentation, and the monitoring and change management practices that help keep the environment stable. The goal is to give IT managers the architectural and operational context they need to lead networking functions effectively, rather than function as a step-by-step operational runbook.

Figure 6.1: Enterprise Network Architecture Overview - LAN, WAN, Wireless, Internet, Cloud Edge.

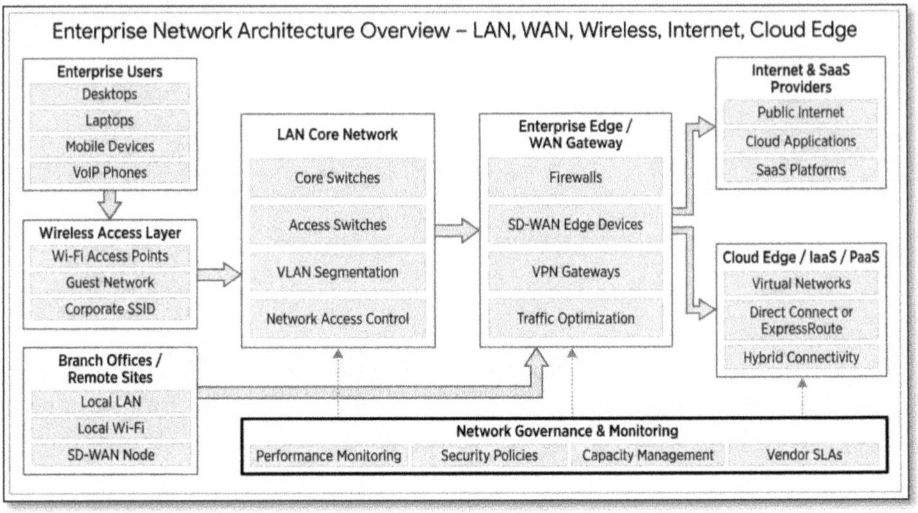

Networking in the Modern Enterprise

The enterprise network has changed in fundamental ways. Traffic no longer flows neatly from users to the data center and back. Users now work from home, branch offices, and mobile devices. Applications run across cloud platforms, SaaS environments, and hybrid infrastructure. The network has to perform across all of those paths, under different conditions, and be managed by a team that often cannot physically access much of what it supports.

The Core Functions of a Modern Network

1. **Connectivity.** Keeps users, systems, and applications linked across the environment, regardless of physical location.
2. **Performance.** Maintains acceptable latency, throughput, and reliability, ensuring workflows don't stall as workloads grow.
3. **Security.** Protects data in transit using segmentation, encryption, and continuous monitoring to limit the blast radius of a breach.
4. **Scalability.** Allows the network to expand (new sites, more users) without requiring a fundamental redesign.

5. **Manageability.** Supports centralized administration and automation so the team spends less time on manual CLI configuration.

Table: Example Network Functions and Their Business Impact

Network Function	Business Impact	Example Metric
Connectivity	Supports day-to-day communication and system access	Link uptime
Performance	Keeps applications responsive so productivity stays high	Latency target under 50 ms
Security	Prevents breaches and protects sensitive data	Number of blocked threats
Scalability	Helps the business expand without redesigning networks	New sites added with minimal reconfiguration
Manageability	Reduces operational overhead and speeds troubleshooting	Devices managed per engineer

Local Area Networks (LAN)

A LAN is where most day-to-day network activity takes place: endpoints connect to switches, traffic moves between application tiers, and wireless devices associate with access points. The design decisions at this layer, including VLAN scope, loop prevention, and uplink design, have a direct effect on how predictably the environment behaves when traffic spikes, hardware fails, or configurations change.

LAN Architecture Layers

1. **Access Layer:** The point where end-user devices connect, including switches and wireless access points.

2. **Distribution Layer:** Collects traffic from access switches and applies routing or policy control.
3. **Core Layer:** The high-speed backbone that moves traffic across the network with redundancy.

Figure 6.2: Example of a Three-Tier LAN Architecture

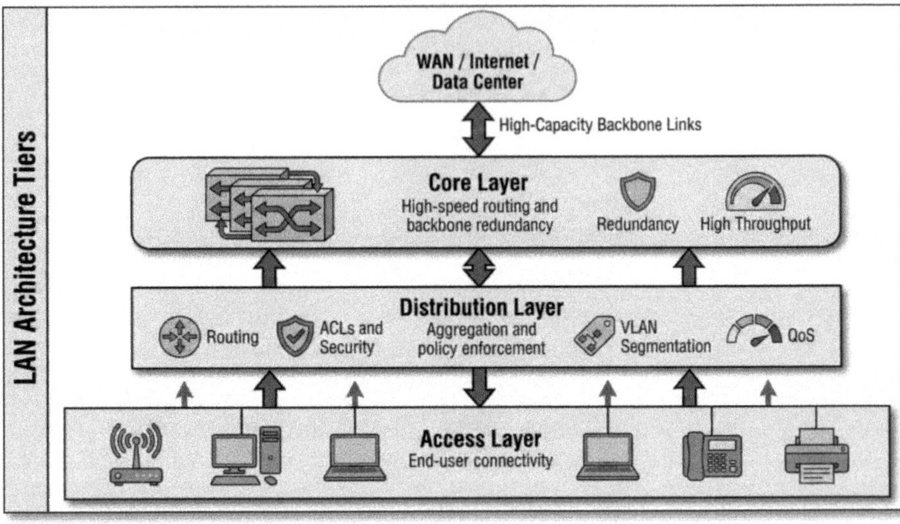

LAN Design Principles

- Use a layered design to help with scalability and fault isolation
- Segment traffic with VLANs to separate teams or application types
- Enable STP or Rapid STP to avoid switching loops
- Use LACP to combine links for added bandwidth and redundancy
- Provide redundant power and uplinks for switches that support critical workloads

Case Example

In one hospital, the LAN was segmented into VLANs for clinical devices, administrative systems, and guest Wi-Fi. This isolation reduced broadcast domains and improved both security and performance.

How the segmentation was implemented safely (what the network lead actually did)

The network lead started by inventorying device types and traffic needs, then mapped them into three zones with clear intent: clinical systems with strict access controls, administrative systems with standard corporate access, and guest access isolated from internal resources. VLANs were only the first layer. Inter-VLAN routing was forced through controlled gateways where ACLs and firewall rules could enforce who could talk to what, and logging was enabled for visibility.

They rolled it out in phases to avoid clinical disruption. One wing was migrated first during a planned window, validating DHCP, DNS, and application reachability for each device class before moving on. Access switch configs were standardized, trunking was locked down to allowed VLANs, and unused ports were disabled to reduce accidental exposure. Broadcast reduction came from tighter VLAN scope and cleaner endpoint placement, and performance improved because high-chatter guest and noncritical devices no longer shared the same layer 2 domains as clinical equipment.

Figure 6.3: Example VLAN Segmentation Map

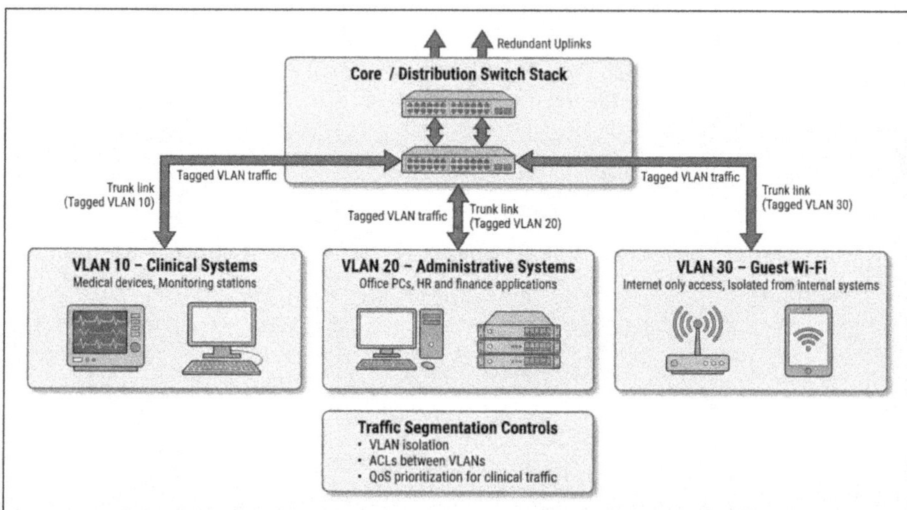

Wide Area Networks (WAN)

Wide area network design shapes the user experience for every application that crosses a site boundary, including SaaS tools, real-time collaboration, ERP access, and any workflow that depends on connectivity between locations. In most organizations, users notice WAN problems before the dashboards do.

Traditional WAN Technologies

MPLS: Became the enterprise WAN standard because it offered traffic prioritization, predictable performance, and carrier-managed reliability. Its drawbacks were cost and limited flexibility. Adding a site or increasing bandwidth usually meant working through provider lead times that could take weeks or months.

Leased Lines: provide dedicated point-to-point bandwidth and are still used where predictability and isolation are critical, although they are costly for the amount of capacity they provide.

IPsec VPNs: Extended connectivity over the public internet at much lower cost, but performance depends on the quality of the underlying internet path, which can vary by carrier, geography, and time of day.

Why Traditional WANs Struggle Today

1. **High ongoing costs for each connected site.** Traditional WAN architectures, particularly those built on MPLS, charge a premium for dedicated bandwidth at every location. As the organization adds sites, branch offices, retail locations, or remote facilities, the recurring cost scales linearly, and bandwidth-heavy workloads like video, backups, and cloud sync make those circuits more expensive to size correctly. The cost structure rewards keeping bandwidth scarce, which works against the demands of modern applications.

2. **Long wait times to provision or upgrade circuits.** Adding a new site or increasing capacity at an existing one often means a carrier provisioning process measured in weeks or months, not days. That lead time becomes a constraint on the business itself: a new office cannot come online until its circuit is delivered, and a

sudden increase in demand cannot be met until an upgrade is scheduled and installed. The network becomes a bottleneck on the organization's ability to move quickly.

3. **Poor flexibility for cloud-first and fast-changing workloads.** Traditional WANs were designed to route traffic back to a central data center, which made sense when applications lived there. In a cloud-first environment, that design forces traffic destined for SaaS platforms and public cloud services to take an inefficient path through headquarters before reaching the internet, adding latency and consuming expensive backhaul capacity. The architecture assumes a traffic pattern that no longer matches how work actually happens.
4. **Hard to apply consistent security policies across different geographic regions.** When each site is configured individually, security policy drifts. A firewall rule updated at one location may never reach another, and verifying that every site enforces the same standards becomes a manual, error-prone exercise. As the footprint grows across regions with different teams and different equipment, maintaining a uniform security posture, and proving it during an audit, becomes increasingly difficult without centralized control.

Figure 6.4: Comparison of Legacy WAN Architecture and Modern SD-WAN Overlay

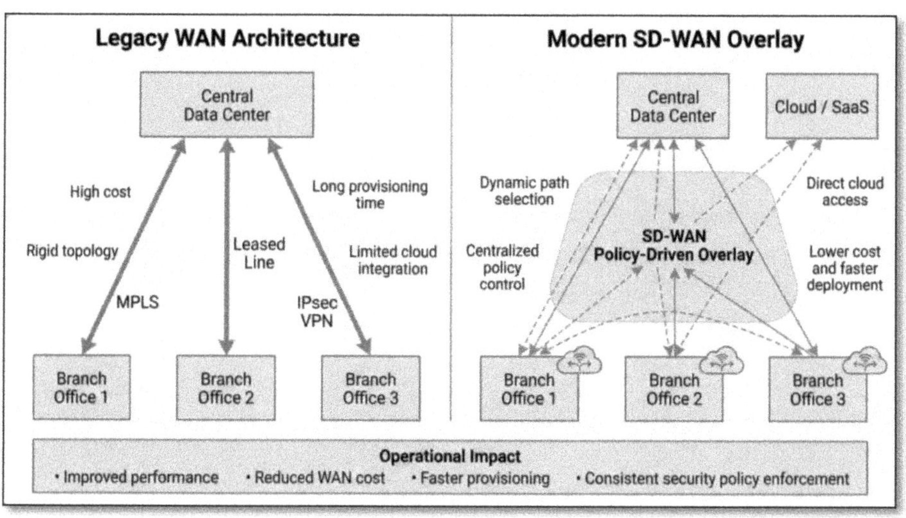

Case Example

A global retail chain running on MPLS experienced bandwidth issues during peak hours. After moving to a hybrid WAN that combined broadband with 4G backup links, the company saw significantly lower monthly costs and more consistent latency.

How the migration was executed without disrupting stores (what the network lead actually did)

They began by baselining traffic and user experience during peak windows, then identified which applications were sensitive to latency and which mainly needed throughput. That allowed them to define routing intent up front, point-of-sale and payment traffic prioritized, corporate tools balanced, guest traffic isolated and rate-limited.

The rollout was phased site by site. Each store received broadband as an additional circuit first, while MPLS stayed as primary. Policies were tested in parallel, and automatic failover to 4G was validated with controlled circuit drops. Only after performance and stability met targets did they change primary routing and later downgrade or remove MPLS where it no longer justified the cost.

To keep operations consistent, they standardized edge configurations, monitored link health and path quality continuously, and used the same cutover checklist at every site. Latency became more consistent because traffic could shift away from congested paths, and cost dropped because broadband carried the bulk of noncritical traffic while 4G covered outages.

The Rise of Software-Defined WAN (SD-WAN)

SD-WAN is now a common architectural choice for multi-site enterprises because it changes how WAN policy is managed. Rather than configuring each edge device independently, teams define policy centrally and push it through a controller. Traffic is also no longer routed only by destination. SD-WAN can steer it based on application type, real-time link conditions, and cost. That is what allows organizations to reduce reliance on expensive dedicated circuits while maintaining control and visibility.

Key Capabilities of SD-WAN

Dynamic Path Selection: SD-WAN evaluates real-time conditions such as jitter, packet loss, and latency to choose the best available path for each application. This keeps performance steady even when one circuit becomes congested.

Centralized Policy Management: Administrators define routing, security, and QoS policies once and push them across all sites from a central controller. This eliminates the need for manual configuration on individual devices.

Application-Aware Routing: Traffic is routed based on the needs of the application, not just destination IP. For example, VoIP and video conferencing can be steered to low-latency links, while bulk file transfers use broadband.

Built-in Security: Many SD-WAN platforms include encryption, segmentation, next-generation firewall functions, and integration with cloud security services.

Hybrid Connectivity: Enterprises can pair existing MPLS links with broadband and 4G/5G connections. This hybrid model reduces dependency on expensive private circuits without compromising reliability.

Typical SD-WAN Benefits

- Better performance for SaaS and cloud applications
- Lower bandwidth costs through broadband and cellular offload
- Faster deployment of new sites
- Consistent security policies across regions
- Improved visibility through unified dashboards

Figure 6.5: Example SD-WAN Architecture Showing Central Controller, Edge Devices, and Hybrid Transport Links.

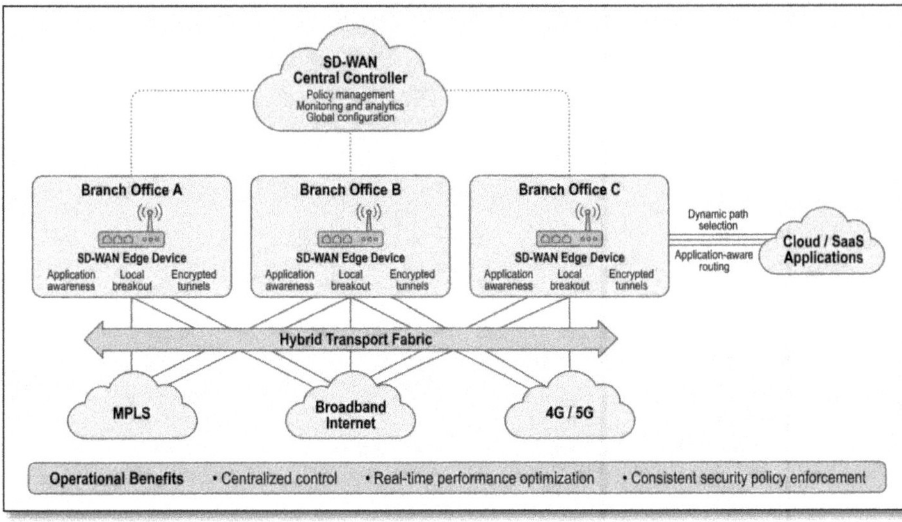

Case Example

A regional manufacturing company replaced its MPLS-only design with SD-WAN at 40 branch locations. By combining broadband and LTE links, the organization improved application responsiveness and cut overall WAN spend. Visibility through a single dashboard also made troubleshooting significantly faster.

How the rollout delivered results (what the network lead actually did)

They started by classifying applications into tiers and defining path rules before deployment, for example ERP and voice prioritized on the best-performing link, bulk transfers pushed to lower-cost broadband. MPLS was not ripped out first. SD-WAN was deployed in parallel, and policies were validated at a small set of pilot sites using real traffic and peak-hour conditions.

Once performance matched targets, they scaled in waves with a repeatable cutover checklist. LTE was configured as automatic failover and tested with controlled outages. Centralized policy templates removed site-by-site configuration drift, and the unified dashboard became the first stop for triage, using link-quality metrics (loss, jitter, latency) to pinpoint whether issues were carrier-related or application-related. Costs dropped as MPLS bandwidth was reduced where broadband proved stable, and responsiveness improved because traffic could steer around congestion automatically.

Wireless and Mobility Infrastructure

Wireless infrastructure has moved from a convenience layer to a primary means of connectivity for most users and a growing number of operational devices. In environments with IoT sensors, clinical equipment, warehouse scanners, or high-density meeting spaces, wireless design and security cannot be treated as secondary concerns. Poor RF planning and weak authentication are common causes of both user complaints and security incidents in modern enterprise environments.

Wi-Fi Standards Overview

802.11n: Delivered major performance improvements over earlier wireless standards and is still found in older deployments, though it is steadily being replaced through normal refresh cycles.

802.11ac: Brought gigabit-capable throughput to enterprise wireless and remains common in many current environments.

802.11ax: Marketed as Wi-Fi 6, was designed to improve performance in dense environments. Where hundreds of devices compete for airtime, it uses more efficient scheduling to improve throughput per device rather than only increasing peak theoretical speed.

802.11be: Marketed as Wi-Fi 7, extends this further with higher throughput ceilings and improved multi-link operation for low-latency applications, although enterprise adoption is still at an early stage.

Table: Wi-Fi Generational Comparison – Throughput, Efficiency, Range

Wi-Fi Generation	Common Standard Name	Release Year	Frequency Band	Maximum Theoretical Speed	Typical Enterprise Throughput Profile	Efficiency in Dense Environments	Range and Coverage Behavior	Notes for IT Managers
Wi-Fi 0	**802.11**	1997	2.4 GHz	2 Mbps	Extremely limited by modern standards, legacy only	Very low	Short range, highly interference-prone	Obsolete in enterprise environments, not suitable for modern production use
Wi-Fi 1	**802.11b**	1999	2.4 GHz	11 Mbps	Low throughput, affected heavily by interference	Very low	Good range but poor spectrum efficiency	Legacy support only, common source of airtime inefficiency if still enabled
Wi-Fi 2	**802.11a**	1999	5 GHz	54 Mbps	Better performance than 802.11b, lower interference	Low	Shorter range than 2.4 GHz due to higher frequency	Early 5 GHz adoption, largely retired in modern deployments
Wi-Fi 3	**802.11g**	2003	2.4 GHz	54 Mbps	Moderate performance, constrained by crowded 2.4 GHz spectrum	Low to moderate	Better range than 5 GHz, but congestion common	Widely used historically, now mainly legacy compatibility
Wi-Fi 4	**802.11n**	2009	2.4 GHz, 5 GHz	Up to 600 Mbps	Moderate, depends heavily on channel width and client mix	Moderate	Good range, performance drops quickly as density rises	Often still present in legacy areas, usually the first target for refresh in high-density spaces
Wi-Fi 5	**802.11ac**	2014	5 GHz	Up to 6.9 Gbps	High, strong for single-client and general office use	Moderate	Good coverage, better throughput than Wi-Fi 4	Common enterprise baseline, can struggle in high-density lecture halls or events without careful RF design
Wi-Fi 6	**802.11ax**	2019	2.4 GHz, 5 GHz	Up to 9.6 Gbps	High and more consistent under load	High	Similar coverage to Wi-Fi 5, but better usable capacity	Better at handling many clients (OFDMA and multi-user improvements), typically the best upgrade point for dense campus and IoT growth
Wi-Fi 6E	**802.11ax**	2020	2.4 GHz, 5 GHz, 6 GHz	Up to 9.6 Gbps	Very high, especially in clean 6 GHz spectrum	Very high	Shorter range on 6 GHz, but dramatically reduced interference	Major improvement for high-density and low-latency environments, requires compatible clients and newer switching/uplink infrastructure
Wi-Fi 7	**802.11be**	2024	2.4 GHz, 5 GHz, 6 GHz	Up to 46 Gbps	Very high, multi-gig capable where supported	Very high	Similar propagation characteristics, capacity improves with spectrum and design	Emerging standard, value depends on client adoption, spectrum availability, and uplink readiness (switching and PoE). Adds multi-link operation and lower latency improvements

Best Practices for WLAN Design

- Perform predictive RF site surveys using dedicated planning tools
- Use separate SSIDs for corporate users, guests, and IoT devices
- Implement WPA3 or 802.1X authentication to strengthen security
- Optimize channel allocation to reduce interference, especially in dense deployments
- Use controller-based or cloud-managed WLAN platforms for better visibility and centralized administration

Case Example

A university standardized its wireless environment by consolidating 1,200 standalone access points into a single controller-based platform. This shift enabled consistent security policies, improved load balancing, and simplified troubleshooting across the entire campus.

How the consolidation was executed (what the network lead actually did)
They began by inventorying every access point, mapping it to building locations, switch ports, and existing SSIDs, then identifying coverage gaps and high-complaint zones. The controller platform was built in parallel with standardized templates for SSIDs, authentication, VLAN mappings, RF settings, and logging, so policy could be applied consistently.

Rollout happened in phases by building. During each cutover, APs were migrated onto the controller, validated for authentication and roaming behavior, and tuned for channel and power to reduce interference. Guest and IoT networks were separated cleanly, and 802.1X policies were enforced centrally instead of relying on per-AP configuration. After migration, troubleshooting improved because the team could see client association, RF health, and authentication failures in one place, which reduced time spent guessing whether issues were device, RF, or identity related.

Pro Tip

Predictive heatmaps are useful, but they lie. Software assumes a wall is just a wall, but it can't see the metal piping, reinforced concrete, or lead-lined X-ray room inside that wall. Never deploy a critical warehouse or campus network based solely on a simulation. You must walk the floor with test gear ("AP on a stick") to validate the signal, or you will spend the next year moving access points.

Figure 6.6: Centralized Wireless Network Architecture

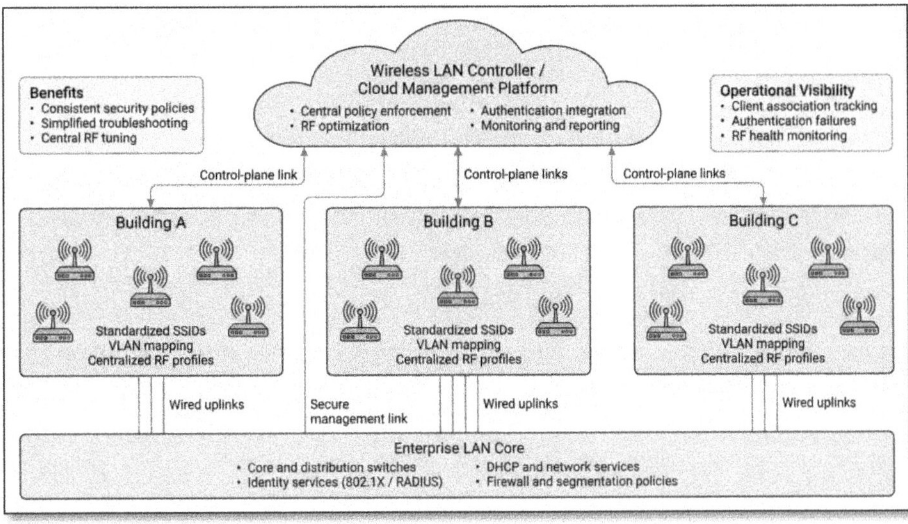

Network Security and Segmentation

Network security is no longer just a perimeter issue. The assumption that a device or user can be trusted once inside the network has been undermined by insider threats, compromised credentials, and lateral movement from breached endpoints. Effective protection requires layered controls: segmentation that limits unnecessary access, encryption that protects data in transit, access controls that verify identity before connectivity is granted, and monitoring that makes unusual behavior visible early.

Network Security Layers

Perimeter Security: Firewalls, intrusion prevention systems, and DDoS mitigation services help filter unwanted traffic before it reaches internal resources.

Internal Segmentation: VLANs, micro-segmentation, and ACLs isolate sensitive systems and reduce the spread of threats inside the network.

Encryption: Protocols such as TLS, IPsec, and MACsec protect data as it moves between network devices or across untrusted paths.

Network Access Control (NAC): Ensures that devices meet security requirements before they are allowed on the network. Authentication and compliance checks are applied consistently.

Monitoring: Security monitoring tools, SIEM platforms, and network behavior analytics provide continuous visibility into activity patterns, anomalies, and potential attacks.

Figure 6.7: Defense-in-Depth Network Security Model.

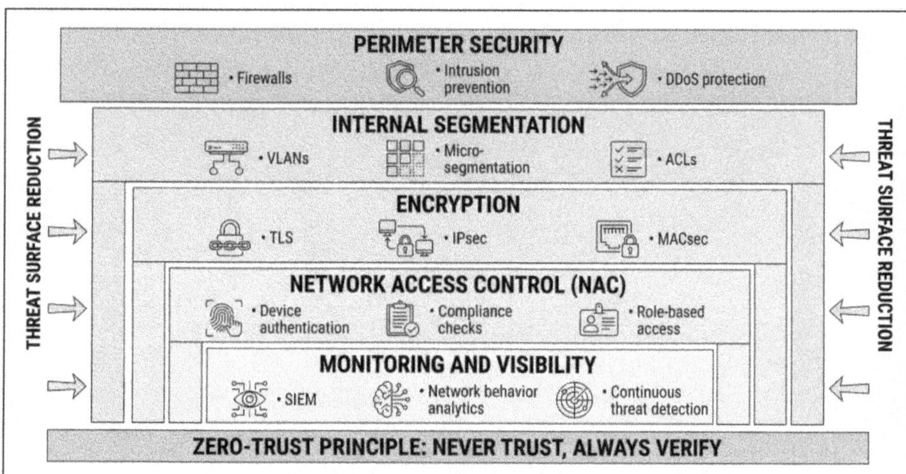

Zero Trust Networking

Zero Trust is an architectural principle based on a simple idea: the network location of a device or user is not enough to trust it. A user inside the corporate perimeter is not automatically safer than one connecting remotely. Under Zero Trust, every access request is evaluated individually, who is making the request, from what device, under what conditions, and what the device posture looks like at that moment. This shifts security away from perimeter-based trust and toward continuous verification, which makes lateral movement much less useful to an attacker who has already compromised one endpoint.

Case Example

A healthcare organization implemented NAC integrated with its Active Directory environment. Devices that failed compliance checks or lacked required patches were automatically placed into a quarantine network. This reduced exposure to vulnerabilities and improved overall security posture.

How the NAC quarantine model was rolled out (what the security lead actually did)

They started with an asset and identity baseline. Endpoints were categorized (clinical devices, corporate workstations, servers, vendor devices), then mapped to AD groups and expected access levels. Compliance checks were defined in plain terms that operations could enforce: approved OS versions, patch level, endpoint protection status, and certificate posture for managed devices.

The rollout was staged to avoid disrupting care. The team ran NAC in monitor mode first to see what would fail and why, then fixed the common issues (stale AD records, unmanaged devices, missing certificates) before enforcement. Quarantine was designed with "allow only what is needed" rules, permitting access to remediation services (patch repositories, endpoint management, AV updates) while blocking lateral access to internal systems.

Exceptions were controlled. Medical and vendor devices that could not meet standard posture were placed into tightly scoped segments with explicit allow lists and review dates. Reporting focused on outcomes leadership understood: how many devices were noncompliant, how quickly they were remediated, and how much the noncompliant population shrank over time.

Network Monitoring, Troubleshooting, and Performance Management

When a WAN link shows green but VoIP calls are dropping, or a switch is reachable while application latency keeps rising, the gap between infrastructure health and user experience becomes a major operational blind spot. Modern monitoring has to close that gap by correlating network telemetry with application performance and user experience data, not just hardware status.

Key Metrics & Modern Telemetry

A well-designed monitoring system should track several key indicators:

- **Link Availability:** The percentage of time each circuit or connection is up and passing traffic. Calculated from monitored uptime and downtime events over a defined period. Used to confirm whether links are meeting SLA commitments and to identify chronic reliability issues before they affect service delivery
- **Application Experience:** Correlates network path health with actual user page-load times to determine if slowdowns are network or app-related
- **Latency and Jitter:** Measures delay and variation in packet delivery
- **Packet Loss:** Identifies congestion, faulty links, or device issues
- **Bandwidth Utilization:** Shows how much traffic is moving through each interface

Monitoring Tools

Organizations typically use a combination of tools to gain full visibility:

- **Infrastructure Monitoring:** Traditional platforms such as SolarWinds and PRTG Network Monitor® rely primarily on SNMP polling and remain common in enterprise environments. Where lower-latency telemetry or higher-volume data collection is needed, SNMP is increasingly being supplemented, or in some cases replaced, by streaming telemetry protocols that send device state data in near real time
- **Flow & Traffic Analysis:** NetFlow/IPFIX for bandwidth usage, and eBPF-based tools for deep visibility into container and cloud traffic
- **Cloud-Native Observability:** AWS CloudWatch and Azure Network Watcher for cloud interconnects
- **Digital Experience Monitoring (DEM):** Tools like Cisco ThousandEyes or Datadog that test the network from the *outside-in*, simulating user behavior

Figure 6.8: Network Monitoring Architecture Diagram.

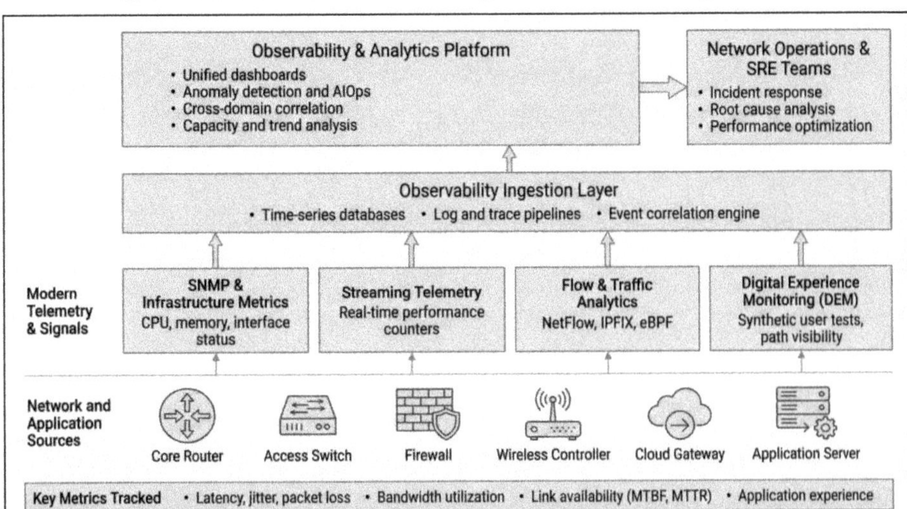

Troubleshooting Framework

A structured approach makes troubleshooting more efficient and repeatable:

1. Define the problem and identify who or what is affected
2. Narrow the issue by isolating layers such as physical, data link, network, or application
3. Test connectivity with traceroute, packet capture, or path analysis tools
4. Review device configurations for errors or inconsistencies
5. Document findings so they can be added to the knowledge base for future reference

Case Example

During intermittent VoIP call failures, engineers noticed short bursts of packet loss tied to peak traffic on a WAN link. After adjusting QoS settings and limiting bandwidth used by background backups, call quality stabilized and the issue was resolved.

How the issue was isolated and fixed (what the network lead actually did)

They first confirmed it was a network symptom, not a handset or PBX problem, by correlating call-quality reports with WAN interface counters and timestamped packet-loss alerts. The loss was not constant; it appeared in short bursts that lined up with backup windows.

Next, they validated the traffic mix. Flow data showed backups consuming large portions of the link during peaks, and queue statistics showed voice traffic occasionally hitting congestion instead of staying in the priority queue. The fix was two-part: tighten QoS classification and queuing so voice stayed protected under load, and cap backup bandwidth (or reschedule it) so it could not starve real-time traffic.

After the change, they monitored jitter, loss, and MOS trends through the next peak period to confirm stability, then documented the root cause, updated the QoS baseline, and added an alert for backup traffic exceeding the agreed threshold.

Pro Tip

The most valuable metric is "Mean Time to Innocence" (MTTI), how fast you can prove the network isn't the problem. Ping is not enough. Implement Digital Experience Monitoring (DEM) to run "synthetic transactions" that simulate a real user logging in. If the network path is green but the synthetic user fails, you have the proof to route the ticket to the application team.

Network Documentation and Change Management

Network documentation and change control are where good operational intent either turns into reliable practice or starts to break down. Most environments have documentation. The problem is that it does not stay current, it is stored in too many places, or it lacks the detail engineers need when pressure is high. The same pattern shows up in change control. The policy exists, but exceptions build up, and over time the network configuration drifts away from the documentation until an outage exposes the gap.

Essential Documents

A well-maintained documentation system typically includes:

- Physical and logical network topology diagrams
- An IP address management (IPAM) database
- VLAN and subnet allocation tables
- Routing protocol configurations and peer relationships
- Firewall, ACL, and security rule inventories
- Circuit information, bandwidth details, and vendor contacts

Figure 6.9: Sample Logical Network Topology Diagram.

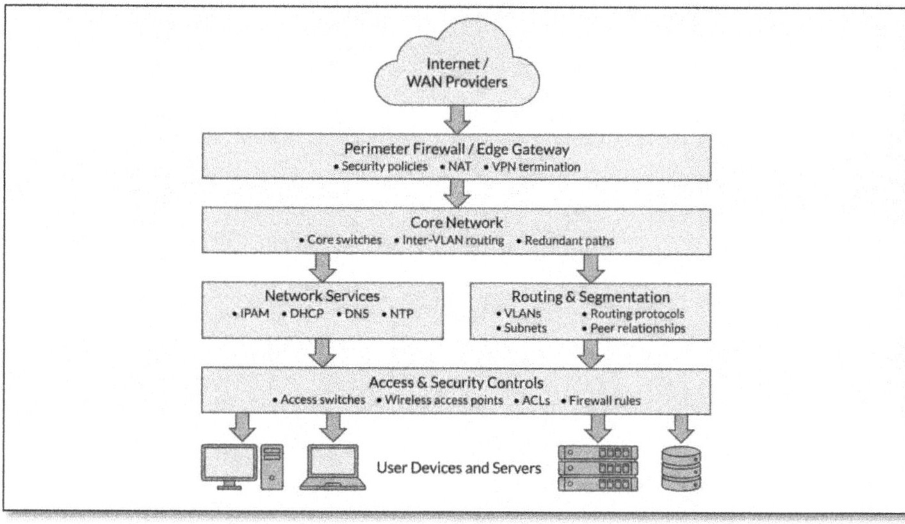

Change Management Process

Change control helps prevent outages and configuration drift by ensuring every modification is reviewed, approved, and traceable. A strong process includes:

1. Documenting the purpose, scope, and potential risks of each change
2. Conducting peer review and obtaining CAB approval for changes that impact operations
3. Scheduling work during maintenance windows to minimize disruption
4. Preparing rollback procedures and validating results after the change
5. Recording the final outcome in the CMDB for future reference and compliance tracking

Case Example

An operations team enforced a strict "no change without a ticket" policy and implemented automated configuration backups. This approach eliminated untracked switch modifications and removed over 90 percent of outages caused by undocumented changes.

How the control was enforced and sustained (what the network lead actually did)

They made the ticket the entry point for any change, even "quick fixes." Access to modify production switch configs was tied to approved change records, with peer review for anything that could affect routing, VLANs, trunks, or security posture. Changes performed outside the process were treated as incidents, captured, reviewed, and corrected.

In parallel, they automated configuration backups on a fixed schedule and after every approved change. When backups detected drift, the system generated a comparison report that showed exactly what changed, when, and on which device. That made unauthorized edits visible immediately and removed the "we are not sure what happened" problem during outages.

Finally, they closed the loop by updating documentation as part of the change closure. If a change modified VLANs, trunks, routing peers, or ACLs, the related diagrams and tables had to be updated before the ticket could be closed. Over time, outage reviews showed a sharp drop in drift-driven failures because the environment became traceable and repeatable.

Vendor and Service Provider Management

External service providers carry a significant share of operational responsibility in most enterprise networks. WAN circuits, cloud interconnects, managed firewall services, and last-mile connectivity are often outside direct IT control. That means vendor management is not just administrative overhead. It is part of how reliability is maintained. When a carrier misses its SLA and the escalation path is unclear, the organization absorbs the risk. When SLAs are specific, scorecards are consistent, and escalation workflows are documented, the provider relationship becomes something the organization can actively manage rather than simply rely on.

Best Practices

- **Define SLAs clearly.** Include latency, packet loss, uptime, and response time requirements so performance can be measured consistently
- **Use monthly scorecards.** Compare actual vendor performance against contractual commitments to highlight trends or gaps
- **Conduct quarterly business reviews (QBRs).** Discuss capacity planning, roadmap updates, service quality issues, and any needed adjustments
- **Maintain redundancy.** Keep backup providers or secondary circuits for critical connections to avoid single points of failure

Table: Example Vendor SLA Metrics and Escalation Procedures.

SLA Metric	How It Is Measured	Typical Reporting Cadence	Target Threshold Example	Escalation Trigger	Escalation Path	Evidence to Attach
Uptime (Availability)	Provider SLA report plus your own monitoring	Monthly, with weekly internal checks	99.9% to 99.99% per circuit	Any breach, or repeated brownouts	NOC, account team, service manager, executive sponsor	Outage timeline, monitoring screenshots, ticket IDs
Latency	Synthetic probes and path monitoring between sites and key apps	Daily trend, monthly summary	Defined per route or app tier	Sustained deviation above baseline	NOC, engineering escalation, vendor performance lead	Probe data, affected apps, timestamps
Packet Loss	Link telemetry, probes, and provider stats	Daily trend, monthly summary	Low single-digit percent or lower by tier	Bursts during peak windows, sustained loss	NOC, carrier escalation desk, regional ops	Interface counters, probe loss charts, PCAP if needed
Jitter	Probes for real-time apps (voice, video)	Daily trend, monthly summary	Defined for voice and UC tiers	Exceeds threshold during business hours	NOC, performance team, account escalation	UC call quality logs, probe jitter data
Mean Time to Respond (MTTR-Response)	Time from ticket open to vendor acknowledgement	Per ticket, monthly rollup	Minutes to hours by severity	Missed response window for Sev1 or Sev2	NOC, duty manager, account manager	Ticket timestamps, chat logs, call records
Mean Time to Restore (MTTR-Restore)	Time from incident start to service restored	Per incident, quarterly review	Hours by severity and site criticality	Missed restore target, repeated incidents	Engineering escalation, leadership QBR	RCA, restoration steps, vendor commit dates
Change Notification and Maintenance Windows	Notice period and adherence to agreed windows	Per change	X days notice, off-hours execution	Unapproved window, insufficient notice	Account team, service manager	Provider notice email, change IDs, impact summary

Case Example

A multinational enterprise negotiated performance-based SLAs with financial penalties for missed uptime targets. The increased visibility improved service quality, strengthened accountability, and helped maintain productive long-term vendor relationships.

How the SLA model was made enforceable (what the manager actually did)

They started by defining measurements in a way that could not be argued later. Uptime, latency, and loss targets were tied to specific circuits, routes, and hours, and the company's own monitoring data was listed as the reference for disputes, not only the vendor's monthly report.

They then built a monthly scorecard that showed trends and business impact, not just raw stats. Breaches triggered a standard escalation workflow and a formal service credit request when applicable. Repeat issues required a corrective action plan from the provider, with dates and named owners reviewed in QBRs.

Finally, penalties were paired with incentives for sustained performance, and chronic offenders faced capacity redesign or secondary-provider deployment. Over time, vendors improved because expectations were measurable, escalations were consistent, and consequences were predictable.

Pro Tip

Buying circuits from two different carriers does not guarantee redundancy. If Carrier A and Carrier B both rent the same conduit from the city to get into your building, a single backhoe will take them both out. Go outside and physically check where the cables enter the facility (the Point of Entry). If they share a trench or a riser, you don't have redundancy; you just have two monthly bills.

The Evolution of Modern Network Management

Network operations are changing in ways that reduce reliance on manual configuration and reactive troubleshooting. Automation platforms now handle provisioning and policy enforcement at scale. AI-assisted tools can identify congestion patterns and anomalies before they affect users. Edge connectivity is also expanding to support IoT, industrial systems, and distributed workloads that traditional network designs were not built to support. IT managers need to understand these trends well enough to evaluate vendor claims, make sound architectural decisions, and manage the transition effectively.

Network Automation

Automation platforms such as Cisco DNA Center and Juniper Apstra simplify provisioning, configuration, and policy updates across large environments. By standardizing changes and reducing manual touchpoints, automation lowers the risk of configuration drift and speeds up deployments.

Network as a Service (NaaS)

Network as a Service, or NaaS, delivers networking functions through a subscription model instead of organization-owned hardware. Organizations pay for connectivity and capacity as a service, which allows them to scale up or down without managing hardware refresh cycles directly. NaaS is often most practical for distributed branch environments, temporary deployments, or organizations that do not have the staff to manage network hardware across many sites. It also introduces dependency on the provider's platform reliability and requires careful review of data sovereignty, performance commitments, and exit options before it is adopted at scale.

AI-Driven Operations (AIOps)

AIOps tools use machine learning to detect anomalies, predict failures, and optimize traffic routing before users experience problems. These platforms analyze telemetry from devices, logs, and flow data to provide proactive insights that traditional monitoring tools cannot.

Edge Networking and 5G

The rise of IoT and real-time applications is pushing more workloads toward the network edge. Combined with 5G connectivity, edge architectures support low-latency services such as industrial automation, sensor networks, and autonomous systems.

Case Example

An energy company implemented AIOps within its SD-WAN environment. The system identified link congestion patterns early enough for engineers to intervene before users felt the impact. Within two quarters, the team reduced unplanned downtime, and the reactive overnight escalations that had defined the previous operating model dropped sharply.

How the AIOps change produced real results (what the network lead actually did)

They first defined what counted as downtime, which sites and apps mattered, and which telemetry would be trusted (loss, jitter, latency, path changes, tunnel resets). The platform was trained on normal patterns by site and time of day so it could flag meaningful congestion trends.

They then built simple playbooks for the common patterns: shift traffic to alternate links, throttle noncritical transfers, or schedule circuit upgrades before peak windows. Each alert had an owner and a documented outcome, and thresholds were tuned to cut noise. Over time, congestion was handled early enough that fewer events reached users as outages.

Figure 6.10: Future Network Management Ecosystem – AIOps,

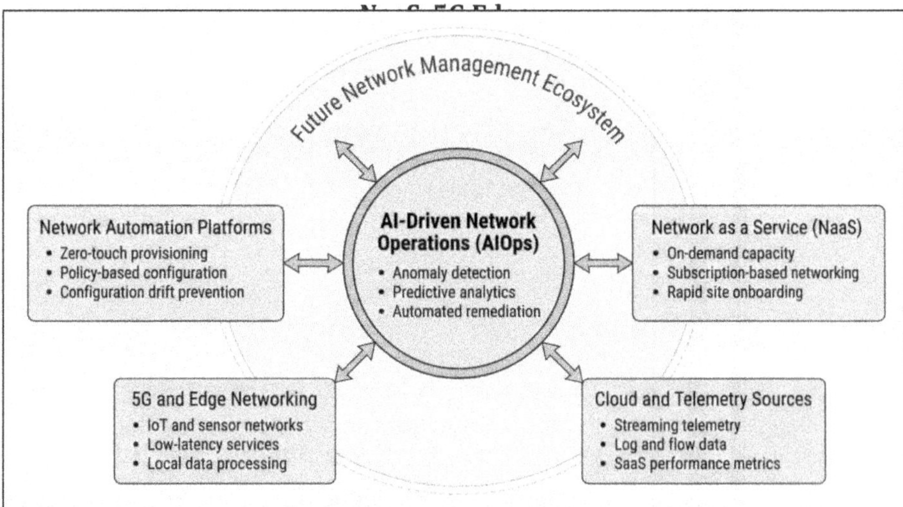

What This Means in Practice

- Network architecture is a design discipline with long-term operational consequences. The VLAN boundaries, routing decisions, and WAN transport choices made today will shape how the environment can be operated for years. Getting those decisions right requires understanding both technical tradeoffs and operational realities

- SD-WAN changes the operating model, not just the hardware. Its value is not limited to cost reduction. It also brings centralized policy control and more consistent visibility across sites that previously required site-by-site configuration and interpretation

- Wireless performance is largely determined during design, not after deployment. RF surveys, channel planning, and authentication architecture need to be done correctly before access points are mounted, rather than corrected later under user pressure

- Monitoring gaps eventually surface as incidents. If telemetry does not cover the full path between the user and the application, the team will spend time troubleshooting the wrong layer. Observability has to be treated as part of infrastructure design

- Change control protects the environment from avoidable mistakes. Many network outages are self-inflicted, caused by changes made outside the review process. A strict no-change-without-a-ticket discipline, combined with automated configuration backups, can remove much of that exposure

- Vendor management is part of reliability management. Carrier SLAs, escalation paths, and physical redundancy validation are not just procurement concerns. They are operational controls that influence whether the network holds up when a circuit fails

Figure 6.11: Summary of Enterprise Network Components – LAN, WAN, WLAN, Security, SD-WAN.

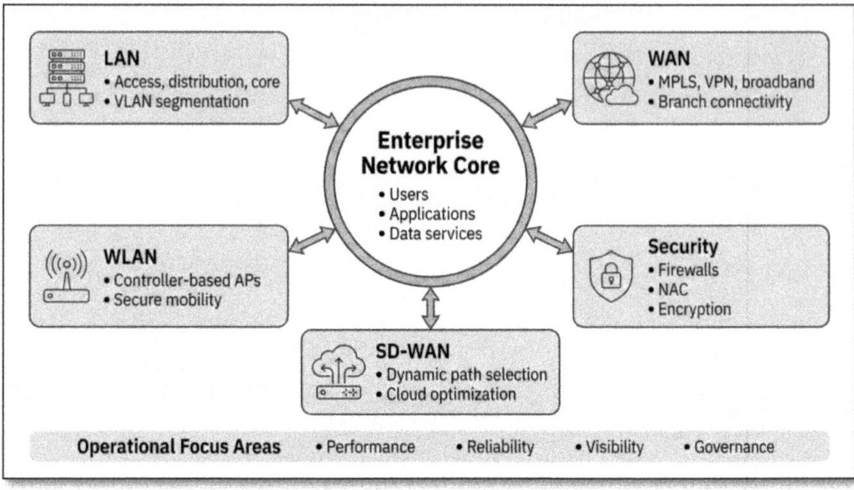

Chapter 7

DATA CENTER OPERATIONS AND MANAGEMENT: POWER, COOLING, CABLING, AND FACILITY STANDARDS

Cloud adoption has not eliminated the data center. It has changed the role the data center plays. Workloads that require predictable latency, strict compliance controls, or tight physical security do not always move well to shared cloud infrastructure. Many organizations have found that a well-run on-premises or colocation environment remains the right fit for certain workloads, even as cloud usage expands elsewhere

Running a data center puts the IT manager between facility engineering, operational discipline, and business continuity. The mechanical and electrical systems that keep servers running are not IT systems, but when they fail, IT still carries the operational impact. The IT manager needs to understand them well enough to govern the environment, work effectively with the engineering teams that maintain it, and make sound operational decisions that keep the facility safe, efficient, and compliant.

This chapter focuses on the operational disciplines that keep a data center running, including power systems and redundancy, cooling design and efficiency, structured cabling, physical security, maintenance controls, and the facility standards that shape design, compliance, and audit readiness.

Figure 7.1: Data Center Operations Ecosystem

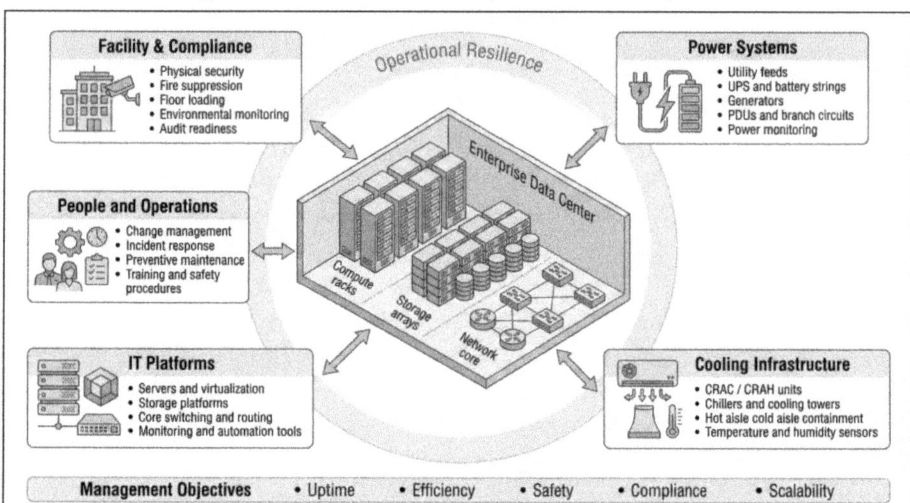

The Role of the Data Center in Modern IT

Despite the shift toward cloud, the data center remains the right environment for many workloads, especially those with strict latency requirements, regulatory limits on data location, or operational characteristics that do not fit well in shared multi-tenant infrastructure. For most enterprises, the real question is not cloud versus data center. It is which workloads belong in each environment. As a result, organizations continue to rely on data centers to host a wide range of essential systems, including:

- On-premises enterprise applications
- Private cloud platforms and virtualized infrastructure
- Colocation deployments supporting hybrid IT strategies
- Edge computing sites positioned near customers or operational hubs

Key Operational Goals

The core operational goals of a data center are straightforward, but each carries significant engineering implications. Reliability means the facility can meet SLA commitments even when individual components fail. Efficiency means power and cooling use stay aligned with IT load, not simply with the size of the facility. Security requires both physical and logical controls to prevent unauthorized access to systems and data. Scalability means new workloads can be added without forcing a redesign of power or cooling paths. Sustainability means the facility operates with the level of environmental and cost efficiency expected in modern regulatory and corporate settings.

Table: Common Data Center Types and Their Use Cases

Type	Description	Example
Enterprise Data Center	Owned and operated by the organization	Financial institutions
Colocation Facility	Third-party hosting with shared utilities	Cloud interconnect hubs

Table: Common Data Center Types and Their Use Cases (Continued)

Type	Description	Example
Edge Data Center	Smaller facilities positioned close to end users	IoT or streaming services
Hyperscale	Massive-scale environments supporting global cloud providers	AWS, Azure, Google DCs

In practice, most organizations do not operate a single data center type in isolation. A large enterprise may own a primary facility for core systems, rely on a colocation provider for connectivity and redundancy, extend to edge sites for latency-sensitive workloads, and consume hyperscale cloud capacity for burst or development environments. This layered model means that the operational goals described above, reliability, efficiency, security, scalability, and sustainability, must be applied consistently across environments that differ significantly in ownership, staffing model, and physical design. The implication for operations teams is that standardizing on common frameworks, monitoring tools, and documentation practices becomes as important as the technical configuration of any individual site. A data center portfolio that functions well as a whole requires deliberate integration, not just capable management of each location in isolation.

Facility Design and Tier Standards

The Uptime Institute Tier Classification System is a common way to describe what a facility's site infrastructure can support, mainly power and cooling, and whether the design can handle maintenance and failures without forcing shutdowns. The practical value for IT leaders is decision clarity. Tier language gives executives and engineering teams a shared way to discuss reliability targets, redundancy cost, maintenance constraints, and how much business risk the organization is willing to carry.

People sometimes talk about Tier like it is only an uptime label, but Tier is really about how the facility is built and what maintenance and failure scenarios it can tolerate. Tier does not replace application resiliency design, strong operations, or disciplined change control. It sets the baseline capability of the environment your IT stack depends on.

The following availability expectations are based on the Uptime Institute Tier Standard. Organizations pursuing formal Tier certification should reference the Uptime Institute's published specifications directly.

Table: Tier, Description, Expected Availability

Tier	Description	Expected Availability
Tier I	Basic capacity with a single path for power and cooling	99.671 percent (about 28.8 hours of downtime per year)
Tier II	Includes redundant capacity components, reducing the impact of individual equipment failures	99.741 percent (about 22 hours of downtime per year)
Tier III	Designed for concurrent maintainability. Systems can be serviced without shutting down operations	99.982 percent (about 1.6 hours of downtime per year)
Tier IV	Fully fault-tolerant design with complete redundancy across all critical systems	99.995 percent (about 26 minutes of downtime per year)

Figure 7.2: Uptime Institute Tier Classification Diagram (Conceptual)

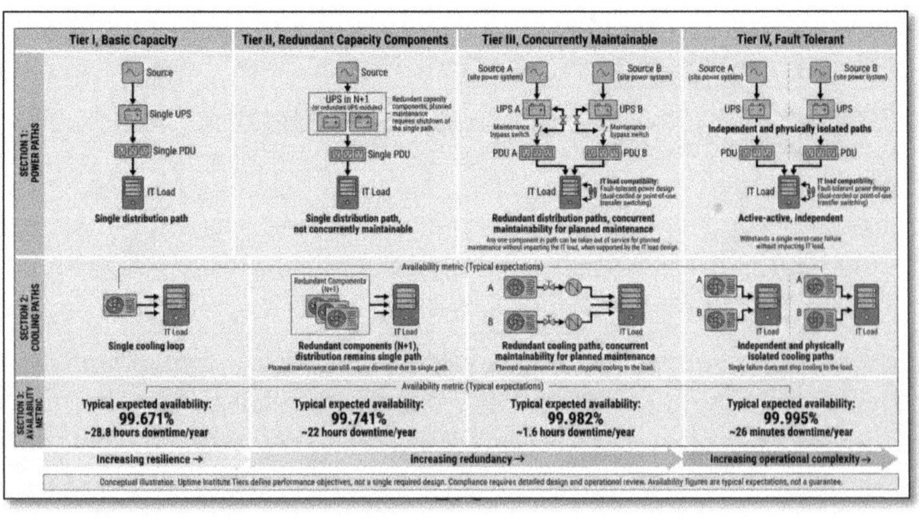

How IT managers should use Tier classifications

Choosing a Tier is a business decision, but it shows up as real engineering constraints, cost, and maintenance limits. The right question is not "What Tier is best," it is "What downtime can the business tolerate, and what is the cost of preventing it." That answer should come from a business impact view (patient care, revenue loss, regulatory exposure, customer trust), then translate into reliability requirements for the facility and the workloads it hosts.

- **Tier I and Tier II:** can be acceptable for dev, lab, training, and non-critical internal services, especially where outages are tolerable and maintenance windows are easy to schedule.
- **Tier III and Tier IV:** are typically pursued when workloads require high availability, predictable maintenance without shutdowns, and stronger failure tolerance, with cost justified by business impact.

One practical reminder: Tier describes what the site infrastructure can support, but actual uptime still depends on day-to-day operations and how applications behave during failures, not only how redundant the building is.

Example

A healthcare organization moved its electronic medical records platform into a Tier III data center. The change reduced annual downtime from more than 15 hours to under 90 minutes, significantly improving both system availability and compliance with patient safety regulations.

How the reliability case was won (what the IT manager actually did)

They tied the decision to patient-facing risk and operational interruption, not to "better infrastructure." The manager documented historical downtime patterns, mapped those outages to clinical impact (access delays, downtime procedures, escalation volume), and showed how concurrent maintainability in a Tier III facility reduced planned-maintenance downtime exposure. They then paired the facility move with operational controls, validated maintenance windows, tested failover and recovery steps, and updated runbooks so the Tier III capability translated into real, repeatable uptime.

Power Systems and Redundancy

Power is the first major failure domain in any data center because every other system depends on it. A weakness in power design, whether in the utility feed, the UPS transition, or the generator start sequence, turns into an outage as soon as a real event exposes it. The goal of power system design is not just to provide backup components. It is to make sure the full chain from utility to rack works correctly under load, and that the backup path has been tested under conditions close to actual failure scenarios.

Key Components of Power Infrastructure

1. **Utility Feed:** The primary electrical supply from the grid.
2. **Uninterruptible Power Supply (UPS):** Provides the critical bridge power during momentary outages or the transition to generators. It also actively conditions power to protect equipment from voltage sags and spikes.
3. **Generators:** Deliver extended runtime when utility power is unavailable. These must start automatically and sustain the load until the utility feed is stable.
4. **Power Distribution Units (PDUs):** Distribute electrical power to racks and IT equipment. Intelligent PDUs are essential for tracking load balance and preventing circuit overloads.
5. **Automatic Transfer Switches (ATS):** The mechanical heart of redundancy, switching the electrical path between utility and generator sources without interrupting downstream systems.
6. **Grounding and Bonding Systems:** A critical safety layer that provides a path for electrical faults, protecting both personnel and sensitive electronics.

Pro Tip

Testing a generator by just turning it on is a waste of time. You have to test the transfer. Most power failures don't happen because the engine failed to fire; they happen because the Automatic Transfer Switch (ATS) seized up or the UPS didn't hold the load during the swap. Schedule controlled "pull the plug" tests to prove the entire chain works under real load.

Figure 7.3: Typical Data Center Electrical Power Flow Diagram.

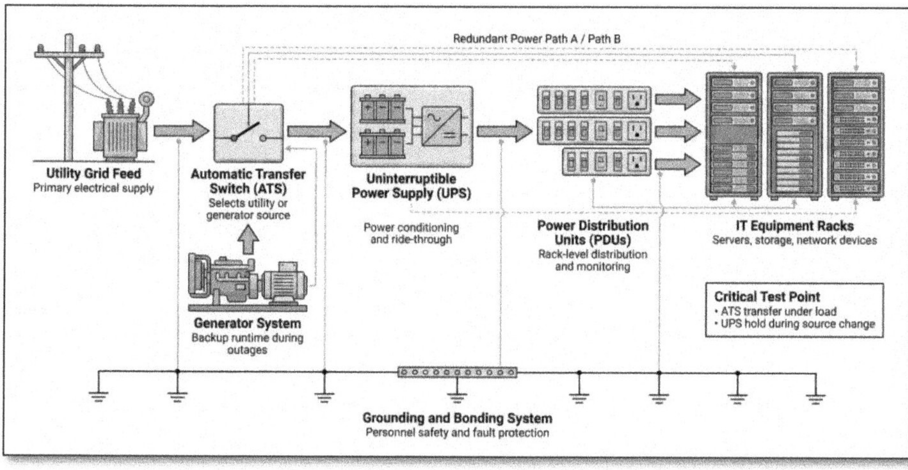

Best Practices

- Design for **N+1** or **2N** redundancy to ensure critical systems remain operational even if a primary component fails
- Conduct **regular load bank testing** of UPS systems and generators to validate performance under real conditions
- Monitor power usage through **intelligent PDUs** for accurate load tracking and capacity planning
- Clearly **label circuits** and maintain accurate documentation to reduce human error
- Establish a **preventive maintenance schedule** and ensure all work is performed by certified electricians

Power Usage Effectiveness (PUE)

Power Usage Effectiveness (PUE) is calculated as total facility energy divided by IT equipment energy ($PUE = \frac{\text{Total Facility Energy}}{\text{IT Equipment Energy}}$)

Many organizations treat a PUE in the 1.2 to 1.4 range as a strong efficiency target, depending on facility design and climate, and tracking PUE over time helps identify waste in cooling, lighting, or power distribution systems.

Case Example

A global bank reduced its electricity costs by 15 percent after consolidating aging UPS systems and deploying real-time power monitoring. These improvements lowered the facility's PUE from 1.9 to 1.5, demonstrating the value of modern power management.

How the cost reduction was delivered (what the manager actually did)

They started with measurement, not assumptions. The facilities and IT leads pulled baseline data for total facility load, UPS efficiency, bypass events, and rack-level consumption from existing meters, then identified which UPS units were running at inefficient load levels and which rooms had the most wasted capacity.

Next, they consolidated the UPS footprint in phases to avoid risk. Loads were shifted during planned windows with clear rollback steps, and the team verified transfer behavior, runtime, and alarm thresholds after each move. At the same time, they deployed real-time monitoring at the UPS and PDU level so power draw and load balance could be seen by feed, room, and rack, not just as a monthly utility bill.

Once visibility improved, they used the data to drive operational changes: rebalancing loads across phases, tightening alert thresholds before overload conditions, and correcting hotspots that were forcing overcooling. As inefficient units were retired and power distribution became better balanced, energy waste dropped and PUE improved in a measurable, repeatable way.

Cooling Systems and Environmental Controls

Cooling is where data center efficiency decisions often have the clearest effect on both operating cost and reliability. Thermal management failures do not always show up as sudden hardware failures. More often, they appear as gradual performance degradation, unexpected throttling, shortened equipment lifespan, and hotspots that force overcooling across the facility just to protect one dense row. Getting the cooling design right from the start reduces all of those outcomes.

Primary Cooling Approaches

1. **CRAC (Computer Room Air Conditioning):** Traditional perimeter cooling units that supply chilled air, often through raised floors. These systems are common in legacy data centers and provide broad room-level cooling.

2. **In-Row Cooling:** Cooling units placed directly between server racks to handle high-density environments. This approach delivers targeted cooling where heat is most concentrated.

3. **Hot Aisle/Cold Aisle Containment:** A design method that physically separates hot exhaust air from cold intake air. Containment improves cooling efficiency, reduces hotspots, and supports higher rack densities.

4. **Liquid Cooling:** Techniques such as direct-to-chip cooling or full immersion cooling used for high-performance computing (HPC) and ultra-dense workloads. Liquid cooling removes heat more effectively than traditional air-based systems.

7.4 Figure: Hot/Cold Aisle Layout Diagram.

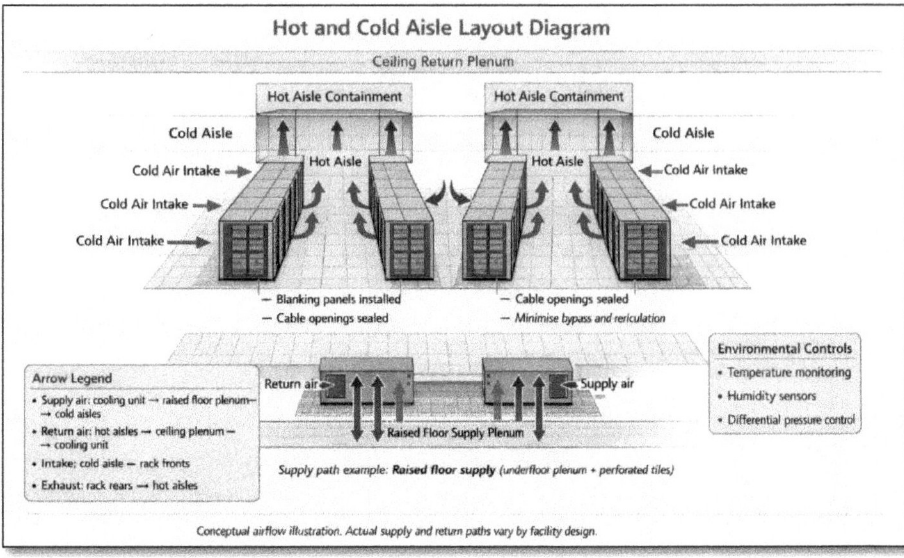

Environmental Monitoring

An effective cooling program relies on continuous environmental monitoring:

- Temperature sensors placed every 3 to 6 meters
- Humidity maintained between **40% and 60%** to prevent static discharge and condensation
- Leak detection systems and airflow sensors integrated with the Building Management System (BMS)

Efficiency Practices

- Use variable-speed fans and economizer modes when outdoor temperatures allow free cooling
- Seal gaps and cable openings to prevent air bypass
- Keep underfloor areas and cooling filters clean to maintain airflow
- Calibrate sensors, thermostats, and airflow tools on a regular schedule.

Example

A media company operating high-density storage racks adopted in-row cooling with full aisle containment. This upgrade significantly reduced hotspot formation and lowered annual energy consumption by approximately 300,000 kWh.

How the cooling upgrade delivered measurable savings (what the facilities lead actually did)
They first mapped hotspots using rack inlet temperature and airflow readings to confirm where hot and cold air were mixing. Containment was installed to stop recirculation, then in-row cooling was added in the highest-density rows.

Setpoints and fan speeds were tuned using inlet temperature targets, and leakage points were closed with blanking panels and grommets. After rollout, hotspot alarms dropped and energy savings were confirmed by comparing metered kWh over similar load periods before and after the change.

Pro Tip

Don't underestimate the humble blanking panel. Leaving empty rack units open destroys your airflow strategy because hot exhaust air gets sucked right back into the cold intake. You can spend millions on high-efficiency cooling, but if you don't seal the rack front with $5 plastic panels, you are just cooling the same hot air over and over.

Structured Cabling and Standards

Cabling is where data center operational quality either holds or starts to break down. A well-documented, well-labeled cabling environment makes changes faster, troubleshooting more systematic, and audits easier to manage. An undocumented or inconsistently labeled environment creates friction with every move, add, or change, and that friction increases as the environment grows. Cabling links power, network, and storage infrastructure, and when it is designed correctly, it supports reliability, airflow, and long-term scalability. Poor cabling practices can lead to signal degradation, overheating, and unnecessary operational complexity.

Cabling Standards

Cabling is where data center operational quality either holds or starts to break down. A well-documented, well-labeled cabling environment makes changes faster, troubleshooting more systematic, and audits easier to manage. An undocumented or inconsistently labeled environment creates friction with every move, add, or change, and that friction increases as the environment grows.

The following standards provide the primary framework for data center cabling design and documentation.

Organizations implementing these standards should consult the current published editions from TIA and ISO/IEC directly, as specifications are updated periodically.

- **ANSI/TIA-942:** A comprehensive data center standard covering cabling design, pathways, redundancy, and performance requirements
- **ANSI/TIA-606-C:** Defines labeling and administration conventions to ensure accuracy, consistency, and effective documentation of cabling systems
- **ISO/IEC 11801:** An international standard specifying structured cabling design, performance classifications, and installation requirements across data center environments

TIA-942-C and ISO/IEC 11801 Structured Cabling Hierarchy

Modern data centers depend on a structured and standards-driven cabling architecture to ensure performance, scalability, and manageability. Two primary standards define this architecture:

- **ANSI/TIA-942-C: Telecommunications Infrastructure Standard for Data Centers**
- **ISO/IEC 11801: Generic Cabling for Customer Premises**

Both describe a three-tiered hierarchy of cabling zones designed to separate backbone, distribution, and horizontal pathways. The figure represents these tiers and their functional relationships within a typical enterprise or hyperscale data center.

1. Core Cabling Pathway (Backbone Layer)

The **Core Pathway** forms the highest tier of the structured cabling system. It carries long-distance, high-bandwidth traffic between major routing domains.

Primary functions:

- Provide high-speed backbone transport between the MDA and core switching layer
- Link data center networks to external carriers, WAN routers, or border gateways
- Support redundant, diverse fiber pathways to improve resilience

Typical components:

- Core routers or spine switches
- DWDM/optical transport systems (in large DCs)
- High-capacity multimode or single-mode fiber trunks
- Diverse pathway conduits and trays

The core layer prioritizes throughput, low latency, and physical path diversity. It is the termination point for Tier-1 routing and external network entry.

2. Distribution Cabling Pathway (Aggregation Layer)

The **Distribution Layer**, located in the Main Distribution Area (MDA), aggregates traffic from multiple equipment areas, server rows, or network pods. It sits between the backbone and access layers.

Primary functions:

- Provide mid-level aggregation between access switches and core routing
- Enforce network segmentation, policy, and security boundaries
- Support both copper and fiber interconnects, depending on architecture
- Maintain a structured, documented cross-connect environment

Typical components:

- Leaf switches (modern architectures) or distribution switches (traditional 3-tier)
- Patch panels and fiber/copper cross-connect frames
- MDA-to-HDA fiber trunks
- Asset and labeling systems aligned with TIA-606-C

This layer allows changes, expansions, and migrations without disrupting core or server-level cabling, improving agility in fast-growing data centers.

3. Access Cabling Pathway (Horizontal Layer)

The **Access Layer** connects the HDA (Horizontal Distribution Area) to endpoint IT equipment located in EDAs (Equipment Distribution Areas).

Primary functions:

- Provide final connectivity to server racks, storage appliances, and network devices

- Support copper and fiber patching through structured pathways
- Enforce consistent labeling, documentation, and equipment identification

Typical components

- ToR/MoR/EoR access switches
- Horizontal copper cabling (Cat6A or higher)
- Fiber patch cords (MMF or SMF)
- Patch panels, zone enclosures, and cable managers
- IT equipment (servers, hyperconverged systems, storage, firewalls)

This is the most frequently touched layer, where operational changes, maintenance, and troubleshooting occur daily. Proper separation of HDA and EDA improves manageability and limits downtime.

4. Cross-Connect Design and MDA Role

The **Main Distribution Area (MDA)** is the structured cabling hub of the data center. It serves as the central cross-connect point for:

- Core routing
- Distribution/leaf switching
- Optical transport systems
- Inter-row and inter-zone connectivity

TIA-942-C strongly recommends using the MDA for all major cross-connects to:

- Reduce cable congestion in IT equipment rows
- Allow flexible patching, re-patching, and migration
- Improve documentation accuracy and change control
- Support clear demarcation points between network domains

In hyperscale environments, the MDA may be replaced or supplemented by POD-based MDAs due to scale.

5. Standards Alignment and Documentation

The structured cabling system must be maintained through consistent documentation and labeling under:

- **TIA-606-C Administration Standard**
- CMDB or asset management integration
- Accurate port-to-port, cable-to-cable tracing
- Clear zone classification (MDA, HDA, EDA, ZDA)

Accurate labeling and documentation ensure cable traceability, simplify troubleshooting, and prevent mispatch errors.

Figure 7.5: Structured Cabling Pathway Diagram – Entrance Room, MDA, HDA, EDA (Optional ZDA)

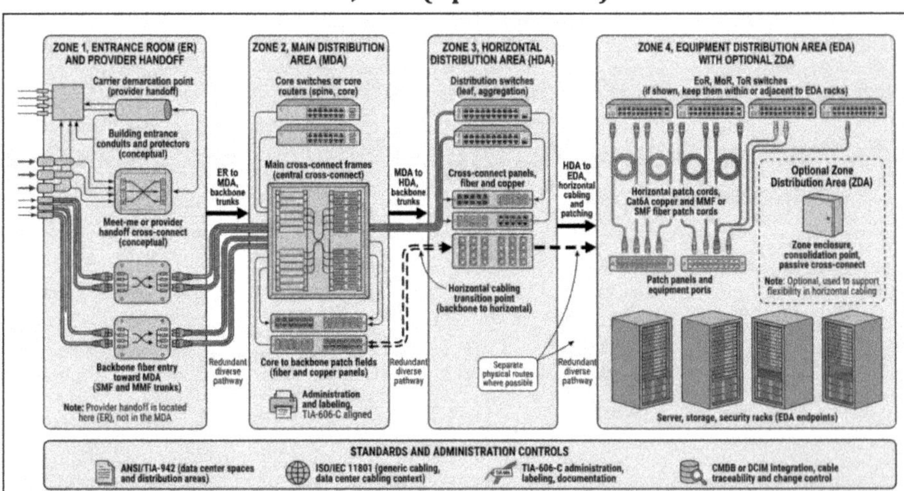

Best Practices

- Keep power and data cabling in separate pathways to reduce interference and improve safety.
- Use color-coded patch cords and trunks so technicians can quickly identify cable types and functions.

- Route cabling through overhead trays or underfloor conduits to maintain airflow and reduce congestion.
- Document every connection in a cable management or DCIM system to improve traceability and speed troubleshooting.
- Follow manufacturer guidelines for bend radius and tension limits to preserve signal integrity.

Case Example

A data center with more than 2,000 connections reduced troubleshooting time by nearly 60 percent after adopting TIA-606-C-compliant labeling and a digital cabling database. The improved organization made maintenance faster and reduced the likelihood of accidental disconnects.

How the improvement was implemented (what the manager actually did)

They started by standardizing the labeling scheme across racks, patch panels, and pathways, then trained technicians on one consistent naming format and where labels had to be placed so they stayed readable during work. Next, they built a digital cabling database that matched the physical layout, each record tied a port to a destination, cable type, and service owner, with change history.

They rolled the change in zones to avoid disrupting production. As each row was cleaned up, technicians verified connections, corrected mislabeled runs, and updated the database immediately. They also made labeling and database updates a close-out requirement for any move, add, or change. Troubleshooting time dropped because techs could trace paths from the record first, then validate physically, instead of tone-and-tagging in live environments.

Pro Tip

Apply color-coding logic to your power cables too. Use Red cables for Power Source A and Blue cables for Power Source B.

When a breaker trips at 3:00 AM, you don't want to be tracing black cables through a dark rack to see which feed is active. Visual distinction prevents the catastrophic error of unplugging the active line while trying to fix the dead one.

Physical Security and Access Control

Physical security is often treated as a facility concern separate from IT security, but in practice the two are tightly linked. A threat actor who can access a rack does not need to bypass the firewall. Physical access controls, access logging, and perimeter security belong in the same risk model as network segmentation and endpoint protection. They require the same governance discipline: documented policies, regular access reviews, audit evidence, and tested procedures.

Security Layers

Perimeter Protection: Fencing, surveillance cameras, controlled gates, and security patrols help secure the outer boundary of the facility.

Facility Access Control: RFID badges, biometric scanners, and secure entry vestibules ensure that only authorized personnel can enter the building.

Mantraps: Two-door, interlocked entry systems that prevent tailgating and verify identity before granting access.

Rack-Level Security: Locking cabinets, access logs, and electronic handle systems protect equipment inside the data hall itself.

Monitoring: CCTV systems with long-term retention and motion-based alerts provide real-time and historical visibility into all access points.

Figure 7.6: Data Center Security Zones Diagram

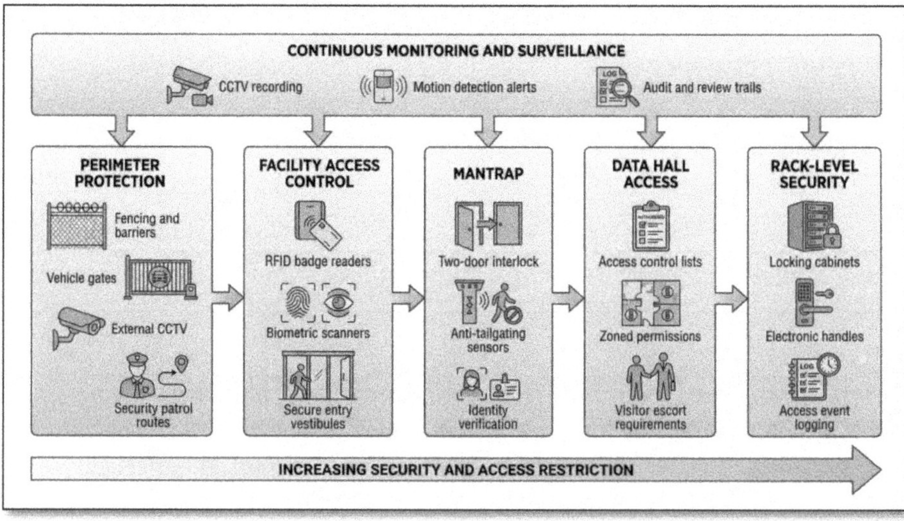

Policies

- Maintain detailed **visitor logs** and escort procedures
- Perform **quarterly reviews** of key-card access to ensure accuracy and remove stale permissions
- Integrate **physical access logs** with logical access reporting to strengthen overall compliance and traceability

Example

A data center integrated biometric access control with its building management platform. Every entry attempt was automatically logged and tied to user credentials, giving auditors complete traceability during compliance reviews.

How the integration improved audit readiness (what the security lead actually did)

They first standardized identity data so the access system and the management platform used the same user records and role definitions. Biometric enrollment was tied to approved access requests, and access was granted by role and zone, not by individual exceptions.

Next, they integrated event logs end to end. Every grant, deny, and forced-door event was forwarded into the central platform with timestamps, door IDs, and user identifiers, then retained under a defined policy. Alerts were tuned for high-risk patterns like repeated denials, after-hours entry, and tailgating events.

For audits, they built a repeatable evidence package. Quarterly access reviews produced a report of active permissions, recent changes, and removed access, and specific access events could be traced back to the approved request and escort records when required.

Facility Maintenance and Operations Management

Maintenance in a data center is not a background activity. The mechanical and electrical systems that keep IT running, generators, UPS units, cooling systems, transfer switches, and power distribution, require scheduled care and validated performance. When that maintenance is deferred or informal, the failure usually stays hidden until the next stress event, often when the facility is already under load.

Preventive and Predictive Maintenance

- **Preventive Maintenance:** Scheduled inspections and equipment servicing performed at regular intervals. This includes tasks such as cleaning air filters, tightening electrical connections, testing generators, and recalibrating sensors
- **Predictive Maintenance:** Uses real-time telemetry and performance data to identify early warning signs before failures occur. Vibration analysis, thermal imaging, and sensor-based monitoring are common tools for predicting issues
- **Standard Operating Procedures (SOPs):** Clear SOPs help maintain consistency across teams and shifts. They define responsibilities, escalation paths, troubleshooting steps, and communication requirements. Well-documented SOPs reduce human error and ensure work is completed safely and reliably

- **Training and Compliance:** Operators should receive ongoing training in safety procedures, equipment handling, and emergency response. Compliance with standards such as NFPA, OSHA, ISO, and TIA must be reviewed regularly to ensure the facility remains up to date

Figure 7.7: Integrated Facility Maintenance Program – Preventive, Predictive, and Corrective Activities

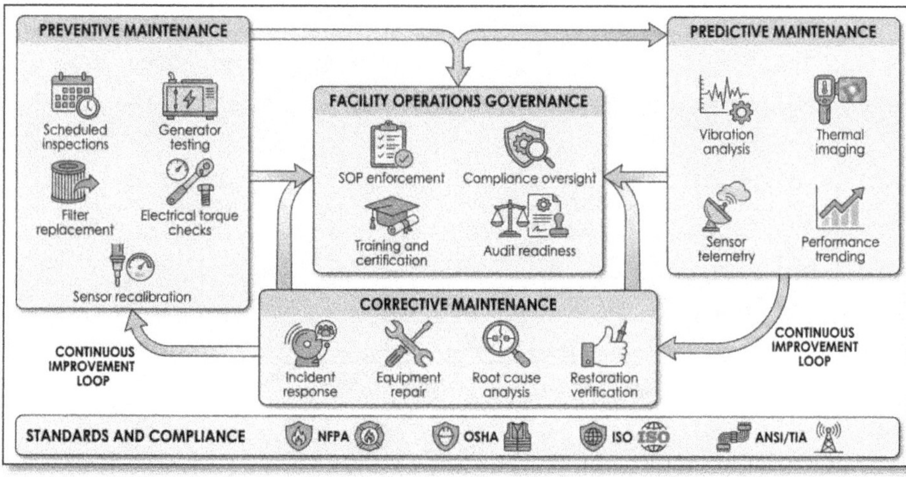

Case Example

A large enterprise introduced standardized SOPs across all its data centers and implemented a central maintenance tracking system. Within a year, equipment-related incidents dropped significantly, and audit readiness improved across multiple facilities.

How the program was implemented (what the operations lead actually did)

They started with the highest-risk procedures, UPS, generator, cooling, breaker operations, and alarm response, and rewrote them into one standard SOP format with safety steps, exact instructions, validation checks, and escalation triggers.

They then rolled out a central maintenance tracking system where every task was logged against an asset ID with measurements and evidence (test results, photos, vendor reports). SOP links were embedded in work orders to prevent outdated local copies. Monthly spot checks and retraining closed the loop, improving audit evidence quality and reducing equipment-related incidents.

Data Center Infrastructure Management (DCIM)

DCIM platforms bring monitoring and management across the mechanical, electrical, and IT layers of the data center into one operational view. Without that integration, power, cooling, and asset data often sit in separate tools or spreadsheets, which leads to capacity decisions based on incomplete information and delays in identifying anomalies. DCIM improves that by making the relationship between load, thermal conditions, and available capacity visible in real time.

Core Functions

- **Real-time monitoring** of power, cooling, and network performance
- **Asset and capacity management** to track rack space, power usage, and equipment lifecycle
- **Environmental sensors** tied to configurable thresholds for temperature, humidity, and airflow
- **Reporting dashboards** that support compliance reviews and SLA verification
- **Change and workflow integration** that links physical infrastructure updates to ticketing systems, ensuring rack moves, adds, and decommissions are reflected in the asset record without manual reconciliation

Table: Example DCIM Dashboard Metrics - Power Load, Rack Utilization, Temperature Trends, Alerts

Metric Category	Specific Indicator	Description and Utility
Power Load	UPS & PDU Load %	Tracks real-time power draw against maximum capacity. Helps ensure redundancy is maintained (e.g., keeping load below 50% on A/B feeds) and prevents breaker trips.
Power Load	Real-Time PUE	Displays the current Power Usage Effectiveness ratio (Total Facility Power / IT Equipment Power) to gauge energy efficiency trends throughout the day.
Rack Utilization	Available "U" Space	Visualizes open rack units (U) across the floor map. It distinguishes between contiguous space (usable for large chassis) and fragmented space.
Rack Utilization	Stranded Capacity	Identifies racks that have available physical space but no remaining power or cooling capacity, preventing unusable provisioning.
Temperature Trends	Max/Min Intake Temp	Monitors the hottest and coldest sensors in the Cold Aisle to ensure compliance with ASHRAE standards (typically 18°C to 27°C) and prevent hotspots.
Temperature Trends	Rate of Rise	Tracks how quickly temperatures increase during a cooling failure, helping to estimate the "ride-through" time available for emergency response.
Alerts & Health	Active Critical Alarms	A consolidated count of devices (CRACs, UPS, PDUs) currently in a failure state requiring immediate dispatch or remediation.
Alerts & Health	Communication Status	Flags devices that have lost network connectivity (SNMP/Modbus timeouts), indicating potential blind spots in the monitoring system.

Example Tools

Common industry platforms include Schneider EcoStruxure, Nlyte, Sunbird DCIM, and Vertiv Environet.

Benefits

- Consolidated visibility across mechanical, electrical, and IT systems
- Earlier detection of anomalies, allowing faster intervention
- Better forecasting for future capacity and asset planning

Figure 7.8: Example of DCIM System Dashboard View.

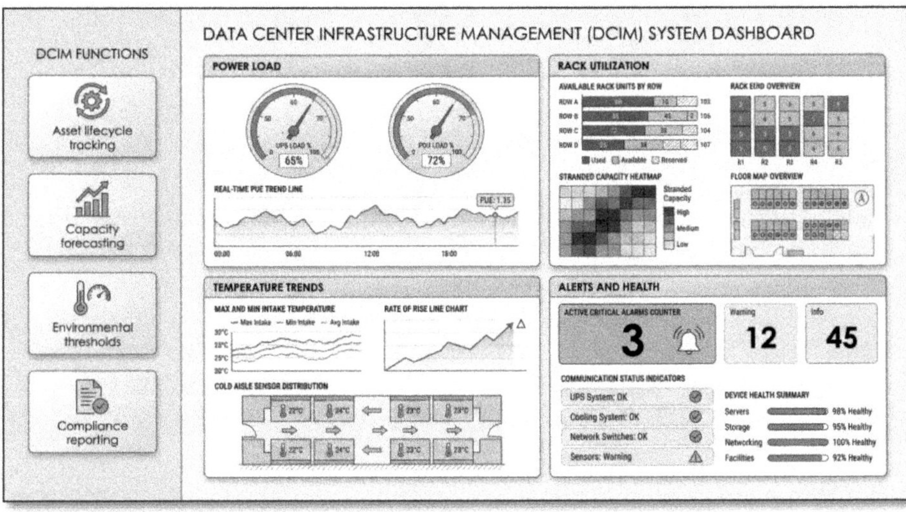

Compliance, Safety, and Risk Management

Compliance and safety requirements in data centers are not abstract obligations. They reflect real failure modes, electrical injuries, fire events, environmental exposure, and data breaches that have occurred in inadequately governed facilities. Standards like NFPA, OSHA, ISO 27001, and ASHRAE exist because the consequences of getting facility operations wrong are serious and often hard to reverse. The IT manager's role is to understand which standards apply, integrate them into operational procedures, and ensure compliance evidence is maintained and ready for audit.

Relevant Standards and Regulations

Several standards shape how data centers are governed and audited. **ISO 27001** provides the management framework for information security. **NFPA 75** and **NFPA 76** address fire protection in IT equipment spaces and telecommunications facilities. **OSHA** and broader **EHS** requirements govern worker safety in electrical and mechanical environments, including lockout/tagout and PPE. **SOC 2 Type II** provides evidence that operational controls are functioning consistently over time, which many enterprise customers expect. **ASHRAE 90.4** focuses on energy efficiency in data center mechanical and electrical systems and is becoming more relevant in sustainability and regulatory reporting.

Risk Management Practices

- Maintain a detailed risk register capturing environmental, equipment, and human factors
- Conduct annual Business Impact Analyses (BIAs) to understand service dependencies and recovery needs
- Perform redundancy tests and failover drills to validate resiliency plans
- Audit all third-party maintenance vendors to verify compliance with safety and operational standards

Case Example

A colocation provider reduced operational risk by requiring all vendors to complete a site-specific safety orientation before beginning work. This policy resulted in zero recorded EHS violations over an 18-month period.

How the control was enforced (what the facility manager actually did)

They treated orientation as an access control, not optional training. Vendor companies had to submit a roster in advance, and each worker completed orientation before receiving any site badge or being allowed past the security checkpoint. The orientation was short but specific: PPE rules, electrical and LOTO boundaries, restricted areas, incident reporting, emergency response, and how work authorization worked on that site.

Compliance was verified on the floor. Escorts and operations staff performed spot checks for PPE and permitted work scope, and any violation triggered immediate stop-work and re-orientation. Orientation records were tied to work orders and access logs so audits could prove who was on site, when, and under what authorization. Over time, consistency improved because vendors knew expectations were enforced the same way every visit.

Sustainability and Future Trends

Data center power consumption is a significant and measurable cost driver. Energy spend often ranks among the top operational expenses in a facility budget, and the link between power efficiency and operating cost is direct. Sustainability efforts in the data center are not driven only by environmental goals. They also overlap with financial discipline, risk reduction, and regulatory requirements that are tightening across multiple jurisdictions.

Emerging Approaches

- **Liquid Immersion Cooling:** A cooling method in which IT equipment is submerged in a thermally conductive dielectric fluid to remove heat more efficiently than air-based systems. Immersion cooling can reduce the energy used by the cooling infrastructure, support higher compute density per rack, and in some designs reduce dependence on traditional CRAC units or chiller systems. It is used most often in high-performance computing and specialized high-density environments, although adoption is gradually expanding

- **AI-Driven Efficiency:** Using artificial intelligence platforms to adjust power and airflow settings in real time, eliminating the lag inherent in manual tuning

- **Renewable Energy Integration:** Incorporating solar, wind, and hydro-sourced power to reduce dependence on traditional electrical grids and meet corporate sustainability goals
- **Modular Data Centers:** Deploying prefabricated, scalable units to expand capacity rapidly without the lead time of traditional construction

Case Example

A cloud provider deployed AI-controlled cooling optimization software across one of its facilities. The system dynamically tuned airflow and power usage, reducing energy consumption by 30 percent while keeping temperature and humidity within required ranges.

How the reduction was achieved (what the facilities lead actually did)

They started by tightening the inputs before trusting automation. Temperature and humidity sensors were audited, recalibrated, and mapped to real rack intake conditions so the platform was optimizing the right points, not room averages. They also defined safe operating guardrails, including hard limits for inlet temperature, humidity bands, and maximum allowed rate of change to avoid control oscillations.

The AI tuning was rolled out in stages. It ran in observe mode first to learn baseline behavior by load and outdoor conditions, then was allowed to make small adjustments during low-risk periods. Setpoints, fan speeds, and economizer usage were tuned gradually, with automatic rollback to static controls if any threshold was approached.

Once stable, they focused on waste removal: reducing overcooling in low-density zones, smoothing fan speed spikes, and balancing airflow so hotspots stopped forcing aggressive cooling across entire rooms. Results were validated using metered energy data over comparable IT loads and weather windows, with alarms and exception reporting built in so savings did not come at the expense of environmental stability.

Figure 7.9: Future Data Center Design Concept – Modular, Sustainable, Intelligent

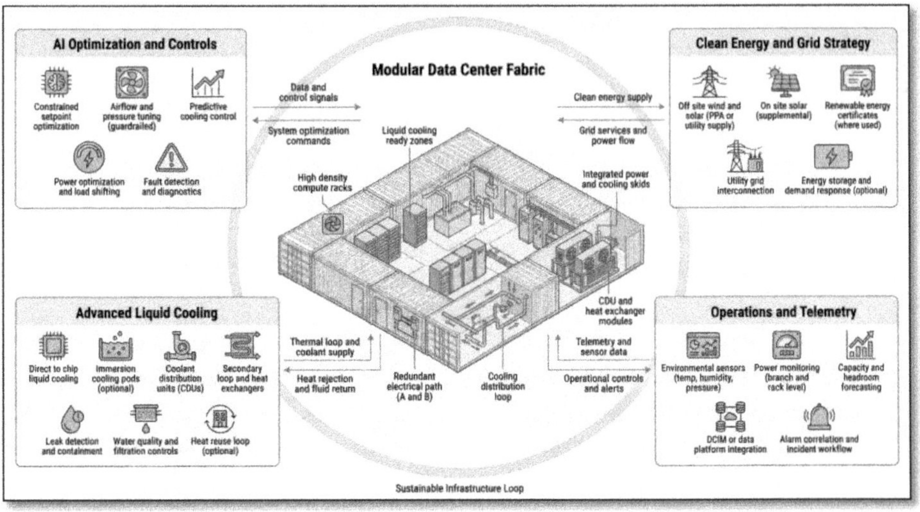

What This Means in Practice

- Data center reliability is an engineering outcome, not something procurement can guarantee on its own. Redundancy in power, cooling, and cabling creates the conditions for uptime, but those systems still have to be tested, validated, and maintained if the design is going to perform as promised
- Tier classification is a starting point, not a guarantee. A poorly operated Tier III facility can underperform a well-run Tier II site. The design sets the upper limit. Day-to-day operations determine where the facility actually performs
- Cooling and power efficiency are directly tied to cost. PUE improvements, hotspot elimination, and load balancing are not peripheral concerns. They affect how much of the facility's energy budget is doing useful work versus compensating for design or operational weaknesses
- Cabling quality is part of infrastructure quality. An unlabeled or poorly documented cabling environment creates operational friction that builds over time, slower troubleshooting, higher change risk, and audit exposure that can take years to correct
- DCIM helps close the gap between assumption and reality. Capacity decisions made without integrated power, thermal, and space data are little more than estimates. The platform adds value only when the data feeding it is accurate and current
- Physical security is part of the overall security posture, not separate from it. Access controls, audit logs, and physical evidence requirements belong in the same governance framework as logical security controls

Figure 7.10: Summary Diagram – Data Center Operational Excellence Model: Power, Cooling, Cabling, People, Process

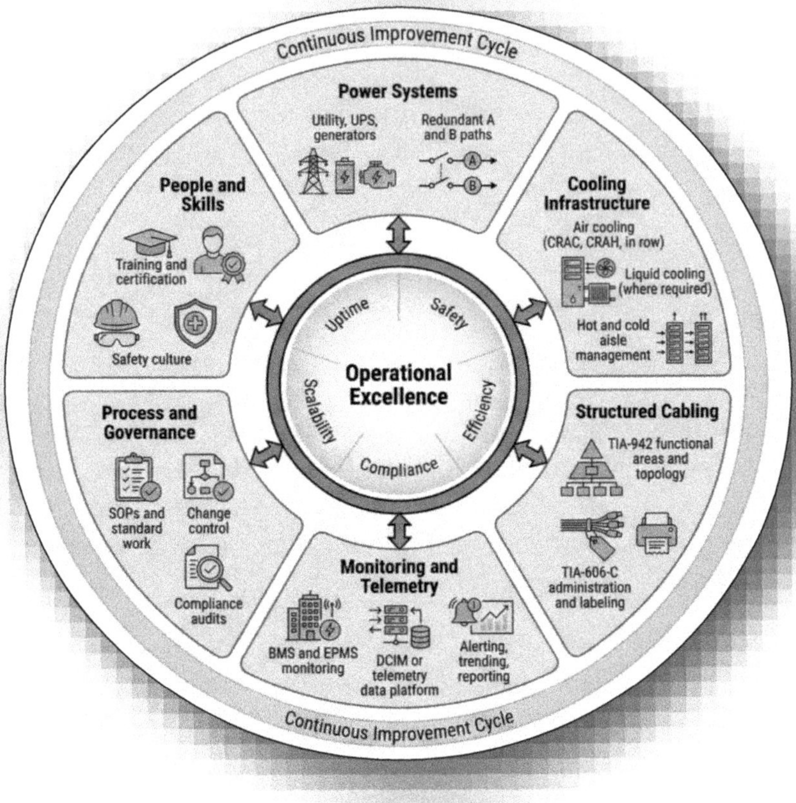

Chapter 8

CLOUD AND VIRTUALIZATION TECHNOLOGIES: HYBRID, MULTI-CLOUD, AND VIRTUAL INFRASTRUCTURE

Virtualization and cloud computing changed the economics of IT infrastructure. Before virtualization, workloads were tied to specific physical servers. Scaling required buying hardware, waiting for delivery, and provisioning it manually. Moving a workload often meant planned downtime and direct physical intervention. Modern environments changed that model by separating workloads from hardware and turning compute, storage, and network into shared resources that can be adjusted without rebuilding the underlying infrastructure. Modern environments run on shared pools of compute, storage, and network capacity that can scale quickly, shift across regions, and support different deployment patterns without rebuilding everything.

For IT managers, the architectural transition is rarely the hardest part. The harder challenge is maintaining cost control and security discipline in an environment that changes faster than governance can adapt. Flexibility creates speed, but it also creates exposure: configurations drift, spending builds up in untagged resources, and access permissions expand quietly over time. The manager's job is to put guardrails in place so the environment can move quickly without losing control.

This chapter focuses on the architectural and operational decisions that shape how virtualized and cloud environments are built, governed, and kept reliable. It moves from the hypervisor layer through containers, cloud service models, and hybrid strategy, then into the cost, security, monitoring, and automation disciplines required to keep complex environments under control.

Figure 8.1: Evolution of Infrastructure - Physical Servers to Virtual Machines to Cloud Services

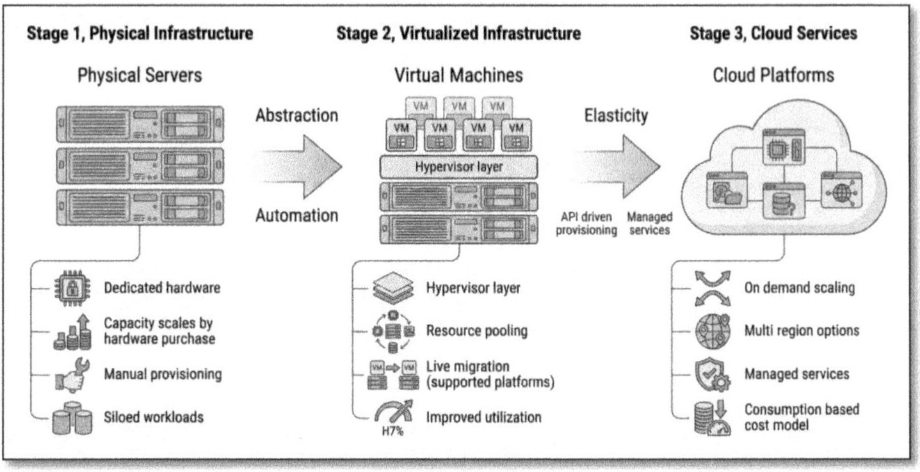

Virtualization Fundamentals

Virtualization separates workloads from physical hardware by turning compute, storage, and network capacity into software-defined resources that can be provisioned, moved, or retired without touching the underlying equipment. That is what makes elastic scaling, live migration, and rapid recovery possible, and it is the foundation on which private cloud, public cloud, and hybrid environments are built.

Core Types of Virtualization

Containers use OS-level process isolation rather than hardware virtualization, but they are grouped here because they serve similar purposes in modern infrastructure: abstracting the application from the underlying environment and enabling workload portability.

- **Server Virtualization:** Multiple virtual machines share one physical host. Hypervisors (like VMware ESXi, Hyper-V, and KVM) handle isolation and resource allocation.
- **Network Virtualization:** Logical networks (VLANs, VXLANs, SDN) operate independently from the physical cabling, improving segmentation and mobility

- **Storage Virtualization:** Combines multiple storage arrays into unified pools, masking the physical complexity from the server and improving resiliency
- **Desktop Virtualization:** Runs user desktops on centralized servers (VDI), keeping data in the data center rather than on unsecured laptops
- **Application Packaging and Isolation:** Containers package applications so dependencies travel with the software, eliminating the "it works on my machine" problem

Figure 8.2: Virtualization Stack — Hardware, Hypervisor, Guest OS, Applications

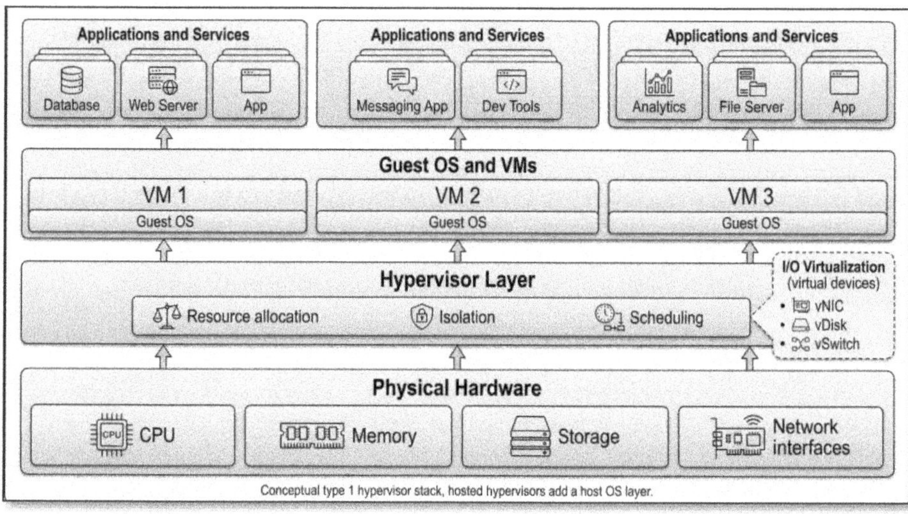

Benefits

The operational benefits of virtualization are concrete. Higher hardware utilization means fewer physical servers are needed to carry the same workload, which reduces both capital spend and facility footprint. Disaster recovery also becomes faster through snapshot-based backups and live migration, reducing recovery time from hours to minutes in many failure scenarios. Provisioning is easier because new servers can be deployed in minutes from a template instead of waiting days for hardware to be ordered and built. Over time, total cost of ownership falls across all of those areas, fewer physical assets to maintain, less rack space, lower power draw, and less manual labor for each deployed workload.

Case Example

An insurance provider reduced its physical footprint by 70 percent by migrating to virtualized clusters, improving backup times from eight hours to less than one.

How the migration delivered both consolidation and faster backups (what the manager actually did)
They started with a workload inventory and right-sizing effort, identifying servers that were overprovisioned, underutilized, or running duplicate functions. Those workloads were grouped into clusters based on performance needs and recovery criticality, then migrated in waves with standard build templates so new VMs were consistent.

Backup improvement came from redesigning how backups were executed. Instead of long agent-based full backups, they moved to snapshot-based backups at the hypervisor layer with incremental changes and a clear retention policy. Backup windows were spread across clusters to avoid I/O spikes, and restore testing was built into the rollout so speed gains were proven, not assumed. Once the majority of workloads were consolidated, entire racks were decommissioned, and the environment became easier to patch, monitor, and recover.

Hypervisors and Virtual Machine Management

A hypervisor is the software layer that makes server virtualization possible. It sits between the physical hardware and the virtual machines, managing how compute and memory resources are allocated, isolated, and shared across workloads running on the same host.

Hypervisor Types

- **Type 1 (Bare Metal)**: ESXi, Hyper-V, XenServer, KVM
- **Type 2 (Hosted)**: VirtualBox, VMware Workstation

Core Functions

- CPU and memory scheduling
- Virtual device emulation
- VM isolation
- Snapshot management
- Integration with orchestration systems

Best Practices

- Standardize host hardware
- Enable clustering for high availability
- Use templates for consistency
- Control configuration drift using automation or IaC

Case Example

A regional government improved uptime to around 99.99 percent after standardizing its virtualization platform and consolidating VM operations under VMware vCenter.

How the uptime improvement was achieved (what the virtualization lead actually did)
They standardized host builds and baselines so clusters behaved consistently, then used vCenter as the single control point for templates, patching, and configuration policy to eliminate drift.

They enabled HA with proper admission control, restart priorities, and maintenance workflows that evacuated hosts before patching. Centralized monitoring and periodic failover tests confirmed the environment could recover automatically, which reduced outages caused by inconsistent changes and manual recovery.

Containers and Orchestration

Containers shift the unit of deployment from the server to the application. Instead of configuring a server for a specific workload, a container packages the application together with the libraries, configuration, and runtime dependencies it needs to run, so it behaves the same way across development, test, and production environments. That consistency is one of the reasons containers work well in microservices architectures and fast release cycles: the same artifact that passes testing is the one deployed to production.

A container is different from a virtual machine in one key way, it shares the host kernel. It isolates processes through namespaces and groups, which is why containers start fast and run efficiently. The tradeoff is that you must be disciplined about image hygiene, runtime security, and cluster operations. If you treat containers like "small VMs," you recreate VM-era sprawl and drift, except it spreads faster.

Core Technologies

- **Docker** remains the most widely used toolchain for building and packaging container images, particularly in development and CI/CD workflows
- **Containerd and Podman** are runtime alternatives used in environments where a cleaner separation between build tools and runtime execution is preferred
- **Kubernetes** has become the standard platform for running containers in production at scale. It handles how containers are scheduled onto nodes, how services find each other, how deployments are rolled out and rolled back, and how the cluster maintains desired state when individual containers or nodes fail
- **OpenShift** builds on **Kubernetes** and adds opinionated enterprise defaults: integrated build pipelines, stricter security policies, and operational tooling that reduces the configuration burden for teams standardizing delivery across multiple application teams

Benefits

- **Rapid deployment.** Containers start in seconds (not minutes), which makes rollouts, scaling, and recovery faster.
- **Consistent environments.** The same image runs in dev, test, and production, reducing environment mismatch failures.
- **High resource efficiency.** Higher density is possible because containers share the host OS, unlike VMs which require a full OS for every app.
- **Strong integration with CI/CD.** Containers align naturally with automated build pipelines. Versioned images and declarative manifests make releases repeatable.

Management Challenges

Containers make shipping easier, but they raise the bar for operational discipline.

- **Image sprawl:** Without standards, teams create dozens of near-duplicate images, inconsistent base layers, and unclear ownership. That increases attack surface and complicates patching
- **Security of registries:** The registry becomes part of your supply chain. If it is not controlled, scanned, and audited, you can deploy risk at scale
- **Complex monitoring:** Traditional host monitoring is not enough. You need visibility across pods, services, ingress, and dependencies. You also need the ability to trace performance issues across layers
- **Multi-cluster operations:** Many organizations end up with multiple clusters across regions or environments. Without a standard approach, policy drift and inconsistent upgrades become a reliability risk

Best Practices

- ✓ **Private image repositories:** Use a controlled registry with clear ownership, image retention rules, and access logging. Standardize base images and enforce tagging conventions so teams can patch consistently and roll back cleanly
- ✓ **RBAC within Kubernetes:** Treat permissions as a first-class control. Grant access by role, namespace, and service account. Keep cluster-admin limited, and review permissions on a cadence. Most Kubernetes incidents are made worse by excessive privileges
- ✓ **Centralized monitoring using Prometheus and Grafana:** Standardize metrics collection and dashboards so teams share the same view of health. Pair metrics with logs and tracing where possible so troubleshooting does not require jumping between disconnected tools

Additional practices that prevent predictable failures

- Use namespaces and network policies to limit lateral movement between services
- Enforce resource requests and limits so noisy neighbors do not destabilize nodes
- Scan images for vulnerabilities and block unapproved images from deployment
- Standardize cluster upgrade cadence and test upgrades like any other change
- Keep manifests and Helm charts under version control with peer review

Example

A fintech company cut its release cycle time by over 90 percent after moving standardized deployments onto Kubernetes.

How the release cycle was reduced (what the platform lead actually did)

They standardized how applications were built and deployed. Teams moved from manual server changes to a container build pipeline that produced versioned images on every merge, with automated tests and a consistent deployment manifest. Kubernetes then handled rollouts using rolling updates, health checks, and fast rollback when metrics degraded.

They also removed the "ticket wall" that slowed releases. Instead of waiting for infrastructure teams to provision hosts, teams deployed into approved namespaces with predefined quotas and policies. RBAC controlled who could deploy, and admission controls blocked unscanned or noncompliant images. Monitoring dashboards and SLO alerts were shared so release readiness could be measured, not debated.

Finally, they forced consistency across environments. The same deployment patterns were used in dev, staging, and production, and releases were promoted through environments rather than rebuilt. Over time, the bottleneck shifted away from provisioning and manual validation and toward the work that should be the bottleneck: testing, quality, and change discipline.

Cloud Computing Overview

Cloud computing delivers infrastructure, platforms, and software as on-demand services, with costs tied to usage rather than capital purchase. The operational impact is substantial. Teams can access compute capacity globally without waiting through hardware procurement cycles, scale resources in line with actual demand instead of forecasted peaks, and deploy new services without waiting for underlying infrastructure to be built.

Cloud platforms remove much of the operational overhead involved in managing underlying hardware and infrastructure layers, but they replace it with a different set of demands: cost visibility, access governance, configuration compliance, and the ability to manage an environment that changes faster than traditional IT processes were designed to support. The speed advantage of cloud only creates lasting value when governance keeps pace with it.

Service Models

The IaaS, PaaS, and SaaS service model definitions below are based on widely adopted industry terminology formally documented in NIST SP 800-145. The practical descriptions and examples are adapted for an operational context.

1. **Infrastructure as a Service (IaaS):** Delivers raw compute, storage, and networking as a managed service. The customer controls the operating system and above; the provider manages the physical hardware and virtualization layer.

   Examples: AWS EC2, Azure Virtual Machines, Google Compute Engine. IaaS is typically used for lift-and-shift migrations, flexible development environments, and workloads that require operating system-level control.
2. **Platform as a Service (PaaS):** Removes the OS and runtime management burden from the customer. The provider manages the platform; the customer focuses on application code and configuration.

   Examples: Azure App Service, Google App Engine, and AWS Elastic Beanstalk are common examples. PaaS suits teams that want to deploy and scale applications without managing servers.
3. **Software as a Service (SaaS):** Delivers complete applications over the internet, with the provider managing everything from infrastructure to application updates.

   Examples: Microsoft 365, Salesforce, and Workday are standard examples. SaaS is the right model for standardized business functions that do not require significant customization.

Pro Tip

"Lift and shift" is the most expensive way to use the cloud. If you move your on-premise virtual machines directly to the cloud without resizing them or shutting them down at night, you will likely double your infrastructure bill. Cloud economics only work if you use elasticity (turning things off) or refactoring (using PaaS). If you treat Amazon or Azure like just another data center, you are paying a premium rent for a space you never clean up.

Figure 8.3: Cloud Service Model Stack - IaaS, PaaS, SaaS

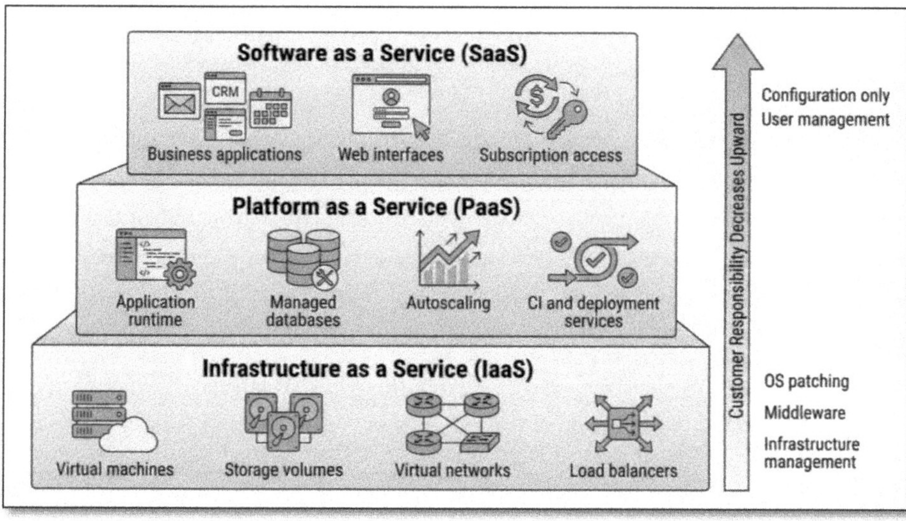

Deployment Models

- **Private Cloud:** Infrastructure deployed and operated by the organization, either on-premises or in a dedicated colocation environment. Provides full operational control, consistent performance, and strong alignment with data residency and compliance requirements. Best suited for workloads that cannot move to shared infrastructure due to regulatory, latency, or security constraints

- **Public Cloud:** Compute, storage, and managed services delivered by providers such as AWS, Azure, and Google Cloud. Resources are billed on consumption and accessible globally without capital investment. Best suited for variable workloads, fast-moving development, and applications that benefit from managed service abstractions
- **Hybrid Cloud:** Combines on-premises or private cloud infrastructure with public cloud resources. Workloads are placed based on performance, compliance, and cost requirements, and connectivity between environments is managed through dedicated links, VPNs, or cloud interconnects. Best suited for phased migrations, data residency constraints, and workloads that span both environments
- **Multi-Cloud:** Uses more than one public cloud provider simultaneously. Motivations include access to provider-specific services, avoiding dependency on a single vendor, regional availability requirements, and cost optimization across workload types. Requires consistent governance, identity federation, and operational discipline across providers

Case Example

A media company adopted Azure for cloud bursts during rendering peaks while keeping regulated assets on-premises. This hybrid approach balanced compliance needs with scalable compute power.

How the hybrid burst model was made workable (what the cloud lead actually did)

They separated workloads by constraint. Regulated assets and licensing-bound data stayed on-prem, while compute-heavy rendering jobs were packaged so they could run stateless in the cloud without pulling sensitive datasets across boundaries.

They then built a predictable "burst" workflow. Rendering queues monitored utilization, and when thresholds were reached, jobs were dispatched to Azure using pre-approved images, network rules, and identity controls. Data movement was tightly controlled, only the minimum inputs were staged, outputs were validated, and then stored back into approved repositories.

Cost and performance were governed like operations. The team set spend guardrails, tagged resources by project, and tracked render time per job so leadership could see when bursting was cheaper than expanding on-prem capacity.

Hybrid and Multi-Cloud Strategies

Hybrid and multi-cloud strategies exist because no single environment is the right fit for every workload. Some applications belong on-premises because of latency requirements, data sovereignty rules, or licensing constraints. Others fit better in public cloud because of variable demand, global reach, or access to managed services. The challenge is making those placement decisions deliberately and managing them consistently as workloads and requirements evolve.

Benefits of Hybrid and Multi-Cloud

- Avoid vendor lock-in and increase flexibility
- Place workloads based on performance, cost, or regulatory needs
- Leverage geographic redundancy for resilience
- Use multiple providers to optimize pricing

Challenges

- Governance and policy alignment across platforms
- Differences in API models and security controls
- Data egress costs and latency considerations
- Operational complexity in monitoring and troubleshooting

Best Practices

- ✓ **Cloud Management Platforms (CMPs)** for unified visibility

- ✓ **Identity federation** for consistent access control policies
- ✓ **Standardized tagging and cost allocation** across all environments
- ✓ **Regular performance and cost reviews** to optimize workload placement
- ✓ **Adopt consistent guardrails** such as landing zones and baseline architectures

Case Example

A global manufacturer deployed IoT analytics on AWS for edge processing while using Azure for visualization dashboards. A centralized CMP reduced operational overhead by 30 percent.

How the multi-cloud split stayed manageable (what the cloud lead actually did)

They made the split deliberate: AWS handled edge ingestion and analytics close to the device pipeline, while Azure hosted dashboards to align with existing identity and reporting tooling. Data movement rules were defined up front to control latency and egress.

A centralized CMP enforced standard tagging, naming, and baselines across both clouds, with federated identity so access followed the same role model. Monitoring and alerts fed one incident workflow. Monthly reviews caught cost or performance drift and drove refactoring or workload moves, which is where most of the overhead reduction came from.

Pro Tip

Don't let the fear of "vendor lock-in" drive you into a multi-cloud strategy you can't support. Running AWS and Azure simultaneously doubles your training requirements, security complexity, and networking costs. For most mid-sized organizations, the operational overhead of managing two clouds far outweighs the theoretical risk of being stuck with one. Pick one provider, master it, and only branch out if a specific business capability demands it.

Cloud Governance and Security

Cloud governance is what keeps the speed of cloud from turning into operational risk. Without enforced guardrails, access expands over time, configurations drift away from approved baselines, spending builds up in untagged resources, and sensitive data ends up in locations it was never meant to reach. Many cloud security incidents are not the result of sophisticated attacks. They come from preventable misconfigurations that governance controls are designed to catch.

Key Governance Components

1. **Access Management:** Implement least-privilege access using RBAC, IAM roles, MFA, and conditional access policies.
2. **Policy Enforcement:** Use tools like Azure Policy, AWS Config, and Google Organization Policies to enforce configuration baselines.
3. **Cost Governance:** Monitor usage with dashboards, alerts, anomaly reports, and automated optimization recommendations.
4. **Compliance Alignment:** Map cloud environments to frameworks such as ISO 27017, SOC 2, NIST, and GDPR. Ensure continuous compliance through automated scanning.
5. **Backup and Disaster Recovery:** Cross-region replication, automated snapshot policies, and tested failover procedures.
6. **Zero Trust in the Cloud:** Verify all access attempts, apply micro-segmentation, monitor continuously, and integrate with SIEM tools such as Splunk or Microsoft Sentinel.

Case Example

A healthcare organization used AWS Organizations and Service Control Policies to require encryption and limit deployments to approved regions. Reported compliance violations fell sharply (around 80 percent) once misconfigurations were blocked up front and drift was handled consistently.

How the controls were enforced (what the cloud security lead actually did)
They defined a short list of non-negotiables: encryption required, approved regions only, and no public resources without explicit approval. Those were enforced with SCP guardrails at the org and account level, so teams could not bypass them with local IAM permissions.

Accounts were separated by environment and risk level (prod, non-prod, regulated) with different control strength. AWS Config flagged drift, findings were assigned to owners, and repeat violations tightened guardrails or fixed the deployment pipeline. Violations dropped because most misconfigurations were blocked up front and the rest were handled consistently.

Pro Tip

Implement a strict "No Tag, No Deploy" policy from day one. If an engineer tries to provision a resource without an "Owner" and "Cost Center" tag, the automation should block it. If you allow resources to be created as "unallocated" with the intention of tagging them later, you never will. You will end up with a "General IT" bucket that consumes no less than 30% of your budget, and you won't be able to shut it off because you don't know what it breaks.

Virtual Infrastructure Monitoring and Automation

Cloud and virtualized environments generate telemetry at a scale that makes manual monitoring impractical. The challenge is not the amount of data. It is the gap between what the data shows and what it actually means operationally. Monitoring strategy in these environments has to define which signals require action, at what threshold, and by whom. Everything else becomes noise, slowing response time and training teams to ignore alerts.

In traditional environments, monitoring often focused on device health and uptime. In virtual and cloud environments, the same workload can move between hosts, scale horizontally, or be rebuilt automatically. That changes what matters. You still watch CPU and memory, but you also need to watch service behavior, dependency health, and cost signals that can spike faster than any hardware alarm.

Monitoring Focus Areas

- **Resource Utilization: CPU, memory, disk, storage IOPS:** Watch for sustained saturation, noisy-neighbor effects, storage queue depth, and IOPS spikes that correlate with batch jobs or backups. In virtual clusters, utilization trends matter more than point-in-time snapshots because contention builds over time
- **Application Performance: latency, throughput, dependency mapping:** Infrastructure metrics alone do not explain user impact. Monitor request latency, error rates, and service-to-service dependencies so you can isolate whether the bottleneck is network, storage, database, or application logic
- **Cost and Usage Trends: anomalies, sudden consumption spikes:** In cloud, cost is a reliability signal. Unexpected spend often means runaway scaling, misconfigured logging, or data egress. Anomaly detection and budget alerts should be treated like operational alarms, with clear owners and response expectations
- **Security Signals: unauthorized changes, IAM events, suspicious API calls:** Cloud control plane activity is as important as dataplane health. Alerts should focus on high-risk patterns, privilege escalations, policy changes, new public exposure, and unusual access paths, not just "someone logged in

Tools and Platforms

Most organizations use multiple tools because no single platform covers everything cleanly.

- **Observability** platforms such as Dynatrace, Datadog, and New Relic provide end-to-end visibility across distributed systems, including distributed tracing, service dependency mapping, and anomaly detection
- **Cloud-native monitoring** tools like AWS CloudWatch and Azure Monitor are essential for collecting provider-level metrics, triggering alerts on service health, and integrating with cloud-native automation
- **Log aggregation** platforms such as the Elastic Stack and Splunk centralize log data from across the environment, making it possible to correlate events across services and support security investigations. Most production environments use a combination of these layers because no single tool covers every visibility need cleanly
- **Automation Platforms:** (Terraform, Ansible, Azure DevOps): Used to enforce infrastructure standards and deploy changes consistently

One practical risk is tool sprawl. If every team has a different dashboard and alerting scheme, you will lose time during incidents. Standardize where possible and make sure the escalation path is clear.

Automation Use Cases

- **Auto-scaling of applications during peak usage:** Scaling policies should be tied to service-level indicators, not just CPU. Add guardrails to prevent runaway scaling and ensure scaling does not break downstream dependencies
- **Automated configuration compliance scanning:** Scan for drift against approved baselines. The best programs make

violations visible and assignable, then block the worst misconfigurations at deploy time

- **Infrastructure provisioning using IaC pipelines:** IaC reduces drift and improves repeatability. It also creates a change record through commits, reviews, and pipeline logs, which improves auditability

- **Automated remediation of common incidents:** Automation should focus on low-risk, high-frequency issues first. Examples include restarting failed jobs, recycling unhealthy instances, rolling back failed deploys, fixing certificate renewal failures, or detaching and reattaching a broken endpoint. Anything with high blast radius should require approvals or be limited to safe actions

A simple rule that holds up: if you cannot define the trigger, validation checks, and stop conditions, do not automate it.

Case Example

A large online retailer rolled out real-time anomaly detection across its multi-cloud environment and paired it with automated runbooks. Many repeat, low-risk incidents, those with clear triggers and safe automated responses, were resolved without human intervention once guardrails and validation steps were put in place. The improvement was sustained because the automation was bounded and results were reviewed weekly rather than accepted without review.

How the automation was made reliable (what the operations lead actually did)

They limited automation to a defined list of repeatable events, unhealthy nodes, failed deployments, stuck queues, certificate issues, and runaway logging. Baselines were learned per service and environment so alerts reflected real deviations, not expected spikes.

Runbooks were built with guardrails: pre-checks, maximum scope, stop conditions, and post-action validation. Automated actions were restricted to safe moves first, restart, recycle, roll back, scale within limits, and escalate if health did not recover. Every automated action wrote back to the incident record with what changed and whether validation passed. Weekly reviews tuned thresholds and improved runbooks based on outcomes, which is why the reduction held instead of turning into noisy automation that nobody trusted.

What This Means in Practice

- Virtualization changed the unit of infrastructure from physical hardware to software-defined resources. That shift is what makes everything else in this chapter possible: containers, cloud, hybrid design, and elastic scaling all depend on the abstraction layer virtualization provides.
- Containers and Kubernetes raise the bar for operational discipline. They make software delivery faster and more consistent, but only if teams govern image hygiene, RBAC, resource limits, and cluster upgrades with the same rigor they apply to other production infrastructure.
- Cloud service model selection is a workload decision, not a trend decision. IaaS, PaaS, and SaaS each carry different cost structures, operational responsibilities, and governance implications. Choosing the wrong model for a workload creates both cost inefficiency and operational complexity.
- Hybrid and multi-cloud strategies add operational overhead that has to be justified. The benefits of workload placement flexibility and redundancy are real, but so are the costs of managing multiple identity systems, API models, and governance frameworks simultaneously.
- Cloud governance is preventive infrastructure. Access controls, policy guardrails, tagging standards, and cost monitoring are not cleanup activities. They are the controls that prevent the most common and costly cloud failures before they happen.
- Monitoring and automation in cloud environments require a different approach than traditional infrastructure. The goal is not comprehensive coverage of every metric. It is defining which signals drive decisions and automating the responses that are safe, repeatable, and well-bounded."

Figure 8.4: End-to-End Cloud and Virtual Infrastructure Landscape

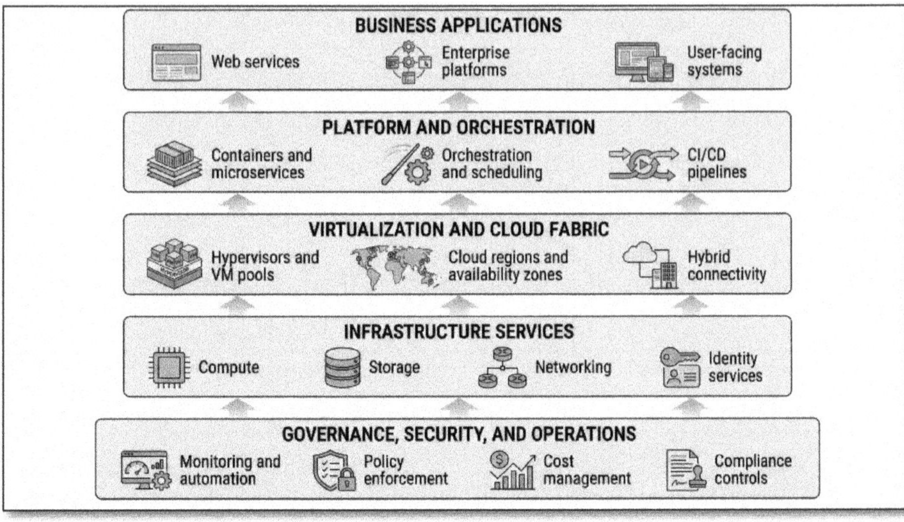

Part III

OPERATIONAL CONTROL AND RESILIENCE

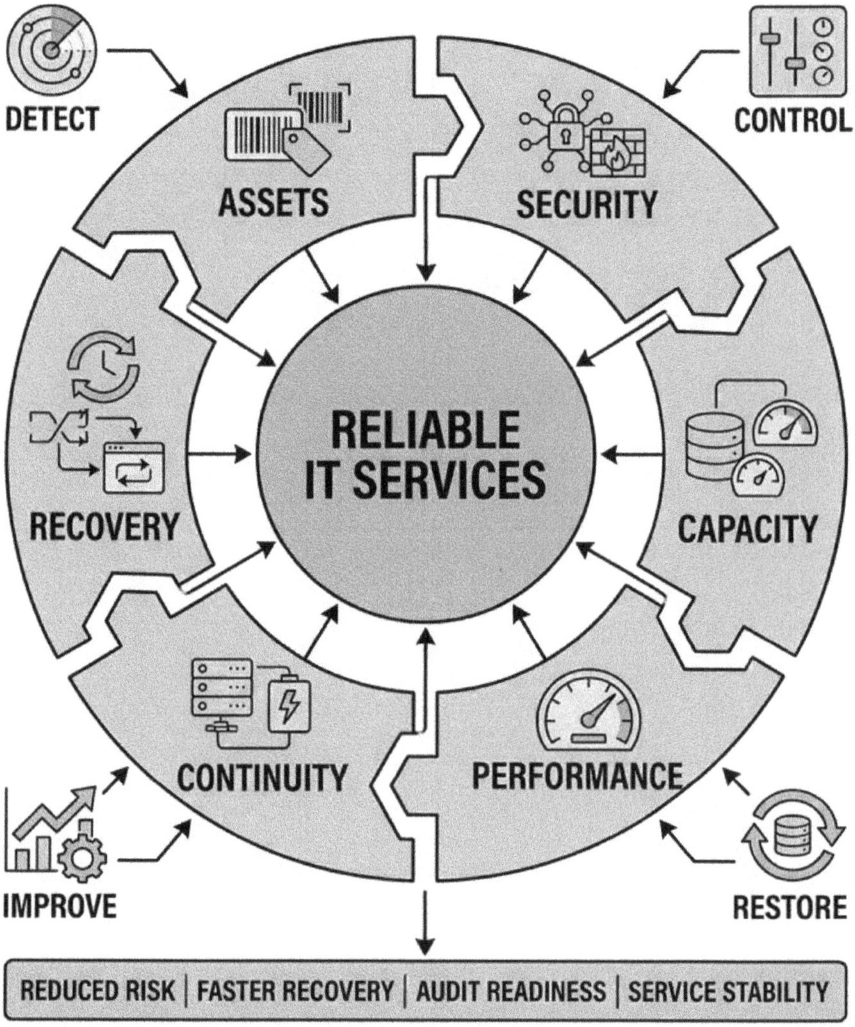
DETECT
CONTROL
ASSETS
SECURITY
RECOVERY
RELIABLE
IT SERVICES
CAPACITY
CONTINUITY
PERFORMANCE
IMPROVE
RESTORE
REDUCED RISK | FASTER RECOVERY | AUDIT READINESS | SERVICE STABILITY

Chapter 9

MONITORING, CAPACITY PLANNING, AND PERFORMANCE OPTIMIZATION

Architecture decisions and infrastructure investments only matter if systems perform reliably under real conditions. Monitoring is what closes the gap between a system that is well designed and one that is well run. It is the discipline of watching how systems behave, catching drift before it becomes degradation, and acting on signals before users notice the impact. Monitoring has moved far beyond status boards and uptime checks. In complex distributed environments, it is one of the main ways IT understands system behavior, detects degradation early, and maintains the level of operational awareness needed to respond before the business feels the impact.

Capacity planning extends the value of monitoring by looking ahead. Where monitoring shows what is happening now, capacity planning uses that data to project what is likely to happen next, when resources will become constrained, where growth will create bottlenecks, and how far in advance procurement decisions need to be made. Together, they shift the operating model away from pure incident response and toward anticipation, reducing both the frequency and cost of performance-related events.

This chapter focuses on the monitoring, capacity, and optimization disciplines that keep IT environments stable and responsive to business demand. It explains how to design monitoring that spans infrastructure, application, and user experience layers, how to use KPIs and SLAs in ways that actually guide action, how to build capacity forecasts early enough for teams to respond, and how to approach performance optimization systematically instead of reactively.

Figure 9.1: Performance Management Cycle - Monitor, Analyze, Predict, Optimize

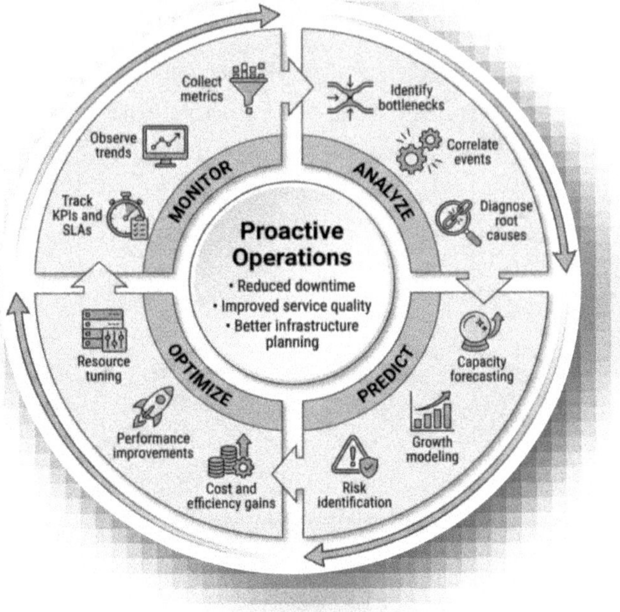

The Role of Monitoring in IT Operations

Monitoring is the operational discipline that connects system behavior to management decisions. It is not simply about collecting metrics. It requires correlating signals across infrastructure, application, and network layers, establishing baselines that reflect normal behavior, and routing the right information to the right people quickly enough to act. As environments become more distributed, monitoring architecture becomes as important as infrastructure architecture. Without it, teams lose the visibility needed to troubleshoot, plan, and improve. Workloads span physical servers, virtual machines, public clouds, SaaS platforms, and edge locations. Without a common monitoring approach, teams end up with data silos, blind spots, and fragmented troubleshooting.

Objectives of Monitoring

1. **Availability:** Monitoring must detect outages or degradation immediately. This includes service uptime, component failures, process health, and connectivity issues. High availability depends on rapid detection, accurate classification, and streamlined escalation.

2. **Performance:** Performance metrics capture how quickly applications respond, how consistently transactions complete, and how efficiently systems handle load. Response times, throughput, and latency all reveal bottlenecks that may not yet appear as outages.

3. **Capacity:** Resource constraints often surface gradually. CPU saturation, memory exhaustion, storage growth, and network congestion are predictable when tracked correctly. Monitoring highlights these patterns long before they become emergencies.

4. **Security:** Unauthorized activity, access anomalies, and unexpected configuration changes can signal security breaches. Integrating monitoring with event logging strengthens early detection and supports a zero-trust model.

5. **Compliance:** Regulated industries rely on monitoring to maintain audit trails. Tracking performance history, access logs, and data retention supports internal governance and external requirements.

Table: Monitoring Objectives and Corresponding Metrics

Objective	Core Focus	Key Metrics & Indicators
Availability	Detecting outages, component failures, and service degradation immediately.	• Service uptime • Component status (up/down) • Process health • Connectivity status
Performance	Measuring responsiveness, transaction consistency, and system efficiency.	• Response times • Throughput (requests per second) • Latency • Transaction completion rates
Capacity	Tracking resource usage patterns to predict constraints before they become emergencies.	• CPU saturation • Memory exhaustion • Storage growth rates • Network congestion
Security	Identifying unauthorized activity, anomalies, and potential breaches.	• Access anomalies • Unexpected configuration changes • Event logs • Failed login attempts
Compliance	Maintaining audit trails for internal governance and external regulatory requirements.	• Performance history retention • Access logs • Data retention status • Audit trail integrity

Figure 9.2: End-to-End Visibility Dashboard example - Server, Network, Application, Cloud

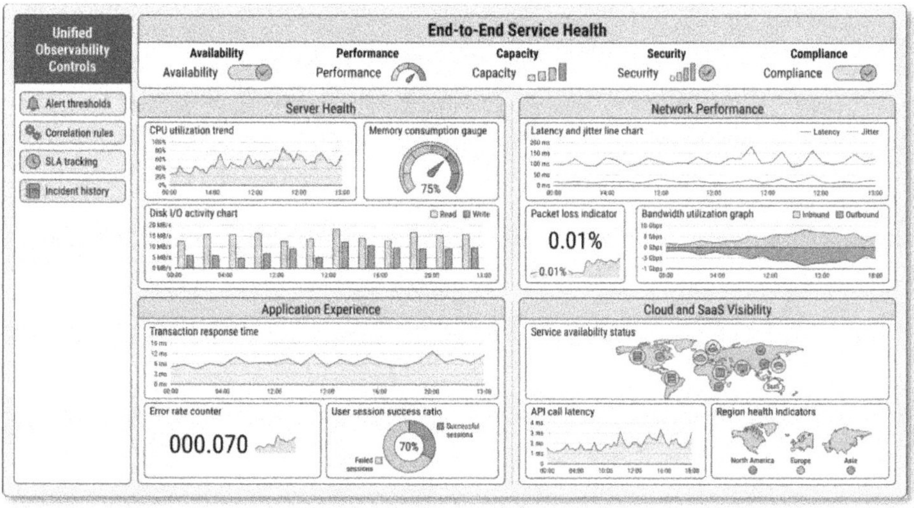

Designing a Monitoring Architecture

A monitoring architecture works when it provides a coherent view across all layers, not a collection of disconnected tools that engineers have to reconcile manually during an incident. The goal is unified visibility, one place where infrastructure status, application performance, network health, and user experience data can be analyzed together so the platform does the correlation work before the team is forced to do it under pressure.

Core Monitoring Layers

1. **Infrastructure Monitoring:** Focuses on CPU, memory, disk I/O, storage capacity, network interfaces, system processes, and hardware health. These metrics form the foundation for performance analysis and capacity planning.

2. **Application Performance Monitoring (APM):** Tracks transaction paths, code-level execution times, database queries, external service dependencies, and error patterns. APM reveals how applications behave under different loads and identifies where performance actually breaks down.

3. **Network Monitoring:** Uses SNMP polling, NetFlow, packet capture, and link analysis to track latency, bandwidth usage, route stability, and interface saturation. With hybrid IT, network health becomes as important as compute performance.

4. **User Experience Monitoring:** Captures real session traffic or runs synthetic transactions to simulate login flows, web requests, or API calls. This ensures teams measure performance as users actually experience it.

5. **Security and Event Monitoring:** Centralized logging and SIEM platforms collect authentication records, configuration changes, and event anomalies. Security insights become part of operational monitoring rather than an isolated specialty.

Figure 9.3: Layered Monitoring Architecture Model

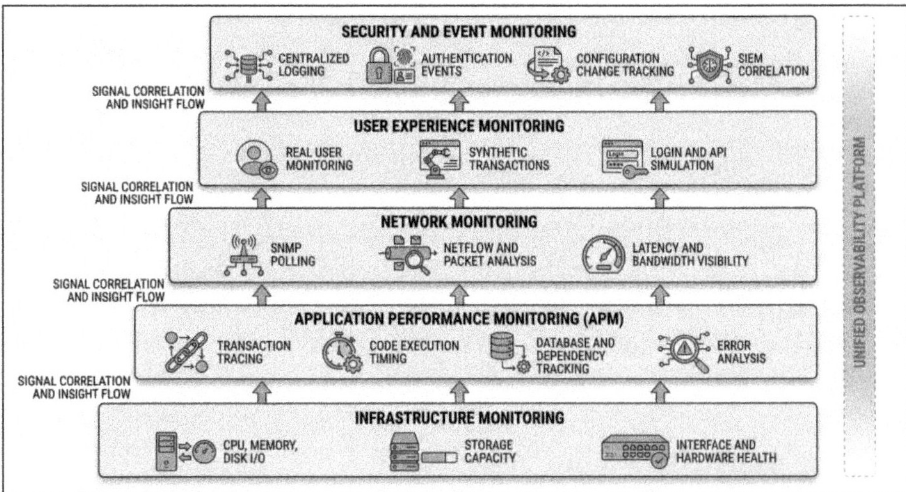

Tool Categories

- **Open Source Tools:** Zabbix, Prometheus, Grafana, and Nagios provide customizable dashboards and flexible alerting for technical teams

- **Enterprise Tools:** SolarWinds, PRTG, Datadog, New Relic, and Splunk offer broad visibility, enterprise integrations, and scalable analytics

- **Cloud-Native Tools:** AWS CloudWatch, Azure Monitor, and Google Operations Suite provide telemetry for cloud resources, serverless functions, and managed services
- **AIOps Platforms:** Dynatrace, Moogsoft, and LogicMonitor leverage machine learning to correlate events, reduce noise, and identify root causes

Best Practices

- **Establish alert thresholds tied to service-level objectives (SLOs).** Thresholds must reflect business impact rather than arbitrary values
- **Use dynamic baselining.** Systems rarely behave identically every day. Baselines adjust automatically based on historical patterns
- **Aggregate data into a single pane of glass.** Consolidated dashboards reduce tool switching and speed up decision-making
- **Automate incident creation.** Integrate monitoring with ITSM platforms to ensure important events trigger workflows, escalations, and documentation

Example

An e-commerce provider deployed AIOps to analyze API latency, service dependencies, and infrastructure signals. During a flash promotion, the AI engine identified one backend node as the bottleneck and isolated the problem automatically, preventing a costly outage during peak demand.

How the outage was avoided (what the incident lead actually did)
They made sure the platform had the right context before the promotion. Key APIs were tagged to services and dependencies, baselines were built from prior peak periods, and alerts were tied to user-impact signals (checkout latency and error rate), not raw CPU thresholds.

When latency climbed, the AIOps correlation grouped the symptoms to one dependency path and flagged a single backend node with abnormal response time and retry patterns compared to its peers. The incident lead confirmed it quickly by checking node-level metrics and recent change history, then removed that node from rotation and shifted traffic to healthy highlights using standard load balancer controls.

After stability returned, they captured the root cause and prevented recurrence by adding a targeted health check for the failing condition and tightening deployment validation so a similar node-level degradation would be caught before entering service.

Pro Tip

A dashboard that is always red is as useless as one that is always green. If a warning light stays on for weeks and nobody fixes it because "it's just a false positive," you are training your team to ignore real outages. Be ruthless: tune the threshold or fix the root cause. If you can't do either, delete the alert. "Normalization of deviance" is the fastest way to miss a catastrophe.

Defining KPIs and SLAs

KPIs and SLAs serve different purposes, but they need to work together. KPIs are the operational signals IT teams track continuously to understand system performance. SLAs are the commitments the business makes to users and customers about what those systems are expected to deliver. The link between them matters. If IT tracks the wrong KPIs, it can hit every internal target and still miss every SLA. Alignment starts by defining KPIs that reliably indicate whether SLA thresholds will be met, not just whether the infrastructure appears healthy.

Common Infrastructure KPIs

- CPU, memory, and disk utilization
- Network latency, jitter, and packet loss

- Disk IOPS and storage latency
- Application response times and throughput
- Backup and replication success rates

The table below summarizes each monitoring objective and the core indicators teams typically track to measure it.

Table: Example SLA and KPI Mapping

Service Area	Business SLA Commitment	KPI Signals Tracked by IT	Early Warning Threshold	Typical Owner
Customer-facing web app	Availability (monthly uptime)	Synthetic uptime, error rate, health checks	Error rate rise or failed synthetic checks	App Ops, SRE
Checkout or transaction flow	Transaction success rate, response time	P95 latency, timeout rate, DB query time	P95 latency trending up, timeouts increasing	App Ops, Database
WAN connectivity to sites	Link availability, performance	Packet loss, jitter, latency, interface errors	Loss bursts or jitter above baseline	Network Ops
Storage platform	Performance and data availability	Storage latency, IOPS, replication status	Latency above target, replication lag	Storage Ops
Backup and recovery	RPO, backup success	Backup job success rate, restore test results	Failures above threshold, missed restore tests	Backup Owner
Identity and access	Authentication availability	Login success rate, token failures, directory latency	Spike in failed logins, auth latency rise	IAM Team

Best Practices

- ✓ **Collaborate with business owners.** KPIs must reflect user experience and business priorities, not just technical preferences
- ✓ **Set alert thresholds well before SLA violations.** Teams should have room to resolve degradation before it becomes an incident
- ✓ **Define clear escalation paths.** Everyone should know who acts when a metric crosses a threshold
- ✓ **Review SLAs quarterly.** As workloads change, SLAs need to evolve. Static agreements become outdated quickly

Example

A logistics company increased its SLA from 99.5 percent to 99.9 percent after automating recovery processes and adding redundant routing paths. This provided stronger continuity for delivery-critical applications.

How the SLA uplift was made achievable (what the operations lead actually did)

They first quantified what 99.9 percent meant operationally, then identified the top outage drivers that were consuming the error budget. Recovery steps were converted into automated runbooks for the repeatable failures, including service restarts, route failover, and dependency checks with validation gates.

In parallel, they removed single points of failure in network paths for the delivery applications by adding redundant routes and testing failover during planned windows. Monitoring thresholds were tightened to trigger response before user impact, and post-incident reviews focused on shaving recovery time, not just documenting causes. The SLA increased because detection was faster, recovery was more consistent, and routing resilience reduced the number of incidents that could take the service down.

Capacity Planning: Anticipating Growth

Capacity planning helps IT stay ahead of demand instead of chasing it. It is meant to show when resources will become constrained, how much time is needed to address those constraints, and what decisions need to be made around procurement and funding. Done well, it reduces the need for reactive purchases and emergency expansions that raise cost and make the environment less stable.

Core Steps of Capacity Planning

1. **Baseline Collection:** Before forecasting, the team needs accurate data on how systems actually behave, not how they were expected to behave on paper. That means collecting utilization data across compute, storage, and network during peak demand, seasonal cycles, and normal operating periods. A strong baseline helps separate real growth from background noise and gives the forecasting model a reliable starting point.

2. **Trend Analysis:** The next step is to examine how consumption has changed over time and what caused those changes. Steady organic growth needs to be separated from short-term event-driven spikes, and workloads growing faster than the rest of the environment need to be identified early. The most important patterns are the ones that repeat.

3. **Forecast Modeling:** Growth trends then need to be applied to estimate when each resource type will approach saturation. Linear regression can work in steady environments, while time-series methods are better suited to seasonal or cyclical demand. The output should not be a single date with false precision. It should be a projected saturation window for each constrained resource, with an appropriate confidence range.

4. **Scenario Planning:** Forecasting also has to account for planned business changes before they happen. New application onboarding, customer growth, or a cloud migration can all change the resource picture. Scenario planning makes those effects visible early enough for the organization to respond.

5. **Budget Integration:** The final step is turning forecast output into a funding case. The discussion with finance should cover the expected saturation date, procurement lead time, the cost of available options, and the operational impact of delaying the investment. Infrastructure spending that is not tied to a forecast is often either too late or unnecessarily wasteful.

Pro Tip

Don't confuse "exhaustion date" with "decision date." If your forecast shows you will run out of storage in six months, you might think you have time. But if it takes one month to get a quote, two months to approve the budget, and three months for the vendor to ship the hardware, you are already too late. Always subtract the "procurement lag" from your forecast to find the real deadline.

Data Sources for Capacity Planning

- Infrastructure monitoring platforms such as vRealize, SolarWinds, and Datadog
- Log analytics systems like Splunk or ELK
- CMDBs for asset inventory and lifecycle data
- Business growth forecasts and technology roadmaps
- ITSM platforms for change and incident history

Example

A SaaS provider anticipated 25 percent annual growth after a successful product launch. Capacity modeling showed that current compute clusters would reach saturation within nine months. By identifying this early, the engineering team secured funding for scaling and avoided emergency purchasing and potential outages.

How the capacity risk was prevented (what the capacity lead actually did)

They built a baseline from peak-hour telemetry and separated steady growth from launch-driven spikes, then modeled saturation using CPU ready time, memory pressure, and storage IOPS rather than simple average utilization. Procurement lead times were added to the plan so the decision date came well before the exhaustion date.

They packaged the forecast into a short business case with options: add nodes to existing clusters, shift selected workloads to cloud, or reduce demand through tuning and right-sizing. Each option included cost, timeline, and the risk of doing nothing. Funding was approved because the plan showed a clear deadline, a measured impact to customer experience if capacity ran out, and a phased scale approach that could be executed without a risky big-bang expansion.

Performance Tuning and Optimization

Monitoring shows where performance is degrading. Optimization is how IT responds. The two disciplines are tightly linked: monitoring without optimization leads to dashboards with little operational value, and optimization without monitoring turns into guesswork. Performance management has to be continuous rather than project-based because workloads shift, usage patterns change, and the gains from one round of tuning can be offset by the next round of growth or new deployments.

Optimization Domains

1. **Server Optimization:** Improve CPU scheduling, rebalance workloads, update firmware, and tune OS parameters. Virtual machines should be right-sized based on actual usage rather than theoretical requirements.

2. **Storage Optimization:** Use caching, tiered storage, deduplication, and compression to reduce latency and improve IOPS. Storage contention should be monitored closely because it often becomes a silent bottleneck.

3. **Network Optimization:** Apply QoS policies to prioritize critical traffic, tune MTU sizes, remove unnecessary hops, and ensure routing is optimal. Regular audits help identify misconfigurations or outdated hardware.
4. **Database Optimization:** Analyze slow queries, improve indexing strategies, and monitor connection pooling. Proper schema design and periodic index maintenance can dramatically improve performance.
5. **Application Optimization:** Reduce unnecessary round trips, improve API interactions, and eliminate inefficient code paths. Modern applications may require profiling tools to identify hidden bottlenecks across microservices.

Optimization Action Table

Domain	Optimization Action	Typical Benefit
Server	Tune vCPU allocation and rebalance workloads	10 to 15 percent faster processing
Storage	Add SSD tiers for frequently accessed data	Up to 4 times improvement in IOPS
Network	Apply QoS for latency-sensitive traffic	Around 50 percent reduction in jitter
Database	Rebuild indexes and optimize queries	Roughly 20 percent faster query execution
Application	Implement caching and reduce network calls	Up to 40 percent faster response times

Case Example

A large enterprise struggled with ERP performance issues caused by high IOPS on legacy HDD arrays. After migrating hot data to SSD storage, performance improved dramatically, and user complaints dropped to nearly zero.

How the Storage Migration Was Executed (What the Performance Lead Actually Did)

They began by identifying which data was truly hot rather than migrating everything at once. APM traces and storage performance counters were used to identify the specific LUNs and workloads generating the highest IOPS and longest queue depths. Those workloads were prioritized for the first migration wave to SSDs, with validation checks after each move to confirm improvements in latency and IOPS. Less frequently accessed data remained on HDD arrays and was later reviewed for archival tiering. Monitoring was updated to alert on queue depth and latency thresholds for the migrated volumes, and the storage team added a recurring review to catch new workloads that were being placed on spinning disk when they should not have been.

Figure 9.4: Performance Optimization Framework - Identify, Analyze, Execute, Measure

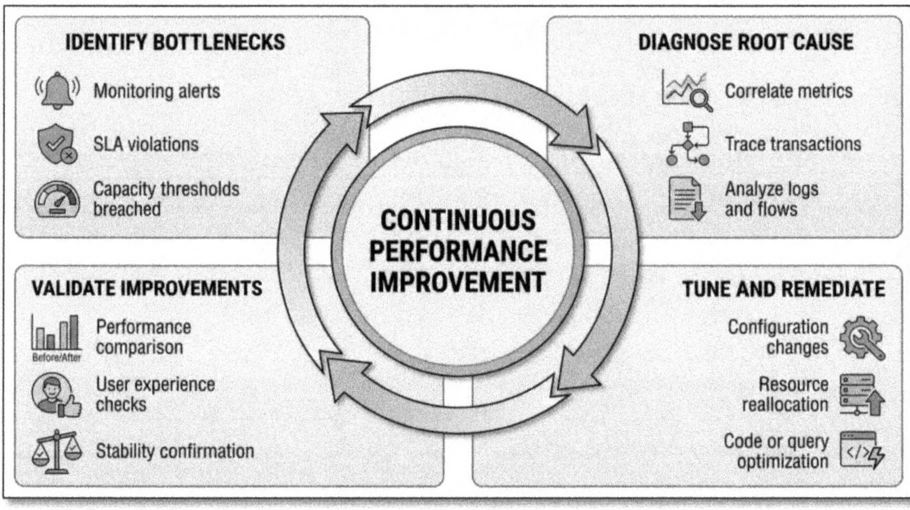

Monitoring Automation and AIOps

Alert volume in large environments often reaches a level where manual triage is no longer practical during an active incident. The result is that teams either ignore lower-priority alerts, which creates blind spots, or spend too much time filtering noise before they identify the real problem. AIOps platforms address this by correlating related alerts into a single incident, applying learned baselines to reduce false positives, and, when properly governed, triggering automated responses for low-risk and well-understood failure patterns.

Key Capabilities of AIOps

- **Alert Correlation:** AIOps platforms group related alerts into unified incidents, reducing noise and improving clarity
- **Predictive Analytics:** Machine learning models forecast capacity exhaustion, identify degrading performance, and reveal patterns invisible to human analysts
- **Automated Remediation:** AIOps can trigger scripts or workflows to address common issues automatically, such as restarting a service, clearing a queue, or shifting traffic
- **Real-Time Root Cause Analysis:** Correlated data from logs, telemetry, and infrastructure health helps identify the true source of issues faster

Best Practices for Implementing AIOps

- Provide enough historical data to cover multiple cycles of both normal and abnormal behavior, including seasonal patterns, peak periods, and prior incidents. In most environments, that means at least several months of reliable telemetry before automated responses are enabled. The more varied the historical record, the better the platform can distinguish true anomalies from normal variation
- Combine automation with human approval for highly sensitive systems
- Continuously refine filters to eliminate false positives
- Integrate AIOps outputs with ITSM workflows for governance and traceability

Case Example

A telecommunications provider noticed recurring latency spikes every Friday night. Their AIOps platform identified the pattern, traced it to a weekly security scan, and automatically rescheduled the task. This eliminated recurring outages and improved service stability.

How the recurring latency pattern was identified and resolved (what the operations lead actually did)

They treated the recurring spike as a pattern-detection problem first, not a guess-and-check exercise. The AIOps platform was fed the right signals (latency, error rate, queue depth, and task schedules), then tuned to correlate the Friday-night degradation to a specific change window and a consistent workload signature. Once the platform flagged the security scan as the trigger, the lead validated it by comparing timestamps, resource contention signals, and the affected dependency path. The fix was operational and controlled: the scan was rescheduled to a lower-impact window, throttled where possible, and paired with monitoring guardrails so any future scan-driven contention would alert early. They then documented the new schedule, added a change control requirement for future scans, and verified stability over multiple weeks to confirm the pattern was actually gone.

Figure 9.5: AIOps Integration Workflow - Data Ingestion, Correlation, Action, Feedback Loop

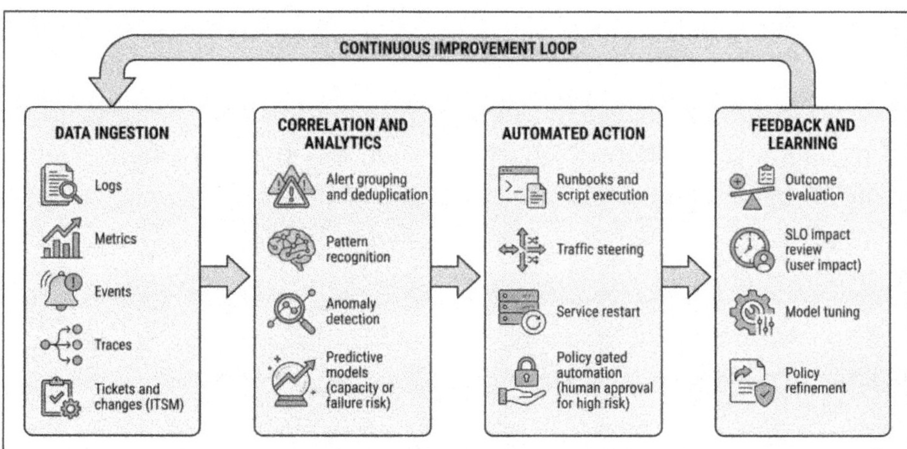

Monitoring Across Hybrid and Cloud Environments

Monitoring hybrid environments is harder than monitoring a single environment because the data is fragmented by design. On-premises infrastructure produces one set of telemetry. Cloud platforms produce another. SaaS tools produce a third, often with limited visibility below the application layer. When a performance issue spans two or more of these environments, the team has to correlate signals across systems that were not built to work together natively. Without deliberate architecture to connect them, that correlation happens manually, takes too long, and often begins only after the incident has escalated.

Challenges in Hybrid Monitoring

- Multiple monitoring tools using different data formats and APIs
- Limited access to cloud provider telemetry compared to on-prem metrics
- Latency between environments impacting user experience
- Increased complexity in correlating events across boundaries

Solutions

- **Use Cloud-Native Integrations:** AWS CloudWatch, Azure Log Analytics, and Google Operations Suite provide deep insight into cloud workloads
- **Adopt Multi-Cloud Monitoring Platforms:** Centralized tools consolidate metrics across AWS, Azure, Google Cloud, and on-prem systems.
- **Implement Synthetic Monitoring:** Simulated transactions test end-to-end user paths across external and internal services
- **Centralize Logs:** Aggregating logs improves forensic analysis and ensures consistent visibility

Case Example

A global manufacturer consolidated monitoring across Azure services and on-premises VMware clusters. Standardizing on a single monitoring platform reduced redundant tools and overlapping licenses, lowered monitoring costs, and gave the team a more consistent view of incidents spanning both cloud and on-premises environments.

How the consolidation improved hybrid troubleshooting (what the monitoring lead actually did)

They started by standardizing what had to be monitored for every service: availability, latency, error rate, dependency health, and key infrastructure signals. Azure logs and metrics were onboarded alongside VMware host and guest telemetry, and naming and tagging were normalized so a service in cloud and a service on-prem could be viewed under the same ownership and environment labels.

Next, they removed duplicate alerting. Thresholds and routing were rebuilt so incidents were created by service impact, not by individual device alarms. Correlation rules linked app symptoms to infrastructure signals across boundaries, for example, a SaaS slowdown tied to a specific ExpressRoute path, or a VM performance issue tied to storage latency on-prem.

Finally, they rationalized tooling and licenses. Dashboards were consolidated, legacy tools were retired in phases, and any remaining specialist tools were configured to forward events into the central platform. Cost dropped because overlapping licenses were eliminated, and incident response improved because engineers stopped losing time switching tools during the first minutes of triage.

Reporting, Analytics, and Continuous Improvement

Monitoring data only becomes operationally useful when it reaches the right people in a form they can act on. For engineers, that usually means real-time dashboards and actionable alerts. For leadership, it means trend summaries, SLA performance, and a clear connection between system behavior and business outcomes. Reporting closes that gap by translating operational signals into forms each audience can use to make decisions.

Key Report Types

1. **Operational dashboards** are built for the teams running the environment. They provide real-time system status, active alerts, and resource utilization so engineers can see current conditions and respond quickly.

2. **Executive summaries** serve a different audience and answer a different set of questions. Is the service meeting its commitments? What direction are performance and reliability trending? Where are the current risks? These reports translate operational data into business-facing terms, emphasizing SLA performance, customer impact, and cost rather than raw technical metrics.

3. **Trend reports** look backward so the organization can make better forward decisions. Recurring failure patterns, sustained growth in resource consumption, and longer-term shifts in performance are the signals that inform infrastructure planning and targeted improvement work.

4. **Incident analytics** focus on what failed, how long recovery took, and what was done to prevent the issue from happening again. Over time, these reports show whether post-incident actions are actually closing gaps or whether the same patterns continue to repeat.

Best Practices

- ✓ **Automate report generation** so data is delivered consistently. Weekly or monthly reports help stakeholders stay informed without manual effort

- ✓ **Use visualization platforms** to present trend data in a format non-technical audiences can understand easily. Business intelligence tools such as Power BI and Tableau work well for executive reporting and financial analysis. Observability-focused dashboards like Grafana are better suited for operational monitoring. The specific tool matters less than making sure the output is clear, consistent, and updated on a dependable schedule

- ✓ **Link performance metrics to financial or business impact**, highlighting how uptime, stability, and optimization support revenue, customer satisfaction, or cost savings
- ✓ **Report performance in business terms.** Instead of stating "CPU utilization exceeded 90 percent," translate it to "Capacity limits risked delays during order processing

Case Example

A CIO instituted a monthly "IT Pulse Report" that consolidated uptime metrics, cloud spending, and incident trends. Linking performance to revenue-producing systems improved executive trust and helped secure budget for infrastructure modernization.

How the report became a decision tool (what the CIO actually did)

They kept the format consistent and short: one page of executive metrics, one page of trend views, and a short appendix for technical detail. Every metric was tied to a service that leadership cared about, with plain-language impact and a clear owner.

Cloud spend was broken down by product line and environment with month-over-month deltas, and incident trends highlighted repeat drivers with the specific corrective actions underway. The report ended with a small set of decisions needed, approvals, tradeoffs, and timeline, so leadership could act in the same meeting instead of asking for follow-up decks.

Pro Tip

Beware of "Watermelon Metrics" dashboards that are green on the outside (SLA met) but red on the inside (users are unhappy). You can have 100% server uptime while a database lock prevents anyone from logging in. If your report says "All Systems Green" but the Service Desk is flooded with calls, your report is lying. Always prioritize User Experience metrics over raw infrastructure stats to keep your reporting honest.

Building a Performance Optimization Culture

Performance does not remain steady on its own. Workloads grow, applications change, and teams turn over. If optimization is treated as a project to finish rather than an ongoing part of operations, the gains from one improvement cycle are quickly eaten away by the next round of growth or accumulated technical debt. The manager's role is to build an environment where performance improvement stays visible, valued, and repeatable.

Steps to Develop a Performance Culture

- ✓ **Set Clear Standards:** Define performance baselines for applications, network components, compute platforms, storage arrays, and cloud workloads. Make sure teams understand what "good performance" means and why it matters
- ✓ **Empower Teams:** Give engineers and operators access to monitoring tools, dashboards, and automation platforms. Empower them to identify issues, act on findings, and propose improvements without waiting for escalations
- ✓ **Celebrate Improvements:** Recognize teams that deliver measurable gains in performance, scalability, or cost efficiency. Incremental improvements matter because they build over time. Specific recognition, naming the problem solved and the measurable outcome achieved, shows what the organization values and encourages others to bring similar

work forward instead of treating it as routine maintenance that goes unnoticed

- ✓ **Review Performance Regularly:** Quarterly "performance summits" allow teams to present findings, analyze long-term trends, and share improvement strategies. These sessions help build collective expertise
- ✓ **Link Metrics to Recognition:** Performance improvement becomes a cultural habit only when the organization shows that the work matters. Recognition should be specific and tied to outcomes, what improved, by how much, and why it mattered. Recognition tied to a 15% reduction in backup window time is more meaningful than a generic "great work" acknowledgment. The goal is not to gamify operations. It is to make improvement work visible so teams can learn from one another and see that the effort leads to results

Case Example

An IT operations department introduced quarterly Optimization Awards to recognize improvements that produced measurable results across the environment. Nominations had to include documented outcomes, and winners shared approaches that other teams could reuse. Over time, those steady improvements led to meaningful reductions in CPU waste, storage inefficiency, and backup window length across the compute environment.

How the program drove real behavior change (what the ops manager actually did)

They made the awards measurable and tied to outcomes, not effort. Each nomination had to include a baseline, the change implemented, before-and-after metrics, and proof the improvement held for a full month. Categories were aligned to what leadership cared about: customer experience, reliability, and cost efficiency.

To avoid "heroics", improvements had to be repeatable. Winners were required to publish a short runbook or template, so other teams could reuse the same approach. The manager also reserved time each quarter for teams to implement one small optimization from the shared backlog.

CPU waste dropped because the program pushed consistent actions into normal operations: right-sizing VMs, tightening resource limits in clusters, cleaning up idle environments, and fixing scheduling or scaling policies that kept capacity reserved but unused.

What This Means in Practice

- Monitoring is not a tool decision. It is an architecture decision. The layers covered, the signals correlated, the baselines established, and the escalation paths defined determine whether the team can see problems early or only discovers them when users call.
- KPIs and SLAs only work together if KPIs are chosen because they predict SLA outcomes, not because they are easy to measure. The most common failure is tracking infrastructure health metrics that look good while service quality quietly degrades.
- Capacity planning requires procurement lead time, not just resource headroom. The decision date for an infrastructure investment is not the day resources run out. It is months earlier, accounting for approval cycles, procurement timelines, and deployment work.
- Performance optimization produces diminishing returns without sustained discipline. The same tuning gains get eroded by the next release, workload shift, or period of deferred maintenance. Optimization has to be embedded in normal operations, not treated as a recovery project.
- AIOps and automation raise the floor for the whole team. Correlation and automated remediation work only when the underlying monitoring is accurate and the automation is bounded. Noisy monitoring plus automation produces faster failures, not faster recovery.
- Performance culture is built by making improvement visible and rewarding outcomes. Engineers optimize what gets measured and recognized. If performance work is invisible or unrewarded, it will not happen consistently regardless of what the policy says.

Figure 9.6: Summary Diagram - IT Performance Management Framework

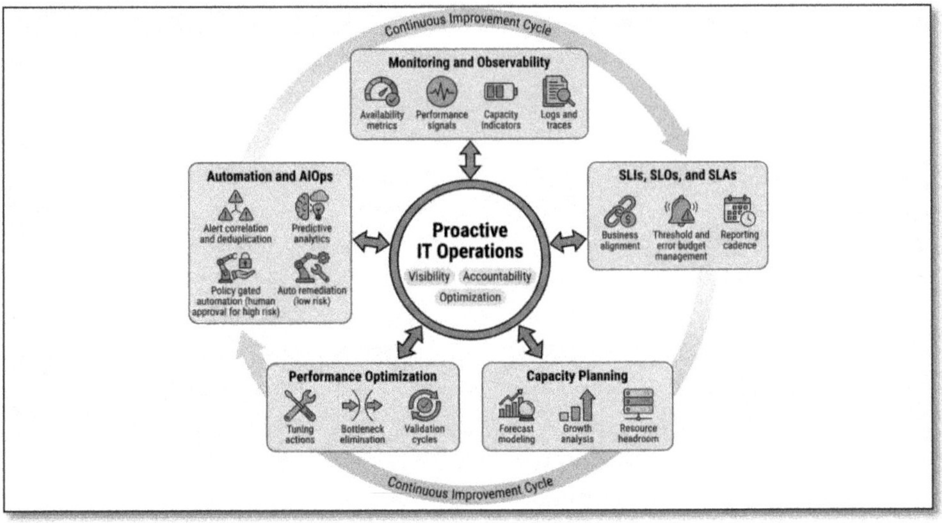

Chapter 10

SECURITY, COMPLIANCE, AND RISK MANAGEMENT IN IT OPERATIONS

Security is not a separate function bolted onto IT operations. It is a property of well-run operations. Environments with strong change control, clean documentation, current patching, defined ownership, and tested recovery plans are also environments that detect threats faster, contain breaches more effectively, and produce credible evidence for auditors without scrambling. Environments without those operational disciplines cannot be secured through tooling alone, no matter how much is spent on security products.

This integrated view of security matters because the threats IT environments face have shifted faster than most security programs have. Ransomware is now an operational disruption event, not just a security incident. Cloud and SaaS adoption has dissolved the traditional perimeter that security architectures were built around. Supply chain attacks compromise vendors who were assumed trustworthy. Regulatory expectations have grown sharper, with frameworks like GDPR, HIPAA, PCI DSS, and SOC 2 demanding continuous evidence rather than point-in-time compliance. The IT manager's role in this environment is not to run security as a parallel discipline, but to ensure that security, compliance, and risk management are built into how the operation runs every day.

This chapter examines security, compliance, and risk management as integrated operational disciplines. It covers how security responsibilities are structured across the IT organization, how identity and access management forms the foundation of modern security architecture, how vulnerability and patch management programs are designed to actually reduce risk rather than generate scan reports, how compliance frameworks intersect with operational practice, and how risk is identified, assessed, and managed across the IT environment. The goal is to give IT managers the operational vocabulary and decision frameworks needed to lead security as part of operations, not as a separate function.

Figure 10.1: Integrated Security, Compliance, and Risk Management Model - Operational Controls, Compliance Evidence, Risk Posture

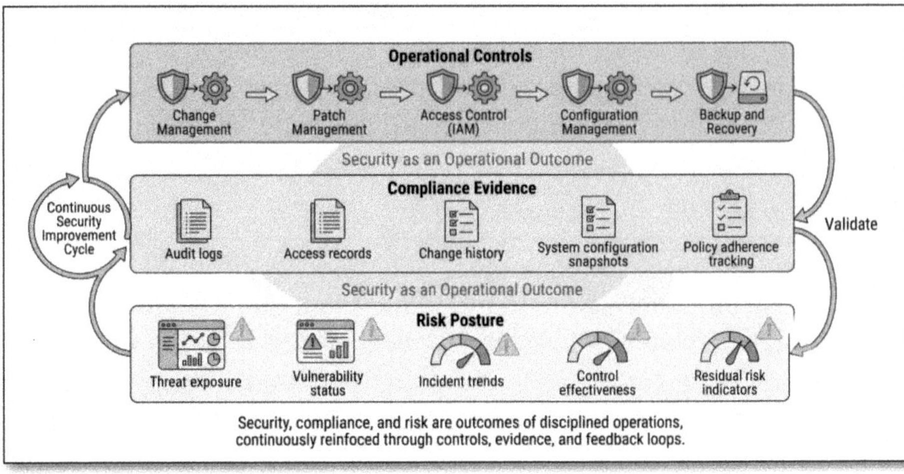

Security Frameworks and Compliance Standards

Compliance frameworks are not interchangeable. Each one was designed for a specific risk domain, data type, or regulatory context. Most organizations operate under more than one at the same time, which means the same control may need to satisfy multiple frameworks with different evidence requirements, audit cycles, and ownership expectations. Understanding what each framework requires, and where those requirements overlap, is what prevents duplicate work and last-minute audit surprises.

IT managers who understand these frameworks are better able to design controls that meet multiple requirements without duplication, maintain evidence continuously rather than rushing before audits, and communicate clearly with legal, compliance, and executive stakeholders about the organization's actual risk posture.

Common Frameworks

- **ISO/IEC 27001** provides a structure for building and maintaining an information security management system. Its main strength is flexibility. Because it uses a risk-based approach, organizations select controls based on their actual risk profile instead of applying the same controls in every case.

- **NIST SP 800-53** is one of the most detailed security control catalogs in use today. Although it was developed for federal agencies, it is also widely used in highly regulated environments because it covers a broad range of areas, including access control, system integrity, incident response, and privacy.
- **SOC 2 Type II** is especially important for service providers that handle customer data. It is not a certification. Instead, it is an attestation that evaluates whether controls were not only designed appropriately, but also operated consistently over a defined review period, often six to twelve months.
- **PCI DSS** focuses specifically on protecting payment card data. It requires organizations to implement technical and operational safeguards such as segmentation, encryption, restricted access, and continuous monitoring of cardholder environments.
- **HIPAA** governs how healthcare organizations and their business associates protect protected health information. The Security Rule focuses on safeguards for securing the data, while the Privacy Rule addresses how that data may be used and disclosed.
- **GDPR** applies to any organization that collects or processes personal data belonging to EU residents, even if the organization is located outside the EU. It gives individuals specific rights over their data and imposes clear requirements around consent, transparency, breach notification, and enforcement.

Table: Compliance Frameworks and Primary Objectives

Framework	Primary objective	Where it is most common	What it forces you to prove
ISO/IEC 27001	Build and operate an ISMS using risk-based control selection and continuous improvement	Global enterprises, vendors, multi-region orgs	Documented risk treatment, control ownership, evidence that the ISMS is maintained and improved
NIST SP 800-53	Apply a comprehensive catalog of security and privacy controls across systems and organizations	US federal, regulated, and high-assurance environments	Control implementation evidence across multiple families, tailored to risk context
SOC 2 Type II	Demonstrate that controls related to Trust Services Criteria operate effectively over a defined period	SaaS and service providers handling customer data	Operating effectiveness evidence over time, not just policy statements
PCI DSS	Protect payment card data environments with defined technical and operational requirements	Merchants, payment processors, any org storing or transmitting card data	Segmentation, encryption and monitoring controls, plus testable operational practices
HIPAA	Protect electronic protected health information with required safeguards	US healthcare and business associates	Administrative, physical, and technical safeguards plus documented procedures and auditing capability
GDPR	Govern lawful processing of personal data and enforce data subject rights	Any org processing EU personal data	Lawful basis, transparency, rights handling (including erasure), and accountable data handling practices

Pro Tip

Compliance is not the same as security. You can meet every requirement on paper and still be exposed to a real-world attack path. Use compliance frameworks to earn budget and executive attention, but rely on threat intelligence and strong architecture to protect the data in practice. Audits validate evidence; attackers look for reachable weaknesses.

Best Practices for Compliance

- ✓ Maintain a detailed compliance calendar tracking audit cycles, assessments, and renewal deadlines
- ✓ Use automated configuration and policy validation tools, such as CIS Benchmark scanners
- ✓ Centralize documentation and evidence in a secure repository to support audit readiness
- ✓ Provide annual training for staff on regulatory obligations, ensuring alignment across departments
- ✓ Map compliance requirements to technical controls to avoid duplicate effort during audits

Case Example

A financial organization automated PCI DSS verification through scripted checks. The system performed daily scans for encryption settings, exposed ports, and password compliance. This reduced manual audit preparation work by 75 percent and improved real-time oversight of cardholder data controls.

How the automation reduced audit prep (what the compliance lead actually did)

They translated PCI requirements into testable checks with clear pass or fail criteria, defined where evidence would come from, and assigned control owners.

Daily scripts validated high-impact areas auditors sample often: encryption settings, exposed ports, privileged access, and password policy compliance. Results were stored centrally with timestamps, and exceptions required an approved ticket with an expiration date.

Findings routed to system owners for remediation, and repeat failures were fixed at the source by updating templates and baselines. Audit prep dropped because evidence was collected continuously and gaps were closed throughout the year, not during the audit window.

Risk Management Framework

A structured risk management program does not remove risk. It makes risk visible, owned, and manageable before it becomes an operational or regulatory event. Its value is not in the register itself, but in the behavior it drives, surfacing exposure early, assigning accountability, and making sure the most serious risks are addressed before they turn into incidents.

Risk Management Lifecycle

1. **Identify:** Catalog threats, vulnerabilities, and asset dependencies across the environment. This includes technical assets, third-party systems, business processes, and critical data flows.

2. **Assess:** Evaluate the likelihood and business impact of the identified risks. Consider financial loss, regulatory penalties, operational disruption, and reputational damage.

3. **Prioritize:** Use a structured matrix to rank risks so that the highest-impact items receive attention first. Prioritization ensures resources are used effectively.

4. **Mitigate:** Determine and implement appropriate controls. These may include technical safeguards, process improvements, training programs, or compensating measures.

5. **Monitor:** Risk evolves as environments change. Continuous reassessment, updated scoring, and visibility into new threats keep the risk program aligned with reality.

Risk Classification Examples

- **Operational Risk.** Driven by system failure, equipment outages, human error, or unexpected power loss
- **Cybersecurity Risk.** Exposure to malware, ransomware, phishing, and active intrusion attempts
- **Compliance Risk.** The threat of regulatory fines or contractual penalties due to control violations
- **Third-Party Risk.** Vendor breaches or a partner's failure to meet established service agreements
- **Strategic Risk.** Poorly aligned IT initiatives, incorrect investments, or compounding architectural debt

Case Example

A telecommunications company identified their reliance on a single internet service provider as a top operational risk. Mitigation involved adding a second carrier, implementing automatic failover, and monitoring both circuits for performance degradation.

How the redundancy risk was mitigated (what the operations lead actually did)

They first mapped all services dependent on the single ISP and quantified the impact of failure to justify the change. A second carrier was selected based on true path diversity, ensuring it did not share upstream infrastructure or physical routes with the primary link.

Failover was implemented using BGP with defined priorities and health checks so traffic would automatically reroute when thresholds were exceeded. The team validated both automatic and manual failover through controlled testing, not just configuration.

Continuous monitoring tracked latency, packet loss, and availability on both circuits, with alerts tied to degradation, not just outages. This ensured issues were addressed early and that redundancy functioned as an operational capability, not just a design assumption.

Security Controls and Defense Layers

Security controls turn risk management decisions into operational practice. They include technical measures such as firewalls and encryption, administrative measures such as access policies and training, and physical controls such as data center access restrictions. The logic behind layering them, often described as defense in depth, is that no single control can be trusted on its own. When one layer fails, the next helps contain the impact. The goal is to make lateral movement more difficult and to limit the business impact of any single control failure.

Control Categories

1. **Preventive Controls:** Designed to stop threats before they occur. Examples include firewalls, encryption, access control lists, endpoint hardening, and multi-factor authentication.
2. **Detective Controls:** Used to discover incidents or anomalies that bypass your preventive measures. These include monitoring systems, intrusion detection tools, log analysis, and alerting mechanisms.
3. **Corrective Controls:** Triggered after an issue occurs to contain the blast radius and restore systems to normal operations. Backups, patching, configuration rollbacks, and disaster recovery processes fall into this category.

Figure 10.2: Defense-in-Depth Security Model

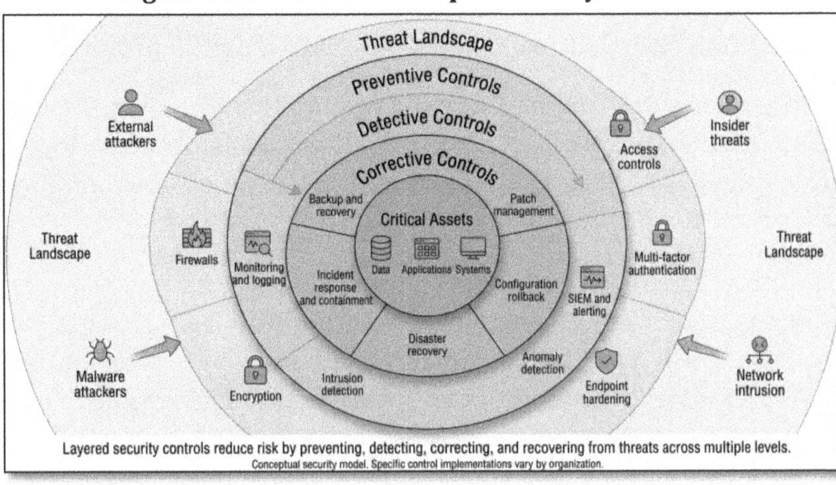

Layered security controls reduce risk by preventing, detecting, correcting, and recovering from threats across multiple levels.
Conceptual security model. Specific control implementations vary by organization.

Operational Controls

1. **Patch Management:** Regular updates for operating systems, firmware, and applications ensure known vulnerabilities are addressed before they can be exploited
2. **Identity and Access Management (IAM):** Role-based access models, multi-factor authentication, privileged access controls, and periodic access reviews help maintain precise and secure user privileges
3. **Endpoint Protection:** Antivirus, endpoint detection and response (EDR), and device posture monitoring protect laptops, servers, and IoT devices from malware and unauthorized changes
4. **Network Security:** Segmentation, VPN enforcement, intrusion prevention systems, and traffic inspection reduce attack paths and strengthen boundary protections
5. **Data Protection:** Encryption in transit and at rest, data classification, and data loss prevention tools help control and monitor the movement of sensitive information

Case Example

An energy provider implemented micro-segmentation across its operational technology network. This prevented lateral movement between industrial control systems and reduced attack surface exposure by 80 percent.

How micro-segmentation reduced the attack surface (what the security architect actually did)
They began by mapping all OT systems and communication paths to understand existing trust relationships. Systems were then grouped into functional zones, with strict rules defining which systems could communicate and how.

Segmentation was enforced using software-defined controls and host-level policies, limiting east-west traffic and removing implicit trust between systems. Only explicitly required communication was allowed, with all other traffic blocked by default.

Monitoring and logs were used to validate behavior and identify unexpected traffic, allowing continuous refinement of policies. The reduction in attack surface came from enforcing least-privilege communication and eliminating unnecessary connectivity.

Vulnerability and Patch Management

Vulnerability management is the operational discipline that keeps known exposure from turning into unmanaged risk. In complex environments with thousands of software components, cloud services, containers, and third-party dependencies, new vulnerabilities appear constantly. A defined lifecycle, from discovery through remediation and verification, helps the organization reduce exposure in a controlled way rather than letting risk build faster than it can respond.

Lifecycle Process

1. **Discovery:** Continuous scanning identifies vulnerabilities across servers, containers, applications, network devices, and cloud resources. Tools such as Qualys, Tenable, and Rapid7 help maintain an up-to-date inventory of weaknesses.

2. **Prioritization:** Vulnerabilities are rated using industry-standard scoring models such as CVSS. Teams must weigh factors like exploitability, asset importance, exposure level, and business impact.(3)

3. **Remediation:** Patching is the primary method of remediation. When patches are not immediately available or cannot be applied due to business constraints, organizations may implement compensating controls such as firewall rules, isolation, or configuration changes.

---

[3] CVSS scores referenced in the severity table below are based on the Common Vulnerability Scoring System, maintained by FIRST (Forum of Incident Response and Security Teams). Score ranges and severity labels may vary slightly between CVSS versions.

4. **Verification:** After remediation, rescans confirm that issues have been resolved and that no new gaps emerged during the process.
5. **Reporting:** Dashboards and trend reports help leadership understand patch progress, aging vulnerabilities, system health, and long-term patterns.

Table: Vulnerability Severity Rating and Response Targets

Severity	Typical CVSS Range	Response Target	Remediation Target	Minimum Compensating Controls if Patch Delayed	Escalation Trigger
Critical	9.0 to 10.0	Acknowledge within 4 hours	Patch within 72 hours	Isolate asset, restrict ingress/egress, tighten IAM, enable additional monitoring	Internet exposed, active exploit, patient or payment data scope
High	7.0 to 8.9	Acknowledge within 1 business day	Patch within 14 days	Firewall or WAF rules, segmentation, disable vulnerable service, config hardening	Repeated missed SLA, high value asset, lateral movement risk
Medium	4.0 to 6.9	Acknowledge within 3 business days	Patch within 30 to 60 days	Hardening, least privilege review, increased logging	Aging over 60 days, multiple related findings
Low	0.1 to 3.9	Acknowledge within 5 business days	Patch within 90 days or next cycle	Track for bundling, document risk acceptance if deferred	Large volume accumulating, dependency risk

Case Example

A government data center implemented automated patch compliance tracking. Dashboards showed real-time compliance by operating system and department, with weekly digests sent to service owners and automatic escalation for overdue critical items. Within a few months, patch compliance improved substantially, supported by consistent visibility, clear ownership, and time-bound exception handling.

How the compliance jump was achieved (what the security lead actually did)

They standardized patch states and ownership first: every server was mapped to a department owner, an OS family, a maintenance window, and a severity target. Compliance was calculated the same way for everyone, based on patch age against the agreed SLAs, not on self-reported status.

Dashboards were then used as an accountability tool, not just a report. Weekly digests went to service owners showing what was due, what was overdue, and what would breach next. Overdue critical and high items auto-created tickets and escalated to management when SLAs were missed.

Exceptions were controlled tightly. Systems that could not patch on time required a documented reason, a compensating control, and an expiration date. Compliance rose because the process made gaps visible immediately, assigned a real owner, and forced either remediation or time-bound risk acceptance.

Pro Tip

Stop chasing "zero vulnerabilities." At enterprise scale, the realistic goal is continuous risk reduction, not a perfect scoreboard. If you tell your team to fix everything, effort shifts to low-friction items while the high-risk, high-effort work gets deferred, the systems that are hardest to patch are often the ones that matter most. Prioritize based on *exposure*, not just the CVSS score. A medium vulnerability on a public-facing web server is an emergency; a critical vulnerability on an air-gapped lab server is a Tuesday project.

Incident Response and Business Continuity

Every IT organization will experience incidents. The question is not whether a response will be required, but how ready the team will be when it happens. Organizations with defined roles, pre-approved actions, tested runbooks, and rehearsed communication flows recover faster and with less disruption than those forced to make those decisions in the middle of an event. The plan exists to remove ambiguity when the pressure is highest.

Incident Response Stages (4)

1. **Preparation:** Define all roles, escalation procedures, communication plans, and response playbooks before the crisis hits. Preparation includes ensuring tools, logs, and contacts are ready and accessible.

2. **Detection:** Use monitoring tools, alerts, log analytics, and user reports to identify anomalies or suspicious activity quickly. Fast and accurate detection reduces time to containment.

3. **Containment:** Implement short-term isolation to prevent the threat from spreading, followed by long-term containment to ensure attackers cannot regain a foothold during cleanup.

4. **Eradication:** Eliminate the root cause by removing malware, revoking compromised access, and patching the exploited vulnerabilities.

5. **Recovery:** Restore normal operations from trusted backups, validate system integrity, and closely monitor the environment for recurring issues. Recovery timelines must align with RTO and RPO requirements.

6. **Lessons Learned:** Conduct a review to document what occurred, what controls worked well, and what improvements are needed to strengthen future responses.

---

[1] The following incident response stages are based on the lifecycle model described in NIST SP 800-61 and widely applied across industry frameworks. Organizations pursuing formal incident response program development should consult the current NIST publication directly.

Figure 10.3: Incident Response Lifecycle Diagram

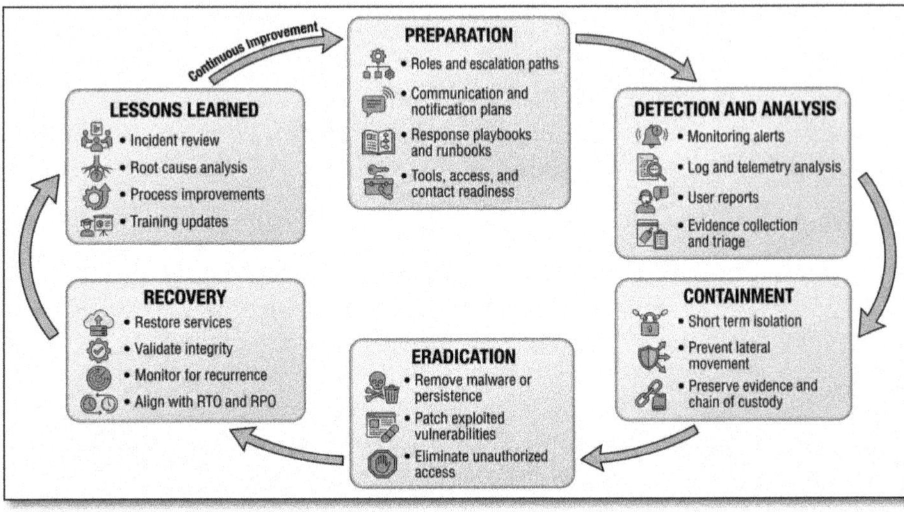

Case Example

A university experienced a large-scale DDoS attack targeting its student portal. Automated traffic redirection and cloud-based filtering were enabled through the institution's incident response plan. Service was restored within 20 minutes, compared to several hours during previous attacks when no structured plan existed.

How the 20-minute recovery happened (what the incident commander actually did)

They treated the DDoS runbook as a switch, not a discussion. As soon as thresholds were hit, the on-call declared an incident, opened the bridge, and executed the pre-approved traffic diversion to the scrubbing provider using scripted routing and DNS actions.

While traffic was being filtered, they applied short-term containment controls, rate limits, tightened WAF rules for abusive patterns, and temporarily disabled nonessential portal features that were amplifying load. Communications were handled in parallel using prepared templates to update leadership and users without slowing technical response.

After stabilization, they monitored for attack shifts and validated portal integrity and performance. The key difference from past events was that approvals, contacts, and routing changes were already preauthorized and rehearsed, so containment and recovery started immediately instead of waiting on ad hoc decisions.

Business Continuity Integration

- Maintain and regularly update the disaster recovery (DR) plan
- Schedule annual failover drills to validate readiness
- Replicate backups to multiple regions for resilience
- Define clear RTO and RPO values that reflect business expectations
- Test failback procedures as thoroughly as failover

Third-Party and Supply Chain Security

Third-party risk is operational risk, not just procurement risk. Vendors, subcontractors, and partners may have access to systems, data, and infrastructure that can be exploited as an attack path or fail in ways that disrupt your services. The same controls applied to internal operations, including access governance, change management, incident response, and compliance evidence, also need to extend to third parties through contractual requirements, periodic assessments, and active monitoring.

Third-Party Risk Management Steps

- Conduct due diligence before onboarding any vendor, including reviewing certifications, security posture, and data protection capabilities
- Require contractual clauses that mandate compliance with standards such as SOC 2 and ISO 27001
- Request regular penetration test reports, vulnerability scans, or independent assessments from vendors
- Monitor for breaches or security incidents affecting vendors and enforce notification requirements within 24 to 48 hours
- Review vendor offboarding steps, ensuring data is securely deleted and access is fully revoked

Case Example

A cloud hosting provider's subcontractor exposed a configuration file containing sensitive metadata. Because the enterprise had a strict notification SLA and continuous third-party monitoring, the issue was identified and resolved within one hour, preventing customer impact and ensuring transparency with stakeholders.

How the issue was contained quickly (what the security lead actually did)

They received the alert from the third-party monitoring feed and treated it as an incident, not a vendor ticket. The subcontractor was contacted through the pre-defined escalation path, and the notification SLA forced immediate engagement instead of "we will look tomorrow."

Containment was executed in parallel: the exposed file was removed or access-restricted, any public endpoints were locked down, and credentials or tokens referenced by the file were rotated. Logs were reviewed to confirm whether the file was accessed externally and to scope what data could have been exposed.

After containment, they documented the event for stakeholders and enforced corrective actions with the vendor, including tightening configuration controls, validating deletion, and updating the vendor's runbooks so similar exposures would trigger faster detection and the same one-hour response path.

Figure 10.4: Third-Party Risk Management Workflow

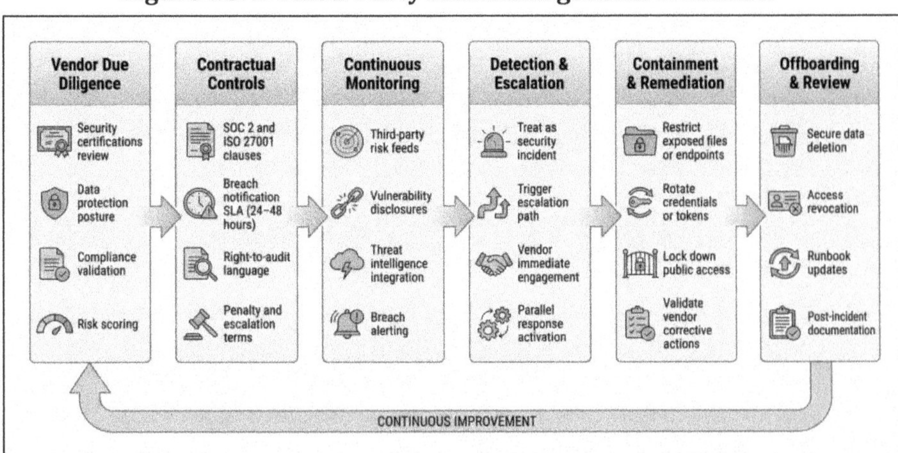

Security Awareness and Human Factors

Technical controls have limits, and human behavior often exposes them. Phishing succeeds not because firewalls fail, but because users are deceived. Credential theft often succeeds not because access controls are weak, but because someone entered credentials into the wrong page. Security awareness training exists to address the part of the attack surface that tools cannot fully control: how people behave under time pressure, when handling unfamiliar requests, or when they fail to pause and verify. When treated as an ongoing operational program rather than a once-a-year requirement, awareness training can reduce the behaviors attackers most often exploit.

Awareness Program Components

Mandatory Annual Training: Annual training sets the baseline. It should cover password hygiene, MFA expectations, email verification, data handling, and what to do when something feels off. Keep it practical and role-aware, a finance team needs different examples than a data center technician. Tie it to real workflows: approving invoices, sharing files, using admin tools, handling customer data, and working remotely.

Simulated Phishing Tests: Simulations are how you measure behavior, not just knowledge. Run them monthly or quarterly, rotate scenarios, and keep difficulty realistic. Track click rate, credential entry rate, and reporting rate. The reporting rate is the metric that tells you whether the culture is working. A good program does not just reduce clicks, it increases fast reporting.

Regular Communication and Campaigns: Short, frequent reminders work better than long memos. Use quick tips, micro videos, posters in high-traffic areas, and brief write-ups of "what happened and what to do next time" after internal incidents. Keep messages consistent: verify the sender, pause before acting, report fast, and do not self-remediate in silence.

Clear Escalation Paths: Users need one simple action that always works. A dedicated "report phishing" button, a single short email alias, or a Service Desk shortcut that routes directly to security triage. Define what happens after reporting so users trust the process: acknowledgment, quick triage, and clear next steps.

Recognition Programs: Positive reinforcement changes behavior faster than punishment. Recognize people who report fast, question unusual requests, and follow secure processes under time pressure. Keep recognition lightweight and consistent. The message should be that safe behavior is part of doing the job well.

Case Example

A logistics organization introduced monthly simulated phishing tests paired with short, targeted refresher videos tied to each simulation scenario. Over several months, click rates declined and reporting rates improved. The team viewed the increase in reporting as a stronger indicator of cultural change than click reduction alone.

How the improvement was delivered (what the security manager actually did)

They treated phishing like a measurable operational KPI. The program started with a baseline campaign to establish the current click and reporting rates. Simulations were then scheduled monthly with rotating themes that matched the company's reality, shipment exceptions, invoice changes, HR updates, and password resets.

Each simulation triggered targeted follow-up. If someone clicked, they received a short refresher video tied to the exact mistake pattern, urgency cues, spoofed domains, or attachment behavior. If someone reported the phish correctly, they received recognition and the report was used as a teaching moment for the broader group without naming individuals.

They also reduced friction in reporting. A single-click reporting button routed directly to a triage queue, and the Service Desk had a simple script for immediate containment steps if credentials were entered. Success was tracked through three metrics: fewer clicks, fewer credential submissions, and faster reporting. The big gain came from shifting behavior toward early reporting, which limits blast radius even when mistakes happen.

Pro Tip

Never weaponize your phishing simulations. If you publicly shame employees who click the fake link, or threaten their jobs, you are training them to hide their mistakes. When a user clicks a real malicious link (and they will), you want them to call the Service Desk immediately, not delete the email and pray no one noticed. Fear creates silence, and silence allows breaches to spread.

Metrics and Continuous Improvement

A security program that reports activity alone, scans run, policies updated, training completed, does not tell leadership whether risk is actually going down. Metrics move reporting from activity to outcomes: whether critical vulnerabilities are being resolved within SLA, whether detection time is improving, and whether incidents continue to trace back to the same root causes. That is what makes security reporting credible to leadership and useful for investment decisions.

Security KPIs

- Number of critical vulnerabilities unpatched
- Mean time to detect (MTTD)
- Mean time to respond (MTTR)
- Percentage of endpoints with updated antivirus or EDR
- Incident recurrence rate
- Phishing success reduction over time
- Compliance audit pass rate

Risk Management Metrics

- Residual risk level after control implementation
- Cost of mitigation compared to potential impact
- Frequency and quality of risk review updates
- Percentage of risks with defined treatment plans

Table: Sample Security and Risk KPI Dashboard

Metric Area	KPI	Definition	Target	Reporting Cadence	Primary Owner
Vulnerability	Critical vuln aging	Count of critical findings older than X days	0 over 30 days	Weekly	Vulnerability Manager
Vulnerability	Patch compliance	Percent of in-scope systems patched within SLA by severity	95 percent or higher	Weekly	Platform Owners
Detection	MTTD	Average time from event start to detection	Improve quarter over quarter	Monthly	SOC Lead
Response	MTTR	Average time from detection to containment or recovery	Improve quarter over quarter	Monthly	IR Lead
Endpoint	EDR coverage	Percent of endpoints reporting healthy EDR status	98 percent or higher	Weekly	Endpoint Lead
Identity	Privileged account hygiene	Percent of admin accounts with MFA and just-in-time access	100 percent	Monthly	IAM Lead
Incidents	Incident recurrence	Percent of incidents repeating same root cause within 90 days	Under 10 percent	Monthly	Ops, SecOps
Awareness	Phishing outcome	Click rate and reporting rate from simulations	Click down, reporting up	Monthly	Security Awareness Owner
Risk	Residual risk level	Risk rating after controls applied	Downtrend	Quarterly	Risk Owner
Risk	Treatment plan coverage	Percent of top risks with current plan and due dates	100 percent	Quarterly	Risk Committee

Case Example

A financial CIO implemented a dashboard correlating vulnerability aging, patch compliance, and incident frequency. By demonstrating that incident volume decreased as patching improved, the leadership team approved additional automation and staffing for vulnerability management. Manual patch work decreased by 40 percent as a result.

How the dashboard drove investment (what the CIO actually did)
They kept it outcome-based: what was overdue, who owned it, and where incidents tied back to unpatched weaknesses. Monthly reviews forced clear exception handling and committed dates. Once the trend held, the CIO funded patch pipelines and automated verification, which removed a large portion of manual patch coordination and follow-up.

Case Study: Integrated Risk and Compliance Framework

This case examines how a large enterprise moved from fragmented compliance execution to a unified operating model. The focus is not on tool selection, but on how governance, ownership, and continuous evidence collection were structured to reduce audit friction and improve visibility into risk.

Case Example

A multinational enterprise struggled with fragmented security tools, inconsistent audits, and unclear accountability across its regional teams.

How the Transformation Was Executed (What the Governance Lead Actually Did)
The governance lead started by defining the problem clearly. They inventoried the existing security and compliance tools across all regions and grouped the gaps into three categories: tools that duplicated the same function across teams, processes that varied from one region to another, and accountability models where no clear owner existed for a control or audit requirement.

The GRC platform was selected to consolidate audit logging, policy management, and incident tracking into one system, but the platform alone was not the transformation. The real change came from the operating model built around it. Each policy was assigned a named owner, a review cycle, and defined evidence sources. Each audit requirement was mapped to the control that satisfied it, allowing evidence to be collected continuously instead of during a pre-audit scramble. Automated monthly checks replaced the manual spot-checks that had been inconsistent across regions.

The Cybersecurity Governance Council gave the program cross-functional authority. IT, compliance, legal, and business leadership reviewed the same risk data on the same cadence, which reduced the common problem of each group working from a different view of risk.

Results became visible within the first two quarters. Duplicate audit requests declined because controls were mapped to multiple frameworks in one place. Certification renewals moved faster because evidence was already current when auditors arrived. Board-level reporting also became more credible because it came from the same operational data the team used every day, rather than from a separate summary built just for the occasion.

What This Means in Practice

- Compliance frameworks define what evidence is required. Security architecture determines how well the organization is actually protected. Both matter, and neither replaces the other. A manager who treats compliance as security is relying on a false sense of assurance

- Risk management delivers the most value before an incident occurs. A risk register that is reviewed and updated regularly helps prevent the common situation in which leadership recognizes a known risk only after it has caused a breach or outage

- Vulnerability management depends on prioritization, not just scanning coverage. High scan volume with weak prioritization pushes effort toward easier findings while leaving the highest-risk exposures unresolved. Exposure and reachability usually matter more than CVSS score alone

- Incident response is a rehearsed capability, not just a document. The difference between a 20-minute recovery and a multi-hour outage often comes down to whether the team had pre-approved decisions, tested runbooks, and practiced communication before the incident began

- Third-party risk requires active governance, not just contract language. Vendors need to be monitored, assessed, and held to notification and remediation SLAs with accountability that matches the standards applied to internal controls

- Security metrics only drive investment when they are tied to business outcomes. Patch compliance rates and MTTD improvements need to be translated into trends in incident frequency and reductions in business impact before leadership can act on them

Figure 10.4: Summary Diagram – Integrated Security and Risk Governance Framework

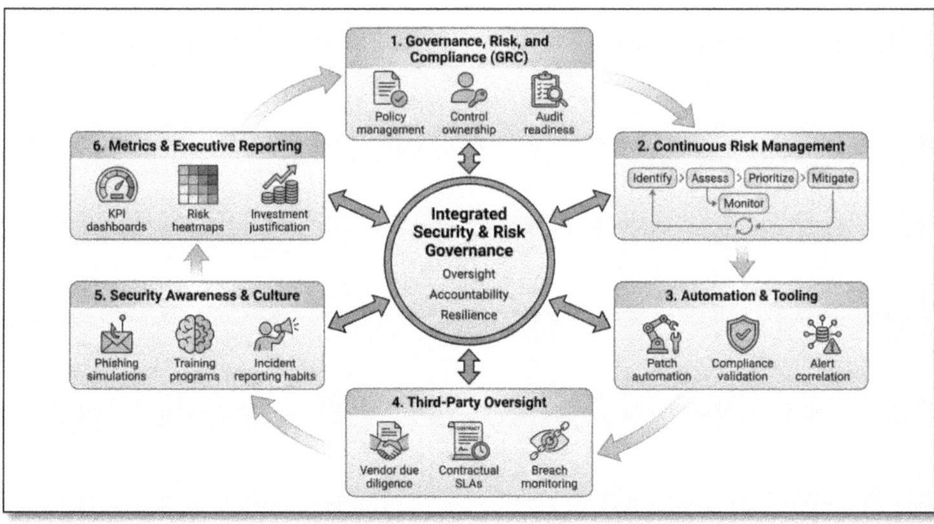

Chapter 11

IT SERVICE MANAGEMENT (ITSM): INCIDENT, PROBLEM, AND CHANGE CONTROL

IT Service Management defines how technology services are delivered, supported, and improved across their lifecycle. The key distinction is in how the work is framed. ITSM treats technology as a set of services that must deliver measurable business outcomes, rather than as isolated technical activities. That framing changes how processes are designed, how performance is measured, and how teams are held accountable for what users and business stakeholders experience.

For IT managers, ITSM turns informal, person-dependent operations into something governed, measurable, and capable of improving over time. When applied with the right level of discipline, it makes the environment more predictable, strengthens trust with business stakeholders, and shifts the team's time away from recurring firefighting and toward prevention.

This chapter introduces the core principles of IT Service Management, the ITIL lifecycle framework, and the three operational processes most responsible for day-to-day service stability: Incident Management, Problem Management, and Change Management. It also explains how those processes connect, and how automation, metrics, and role clarity turn process design into consistent operating practice.

Figure 11.1: ITSM Lifecycle - Design, Transition, Operation, Improvement

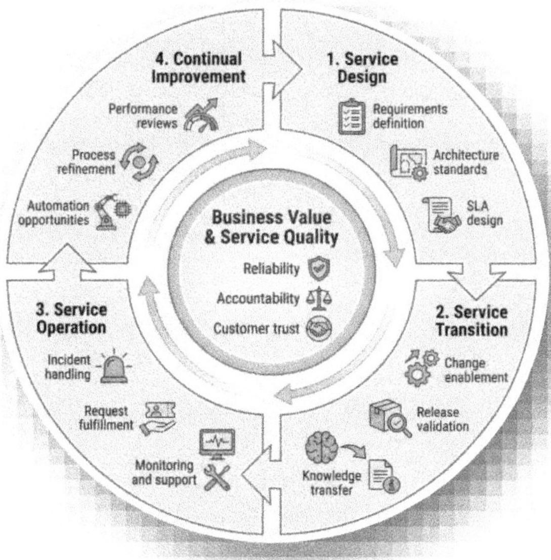

Principles of IT Service Management

ITSM is built on a foundational assumption: IT operates as a service provider to the business, not as a technical function that delivers best-effort results. That assumption requires consistent processes, documented standards, and shared definitions of what acceptable service delivery looks like. The scale changes, a ten-person IT team and a global operations center have different complexity, but the principles that make service management reliable are the same across both.

Core ITSM Principles

1. **Value Creation:** All ITSM processes must produce measurable value. That value may be uptime, faster delivery, reduced risk, improved user satisfaction, or financial savings. ITSM measures success by how effectively services contribute to organizational goals.

2. **Accountability:** Every service, process, and metric must have clearly defined owners. Accountability ensures timely decisions, consistent execution, and clear escalation paths. Without ownership, issues linger and improvements stall.

3. **Standardization:** Standardized procedures reduce risk, eliminate guesswork, and minimize the variability that leads to outages. Templates, defined workflows, and documented SOPs help ensure that repeated tasks are performed the same way every time.

4. **Continuous Improvement:** IT services evolve constantly. Post-incident reviews, KPI analysis, stakeholder feedback, and regular audits help identify weaknesses and opportunities. Continuous improvement transforms processes from static documents into living, adaptive workflows.

5. **Integration:** ITSM succeeds only when teams collaborate. Infrastructure, networking, development, cybersecurity, and support teams must work together, sharing knowledge and aligning processes to avoid silos.

Table: ITSM Principles and Corresponding Operational Benefits

ITSM Principle	What It Means in Practice	Corresponding Operational Benefits	Example Metrics to Track
Value Orientation	Prioritize work based on business impact, define service outcomes, measure results against goals	Higher service reliability, better user experience, faster delivery, clearer ROI for investments	SLA attainment, customer satisfaction (CSAT), change success rate, cost per ticket
Accountability	Assign clear service owners, define escalation paths, enforce ownership for incidents and problems	Faster escalation, fewer stalled tickets, more consistent execution, better audit readiness	Mean time to acknowledge (MTTA), backlog aging, ownership compliance rate, escalation accuracy
Standardization	Use runbooks, templates, and SOPs for repeatable work, enforce change controls and configuration baselines	Reduced human error, fewer outages from process drift, easier onboarding, predictable operations	Repeat incident rate, change failure rate, configuration compliance, first-time fix rate
Continuous Improvement	Run post-incident reviews, trend analysis, and regular service reviews, maintain a visible improvement backlog	Lower recurrence, improving stability over time, reduced MTTR, stronger operational maturity	MTTR trend, problem closure rate, recurring incident count, improvement backlog burn down
Integration	Align workflows across teams (Ops, Sec, Dev, Network), share tooling and data, coordinate releases and dependencies	Less silo-driven friction, faster troubleshooting, fewer handoff delays, improved end-to-end service quality	Handoff count per incident, cross-team resolution time, incident reopen rate, dependency-related incident rate

Example Benefits by Principle

- Value Creation → Higher ROI on IT initiatives
- Accountability → Faster resolution and clearer ownership
- Standardization → Fewer errors and predictable outcomes
- Continuous Improvement → Reduced recurrence of incidents
- Integration → Better coordination during changes and incidents

These principles set the baseline for the ITSM processes in the rest of this chapter.

ITIL Framework Overview

ITIL (Information Technology Infrastructure Library) is the most widely used framework for IT service management. It organizes service delivery practices across a lifecycle, from strategy through continuous improvement, and provides a common vocabulary, defined process roles, and structured workflows that help make IT operations more consistent and auditable. Its value is not in adopting the framework in full, but in understanding which practices address the specific gaps in how the organization delivers and manages services today.

The Five ITIL Lifecycle Stages [5]

1. **Service Strategy:** Defines the value proposition, organizational priorities, and how IT will deliver measurable outcomes. This stage ensures that services directly support business strategy.
2. **Service Design:** Focuses on architectures, service catalogs, SLAs, capacity planning, availability design, security controls, and overall service quality. Good design prevents many operational issues before they occur.
3. **Service Transition:** Handles change control, configuration management, release and deployment planning, and validation. It ensures changes are introduced smoothly and safely.
4. **Service Operation:** Covers day-to-day activities including incident handling, request fulfillment, operations monitoring, and routine maintenance. This is the frontline of ITSM.

---

[5] The following lifecycle stages are based on the ITIL v3/2011 framework published by Axelos. ITIL 4, the current version, reorganizes this model around a Service Value System and four dimensions rather than five sequential lifecycle stages. Organizations implementing ITIL should consult current Axelos documentation for the most up-to-date guidance

5. **Continual Service Improvement (CSI):** Uses metrics, audits, feedback, and post-incident reviews to improve services, reduce costs, and strengthen operational maturity.

Figure 11.2: ITIL Service Lifecycle Diagram (ITIL v3 /2011)

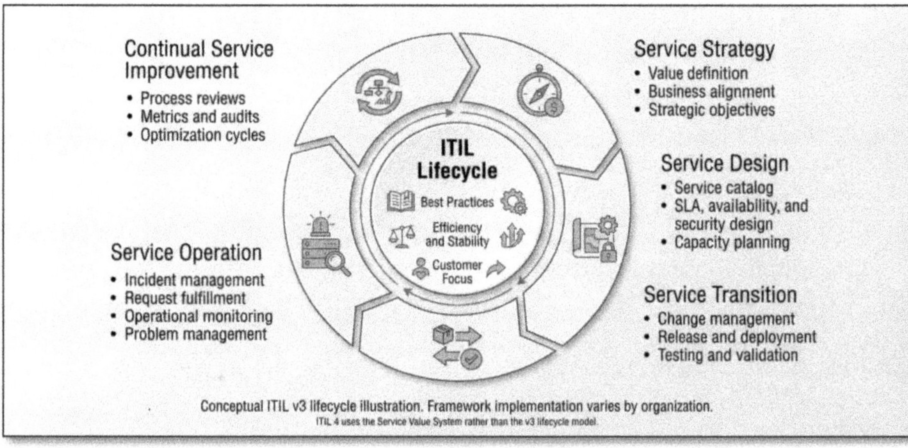

Example

A global enterprise deployed ITIL-based workflows across 14 data centers. Standardizing Incident, Problem, and Change processes improved SLA compliance across all sites and reduced the regional process inconsistencies that had been creating duplicate work and delayed escalation.

How the improvement happened (what the ITSM lead actually did)

They set one global baseline for Incident, Problem, and Change, severity definitions, required fields, ownership, and escalation timelines, then mapped each site's local process to that baseline and removed duplicate workflows.

They standardized the ITSM tooling and reporting so every site used the same forms, CAB expectations, and closure requirements, including CMDB updates tied to change completion. Performance dashboards made gaps visible by site and service, and weekly reviews during rollout corrected drift quickly. SLA improved because routing and escalation became consistent and change quality increased across all sites.

Roles and Responsibilities in ITSM

Clear roles create accountability, reduce confusion, and make multi-team coordination smoother. ITSM relies on defined responsibilities because every process interacts with others. Without role clarity, incidents escalate inefficiently, problems remain unresolved, and changes increase operational risk.

Core ITSM Roles

1. **Service Desk Analyst:** Acts as the first point of contact for incident logging, triage, and user communication. Analysts ensure accurate categorization and provide initial troubleshooting or routing.
2. **Incident Manager:** Owns high-priority incidents, coordinates resolver teams, manages communication, and oversees restoration efforts. Their goal is minimized impact and rapid recovery.
3. **Problem Manager:** Leads root cause analysis, documents findings, manages the Known Error Database (KEDB), and ensures preventive actions are implemented.
4. **Change Manager:** Oversees the change lifecycle, facilitates CAB meetings, evaluates impact and risk, and ensures proper documentation and communication.
5. **Service Owner:** Accountable for the full performance and health of a specific service. They manage SLAs, ensure improvements, and align technical decisions with business goals.
6. **ITSM Process Owner:** Defines policies, ensures process compliance, performs audits, and initiates periodic improvements across Incident, Problem, and Change processes.

Figure 11.3: ITSM Role Relationship Diagram – Process Owners and Stakeholders

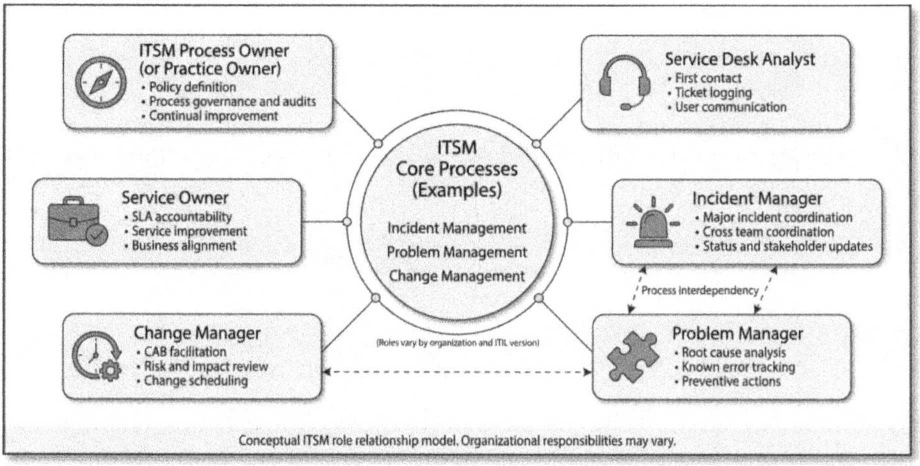

Why Roles Matter

- Clear ownership prevents delays
- Consistency improves user experience
- Escalations follow predictable paths
- Responsibility supports auditability
- Teams understand the business impact of their work

Incident Management

Incident Management is the process that defines how IT responds when services are disrupted. Its primary objective is to restore normal service as quickly as possible while minimizing business impact. It is the most visible ITSM process because users experience its performance directly, how quickly an outage is acknowledged, how clearly updates are communicated, and how fast service is restored.

Definition

An incident is any unplanned event that disrupts or degrades an IT service, such as a system outage, a performance drop, or an application error. It includes any condition that prevents users from receiving the service they depend on at the expected level.

Objectives of Incident Management

- Detect and log incidents accurately, regardless of whether they originate from automated alerts or user reports.
- Prioritize incidents based on business impact and urgency, not just technical severity.
- Restore service quickly using documented procedures or temporary workarounds.
- Maintain consistent and transparent communication with users and stakeholders.
- Capture final resolutions to support future troubleshooting and knowledge reuse.

Figure 11.4: Incident Management Workflow - Detection, Logging, Categorization, Resolution, Closure

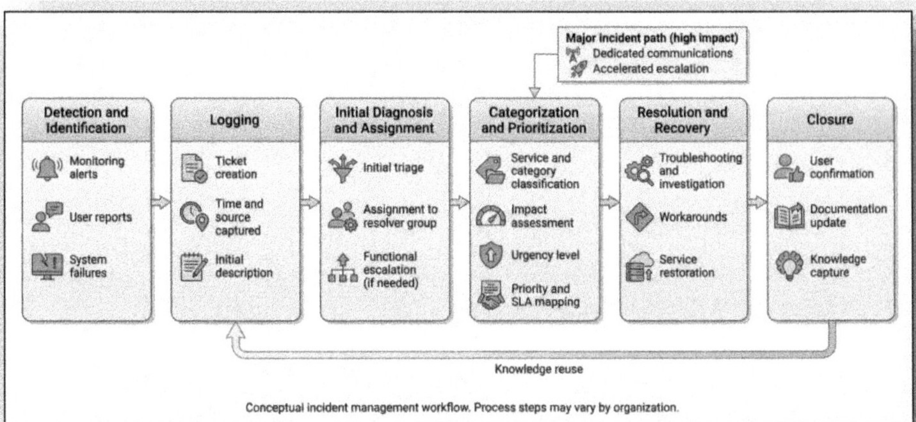

Incident Lifecycle

1. **Detection and Recording:** Incidents may originate from monitoring tools, NOC alerts, or user tickets. Tools like ServiceNow, Remedy, and Jira Service Management help ensure events are captured consistently.

2. **Categorization and Prioritization:** Incidents are categorized by service and assigned urgency based on business impact. Accurate categorization helps route incidents to the correct team.

3. **Investigation and Diagnosis:** Resolver teams diagnose issues using internal knowledge bases, logs, dashboards, or by escalating to experts.

4. **Resolution and Recovery:** Teams apply temporary or permanent fixes to restore service. Speed is crucial, but changes must remain controlled and safe.

5. **Closure:** Analysts confirm with users, document the resolution, and record any follow-up actions.

Example

A financial trading platform experienced sudden latency during market hours. Automated alerting escalated the issue immediately, and the NOC initiated triage and executed a predefined workaround. Normal service was restored within 12 minutes, avoiding SLA penalties and customer complaints.

How the 12-minute restoration happened (what the incident lead actually did)

The alert was tied to a service-level trigger (order entry latency) and auto-created a P1 with the correct resolver group already paged. The NOC lead declared the incident, opened the bridge, and used a standard triage checklist to confirm the scope, which regions, which order flows, and whether the issue was internal or upstream.

Dashboards and traces pointed to saturation on one middleware node. Instead of waiting for a full root-cause analysis, the team executed the pre-approved workaround: draining traffic from the degraded node, shifting load to healthy capacity, and applying a temporary throttling rule for the noisiest background calls. Once latency normalized, they kept the incident open long enough to validate stability and capture the key details for the follow-up review.

Best Practices

- Define SLAs with clear response and resolution targets.
- Use AIOps for alert correlation to reduce noise
- Maintain communication templates for consistent stakeholder updates
- Conduct post-incident reviews for major incidents to capture lessons learned
- Use dashboards to visualize incident volume and response performance

Table: Sample Incident Priority Matrix – Impact vs. Urgency

Impact \ Urgency	Low Urgency	Medium Urgency	High Urgency
High Impact	P2, Respond within 30 minutes, Restore within 4 hours	P1, Respond within 15 minutes, Restore within 2 hours	P1, Respond within 5 minutes, Restore within 1 hour
Medium Impact	P3, Respond within 4 hours, Restore within 2 business days	P2, Respond within 1 hour, Restore within 8 hours	P2, Respond within 30 minutes, Restore within 4 hours
Low Impact	P4, Respond within 1 business day, Restore within 5 business days	P3, Respond within 8 hours, Restore within 2 business days	P3, Respond within 4 hours, Restore within 1 business day

Problem Management

Where Incident Management measures success by how quickly service is restored, Problem Management measures success by whether the same failure happens again. The two processes operate on different timescales. Incident Management works in minutes and hours, while Problem Management works in days and weeks, tracing recurring patterns back to the underlying cause that incident response only addresses at the surface.

Definition

A problem is the root cause behind one or more incidents. Where an incident is a symptom that requires immediate response, a problem is the condition causing those symptoms to recur until it is identified and resolved.

Objectives of Problem Management

- Identify underlying causes of incidents using historical patterns or major outage analysis
- Develop permanent corrective actions that prevent recurrence
- Document known issues and workarounds in a Known Error Database (KEDB)
- Reduce long-term downtime and operational risk

Figure 11.5: Relationship Between Incident, Problem, and Change Processes

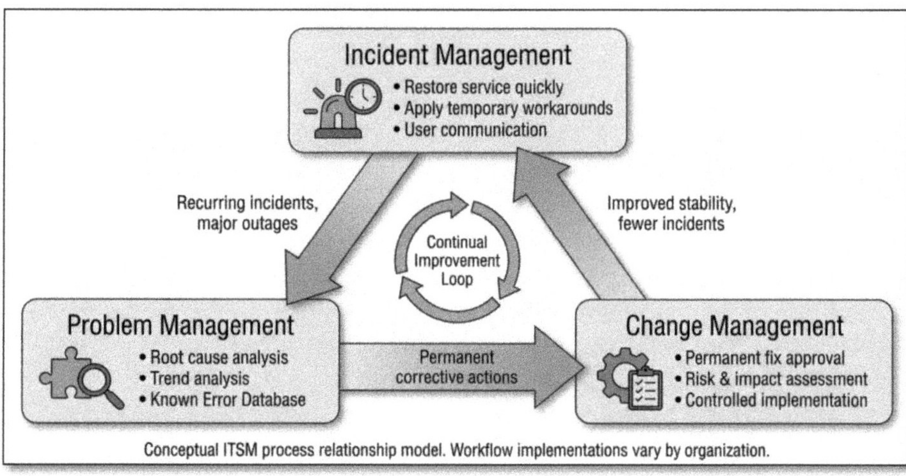

Problem Management Phases

1. **Detection:** Problems arise from recurring incidents, major outages, trend reports, capacity findings, or proactive infrastructure reviews.
2. **Logging and Categorization:** Problem tickets are created and linked to associated incidents for traceability.
3. **Root Cause Analysis (RCA):** RCA techniques include the 5 Whys (a structured questioning method developed within the Toyota Production System), Fishbone diagrams (also called Ishikawa diagrams, developed by quality management pioneer Kaoru Ishikawa), and Fault Tree Analysis. All three are widely adapted for IT incident investigation. The goal in any technique is systematic evidence-based analysis rather than pattern matching or blame assignment.". RCA aims for clarity, not blame.
4. **Resolution:** Engineers implement permanent fixes after evaluating impact, dependencies, and risks. These fixes often require changes to configuration, hardware, or processes.
5. **Closure:** After successful implementation, the issue is closed and documented in the KEDB.

Example

A virtualized server cluster suffered repeated storage disconnects. Trend analysis flagged the issue, prompting a problem investigation. RCA revealed outdated NIC drivers across multiple hosts. A coordinated firmware and driver update eliminated all related incidents.

How the root cause was confirmed and removed (what the problem manager actually did)

They pulled the last 30 days of incident data and matched it against storage path alerts and host logs to confirm a repeatable pattern, same symptom, same cluster, same peak I/O window. Affected hosts were compared against healthy hosts, and a config and driver inventory quickly showed inconsistent NIC driver versions.

To prove causality, they ran a controlled validation: moved a test workload onto an affected host, reproduced the disconnect under load, then repeated the same test after applying the updated driver bundle. Once behavior normalized, they scheduled a coordinated maintenance window to update firmware and drivers across the entire cluster with rollback steps and post-change verification.

They closed the loop by adding a driver compliance baseline, linking it to change closure criteria, and publishing a KEDB entry with symptoms, the temporary workaround, and the verification checks so the issue could be recognized immediately if it ever resurfaced.

Pro Tip

Never accept "Human Error" as a root cause. If an admin types the wrong command and crashes a server, the root cause isn't the typo; it is the system design that allowed a single typo to take down production. If you stop your analysis at "Human Error," you are just blaming a person rather than fixing the guardrails. You will eventually fire that person, hire someone else, and they will make the exact same mistake.

Proactive Problem Management

- Analyze incident trends using dashboards and analytics
- Perform recurring availability and capacity reviews
- Host quarterly RCA workshops for critical services
- Use configuration drift tools to identify hidden vulnerabilities

Deliverables

- RCA reports
- Problem records and linked incident chains
- Known Error Database entries
- Preventive maintenance plans

Table: Problem Management RCA Template - Description, Impact, Root Cause, Solution, Preventive Action

Field	What to Capture	Example Entry
Problem Description	What is happening, where, how often, and what services are affected	"Intermittent storage disconnects on Cluster A, 3 to 5 times per week"
Business Impact	User or customer impact, revenue or SLA risk, operational disruption	"VM restarts during business hours, risk to 99.9% SLA"
Incident Linkage	Related incident IDs, dates, and common patterns	"INC-1241, INC-1310, INC-1398, all during peak I/O"
Timeline	Key events from first detection to resolution	"First seen Jan 4, escalated Jan 20, fixed Jan 28"
Evidence Collected	Logs, metrics, traces, vendor findings, config diffs	"Host logs show NIC reset events, storage path flaps"
Root Cause	Specific technical cause, avoid blame language	"Outdated NIC driver causing intermittent link resets under load"
Contributing Factors	Conditions that increased likelihood or impact	"No driver compliance baseline, mixed host builds"
Workaround	Temporary mitigation used during investigation	"Pinned workloads away from affected hosts, reduced peak replication"
Permanent Fix	What was changed to remove the cause	"Standardized firmware and driver bundle across all hosts"
Validation	How you proved the fix worked	"72-hour soak test, no path flaps, metrics stable"
Preventive Action	Controls to prevent recurrence	"Driver baseline policy, monthly compliance scan, CAB check"
KEDB Entry	What was documented for future response	"Known symptoms, workaround, and verification steps"

Change Management

Change Management is the process that keeps the environment from being modified in ways that create unnecessary risk. Many enterprise outages are not caused by hardware failure or external attack. They result from change, patches applied without testing, configurations modified informally, or deployments that interact unexpectedly with other changes already in progress. A formal change process does not eliminate change. It makes sure change is planned, reviewed for risk, approved by the right people, and carried out with a tested rollback path.

Definition

A change is any action that modifies the IT environment in a way that may affect service delivery, including adding hardware, updating software, changing configurations, modifying network rules, or revising documented procedures. Even changes that appear minor can interact with other components in ways that disrupt service.

Pro Tip

Beware the "Emergency Change" loophole. Teams often label poor planning as an emergency to bypass the Change Advisory Board (CAB) and get code into production faster. Be strict: an emergency is when the business is *currently* losing money or data. If the "emergency" is just that a project manager forgot to submit a ticket on time, make them wait for the next cycle. If you don't, your emergency process will quickly become your standard process.

Core Objectives

1. Maintain a standardized process for all changes.
2. Assess risks, impacts, and dependencies prior to implementation.
3. Obtain formal approval from stakeholders or the Change Advisory Board (CAB).

4. Communicate schedules, risks, and expected downtime to all affected teams.

5. Verify success and maintain documentation for compliance and audit trails.

Change Categories

1. **Standard Change:** Pre-approved, low-risk, repeatable activities with minimal impact, such as routine patching or user provisioning.

2. **Normal Change:** Requires full assessment, documentation, testing, and CAB approval. These changes have potential risk and must be scheduled thoughtfully.

3. **Emergency Change:** Needed to resolve critical failures or prevent near-term outages. They bypass standard approval timelines but require later review to ensure proper governance.

Example

A multinational e-commerce company suffered frequent outages due to informal patching practices. After adopting Change Management with CAB oversight and implementing scheduling guidelines, unplanned downtime dropped by 80 percent within six months.

How the outage reduction was achieved (what the change manager actually did)

They stopped "silent patching" by requiring a change record for any production modification, including patches and configuration updates. A small set of standard changes was created for low-risk, repeatable work with pre-approved steps, testing, and rollback, so teams were not forced into the normal change path for routine tasks.

For higher-risk work, CAB enforced minimum entry criteria: impact assessment, evidence of testing, a timed rollback plan, and clear ownership. Conflicting changes were deconflicted through a shared calendar, and risky work was moved into controlled maintenance windows with stakeholder communications.

Post-implementation validation became mandatory. Changes were not closed until service health checks passed and key metrics stabilized. The 80 percent drop came from fewer conflicting changes, fewer untested patches, and faster rollback when something did slip through.

CAB Responsibilities

- Evaluate risk and potential business impact
- Approve or decline changes based on readiness and clarity
- Review implementation plans for completeness
- Coordinate scheduling to minimize service disruption
- Review post-implementation reports

Figure 11.6: Example CAB Review Template - Change ID, Risk Level, Decision, Next Steps

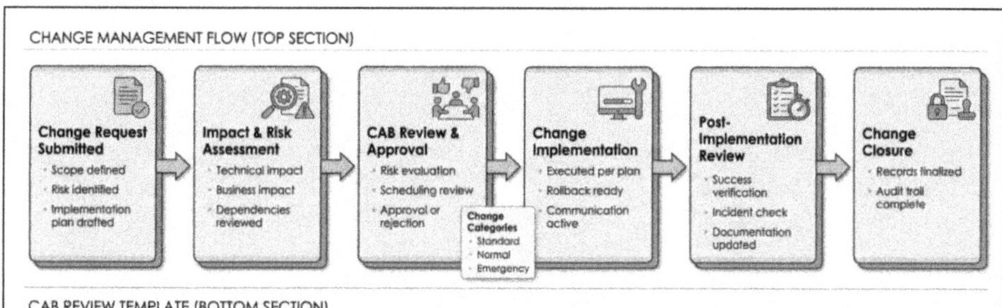

Example CAB Review Template			
Change ID	Risk Level (Low, Medium, High)	CAB Decision (Approved, Rejected, Deferred)	Next Steps
CHG-001	Medium	Approved	Schedule implementation
CHG-002	High	Deferred	Request additional risk analysis
CHG-003	Low	Approved	Proceed as planned

Conceptual Change Management and CAB workflow. Approval processes vary by organization.

Pro Tip

The most dangerous sentence in a CAB meeting is, "It's just a quick config change; nothing should go wrong." When you hear that, pause the meeting. "Should" is hope, not engineering. Ask specifically for the rollback plan. If the engineer cannot explain exactly how to undo the change in under fifteen minutes, deny the request.

Best Practices

- ✓ Enforce a strict "no ticket, no change" policy
- ✓ Maintain a forward schedule of changes (FSC) to track upcoming deployments
- ✓ Perform rollback readiness checks before every change
- ✓ Automate change notifications through ITSM tools for consistent communication

Integration Between ITSM Processes

Incident, Problem, and Change Management are not independent processes. They are meant to work together. An incident surfaces a symptom. Problem Management traces that symptom to a root cause. Change Management implements the permanent fix. When that sequence is repeated consistently and documented properly, organizations reduce both the volume and severity of incidents over time instead of continuing to manage the same failures again and again.

Integration Workflow

- Incidents reveal symptoms that may warrant deeper investigation
- Recurring or major incidents trigger formal Problem records
- Root causes identified in Problem Management lead to Changes for permanent fixes

- Successful Changes reduce future incidents and contribute to continuous improvement
- Lessons learned feed back into documentation, SOPs, and training

Figure 11.7: ITSM Process Interaction Diagram

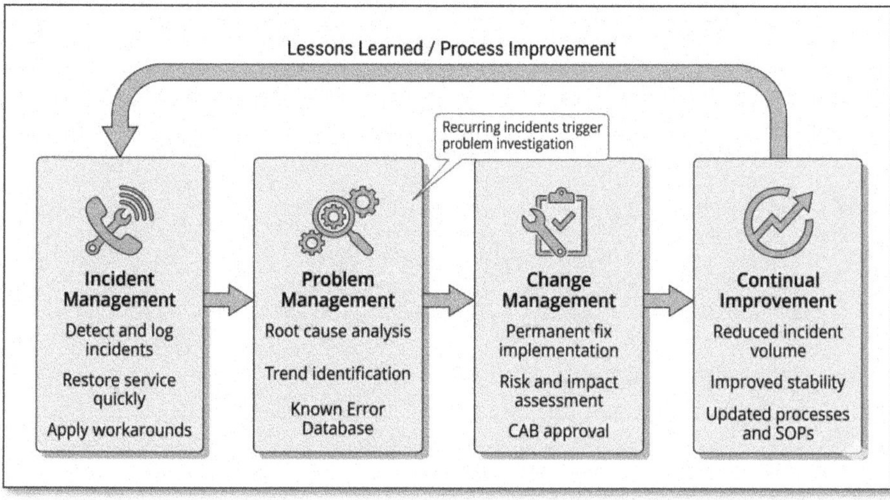

Example

In a data center, multiple high-priority network outages were traced to outdated switch firmware. Incident records led to a Problem ticket, which identified the firmware issue as the root cause. A Change request was created for standardized upgrades, reviewed by CAB, and executed during a planned maintenance window. This documented workflow became a best practice, significantly reducing future outages.

How the integration worked in practice (what the ITSM owner actually did)

They linked every outage incident to the same service and configuration item, which made the pattern obvious in reporting. Once the repeat trend hit the threshold, they opened a Problem record and pulled evidence from incident timelines, device logs, and firmware versions across affected switches.

RCA confirmed the outdated firmware as the common driver, and a normal Change was raised with a tested upgrade sequence, a rollback plan, and a staged rollout list. CAB approval focused on impact and readiness, then upgrades were executed in a controlled window with validation checks after each switch group.

After completion, they updated the KEDB entry and SOPs to include firmware compliance checks, added a recurring review for firmware drift, and tightened change closure criteria to require version verification. Future outages dropped because the root cause was removed and the control was built into normal operations.

Benefits of Integration

- Lower mean time to resolution (MTTR)
- Reduced recurrence of high-impact incidents
- Clear traceability between issues, root causes, and long-term fixes
- Improved predictability and service stability
- Better communication between operations, engineering, and management teams

Tools and Automation

Manual ITSM execution does not scale well. At smaller size, a skilled team can manage incident routing, change scheduling, and problem tracking through discipline and experience. As environments grow, the volume of events, the number of services, and the pace of change quickly exceed what teams can handle manually without creating errors, delays, or inconsistency. Automation is not about replacing judgment. It is about removing repetitive, rule-based work that consumes capacity without improving outcomes.

Common ITSM Platforms

ServiceNow: A leading enterprise platform offering incident, problem, change, request, asset, and configuration management. Highly customizable with strong automation, workflow, and integration capabilities.

Atlassian Jira Service Management: Flexible ITSM solution designed for agile environments, offering fast ticketing, lightweight change workflows, and integration with development pipelines.

BMC Helix Remedy: Long-standing ITSM suite with strong process automation, CMDB integration, and scalability for large enterprises.

Ivanti: Focuses on service desk operations, endpoint management, and process automation for mid-size and large organizations.

ManageEngine ServiceDesk Plus: Cost-effective ITSM platform with core ITIL processes and strong reporting for operational environments.

Automation Opportunities

Incident Auto-Routing and Prioritization: AI and rule-based logic can classify incidents, assign ownership, and predict severity based on historical patterns or real-time telemetry.

Change Impact Assessment: Configuration dependency mappings identify how proposed changes affect systems, applications, networks, or business services.

Automated Remediation: Scripts or runbooks handle common events such as service restarts, cache clearing, or applying predefined workarounds.

Real-Time Dashboards: Service health dashboards visualize SLA countdowns, open incidents, change schedules, and performance metrics in one view, improving transparency.

Insert Figure: Automated ITSM Workflow Example - Alert to Ticket to Resolution

Case Example

An enterprise integrated its monitoring platform with ServiceNow. Critical alerts automatically generated detailed tickets with attached diagnostic logs. Many high-volume, repeatable incidents were resolved through auto-remediation scripts before engineers had to step in, which freed the team to focus on more complex issues that required judgment rather than routine scripted handling. This reduced noise, eliminated repetitive tasks, and allowed engineers to focus on complex issues.

How the automation worked (what the service owner actually did)
They limited ticket creation to actionable alerts and required consistent fields, service, CI, severity, and a standard diagnostic bundle. Alerts automatically attached recent logs and key metric snapshots so triage started with evidence.

They then automated the highest-volume incident types using guarded runbooks: clear triggers, validation checks, stop conditions, and automatic escalation when a script did not fix the issue. Each runbook wrote structured notes back into the ticket showing what ran and what was verified. The 35 percent resolution rate came from a small set of repeatable fixes with tight controls, not broad "automate everything" efforts.

Reporting, Metrics, and Continuous Improvement

ITSM metrics serve two related purposes that are often confused. The first is operational visibility, knowing what is happening, how quickly issues are being resolved, and where breakdowns are occurring. The second is accountability, making performance visible enough that ownership is clear and improvement is expected. A program that tracks metrics but does not use them to guide decisions carries the cost of measurement without getting the value from it.

Key Metrics Across ITSM

Incident Management Metrics

- Mean Time to Resolution (MTTR)
- SLA compliance and breach distribution
- Incident recurrence rate
- Average wait time before triage
- Percentage of incidents auto-resolved

Problem Management Metrics

- Number of root causes identified
- Time to complete RCA
- Percentage of recurring incidents eliminated
- Number of Known Error Database entries created
- Preventive actions implemented per quarter

Change Management Metrics

- Change success rate
- Percentage of emergency changes
- Number of changes with failed or partial implementation
- CAB review adherence
- Number of unauthorized changes detected

Table: Example ITSM KPI Dashboard

Process Area	KPI	What It Measures	Target	Review Cadence	Typical Owner
Incident	MTTR	Time from incident start to service restore	Downtrend, by priority	Weekly	Incident Manager
Incident	SLA compliance	Percent closed within SLA, breach distribution	95%+	Weekly	Service Owner
Incident	Triage wait time	Time from ticket creation to first meaningful action	Under 15 minutes for P1/P2	Weekly	Service Desk Lead
Incident	Auto-resolve rate	Percent resolved by automation or self-heal	Uptrend	Monthly	Ops Automation Lead
Incident	Recurrence rate	Repeat incidents tied to same cause within 30 to 90 days	Under 10%	Monthly	Ops, Problem Mgr
Problem	RCA cycle time	Time to complete RCA for major issues	Under 10 business days	Monthly	Problem Manager
Problem	Root causes identified	Confirmed causes closed per period	Uptrend	Monthly	Problem Manager
Problem	Recurrence eliminated	Percent of repeat incidents removed after fix	30%+ per quarter	Quarterly	Service Owner
Problem	KEDB entries	New known errors with workaround and validation	Uptrend	Monthly	Problem Manager
Change	Change success rate	Percent implemented without rollback or incident	98%+	Weekly	Change Manager
Change	Emergency change rate	Percent of total changes marked emergency	Under 5%	Monthly	Change Manager
Change	Unauthorized changes	Detected changes without approved record	0	Weekly	CAB, Security
Change	CAB adherence	Changes reviewed per policy and closed with evidence	100%	Weekly	CAB Chair

Continuous Service Improvement (CSI)

CSI ensures that ITSM processes remain aligned with organizational needs. It identifies gaps, promotes accountability, and drives incremental improvements.

CSI Activities

- Conduct regular audits of ITSM processes and workflows
- Review stakeholder feedback to understand service perception
- Analyze trends across incidents, problems, and changes
- Implement corrective actions into design or transition processes
- Hold quarterly improvement workshops to ensure cross-team collaboration

Example

A technology company introduced quarterly CSI Workshops that brought engineers, project managers, and ITSM leaders together to review operational data rather than just move through an agenda. By focusing on recurring incident themes and change-related failures, the workshops produced targeted corrective actions that reduced incident recurrence over several quarters.

How the workshops created measurable improvement (what the CSI lead actually did)

They used a fixed agenda tied to data, not opinions: top repeat incident themes, top change-related incidents, and the longest-running backlog items. Each workshop produced a short action list with owners, due dates, and success metrics, then those actions were tracked like a project.

To reduce recurrence, they selected a small number of high-volume incident categories and required each one to leave the workshop with either a Problem record, a KEDB entry, or a planned Change. For change workflow improvement, they tightened entry criteria for high-impact changes, standardized implementation checklists, and added validation steps before closure. Results held because every quarter started by reviewing the previous quarter's actions and whether the metrics moved.

Case Study: ITSM Transformation in a Global Enterprise

Background

A multinational logistics company faced inconsistent incident handling across regions, limited visibility into global changes, and frequent outages linked to poorly executed maintenance activities.

Actions Taken

- Deployed a unified ITSM platform integrated with monitoring tools and a centralized CMDB
- Established global Incident, Problem, and Change procedures aligned with ITIL
- Trained over 600 employees on best practices and new workflows
- Introduced CAB governance and implemented KPI-driven performance reviews

Results

Priority one incident response time improved significantly after the unified workflow was established. Change-related outages dropped sharply due to stronger pre-change assessment and mandatory testing requirements. SLA compliance reached and sustained high levels across the global environment as routing and escalation became consistent across all regions. Centralized dashboards provided real-time visibility that had previously required manual aggregation across regional teams.

Figure 11.8: ITSM Maturity Model – From Reactive to Optimized

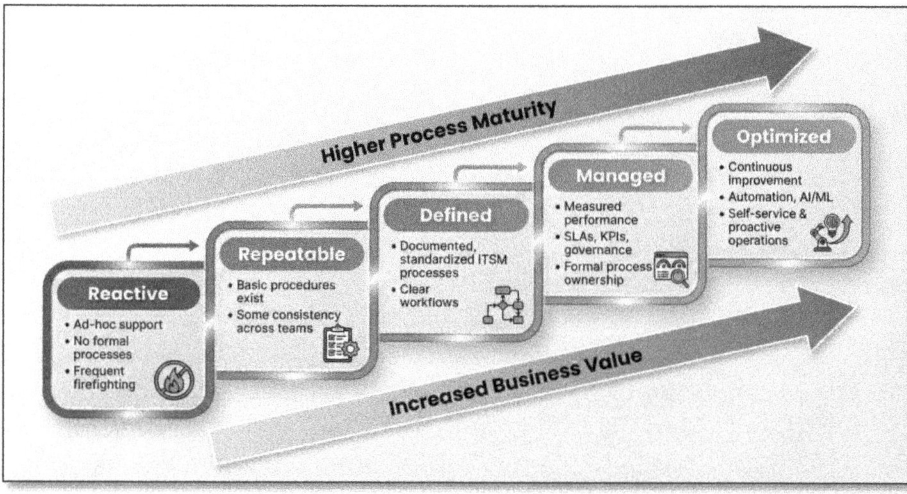

What This Means in Practice

- ITSM only creates value when it changes behavior, not just when it installs process. A well-designed incident workflow that no one follows is not effective service management. The discipline shows up in consistent execution, not in the quality of the documentation alone
- ITIL provides structure and common language, not a rigid prescription. Organizations that adopt it wholesale without adapting it to their operating reality often add process overhead without improving reliability. The goal is to use the practices that fit and make deliberate choices about the ones that do not
- Incident, Problem, and Change Management are most valuable when they work as a system. Incident Management restores service, Problem Management reduces recurrence, and Change Management lowers the chance of introducing new failures. Together, they create operations that become more stable over time
- Role clarity is what allows ITSM to function under pressure. When an incident is escalating, the team cannot stop to decide who owns the bridge, who communicates to stakeholders, or who can approve a workaround. Those decisions need to be made before the incident starts
- Automation in ITSM should be bounded and reviewable. Auto-routing and auto-remediation can reduce response time, but only when the logic is clear, guardrails are tight, and every automated action creates a record of what it did and whether it worked
- Continuous improvement only matters when the loop is closed. Workshops and retrospectives generate action items, but those actions have to be tracked, owned, and reviewed in the next cycle. Improvement that is discussed but not completed does not change the environment

Figure 11.9: Summary Diagram – ITSM Integrated Operations Framework

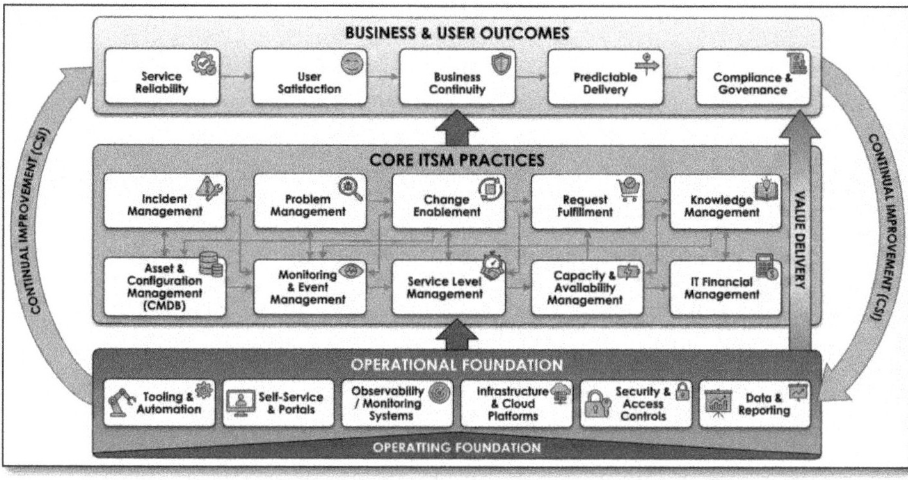

Chapter 12

BUSINESS CONTINUITY, DISASTER RECOVERY, AND RESILIENCE PLANNING

Every IT organization will eventually face a disruption it did not plan for. What varies is timing and severity. Power failures, cyberattacks, hardware failures, and natural disasters all create the same pressure: systems go down, teams mobilize, stakeholders demand answers, and recovery timelines come under scrutiny. The organizations that handle these events best are not the ones with perfect infrastructure. They are the ones that prepared before the event.

Business Continuity, Disaster Recovery, and Resilience Planning are closely connected disciplines. Business Continuity focuses on how the organization keeps functioning during a disruption. Disaster Recovery focuses on how IT systems and data are restored afterward. Resilience design focuses on building systems in ways that reduce the likelihood and severity of disruption before it happens. Each discipline supports the others, and weaknesses in any one of them tend to become visible when pressure is highest.

This chapter focuses on the disciplines that keep organizations operating during and after disruption. It explains how to assess risk and conduct a Business Impact Analysis, how to build a continuity and recovery framework, how to design for high availability and resilience, and how to test, govern, and improve plans that must work under real conditions.

Figure 12.1: Business Continuity and Disaster Recovery Integration

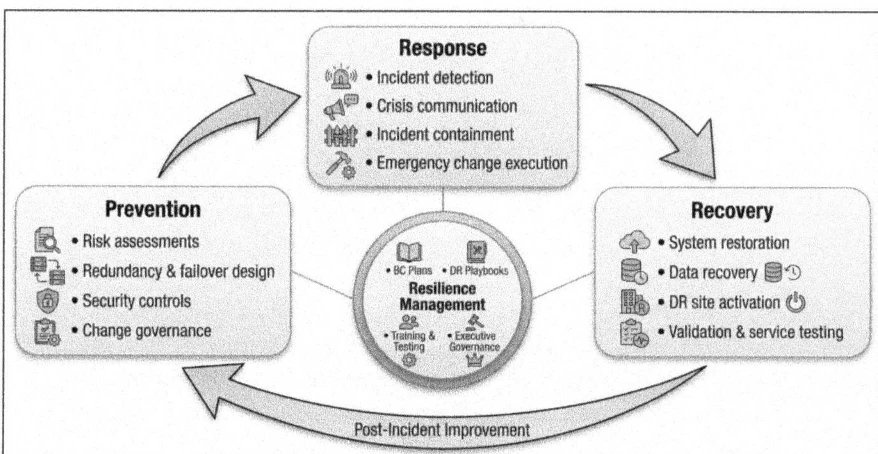

Understanding Business Continuity and Disaster Recovery

Business Continuity (BC): refers to the organization's ability to continue core functions during and after an unexpected event.

Disaster Recovery (DR): focuses specifically on restoring IT systems and data after a disruption.

Table: Key Differences and Relationship

Aspect	Business Continuity	Disaster Recovery
Scope	Organization-wide	IT systems and data
Objective	Maintain critical business operations	Restore systems and services
Timeframe	Immediate to long term	Short to medium term
Ownership	Executive and operations leadership	IT management and technical teams

Figure 12.2: Overlap of BC and DR Functions – Operational Continuity, IT Restoration, Governance

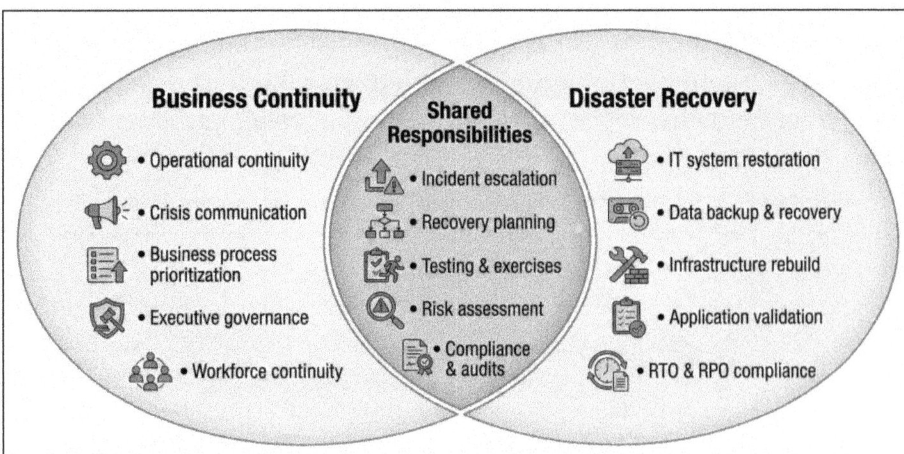

BC and DR together cover the full scope of disruption response. They help keep people working, systems available or recoverable, and organizational commitments to customers, regulators, and partners intact when conditions are under strain.

Risk Assessment and Business Impact Analysis (BIA)

Continuity planning without a clear understanding of actual risk leads to plans built around the wrong scenarios. The starting point is identifying what can realistically go wrong in the specific environment, not working from a generic threat list, and understanding which of those scenarios would seriously affect the business's ability to operate.

Risk Assessment Process

1. Identify threats (natural, technical, human, environmental)
2. Assess likelihood of occurrence
3. Evaluate potential business and financial impacts
4. Define existing controls and their effectiveness
5. Prioritize risks for mitigation and planning

Common Risks

- Power and utility failure
- Hardware or network outages
- Cyberattacks and data breaches
- Fire, flood, or natural disasters
- Supply chain disruption
- Human error or insider threat

Business Impact Analysis (BIA)

The BIA quantifies how disruptions affect business operations, defining:

- **Critical Business Functions (CBFs):** The business activities that must continue, or be restored quickly, to avoid significant operational, financial, regulatory, or reputational impact. CBFs are identified based on their direct link to revenue generation, customer commitments, legal obligations, and core service delivery. They establish prioritization, determining which systems, processes, and dependencies receive recovery focus first during a disruption

- **Maximum Tolerable Downtime (MTD):** The maximum duration a business function can be unavailable before the impact rises to an unacceptable level for the organization. MTD is a business determination, not a technical one, and it sets the upper boundary that any RTO target must stay within. An RTO set equal to or greater than MTD means the recovery plan is designed to fail its own business requirement
- **Recovery Time Objective (RTO):** The maximum duration the organization can tolerate before a disrupted service must be restored to operational status. RTO drives the technical design of recovery solutions; a one-hour RTO requires different infrastructure than a 24-hour RTO.
- **Recovery Point Objective (RPO):** The maximum age of data the organization can recover to without unacceptable business impact. An RPO of 15 minutes means the organization must be able to restore to a state no older than 15 minutes before the disruption. RPO drives replication frequency and backup cadence decisions

Table: Sample BIA Matrix – Function, MTD, RTO, RPO, Owner

Function	MTD	RTO	RPO	Owner
Email & Communication	8 hours	2 hours	15 minutes	IT Operations
ERP/Finance	24 hours	4 hours	30 minutes	Finance IT Lead
CRM	48 hours	6 hours	1 hour	Sales Director
Data Warehouse	72 hours	8 hours	4 hours	Data Team

Case Example:

A global logistics company performed a BIA and identified its shipping system as the most critical dependency. After defining a 1-hour RTO and 15-minute RPO, the company invested in high-availability replication across two regions, preventing multimillion-dollar losses during later outages.

How the BIA drove the decision (what the continuity lead actually did)
They mapped the end-to-end shipping workflow and quantified the cost of downtime in real terms: delayed orders, missed cutoffs, penalty fees, and customer churn risk. That analysis showed the shipping system created immediate business impact, so it received the tightest targets.

With the 1-hour RTO and 15-minute RPO approved, they compared recovery options and rejected backup-only designs that could not meet the window. The chosen approach paired cross-region replication with documented failover steps and routine testing. When a later outage hit one region, the team failed over quickly with minimal data loss, keeping shipments moving and avoiding large downstream costs.

Pro Tip

When interviewing business leaders, never ask, "How much downtime can you tolerate?" The answer will always be "Zero." Instead, ask, "What is the specific financial impact of being down for 4 hours versus 24 hours?" By shifting the conversation from *tolerance* (an emotion) to cost (a metric), you force them to prioritize which systems truly justify the expense of a zero-downtime architecture.

Figure 12.3: Business Impact Analysis

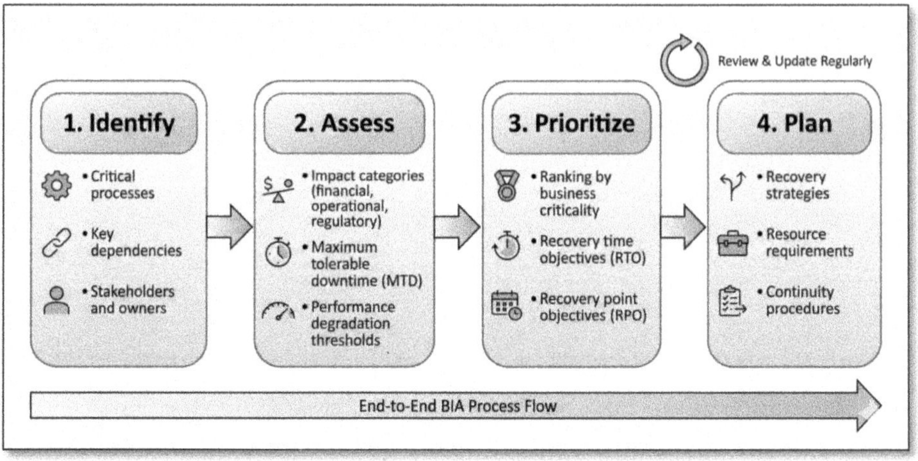

Continuity and Recovery Planning Framework

BC and DR plans must be formal, documented, and regularly maintained.

They define how the organization prepares for, responds to, and recovers from major disruptions.

Key Components of a BC/DR Framework

1. **Policy and Objectives:** Define scope, governance, and leadership commitment.
2. **Risk and Impact Analysis:** Results of assessments and BIAs.
3. **Recovery Strategies:** Technical and procedural measures.
4. **Response Procedures:** Communication, escalation, and roles.
5. **Testing and Maintenance:** Validation through exercises.

Figure 12.4: Business Continuity Management System (BCMS) Framework

Best Practice Standards[6]

- **ISO 22301:** International standard for business continuity management
- **NIST SP 800-34:** Federal guidelines for contingency planning
- **FFIEC (Financial Institutions):** Guidance for operational resilience

Case Example:

A bank aligned its BC/DR program with ISO 22301, establishing governance committees, regular tabletop exercises, and third-party audits. Within a year, audit compliance improved, supported by formalized evidence collection, standardized test documentation, and corrective action tracking that kept the program ready on an ongoing basis instead of forcing teams to scramble before each assessment.

---

[6] The following standards provide recognized frameworks for BC and DR program design. Organizations pursuing formal certification or compliance should consult the current published versions directly.

How the improvement was achieved (what the program owner actually did)

They started by formalizing governance: named executive sponsors, assigned control owners for each BC/DR domain, and set a fixed review cadence with documented decisions and action tracking. Next, they standardized evidence collection, aligning runbooks, test records, and recovery metrics to specific audit requirements so proof was consistent and easy to retrieve.

They then ran targeted tabletop exercises focused on high-risk scenarios and used the outputs to close gaps with clear due dates, owners, and follow-up validation. Finally, independent audits were used as a quality check between major regulatory exams, which kept the program in a steady "always ready" state instead of last-minute prep.

Developing a Disaster Recovery Strategy

A DR strategy is more than a backup plan. It is a documented set of decisions covering which systems are recovered, in what order, to what recovery state, within what timeframe, and by which team. Those choices have to be made before the disruption, because once pressure is high, organizations tend to fall back on whoever is present first and whatever they remember.

Steps to Develop a DR Strategy

1. **Inventory Critical Assets:** Identify applications, databases, and dependencies.
2. **Define Recovery Objectives:** Assign RTO/RPO based on business priority.
3. **Select Recovery Solutions:** Choose between active-active, active-passive, or cold standby configurations.
4. **Design Network and Data Replication:** Implement synchronous or asynchronous replication.
5. **Define Failover Procedures:** Automate where possible.

6. **Establish Communication Channels:** Ensure stakeholder awareness during activation.

Figure 12.5: Disaster Recovery Architecture - Primary Site, DR Site, Cloud Backup, Failover Paths

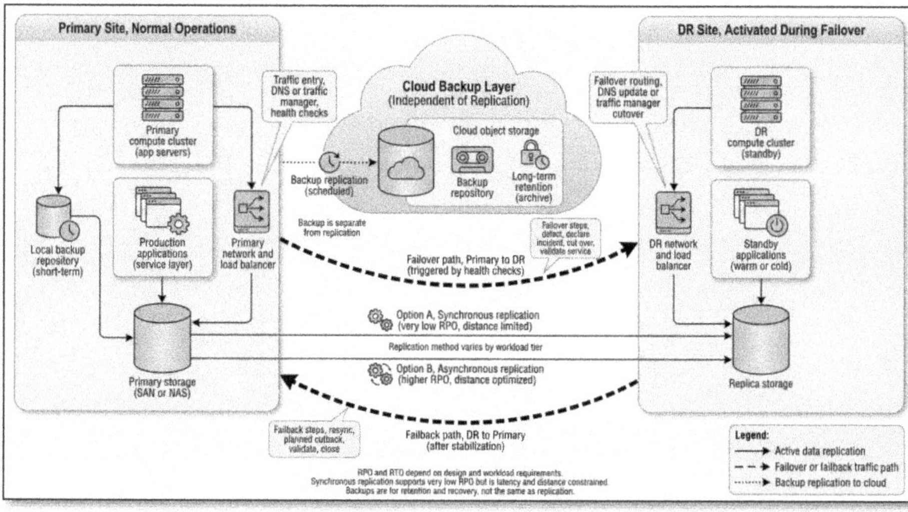

DR Infrastructure Models

- **Cold Site:** A pre-identified location with basic physical facilities but no pre-deployed IT infrastructure. Systems have to be procured, installed, and configured after a disaster is declared. Cold sites have the lowest ongoing cost, but they also have the longest recovery times, often measured in days or weeks

- **Warm Site:** A facility with some infrastructure already in place and data replication already established. Recovery still requires final configuration, validation of replication currency, and cutover of application traffic. Warm sites balance cost and recovery speed, and typically support RTOs measured in hours

- **Hot Site:** A fully operational mirror of the primary environment with live replication and failover capability. Hot sites have the highest ongoing cost, but they also support the shortest RTOs, sometimes measured in minutes

- **Cloud DR:** A recovery model that uses cloud infrastructure to replace or supplement physical DR sites. Cloud DR allows organizations to provision recovery capacity on demand instead of maintaining idle infrastructure, which can reduce cost for workloads that do not require always-on standby. The tradeoff is that recovery speed depends on provisioning time and available data transfer bandwidth

Case Example:

A healthcare organization adopted a warm-site DR model using Azure Site Recovery. The DR system replicated data every 10 minutes and enabled application recovery within 2 hours.

How the DR capability was made reliable (what the DR lead actually did)
They began with a dependency map for the clinical applications, then set RTO and RPO targets per tier so the warm site scope stayed realistic and fundable. Replication policies were tuned to the 10-minute window, and recovery plans were built in the correct sequence, database first, application tiers next, then supporting services.

They automated failover steps where possible and created a short, role-based runbook for the remaining manual actions, including validation checks and a clear decision point for cutover. DR tests were scheduled on a fixed cadence, and each test produced a gap list that fed back into configuration updates, runbook edits, and training so the 2-hour recovery target could be met consistently, not just on paper.

High Availability and Resilience Design

Resilience means building systems that can take a hit without going down. In practice, this is less about "never failing" and more about failing in a controlled way, isolating the blast radius, and recovering automatically when something breaks. High availability is the outcome. Resilience is the design discipline that makes that outcome repeatable.

A resilient design starts by treating the environment as a set of dependencies, not a set of servers. If a single DNS service, identity provider, database, or network path can interrupt transactions, that dependency must be made redundant, or the service must be designed to operate through its temporary loss. The goal is to remove single points of failure and reduce single points of management.

Key Concepts

Redundancy: Duplicate components (N+1 or 2N). Redundancy only matters if it is implemented end to end. A second server does not help if both servers rely on the same upstream power feed, the same top-of-rack switch, or the same storage controller. When assessing redundancy, evaluate compute, storage, network, power, and control plane dependencies as one chain.

Failover Clustering: Automatic rerouting to standby nodes. Clustering should include health detection, quorum behavior, and clear ownership of failover decisions. Poorly tuned failover can create "flapping," where services bounce between nodes and become less stable than a manual recovery.

Load Balancing: Distributes workload evenly for performance and fault tolerance. Load balancers are not just traffic routers, they enforce health checks, drain behavior, and routing rules that determine whether a failing node is isolated quickly or continues to take traffic while degraded.

Geo-Redundancy: Multiple sites in different regions. Geographic separation reduces correlated risk, power events, fiber cuts, and regional cloud service issues. Geo-redundancy requires data replication choices that match RPO goals and application behavior, especially for stateful services.

Distributed Architecture: Decouples components for isolation and scalability. Decoupling reduces blast radius. If one component fails, the rest of the service should degrade gracefully rather than collapse. This often means asynchronous patterns, queues, circuit breakers, and retry logic that is designed, rate-limited, and observable.

What "Resilient" Looks Like in Operations

A resilient design is measurable. You should be able to answer, with evidence:

- What happens if a node fails, a zone fails, or a region fails?
- How quickly does traffic shift, and who gets paged?
- What is the expected customer impact during failover, if any?
- How often is failover tested, and what was the last test outcome?
- What is the actual RTO and RPO achieved during drills, not the target on paper?

Resilience also requires operational controls: change discipline, configuration consistency, and monitoring that can distinguish between partial degradation and full outage. Without these, the design may be theoretically redundant but practically fragile.

Figure 12.6: High Availability and Resilience Architecture Model

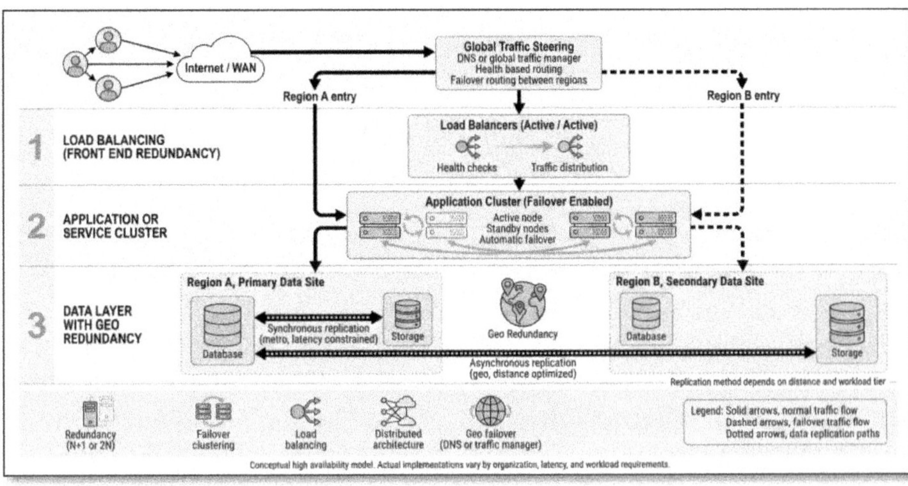

Case Example

A global e-commerce company deployed geo-redundant load balancing across two continents. A regional outage triggered automatic traffic redirection, keeping customer transactions active with no downtime.

How the design prevented downtime (what the engineering lead actually did)
They fronted the service with a global traffic manager using health-based routing, with strict, application-level checks (not just "port open"). Sessions were designed to survive failover, either stateless at the edge or backed by replicated state stores, so shifting traffic did not break checkouts mid-transaction.

They separated dependencies by region, independent ingress, independent identity endpoints, independent database replicas, and independent operational tooling, so a regional control-plane issue did not block recovery. Failover thresholds were tuned to avoid flapping, and traffic draining was validated under load.

Finally, they ran controlled regional failover tests on a schedule and treated failed tests as defects. That testing discipline ensured the automatic redirection worked during a real outage because it had already been proven in production conditions.

Communication and Crisis Management

During a major disruption, communication is as important operationally as recovery. Stakeholders need accurate updates on a consistent cadence. Leadership needs enough control over messaging to avoid reacting to speculation or conflicting information. That is why a pre-designed communication plan matters, pre-approved messages, defined roles, clear escalation paths, and channels that still work when primary systems are Impaired.

Communication Plan Components

- **Crisis Response Team (CRT):** Cross-functional leadership group (IT, HR, Facilities, PR)

- **Contact Directories:** Up-to-date phone numbers, emails, and escalation levels
- **Communication Channels:** Phone, SMS, Teams, internal emergency site
- **Templates:** Pre-approved statements for internal and external stakeholders
- **Public Relations Protocols:** Coordinate media response to protect reputation

Table: Example Escalation Matrix – Severity Level, Response Time, Notified Roles

Severity Level	Typical Trigger	Initial Response Time Target	Update Cadence	Notified Roles
Sev 1, Critical	Service down, safety risk, major customer impact, regulatory exposure	5 to 10 minutes	Every 15 to 30 minutes	Incident Commander, IT Ops Lead, Facilities, Security, Comms or PR, Executive On-Call
Sev 2, High	Partial outage, major degradation, multiple sites affected	15 minutes	Every 30 to 60 minutes	IT Ops Lead, Service Owner, Facilities as needed, Comms lead for internal updates
Sev 3, Medium	Limited user impact, workaround available	30 to 60 minutes	Every 2 to 4 hours	Service Owner, Service Desk Lead, Relevant engineering teams
Sev 4, Low	Minor issue, no material business impact	1 business day	Daily, as needed	Service Desk, owning team

Case Example:

During a regional data center outage, a university's crisis team used pre-scripted communications through its notification system. Stakeholders received status updates every 30 minutes until restoration, maintaining transparency and confidence.

How the communication stayed controlled (what the crisis lead actually did)
They activated the crisis response team, assigned a single spokesperson, and locked updates to one source of truth, the incident timeline and current status. Pre-approved templates were used for each audience, executives, staff, students, and external partners, so messages stayed consistent and did not speculate on root cause. Every 30 minutes, the team sent a short update with what is impacted, what is working, what changed since last update, and the next checkpoint time.

Pro Tip

Your primary communication tool will likely fail during a major crisis. If your Identity Provider (like Azure AD or Okta) goes down, you lose access to Email, Teams, and Slack all at once. Always establish an "out-of-band" emergency channel, such as a dedicated WhatsApp group or an external mass-texting service that is completely totally decoupled from your corporate infrastructure.

Testing, Training, and Exercising the Plan

A BC/DR plan that has never been tested is still an assumption, not a proven capability. Testing is what turns documented procedures into practiced execution. It exposes gaps in runbooks, reveals single points of failure in the recovery process itself, and confirms that the people responsible can perform their roles under conditions close to a real event.

Types of Tests

1. **Tabletop Exercises:** Discussion-based simulations in which the recovery team walks through a hypothetical scenario, makes decisions, and identifies gaps without touching production systems. Tabletop exercises are low-cost and repeatable, which makes them useful for new plans, new team members, and scenario variations. Their limitation is that they test decision-making and familiarity with the plan, not technical execution.

2. **Functional Tests:** Targeted validations of specific recovery components, such as failing over a single application, restoring a database from backup, or testing DNS cutover. Functional tests require more effort than tabletops, but they provide direct evidence that specific recovery steps work. They are especially useful for addressing gaps identified in tabletop exercises or correcting findings from earlier full-scale tests.

3. **Full-Scale Tests:** End-to-end simulations of a full recovery scenario, often involving production-like traffic, full team activation, and validation against all recovery objectives. Full-scale tests provide the highest level of realism, but they also carry the greatest cost and operational risk. They should be performed at least annually and after major environmental changes.

4. **Unannounced Tests:** Recovery exercises conducted without advance notice in order to assess actual readiness rather than rehearsed performance. These tests reveal whether the plan depends too heavily on specific individuals, whether documentation can be accessed without preparation, and whether the team can respond under real uncertainty. They should be used selectively and with appropriate organizational safeguards to avoid introducing unnecessary risk.

Figure 12.7: BC/DR Testing Maturity Levels – Basic to Advanced

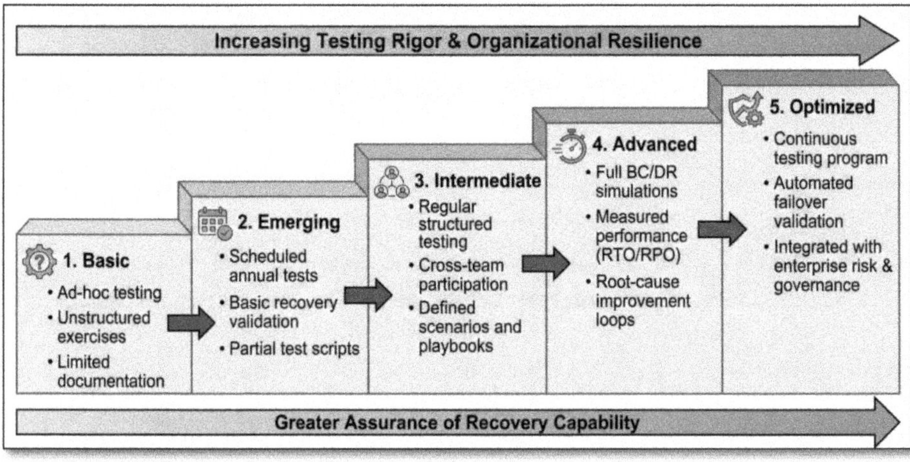

Best Practices

- ✓ Test at least annually or after major changes
- ✓ Document results and corrective actions
- ✓ Review lessons learned and update procedures
- ✓ Train new employees on BC/DR roles during onboarding

Case Example:

A manufacturing company's annual failover test revealed that critical DNS updates were missing from its DR scripts. The team corrected the gaps by pre-staging DNS records, automating cutover steps, and adding validation checks to confirm name resolution before system bring-up continued. Those changes reduced recovery time in the next test cycle.

How the recovery time dropped (what the DR lead actually did)
During the test, they captured exact timestamps for each recovery step and found the longest delay came from manual DNS fixes and propagation waits. The team updated the DR runbook to include pre-staged DNS records, automated cutover steps, and validation checks that confirmed name resolution before application bring-up continued.

They then reran a focused functional test on DNS and application dependencies, tuned the script order, and added a final checklist item that blocked "service restored" until DNS health checks passed. In the next annual cycle, the failover sequence ran without the DNS bottleneck, cutting total recovery time by about 40%.

Pro Tip

Run your next disaster recovery drill with a "Bus Factor" constraint: assume your Lead Architect and IT Director are stuck on a flight and cannot be contacted. If the junior staff cannot execute the failover using only the documentation, your plan failed. A recovery strategy that relies on a specific person's memory is not a strategy; it is a single point of failure.

Third-Party and Supply Chain Resilience

Many recovery plans treat vendor dependencies as a secondary concern. In practice, a vendor failure can trigger a disruption that internal redundancy alone cannot prevent. If a critical supplier's backup process is untested, its notification SLA is undefined, or no alternate path exists, the organization's recovery target becomes only as realistic as the vendor's weakest point. Third-party resilience planning has to be an explicit part of the BC/DR program, not something left to assumption.

Best Practices

- Require suppliers to maintain documented BC/DR plans
- Include BC/DR clauses and RTO/RPO requirements in contracts
- Review supplier test results and certifications annually
- Maintain alternate vendors for critical components

Case Example:

A logistics firm suffered downtime due to a vendor's untested backup process. The company added BC/DR verification to all supplier audits, ensuring redundancy across logistics and cloud providers.

How the resilience gap was closed (what the continuity lead actually did)

They treated the vendor as a dependency with measurable targets, then required evidence, not promises. The supplier audit checklist was updated to include last test date, test scope, achieved RTO and RPO, and proof of restore or failover results. Contracts were revised to add notification timelines, minimum test frequency, and a right-to-audit clause tied to service criticality.

For the most critical services, they implemented a secondary path, either an alternate provider or a validated workaround that could keep operations moving during vendor failure. Each year, supplier reviews included a tabletop exercise that walked through escalation and failover steps so handoffs were clear before the next outage.

Figure 12.8: Vendor Continuity Assurance Framework

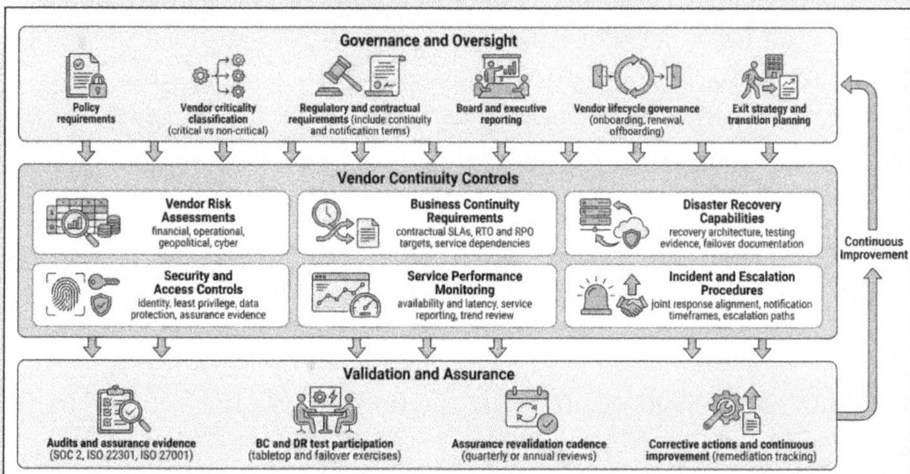

Documentation and Version Control

Every BC/DR program relies on comprehensive, accurate, and accessible documentation. When a disruption happens, you do not have time to debate which runbook is current, who owns a system, or where the last test results live. Documentation is the control plane of continuity, it turns recovery from tribal knowledge into repeatable execution.

BC and DR documentation should be treated as production artifacts. It needs defined ownership, a review cadence, and change control. A plan that is "mostly correct" is unreliable, because the gaps only show up under stress. Teams should be able to open a single location and answer three questions fast: what is impacted, who is responsible, and what steps restore service.

Core Documents

1. **BC and DR policies and procedures:** Scope, activation criteria, roles, decision authority, and minimum testing expectations.
2. **Risk assessment and BIA reports:** Current threats, assumptions, critical business functions, RTO and RPO targets, and priority tiers.
3. **Recovery site configurations:** Network diagrams, identity and access dependencies, replication settings, DNS and routing cutover details, and capacity baselines.
4. **Contact lists and escalation trees:** Named owners, alternates, after-hours escalation paths, vendor contacts, and executive communication routes.
5. **Test reports and audit logs:** What was tested, what failed, what changed, evidence of results, and signed closure of corrective actions.

Documentation Standards

- **Store in both on-prem and cloud repositories:** Continuity documentation should not disappear when a single platform fails. Use a primary repository with a defined secondary mirror, and make the mirror part of the test scope

- **Version-controlled with update timestamps:** Track changes the same way you track production configuration. Every document should show owner, last review date, version, and an audit trail of edits
- **Accessible even during network outages (print or offline copies):** Maintain offline access for the minimum set of documents required to activate and run recovery, including contact trees and the first-hour runbook. Offline access must be validated, not assumed

Case Example

An oil company maintained a mirrored documentation server accessible via satellite in emergencies, ensuring operational continuity during regional disasters.

How access was ensured (what the continuity lead actually did)
They identified the "minimum viable docs" needed to run the first 24 hours of response, activation criteria, contact trees, recovery runbooks, network and dependency maps, and stored that set in a hardened mirror. The mirror synchronized on a schedule, kept prior versions, and exposed a read-only interface so critical procedures could not be edited during a crisis. Satellite connectivity and credentials were tested during exercises, and the team kept an offline bundle as a final fallback in case both primary networks were unavailable.

Continuous Improvement and Governance

BC and DR programs do not stay current on their own. Every major change to the business, a new application, a cloud migration, a vendor change, or a staffing shift, changes the organization's real recovery posture. If the plan is not updated to reflect those changes, it quickly stops matching the environment it is supposed to protect. Governance prevents that decay by making review, testing, and plan updates part of normal operations rather than a once-a-year exercise. New applications, cloud migrations, vendor shifts, staffing changes, and evolving threats all change your real recovery posture. Without governance, BC and DR becomes outdated quietly, then fails loudly when it is needed most.

Continuous improvement means the program has defined ownership, a decision forum, measurable targets, and a closed-loop process for fixing gaps. Testing is not the finish line, it is an input. Each exercise, incident, and audit should produce corrective actions that are tracked to completion and verified through a follow-up test or validation step.

Governance also protects BC and DR from becoming purely technical. Recovery targets are business decisions. They affect cost, acceptable downtime, and customer impact. Executive oversight is what keeps those tradeoffs explicit and funded.

Governance Practices

- **Establish a Business Continuity Steering Committee** Include IT, security, facilities, HR, legal, and key business owners. Define decision authority, quorum, and escalation paths for urgent exceptions
- **Conduct quarterly risk and readiness reviews** Review changes in the environment, new dependencies, last quarter's incidents, test results, and open corrective actions. If a critical control owner changes roles, ownership and backups must be updated immediately
- **Align BC and DR metrics with corporate KPIs** Tie readiness to outcomes leadership already tracks, revenue continuity, customer experience, safety, regulatory exposure, and operational throughput. This prevents BC and DR from being viewed as "IT paperwork."
- **Audit annually against ISO 22301 or internal standards** Use audits to validate evidence quality, test realism, and control effectiveness. Treat findings as program work, not as a compliance exercise

- **Report BC and DR maturity levels to the executive board:** Use a simple maturity model that leaders can understand, current state, target state, gaps, and funding needs. The point is decision support, not scorekeeping

Metrics and Key Performance Indicators

BC and DR metrics answer the question documentation alone cannot: does the plan actually work? Coverage metrics show scope. Test outcome metrics show how well the organization executes. KPI trends over time show whether the program is improving or drifting. Without those measures, leadership is left assessing BC and DR readiness through confidence and assumption, neither of which holds up in a real event. KPIs give leadership a way to see coverage, test quality, and whether recovery targets are achievable in real conditions. They also expose the gap between "plan exists" and "plan works."

Good BC and DR metrics have three traits. First, they are tied to business-critical services, not generic infrastructure counts. Second, they reflect execution evidence, test outcomes, real incident performance, and validated runbooks, not self-reported confidence. Third, they drive action by making ownership and aging visible.

Example BC/DR KPIs

- **Average RTO and RPO compliance rate:** Percent of tests and real events where achieved RTO and RPO met the approved targets, tracked by tier and service owner
- **Percentage of systems covered by a DR plan:** Coverage should be measured against the service catalog or CMDB, with clear exclusions and documented risk acceptance for anything out of scope
- **Frequency of successful test completions:** Not just "tests scheduled," but tests executed and passed with evidence and corrective actions closed

- **Time between incident detection and recovery start:** Measures activation discipline, decision speed, and readiness of communications and access. Many programs fail here even when technical recovery is strong
- **Vendor compliance rate for BC/DR documentation:** Percent of critical suppliers providing current plans, test evidence, and notification commitments, aligned to contract requirements

Table: BC/DR KPI Dashboard Example

KPI	Definition	Target	Measurement Frequency	Data Source	Owner	Action Trigger
RTO Compliance Rate	Percent of recoveries meeting RTO in tests and real events	95%+ for Tier 1	Quarterly	DR test reports, incident timeline	DR Program Owner	Below target for 2 cycles triggers remediation plan
RPO Compliance Rate	Percent of recoveries meeting RPO, measured by data loss window	95%+ for Tier 1	Quarterly	Replication logs, recovery validation	Platform Owners	Any Tier 1 miss triggers RCA and retest
DR Coverage	Percent of in-scope services with approved DR plan and runbook	98%+	Monthly	CMDB, service catalog	Service Owners	Coverage gap older than 30 days escalates
Test Execution Pass Rate	Percent of planned tests executed and passed with evidence	90%+	Quarterly	Test calendar, test results	BC Coordinator	Missed test requires reschedule within 30 days
Activation Lead Time	Time from detection to DR activation decision and start	Under 15 minutes for Tier 1	Per event, quarterly rollup	Incident records, comms logs	Incident Commander	Over target triggers tabletop and comms review
Vendor BC/DR Compliance	Percent of critical vendors providing current BC/DR plan and test evidence	100% critical vendors	Semiannual	Vendor management records	Vendor Manager	Missing evidence triggers contract escalation
Corrective Action Aging	Percent of open BC and DR corrective actions older than threshold	Under 10% older than 60 days	Monthly	Action tracker	Program Owner	Any Tier 1 corrective action older than 60 days escalates

Case Study:
Business Continuity Transformation in a Financial Enterprise

This case examines how a financial institution strengthened its resilience by aligning business continuity planning with measurable recovery objectives and validated execution. The focus is on how structured analysis, tested failover capabilities, and controlled documentation improved both recovery performance and audit readiness.

Background:

A global financial firm experienced multiple outages where recovery efforts were delayed by incomplete and inconsistent documentation. System dependencies were not clearly mapped, failover procedures varied across teams, and key recovery steps relied on tribal knowledge rather than validated runbooks. During incidents, teams spent critical time identifying system owners, confirming recovery order, and validating data integrity, which extended downtime and increased operational risk.

Actions Taken:

How the transformation was executed (what the resilience lead actually did)

They started with an enterprise-wide BIA to reclassify system criticality based on actual business impact, not legacy assumptions. Critical business functions were mapped to supporting systems, and RTO and RPO targets were redefined to reflect operational and regulatory expectations.

Dual-region replication was implemented for Tier-1 systems, with automated failover configured and tested against defined thresholds. Failover was treated as a controlled process, with validation steps ensuring data integrity and application readiness before full cutover.

Documentation was centralized into a controlled repository with version tracking and ownership assigned to each recovery plan. This ensured that runbooks, dependencies, and escalation paths remained current and audit-ready.

Semiannual disaster recovery tests and executive crisis drills were scheduled to validate both technical recovery and decision-making under pressure. Test results were documented, gaps were tracked, and corrective actions were enforced before the next cycle.

Results

- ✓ Tier-1 system availability aligned with 99.99 percent uptime targets, with recovery performance validated through recurring DR tests
- ✓ RTO for critical systems was reduced from several hours to under one hour, with key systems achieving recovery in under 45 minutes
- ✓ Audit compliance was achieved under ISO 22301 and SOC 2, supported by consistent evidence collection and tested recovery procedures

Figure 12.9: Business Continuity Maturity Model – Initial to Optimized

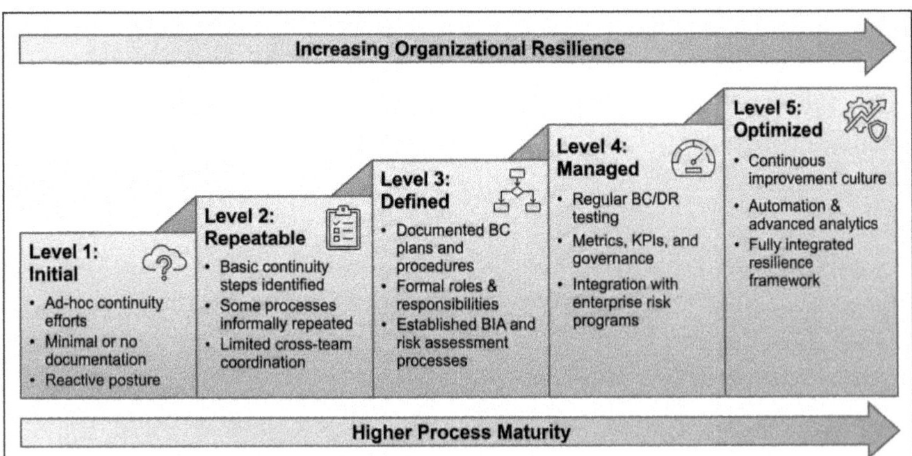

What This Means in Practice

- BC and DR programs only work when they are built around what the business actually depends on. Generic recovery plans protect generic services. The BIA is what turns a generic plan into one that is specific, prioritized, and supportable.
- Recovery targets are business decisions, not just IT decisions. RTO and RPO values carry real cost implications. Without input from business owners and approval from leadership, IT can end up setting recovery targets the organization has not actually agreed to fund or operate.
- Resilience is a design discipline, not a feature. Redundancy that has not been tested end to end remains theoretical. High availability that still depends on a manual recovery step is fragile. The design is only as strong as the operational controls and testing cadence used to validate it.
- Testing is not an annual compliance exercise. It is how the organization finds out what the plan gets wrong before a real event does. Untested plans contain unknown gaps. Tested plans produce documented gaps with owners and timelines for correction.
- Third-party continuity is part of the program. Vendor SLAs, notification requirements, and alternate-path planning need to be written into contracts and validated through supplier reviews, not assumed to exist.
- Governance is what keeps BC and DR from becoming outdated. The program needs clear ownership, a steering structure, metrics that matter to leadership, and a closed-loop process that takes test findings through to verified corrective action.

Figure 12.10: Business Continuity and Resilience Lifecycle Summary Diagram

Resilience maintained through continuous assessment, testing, and improvement.

Chapter 13

FUNDAMENTALS OF IT PROJECT MANAGEMENT

Every technology initiative" is a broad AI opener. The three-item example list is an AI-standard qualifier. The second sentence uses the AI four-item failure list.

Suggested rewrite: "Technology initiatives fail in predictable ways. Scope expands without a formal decision. Communication breaks down between technical teams and business stakeholders. Risks that were visible in planning are never formally owned or mitigated. A structured project management process is not bureaucratic overhead; it is the mechanism that keeps those predictable failure modes from materializing.

IT project management is what gives technology work enough structure to be reliable while still leaving room to respond when conditions change. What makes IT projects different from general business initiatives is their specific complexity: technical dependencies that only become visible during change, security requirements that evolve mid-project, integration points that require coordination across teams that rarely work together, and cutover windows where late-discovered issues leave almost no room for error.

This chapter focuses on the fundamentals of IT project management: how projects are initiated and structured, the lifecycle stages that guide delivery from planning through closure, the roles that carry accountability, and the practices around risk, communication, documentation, and quality that influence whether a project succeeds in operation as well as in design.

Figure 13.1: Relationship Between IT Operations, Governance, and Project Management

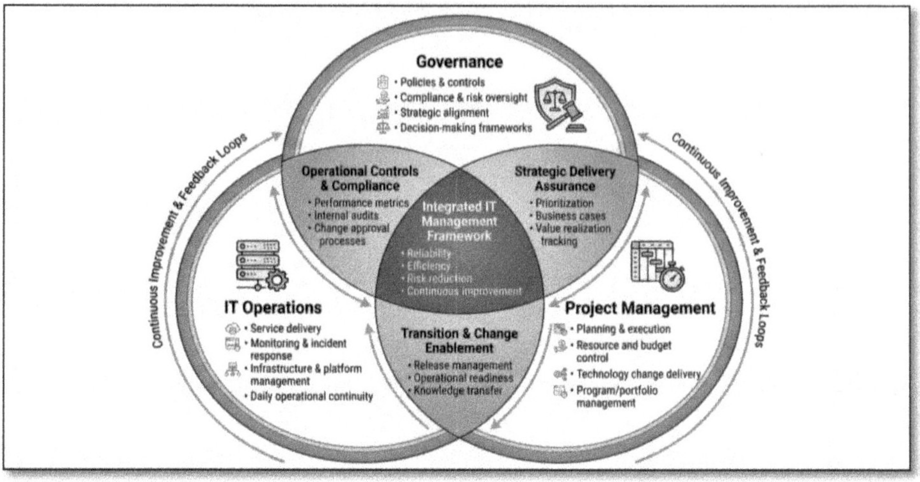

The Nature of IT Projects

An IT project is a defined effort to deliver a specific technology outcome, such as a new system, a platform migration, an infrastructure upgrade, a security deployment, or an application rollout. Unlike ongoing operational work, projects have a clear start, a clear finish, and acceptance criteria that determine when delivery is complete. What makes IT projects distinct is the environment in which they are executed: layered technical dependencies, security constraints, regulatory obligations, and coordination across teams that do not usually operate in the same delivery chain.

IT projects are often more technically and operationally complex than general business initiatives because they involve the integration of hardware, software, networks, cloud services, vendors, and security controls. Rapid technological change also means that requirements evolve quickly, making planning and stakeholder communication even more critical.

Common IT Project Types

1. **Infrastructure Projects:** Data center upgrades, cabling redesigns, hardware refreshes, power and cooling modernization.
2. **Software Projects:** Application development, ERP implementation, CRM customization, API integrations.
3. **Network Projects:** WAN redesigns, SD-WAN rollouts, VLAN restructuring, wireless overhauls.
4. **Security Projects:** Identity management deployments, SIEM implementations, vulnerability management automation.
5. **Cloud Projects:** Migration to public, private, or hybrid cloud platforms, modernization, and re-architecture.

Table: Examples of IT Project Categories and Deliverables

Project Category	Typical Deliverables	Example Duration
Infrastructure	Server rack reconfiguration, new UPS deployment	3 to 6 months
Software	CRM development, API integration	6 to 12 months
Network	SD-WAN rollout, QoS optimization	4 to 8 months
Security	IAM or MFA deployment	2 to 6 months
Cloud	Application migration or refactoring	6 to 18 months

Why IT Projects Differ

1. **Technical Complexity:** Systems are coupled through identity, DNS, routing, shared storage, certificates, APIs, and monitoring. A change in one layer can surface as a failure somewhere else. Dependency mapping is not optional.

2. **Frequent Change:** Priorities shift, vendors deprecate features, security findings force redesign, and capacity needs change. Strong projects plan for controlled change rather than pretending it will not happen.

3. **Higher Risk Profile:** The blast radius includes uptime, data integrity, privacy, and compliance. Many IT failures are not build failures, they are cutover failures, misconfigurations, or missing rollback paths.

4. **Cross-Functional Teams:** Delivery requires coordination between engineering, operations, security, service desk, facilities, vendors, and business owners. Without clear ownership, issues stall in handoffs.

5. **Operational Constraints:** Maintenance windows, freeze periods, and on-call coverage shape the schedule. Plans that ignore operational realities usually slip or create unacceptable risk.

6. **Verification Burden:** Success requires evidence, testing results, monitoring baselines, and acceptance criteria. "It seems fine" is not a closure condition in a mature IT environment.

IT project success depends on managing these variables with discipline and transparency. Strong managers treat delivery as both a technical build and an operational transition, with explicit decisions, controlled change, and validated outcomes.

The Project Management Lifecycle

The project management lifecycle is not administrative structure for its own sake. It provides a consistent set of decision points and delivery stages that reduce variation between projects, make handoffs explicit, and ensure work is properly planned before execution and validated before closure.

The Five PMI Process Groups [7]

The Project Management Institute (PMI) defines five core process groups used globally across industries[8]:

1. **Initiation** Define the project's purpose, value, scope, constraints, and feasibility. This is where the business case and high-level goals are established.

2. **Planning** Develop the detailed roadmap for delivery. This includes scope breakdown, task sequencing, risk planning, budgeting, timeline development, resourcing, and communication strategy.

3. **Execution** Carry out project tasks according to the plan. This involves coordinating teams, resolving issues, managing vendors, executing builds, and maintaining communication with stakeholders.

4. **Monitoring and Controlling** Track project progress against the plan. Adjust timelines, reallocate resources, manage change requests, and monitor risks as the project evolves.

5. **Closure** Complete all deliverables, obtain formal acceptance, release project resources, finalize documentation, and perform lessons-learned reviews to support continuous improvement.

---

[7] The following descriptions are adapted for IT operational context. Organizations pursuing PMP certification or formal PMBOK implementation should consult the current PMBOK Guide edition published by PMI directly.

[8] The following five process groups are defined by PMI in the PMBOK Guide and adapted here for IT operational context.

Figure 13.2: IT Project Management Lifecycle Diagram

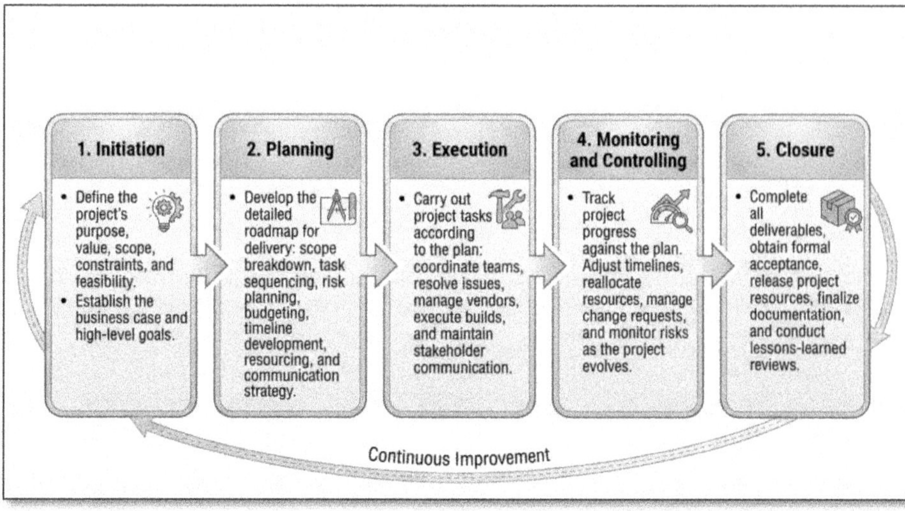

Example

A multinational organization initiated a large-scale mailbox migration to the cloud. The project team created a structured plan with weekly progress reviews, risk dashboards, and pre-defined communication checkpoints. The migration completed within the planned timeline and close to its original budget, outcomes that the PM attributed directly to the risk monitoring and communication cadence built into the plan from the start.

How the migration was executed (what the program manager actually did)

The project team began by segmenting the migration into phased waves based on business unit, mailbox size, application dependencies, and operational risk. Pilot migrations were completed first to validate tooling, bandwidth utilization, authentication behavior, and rollback procedures before broader deployment started.

Weekly governance reviews tracked migration progress, open risks, issue trends, and upcoming cutover activities. Risk dashboards highlighted items such as synchronization failures, legacy application dependencies, licensing gaps, and user readiness concerns so they could be addressed before affecting larger migration waves.

Communication was treated as a formal workstream. End users received scheduled notifications before and after migration events, while technical teams followed predefined escalation and support procedures during cutovers. Executive stakeholders received recurring status updates tied to timeline, budget, adoption progress, and operational impact.

The team also maintained rollback procedures and post-migration validation checks for each wave. Mail flow, calendar functionality, permissions, mobile access, and application integrations were verified immediately after migration to reduce user disruption and support volume

The Project Triangle – Time, Cost, and Scope

Every project operates within three constraints that influence planning and delivery decisions: time, cost, and scope. The relationship between them is not linear. Compressing the schedule usually requires either more budget or less scope. Expanding scope requires more time, more money, or both. This tradeoff is often described as the project management triangle, and in IT projects, the consequences of ignoring it show up quickly and in measurable ways.

Understanding the Three Constraints

1. **Time:** Represents the project schedule, milestones, and delivery dates. Accelerating timelines usually requires additional resources or a reduction in scope.

2. **Cost:** Includes labor, software licensing, hardware purchases, consulting, training, and operational expenses. Cost constraints may lengthen timelines or force prioritization of features.

3. **Scope:** Defines project deliverables, requirements, technical features, and acceptance criteria. Expanding scope increases both time and cost unless trade-offs are carefully negotiated.

Figure 13.3: Project Management Triangle - Balance Between Time, Cost, and Scope

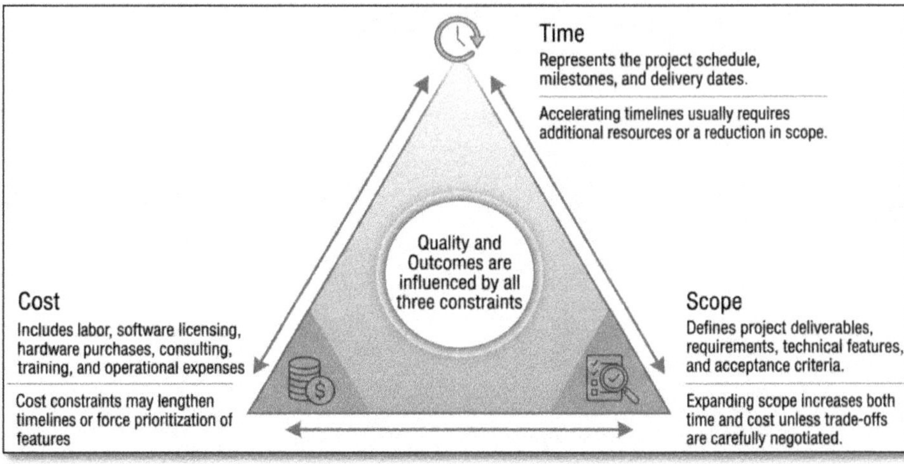

Quality sits at the center of the triangle. A well-managed project maintains equilibrium across all three constraints to protect the integrity of the final product.

Example:

A network modernization project expanded its scope to include redundant carrier links after initial planning. Without adjustment, the new scope would have jeopardized timelines and stability. The project manager worked with executives to extend the schedule and approve additional funding, preserving quality and preventing rushed implementation.

How the triangle tradeoff was managed (what the project manager actually did)

They documented the scope change as a formal decision point, then presented three options to leadership: keep the date and drop lower-priority work, keep scope and extend the schedule, or keep scope and date by adding budget for parallel vendor work and implementation support. They quantified the tradeoffs using outage risk, cutover complexity, and lead times for circuit provisioning. Leadership approved a revised timeline and incremental funding, and the team rebaselined the plan with new milestones for carrier delivery, testing, and cutover, avoiding a rushed change in production.

Roles and Responsibilities in IT Projects

Role clarity in IT projects is an operational control, not just a formality. When an incident occurs during a cutover and no one knows who can approve a rollback, or when a vendor needs a decision and the escalation path is unclear, the delay can cost more than the time saved by skipping proper planning. Defining who owns what, who makes which decisions, and who must be consulted versus informed is the difference between a project that runs on accountability and one that defaults to whoever speaks up first.

Primary Roles in IT Projects

1. **Project Sponsor:** An executive accountable for business justification, funding approval, and organizational alignment. Sponsors remove roadblocks and ensure the project remains a strategic priority.

Pro Tip

Don't treat your Executive Sponsor like a distant ATM. Their job isn't just funding; it is political air cover. When a department head refuses to release staff for testing or a vendor stalls on delivery, do not try to fight that battle alone. Escalate to the Sponsor with a specific "ask." They have the organizational weight to clear roadblocks that would stop a Project Manager cold.

2. **Project Manager (PM):** Responsible for planning, scheduling, communication, risk management, and overall progress. The PM coordinates work across departments, manages vendors, and ensures deliverables align with objectives.

3. **Technical Lead or Architect:** Designs and validates the technical approach. Serves as the primary technical decision-maker and ensures the architecture meets performance, security, and compatibility requirements.

4. **Project Team Members:** Engineers, developers, analysts, and specialists who complete the required technical work. Their output forms the core of project delivery.

5. **Stakeholders:** Individuals or departments affected by project outcomes. They may provide requirements, approve deliverables, or assist with testing and integration.

6. **Change Control Board (CCB):** A formal group responsible for reviewing and approving significant scope, timeline, or resource changes. The CCB ensures changes align with governance standards and do not jeopardize delivery.

Figure 13.4: IT Project Organizational Structure

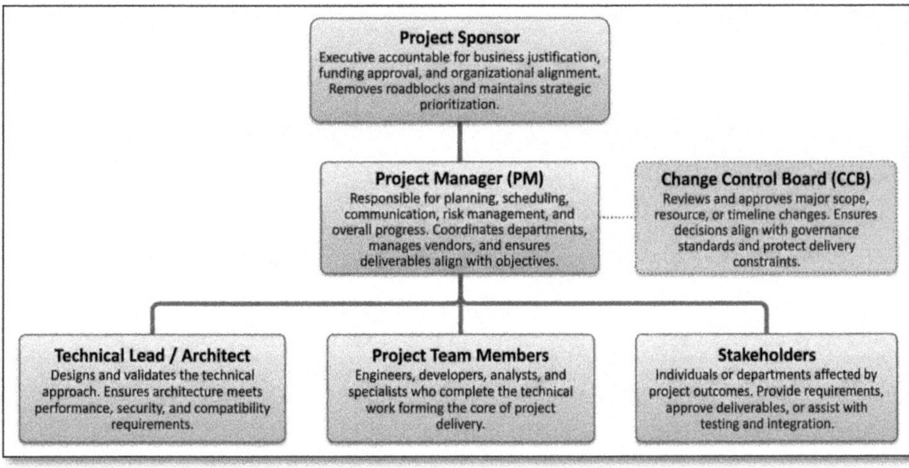

Case Example

During a data center consolidation project, the PM coordinated between facilities engineering, compute administrators, network architects, security analysts, and application owners. Clear sequencing and dependencies were communicated before each migration window, reducing the risk of configuration conflicts or downtime.

How the Consolidation Was Coordinated (What the Project Manager Actually Did)

They started by building a dependency map before scheduling the first migration window. Every application in scope was mapped to its compute, storage, network, identity, and monitoring dependencies, then grouped into migration waves based on shared dependencies and acceptable outage windows.

For each wave, they held a pre-migration checklist review with facilities, compute, network, security, and the application owner in the room. The checklist confirmed connectivity readiness, verified rollback steps, checked monitoring coverage in the target location, and identified any open change conflicts in the shared maintenance calendar.

Communication was handled the same way for every wave. A short pre-migration notice went out three days in advance with scope, expected impact, and the on-call escalation path. After each migration, a confirmation note was sent within an hour, whether the wave completed successfully or had to be rolled back. Configuration conflicts were tracked in a shared issue log and reviewed at the start of each wave so the team was not discovering them in the middle of execution.

This approach reduced configuration conflicts because dependencies were identified before each window instead of during it. It also reduced coordination risk because every affected team was working from the same information.

Core Knowledge Areas in IT Project Management

All ten knowledge areas apply to IT project management, but some carry more weight in complex technical environments where dependencies are layered, teams work across functions, and the operational consequences of errors are immediate.

1. **Scope Management** Defines deliverables, boundaries, and acceptance criteria. Scope management prevents confusion over

what is included in the project and ensures stakeholders have aligned expectations.

2. **Schedule Management** Builds realistic timelines using precedence, dependencies, milestones, and critical path analysis. IT projects often depend on external factors such as vendor deliveries or maintenance windows.

3. **Cost Management** Focuses on estimating, budgeting, and controlling costs. Includes forecasting, variance analysis, and cost baselining to avoid overruns.

4. **Quality Management** Ensures outputs meet performance, reliability, and business requirements. IT quality management often involves code reviews, architecture validation, testing, and configuration audits.

5. **Resource Management** Assigns roles and responsibilities based on skill, availability, and team capacity. This includes managing external vendors or contractors.

6. **Risk Management** Identifies threats, evaluates likelihood and impact, and defines mitigation strategies. Risk management is essential in environments with rapid change, multi-vendor stacks, and complex integrations.

7. **Communication Management** Maintains clarity through structured updates, dashboards, documentation, and stakeholder engagement. Communication failures create project delays even when technical work is on track.

8. **Procurement Management** Handles third-party contracts, software licensing, hardware acquisition, and vendor negotiations. IT procurement timelines often affect overall project schedules.

9. **Stakeholder Management** Manages expectations, gathers requirements, resolves concerns, and ensures alignment across diverse groups.

10. **Integration Management** Creates cohesion among all project processes. This area ensures that goals, changes, and deliverables remain synchronized across teams and lifecycle stages.

Table: Project Management Knowledge Areas and IT Applications

Knowledge Area	IT-Specific Application	Common Tools
Scope Management	Defining technical deliverables and acceptance criteria per system	Project Charter, WBS, Change Log
Schedule Management	Sequencing around maintenance windows, vendor lead times, and freeze periods	Gantt chart, critical path analysis
Cost Management	Tracking hardware, licensing, consulting, and labor against baseline	Budget tracker, variance reports
Quality Management	Configuration validation, testing against acceptance criteria, pilot deployments	Test plans, architecture review checklists
Risk Management	Dependency risk, cutover failure modes, vendor delays, security findings	Risk register, risk matrix
Communication Management	Tailored updates for engineering, security, operations, and executive stakeholders	RACI, communication plan, status reports
Stakeholder Management	Managing expectations across IT, business, compliance, and vendor teams	Stakeholder register, escalation matrix
Resource Management	Allocating engineers across delivery waves and operational constraints	Resource plan, skills inventory
Procurement Management	Hardware acquisition, vendor contracts, software licensing timelines	Procurement tracker, contract log
Integration Management	Coordinating dependencies across systems, teams, and project phases	Integration map, decision log

Case Example

A cloud migration project involving multiple workload types and regulatory constraints required tight coordination across engineering, security, operations, and executive stakeholders. The project manager built risk management and communication cadence into the operating model from the outset, which kept the effort on track through three major scope clarifications and two vendor delays without extending the timeline.

How risk and communication kept the migration on track (what the PM actually did)
They built a risk register tied to each migration wave, with clear owners, triggers, and mitigation steps, not generic "cloud risk" statements. High-impact items were reviewed weekly with security, networking, app owners, and operations, and anything unresolved was escalated early while options still existed.

In parallel, they ran a simple cadence: one weekly cross-functional review for engineering blockers and one short executive update focused on business impact, readiness, and decisions needed. A single decision log captured approvals on scope, data handling, and go-live criteria. By the time each cutover window arrived, security controls, governance requirements, and rollback steps were already agreed and documented, so execution stayed predictable.

Documentation and Governance

Documentation in IT projects is not just a bureaucratic requirement. It is what makes scope decisions traceable, risks clearly owned, and changes auditable. Without it, the project runs on memory and assumption, which may seem workable until the lead engineer takes a two-week vacation or the audit team asks for evidence of a decision made three months earlier. Governance adds the oversight needed to ensure documentation stays current, decisions go through the right approval paths, and the project remains aligned with organizational priorities as conditions change.

Essential Project Documents

1. **Project Charter** Defines the project's purpose, scope, goals, justification, and authority to proceed. It serves as the foundational agreement between business and IT leadership.

Pro Tip

The Project Charter is your primary defense against "scope creep" six months from now. When a stakeholder asks for "just one small feature" later, you don't have to be the bad guy and say "no." You pull up the Charter and say, "That is outside the boundaries we agreed to. We can add it, but it will trigger a change request and delay the launch." The Charter turns a subjective argument into an objective business decision.

2. **Project Plan** A detailed breakdown of tasks, timelines, dependencies, and resource assignments. The project plan guides execution and helps forecast progress and risks.
3. **Risk Register** A living document cataloging risks, likelihood, impact, mitigation strategies, and updates.
4. **Change Log** Tracks all approved modifications to project scope, schedule, or resources. It maintains transparency and supports audit requirements.
5. **Issue Log** Documents problems that require resolution. The log helps prioritize work and ensures accountability for each issue.
6. **Status Reports** Regular summaries provided to stakeholders covering accomplishments, next steps, risks, and decisions needed.

Figure 13.5: IT Project Documentation Framework - Artifacts by Lifecycle Stage

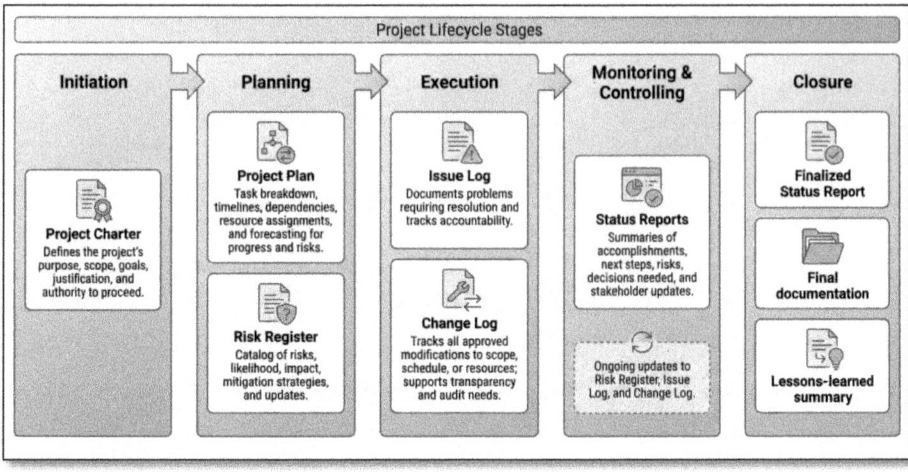

Governance Best Practices

- Establish steering committees to ensure strategic alignment and escalate major decisions
- Conduct monthly reviews of milestones, budget, and risks
- Enforce version control across all project artifacts to maintain accuracy
- Align governance with internal audit and compliance standards
- Use centralized repositories (such as SharePoint, Confluence, or ServiceNow PMO) for documentation

Case Example

An energy company deployed a centralized SharePoint PMO platform to store project documentation, status dashboards, and audit artifacts. This improved reporting consistency across departments and ensured audit readiness for all major initiatives.

How documentation and governance improved execution (what the program owner actually did)

They standardized a small set of required artifacts (charter, plan, risk register, change log, issue log, weekly status) and made them mandatory for every project before kickoff. Each artifact had an owner, a required update cadence, and a simple naming and versioning rule so teams could not store "final v7" files in random folders.

They set up one PMO site per initiative with a consistent folder structure, templates, and permissions, then tied steering committee reviews to the live dashboards and logs. If a risk was rated high or a change affected scope, schedule, or cost, it had to be logged before it could be discussed for approval. Over time, the benefit was not the tool, it was the behavior shift, decisions became traceable, status reporting stopped varying by team, and audit evidence was available without scrambling at the end.

Communication and Stakeholder Engagement

Most IT project delays that cannot be attributed to technical failure trace back to communication breakdown: a stakeholder who did not understand what they were being asked to approve, an executive who was surprised by a scope change, an operations team that was not told how the handoff would work. Communication failures compound because they often go unrecognized until they have already caused a delay. A structured communication plan prevents most of them by ensuring the right information reaches the right audience before a decision is needed, not after it is missed.

Communication Strategies

- ✓ Identify all stakeholders and understand their roles, interests, and communication needs
- ✓ Develop a communication plan specifying message frequency, format, channels, and responsible owners

- ✓ Provide visual dashboards and milestone summaries to present complex information clearly
- ✓ Hold regular stand-ups, status meetings, and technical syncs to maintain transparency
- ✓ Escalate risks and issues early to avoid last-minute surprises

Table: Stakeholder Communication Matrix – Audience, Channel, Frequency, Owner

Audience	Primary needs	Channel and format	Frequency	Owner
Executive sponsor and leadership	Decisions, risk, budget, business impact	1-page dashboard, brief decision log, verbal summary in steering meeting	Biweekly or monthly	Project Manager
Business owners and process leads	Scope clarity, user impact, readiness, adoption	Milestone update, change impacts, training and go-live readiness notes	Weekly	PM plus Business Lead
Technical engineering teams	Detailed requirements, designs, tasks, dependencies	Technical sync, design notes, implementation runbooks, backlog board	2 to 3 times per week	Technical Lead
Security, risk, compliance	Control coverage, exceptions, evidence, signoffs	Risk register, control mapping, approval checkpoints, evidence folder links	Weekly or per stage gate	Security Lead
Operations, NOC, service desk	Support readiness, handoff, monitoring, escalation	Ops readiness checklist, KB articles, on-call plan, comms templates	Weekly during build, daily near go-live	Service Transition Lead
Vendors and third parties	Deliverables, dates, constraints, acceptance criteria	Weekly vendor call, action log, delivery milestones, escalation path	Weekly	Vendor Manager
End users and impacted teams	What changes, when, how to get help	Email or Teams posts, FAQ, training short videos, outage notices	At major milestones and pre go-live	Change Manager

Case Example

A cybersecurity implementation succeeded because the project manager created tailored communication paths: technical engineers received detailed configuration memos, executives received high-level dashboards focused on risk reduction and progress.

How stakeholder engagement prevented delays (what the project manager actually did)
They split communications into two tracks with different artifacts and cadences. For engineers, they published short configuration memos with decisions, standards, and "what changes this week," tied to tickets and rollback notes. For leadership, they used a single dashboard that stayed consistent every review: risk reduced, coverage achieved, exceptions open, and decisions needed.

They also enforced a simple rule: any decision that impacted scope, timeline, or control posture had to be logged and pushed to both tracks in the right format. That kept engineering moving without waiting for approvals, and kept executives informed without flooding them with technical noise.

IT Project Risk Management

Risk in IT projects is not exceptional, it is structural. Dynamic requirements, vendor dependencies, integration complexity, and security constraints all introduce exposure that does not fully appear in the initial plan. Risk management is not about pessimism. It is about converting uncertainty into owned, monitored decisions early enough that options still exist. A risk identified and mitigated in the planning phase costs far less than the same issue surfacing during a cutover window.

Risk Management Steps

1. **Identification** List potential risks, including technical gaps, vendor delays, integration issues, staffing constraints, and security concerns.

2. **Assessment** Evaluate each risk based on likelihood and impact using a structured risk matrix.
3. **Mitigation** Define actions to prevent risks from materializing or reduce their impact. Examples include alternate sourcing, additional testing, or early prototyping.
4. **Monitoring** Review risks regularly, track changing conditions, and update scores based on new information.
5. **Communication** Document risks in accessible tools and ensure stakeholders understand implications and mitigation plans.

Figure 13.6: IT Project Risk Matrix – Likelihood vs. Impact

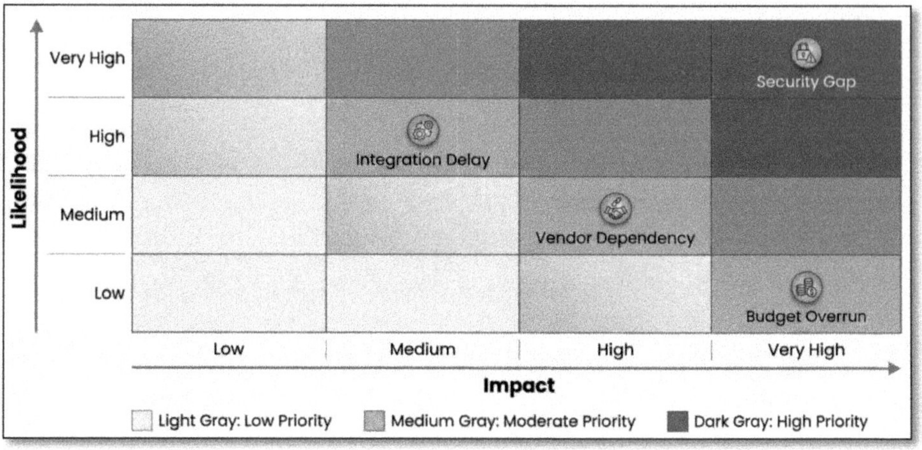

Example Risks

- Delays in vendor deliveries or hardware shipments
- Incompatible system versions during integration
- Budget overruns due to scope expansion
- Staff shortages or turnover of key resources
- Data migration failures or performance issues after cutover

Project Quality and Success Criteria

A project delivered on time and within budget can still be unsuccessful if the system does not perform as expected, creates operational problems after go-live, or needs major rework before it can meet acceptance criteria. Quality management reduces that risk by defining expectations before build starts, validating work at key checkpoints, and requiring evidence of acceptable performance before closure.

Quality Assurance (QA) Practices

- Define acceptance criteria early in planning
- Conduct peer reviews for designs, configurations, scripts, and documentation
- Validate configurations and code through automated or manual testing
- Run pilot deployments or phased rollouts before full-scale implementation
- Measure user satisfaction and operational performance after launch

Figure 13.7: Quality Assurance Integration Points Across Lifecycle

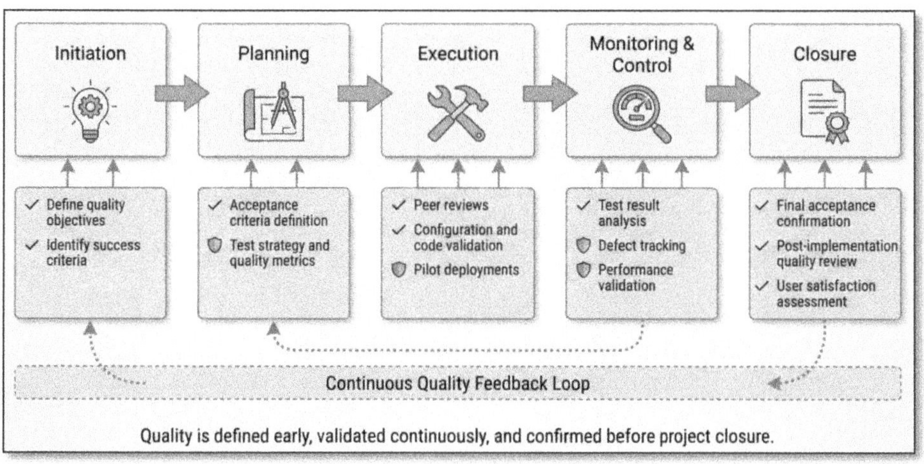

Success Criteria Examples

Technical Success: Meets performance, reliability, and security standards.

Business Success: Delivers expected ROI, reduces operational overhead, or improves user productivity.

Operational Success: Transitions smoothly into production, with minimal post-launch incidents or support escalations.

Case Example

A virtual desktop deployment defined success by tracking help desk tickets before and after implementation. Following rollout, login-related tickets dropped substantially, confirming that the solution improved the user experience and system stability in measurable terms rather than relying on anecdotal feedback.

How quality and success criteria were validated (what the project owner actually did)
They defined "done" in measurable terms before build started, not at go-live. Success criteria included login time targets, session stability thresholds, and a ticket baseline for authentication and profile issues. The team pulled 60 days of service desk data to establish the pre-rollout baseline, then tagged new tickets with a VDI category so post-launch comparisons would be clean.

Before broad rollout, they ran a pilot with a high-variance user group, monitored logon telemetry and profile load failures, and required signoff that acceptance criteria were met. After go-live, they reviewed weekly ticket trends for 4 weeks, validated the 50 percent reduction, and kept a short punch list of remaining issues tied to owners and due dates so quality did not fade once the project closed.

Project Closure and Lessons Learned

Formal project closure is where work is confirmed as complete, resources are released, documentation is archived, and lessons are captured before institutional memory starts to fade. Organizations that treat closure as a formality, signing off quickly so they can move to the next initiative, lose the operational knowledge that makes future projects faster and less error-prone. A lessons-learned review is not just a retrospective exercise. It is an investment in the next project.

Closure Activities

- ✓ Validate that all deliverables meet acceptance criteria
- ✓ Release project resources, close vendor engagements, and finalize payments
- ✓ Update the CMDB and asset records with new system configurations
- ✓ Archive project documentation, including risks, issues, and test results
- ✓ Conduct a lessons-learned workshop to evaluate what worked well and what should change
- ✓ Transition the service or system to operations or managed services

Pro Tip

Operations teams hate "throw-it-over-the-wall" deployments. Never consider a project closed until the Service Desk has successfully resolved a few incidents using only your documentation. If they have to call the project engineers to ask how to fix a basic issue, the project isn't finished; it's just undocumented.

What This Means in Practice

- IT project management is how technology work turns into lasting operational capability, not just a one-time delivery. The difference between a project that succeeds and one that stalls or fails is usually visible in planning, whether scope was defined clearly enough, whether risks were owned instead of just listed, and whether handoffs to operations were designed instead of assumed
- The project triangle is a daily operating reality, not just a conceptual model. Every scope change, budget discussion, and schedule adjustment is a tradeoff across time, cost, and scope. Managing it well means documenting those tradeoffs explicitly instead of letting them disappear into execution
- Role clarity is an operational control. Ambiguous ownership in IT projects shows up at the worst moments, during a cutover decision, a vendor escalation, or a security exception request. Defining decision authority before the project starts is far cheaper than reworking it in the middle of an outage
- Risk management delivers the most value before execution begins. Risks identified, owned, and mitigated during planning cost far less than the same issues discovered during a cutover window with no practical options left
- Closure is not a formality. A project that is technically complete but operationally unready, without documented handoffs, updated CMDB records, and operations teams that can resolve incidents without calling the project team, is not actually finished

Figure 13.8: Summary Diagram – IT Project Management Framework

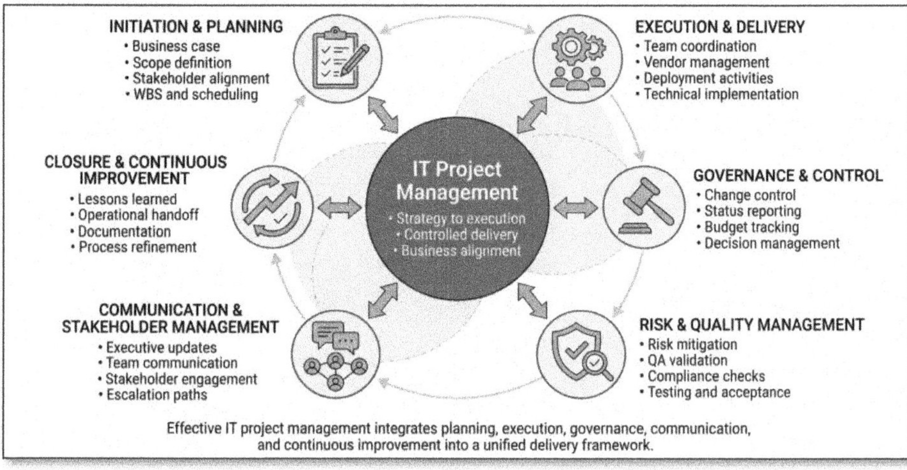

Chapter 14

CHOOSING THE RIGHT METHODOLOGY: WATERFALL, AGILE, HYBRID, AND SAFe

The delivery methodology shapes everything that follows: how teams organize their work, how changing requirements are handled, how risk is surfaced and owned, and how quickly the organization sees usable results. Choosing the wrong methodology does not just slow delivery. It creates friction between how the work is managed and how the organization actually needs to operate. Different IT initiatives require different levels of structure, flexibility, and governance. A data center migration may demand rigid sequencing, strict documentation, and defined change control. A cloud automation rollout or self-service portal, on the other hand, thrives under rapid iteration and continuous feedback.

No methodology fits every project. The goal is not to identify the best framework in theory, but to choose the delivery approach that matches the project's actual needs, requirement clarity, regulatory constraints, team experience, feedback cadence, and the cost of failure. This chapter compares Waterfall, Agile, Hybrid, and SAFe through that lens.

Figure 14.1: Project Methodology Spectrum - Predictive to Adaptive Approaches

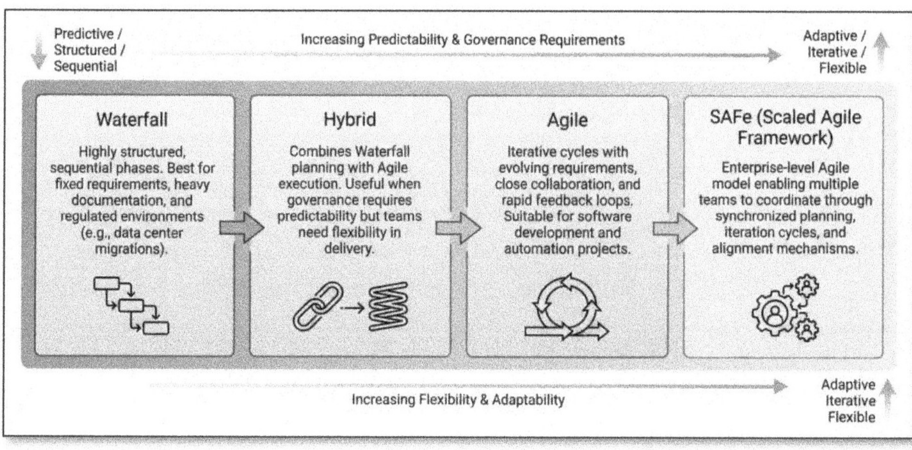

Understanding Project Delivery Methodologies

Project delivery methodologies provide structured, repeatable approaches for planning, executing, and controlling projects. In IT, methodologies typically fall into three categories: predictive, adaptive, and hybrid. Understanding the difference between these categories is the first step in choosing an approach that fits both the project itself and the way the organization needs to operate.

Categories of Methodologies

Methodology Type	Approach	Key Characteristic	Common Examples
Predictive	Sequential and plan-driven	Scope fixed early	Waterfall, PRINCE2
Adaptive	Iterative and responsive to change	Requirements evolve	Agile, Scrum, Kanban
Hybrid	Combine both approaches	Balances governance and flexibility	Hybrid Agile, SAFe

When Predictive Approaches Excel

Predictive methods are ideal when requirements are well-understood, risks are low, and the organization needs strict adherence to schedule and compliance controls. These approaches allow for strong documentation, repeatable sequencing, and high auditability.

When Adaptive Approaches Excel

Adaptive methods shine when requirements evolve rapidly or when user feedback shapes the final product. Agile reduces risk by delivering functionality incrementally, incorporating customer feedback, and adjusting priorities frequently.

When Hybrid Approaches Excel

Hybrid methods are valuable for large enterprises with both regulatory responsibilities and innovation needs. They allow teams to plan predictively while executing iteratively.

The best methodology depends on project scale, technical complexity, organizational maturity, and the amount of flexibility teams require.

The Waterfall Methodology

Waterfall is a linear delivery model in which each phase must be completed and approved before the next begins. It works best when requirements are stable, scope can be defined early, design can be completed with confidence, and implementation can follow in sequence. Under those conditions, Waterfall provides predictability, clear phase-based accountability, and documentation that supports audit and regulatory needs.

Phases of Waterfall

1. **Requirements Gathering** Define the project scope, functional requirements, technical constraints, and acceptance criteria. This phase establishes the foundation for all downstream work.
2. **Design** Architects and engineers create detailed technical specifications, diagrams, and system blueprints. Every component is defined before implementation.
3. **Implementation** Teams build or deploy the solution based on approved designs. Work occurs according to a predefined schedule and resource plan.
4. **Verification** Testing ensures the delivered solution matches documented requirements. Any gaps discovered late in this stage may require significant rework.
5. **Maintenance** After deployment, the system enters operational support. Enhancements or fixes follow structured change control processes.

Figure 14.2: Waterfall Model Phases Diagram

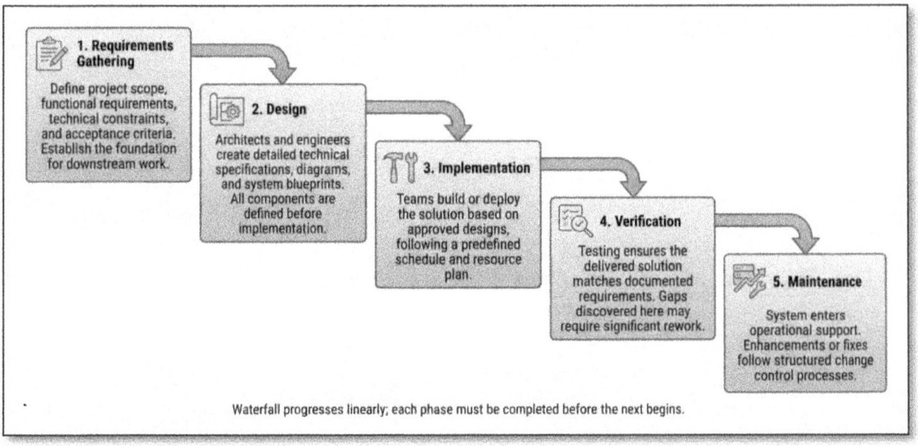

Advantages of Waterfall

- Clear structure and documentation
- Predictable timeline and cost for planning-driven environments
- Ideal for regulatory or audit-heavy projects
- Well-suited for fixed-scope initiatives with little uncertainty

Disadvantages of Waterfall

- Inflexible once requirements are finalized
- Late detection of requirement gaps or defects
- Limited stakeholder involvement during execution
- Adaptation is difficult without formal change approvals

Best Suited For

- Data center infrastructure projects
- Hardware deployments
- Structured compliance-driven upgrades such as PCI DSS, SOX, or regulatory audits
- Projects dependent on sequential engineering tasks

Table: Waterfall Pros and Cons Summary

Area	Pros	Cons
Requirements clarity	Strong fit when scope and acceptance criteria are stable and known up front	Weak when requirements are uncertain or likely to evolve
Planning and predictability	Easier to baseline schedule, cost, and resourcing early	Changes later often require rework, approvals, and schedule resets
Documentation and auditability	Heavy documentation supports audits, safety reviews, and compliance evidence	Documentation can become a workload if it is not used as a working control
Risk and defect discovery	Risks can be identified early through design reviews and sign-offs	Defects and requirement gaps may surface late during verification
Stakeholder engagement	Clear phase gates make leadership decisions straightforward	Business stakeholders may have limited visibility during build until late-stage testing
Delivery speed	Works well for sequential engineering where tasks must be done in order	Slower feedback loops, less ability to course-correct midstream

Case Example

A telecommunications provider used Waterfall for a large power redundancy expansion across multiple sites. The project required structured sequencing, detailed engineering sign-offs, and precise coordination with safety inspectors. Waterfall ensured every task was completed in the correct order with full compliance.

How Waterfall protected sequencing and compliance (what the project owner actually did)

They locked requirements into an approved scope package that included one-line diagrams, load calculations, safety method statements, and acceptance criteria for commissioning. Each phase ended with a formal sign-off, engineering design approval before procurement, site readiness and permits before mobilization, and pre-commission checklists before any cutovers.

To keep execution controlled across sites, they used a master schedule with dependency gates, standard work packages, and a single change path for any field deviation. Weekly reviews focused on three items only: upcoming safety inspections, long-lead material status, and readiness for the next gate. That kept work in sequence, reduced rework, and produced clean evidence for inspectors and auditors.

Agile Methodology

Agile developed as a response to the real-world limitations of plan-heavy sequential methods, late discovery of requirement mismatch, limited stakeholder involvement during build, and feedback loops too slow to catch problems before they grew. It is not a single method, but a family of frameworks built on common principles: short delivery cycles, continuous feedback, adaptive planning, and working software as the main measure of progress.

The Principles Behind Agile

The Agile Manifesto, published in 2001 by seventeen software practitioners, established four value statements that distinguish Agile from more plan-driven approaches. These values do not reject process or documentation. They clarify what should be prioritized when tradeoffs have to be made. The most important ideas include:

1. **Individuals and interactions over processes and tools:** Teams succeed when communication flows freely and people collaborate effectively.
2. **Working solutions over comprehensive documentation:** Teams prioritize delivering functional increments that stakeholders can evaluate.

3. **Customer collaboration over contract negotiation:** Engagement with users is continuous, not confined to milestones.
4. **Responding to change over following a plan:** Plans adapt as new information emerges.

Figure 14.3: Agile Feedback and Iteration Loop Diagram

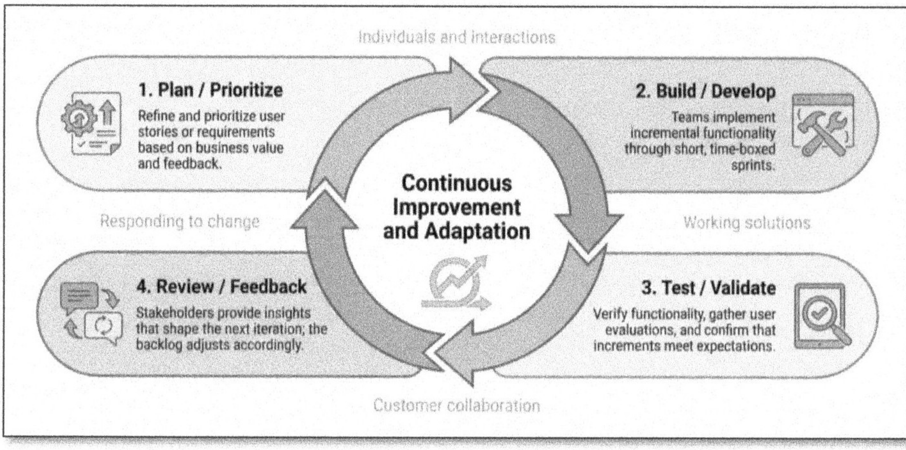

Core Agile Frameworks

Agile includes several frameworks that differ in structure but share the same values.

Scrum

Scrum, as defined by Ken Schwaber and Jeff Sutherland in the Scrum Guide, organizes work into time-boxed sprints that typically last two to four weeks. Each sprint includes planning, daily coordination, a review in which the team demonstrates completed work, and a retrospective in which the team reflects on how the work was done and how the process can improve.

Kanban

Kanban uses a visual board to make work visible, with a focus on managing how much work is in progress at any given time. By limiting active work, teams reduce context switching and improve flow from start to completion. Unlike Scrum, Kanban does not rely on fixed-length sprints. Work is pulled as capacity becomes available.

Extreme Programming (XP)

XP is an Agile framework built around strong technical discipline. Common XP practices include test-driven development, continuous integration, pair programming, and frequent small releases. In enterprise IT, these practices are often adopted selectively within Scrum teams rather than used as a full standalone method. XP is especially valuable for teams building complex software where quality and reliability are critical.

Agile Roles

- **Product Owner**: Defines the product vision, manages the backlog, and prioritizes features
- **Scrum Master**: Facilitates Agile processes and removes roadblocks
- **Development Team**: Cross-functional group responsible for delivering increments

Pro Tip

Watch your team's eyes during the Daily Stand-up. If they are looking at you (the manager), they are giving a status report, not collaborating. To fix this, stop running the meeting. Stand outside the circle or leave the room entirely until they learn to synchronize with each other rather than reporting to you.

Advantages of Agile

- Faster delivery of usable functionality
- High stakeholder engagement throughout the project
- Allows teams to adjust to shifting requirements
- Strong team ownership and morale

Disadvantages of Agile

- Requires dedicated and disciplined teams
- Less predictable for fixed-scope or fixed-date projects

- Documentation may be inconsistent without strong governance
- Can conflict with traditional compliance requirements

Best Suited For

- Software development and iterative product delivery
- Cloud automation and CI/CD pipeline enhancements
- Pilot programs or innovation initiatives
- Projects where requirements evolve rapidly

Table: Agile Roles and Key Responsibilities

Role	Primary responsibility	Key activities	Success indicators
Product Owner	Maximize product value	Owns backlog, prioritizes work, defines acceptance criteria, aligns stakeholders	Clear priorities, fewer rework cycles, features map to user value
Scrum Master	Protect the process and flow	Facilitates ceremonies, removes blockers, coaches team habits, improves delivery	Fewer blockers, stable sprint cadence, better predictability over time
Development Team	Deliver working increments	Builds, tests, reviews, demos, improves quality, estimates work	Working features each sprint, low defect escape rate, reliable velocity trend
Stakeholders and Users	Provide direction and validation	Review increments, give feedback, clarify needs, approve releases	Fast feedback, fewer late requirement changes, higher adoption

Case Example

A software engineering team developing a customer portal adopted Scrum. Every two weeks, customers reviewed new features and provided feedback. Satisfaction scores improved measurably, and the team attributed the improvement to early issue correction and the fact that features were shaped by real user input rather than assumptions made at the start of the project.

How iteration improved outcomes (what the team lead actually did)

They converted the portal requirements into a ranked backlog with clear acceptance criteria, then committed only to the highest-value items each sprint. At the end of every two-week cycle, they ran a live demo with real users, captured feedback as new backlog items, and re-prioritized immediately instead of waiting for a late-stage "UAT surprise."

They also used each retrospective to address one delivery constraint at a time, unclear requirements, test gaps, or handoff delays. By fixing issues early and shaping feature with continuous user input, rework dropped and satisfaction rose by more than 30 percent because customers saw progress and influenced the direction while changes were still cheap.

Hybrid Methodology

Hybrid delivery combines the discipline of upfront planning with the iterative execution model of Agile. It exists because most enterprise IT environments do not fit cleanly into a single delivery model. They often need formal governance for compliance, while also needing the speed and feedback loops that sequential methods struggle to provide. Hybrid is not a compromise. It is a deliberate choice about which parts of the project require more structure and which parts benefit.

Hybrid does not mix Waterfall and Agile at random. It defines which parts of the project operate under each model and where the boundary between them is set. In many cases, that boundary sits between planning and execution: requirements, architecture, budget, and governance commitments are established through a predictive process, while build and test activities run in iterative cycles. The key design decision is where to place that boundary and what governance applies when work moves from one mode to the other.

How Hybrid Works

- Early phases such as requirements, architecture, budgeting, and risk analysis follow structured predictive planning
- Execution phases such as development or testing use Agile techniques like sprints or Kanban boards
- Governance boundaries need to be clearly defined, which decisions require formal approval, and which can be made within sprint execution without creating audit gaps
- Stakeholders receive iterative results while still having clear milestones and delivery gates

Figure 14.4: Figure: Hybrid Project Model - Predictive Front-End, Adaptive Back-End

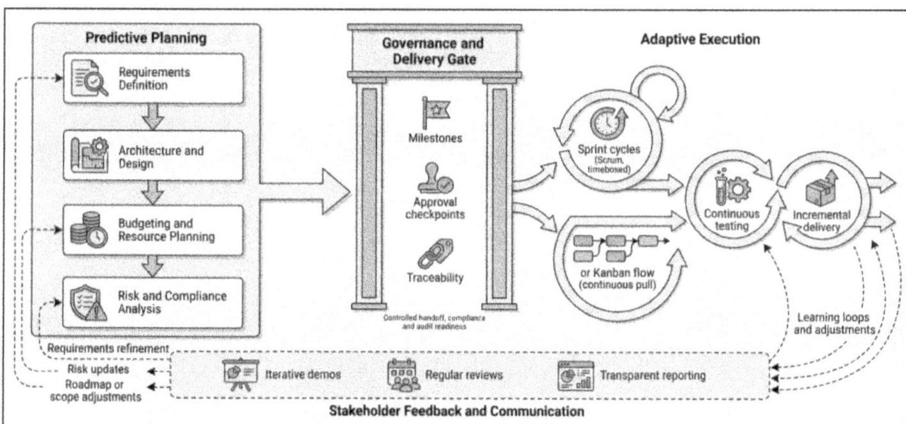

Hybrid delivery combines upfront discipline with execution flexibility to balance compliance, speed, and control.

Advantages of Hybrid

- Offers the governance required for regulated industries
- Supports flexibility for iterative work within stable project boundaries.
- Improves communication between architects, engineers, and business stakeholders
- Reduces friction that occurs when Agile teams interact with traditional governance structures

Disadvantages of Hybrid

- Requires strong project managers who understand both methodologies
- If boundaries are unclear, teams may struggle between structure and flexibility
- May require cultural adjustments across departments

Best Suited For

- Large, multi-phase enterprise programs.
- Projects with fixed deliverables but evolving technical implementation details
- Cloud migration programs mixing infrastructure work with iterative application development
- Transformations that require both compliance and innovation

Case Example

A financial services company used Hybrid for a core banking modernization. Up-front architecture and compliance requirements followed a predictive model, while customer-facing modules were developed in Agile sprints. This approach preserved auditability while increasing delivery speed.

How Hybrid preserved auditability and still moved fast (what the program owner actually did)
They locked the "non-negotiables" early, target architecture, data classifications, control requirements, integration boundaries, and release gates, then got formal signoff so scope and compliance expectations stayed stable.

Execution was split into sprint teams for customer-facing modules. Each sprint produced a demo and test evidence, but releases only progressed through predefined governance gates (security review, change approval, rollback plan, and operational readiness). That let the auditors trace decisions and controls end to end, while the business still saw usable increments on a predictable cadence.

Scaled Agile Framework (SAFe)

SAFe provides a governance and coordination model for organizations where multiple Agile teams are working toward the same product, platform, or business outcome. At the team level, work still runs in short cycles using Scrum, Kanban, or similar practices. Above that, SAFe adds structured planning and alignment so teams working in parallel do not create unmanaged dependencies, integration conflicts, or competing priorities that slow the delivery speed Agile is meant to support.

SAFe Layers

- **Team level** Teams execute using Scrum, Kanban, or XP, delivering increments frequently
- **Program level** Multiple teams align through an **Agile Release Train (ART)**, a long-lived "team of teams" that plans and delivers on the same cadence
- **Portfolio level** Strategy, funding, and governance decisions are managed to keep delivery aligned with business outcomes and capacity

Key SAFe Concepts

- **Agile Release Train (ART)** Coordinates delivery across many teams working toward one mission
- **Program Increment (PI)** A fixed planning and delivery timebox that synchronizes teams
- **Lean Portfolio Management** Aligns work selection and funding to business priorities
- **Continuous Delivery Pipeline** Automation, testing, and release practices that reduce batch size and speed delivery

Advantages of SAFe

- Shared cadence and planning reduces cross-team collisions and late integration surprises
- Portfolio visibility improves prioritization, sequencing, and funding decisions
- Standard events and artifacts can strengthen traceability for regulated environments

Disadvantages of SAFe

- Requires training and leadership discipline, otherwise it becomes ceremony without outcomes
- Adds overhead that is unnecessary for small, single-team efforts
- Can become bureaucratic if roles and decision rights are unclear

Best Suited For

- Enterprises running many teams against one platform or product
- Large modernization programs with heavy dependencies
- Organizations that need Agile execution with portfolio-level governance

Table: SAFe Key Roles

Role	Primary focus	What they do in practice
Release Train Engineer (RTE)	Flow and coordination	Runs PI Planning and ART ceremonies, removes cross-team blockers, keeps dependencies visible, escalates risks early
Product Management	Value and prioritization	Owns feature priorities, aligns roadmap to business outcomes, makes tradeoffs when capacity conflicts with demand
System Architect	Technical alignment	Defines shared architecture direction, sets integration patterns and guardrails, reduces technical divergence across teams

Case Example

A multinational software company implemented SAFe to coordinate a large number of Agile teams across several continents. Release frequency increased significantly after the first two program increments, and the consistent governance artifacts produced through PI Planning made ISO 27001 control evidence easier to generate and maintain.

How SAFe increased release frequency and kept controls auditable (what the program owner actually did)
They first reorganized delivery into a small number of ARTs aligned to products, not org charts. They established one shared cadence, one definition of done, and one integrated system demo requirement, so "done" meant integrated and releasable, not "finished in my repo."

They then ran PI Planning as a decision forum, not a status meeting. Dependencies were mapped in the room, risks were captured as explicit ROAM items, and PI Objectives were approved with business owners present. Anything that could not be integrated inside the increment was de-scoped or split, not carried as hidden work.

To protect security and compliance, the program owner embedded controls into the flow: required evidence checkpoints at the end of each iteration (testing results, approvals, traceability links), automated where possible, and made "no evidence, no promote" a release gate. That is what enabled smaller, more frequent releases without losing audit readiness.

Selecting the Right Methodology

Methodology selection is a strategic decision with daily operational consequences. It shapes how teams communicate, how scope changes are managed, how risk is surfaced, what governance artifacts are required, and how quickly business stakeholders see usable results. Getting it right reduces delivery friction. Getting it wrong creates problems that build throughout execution. IT leaders must evaluate the nature of the project, the maturity of the organization, and the expectations of stakeholders before choosing a delivery approach.

The decision framework below helps connect project characteristics to methodology choices. Each factor narrows the options, and taken together, they usually point more clearly to the right approach than any single factor alone.

Key Decision Factors

1. **Project Complexity:** Highly complex projects with multiple dependencies benefit from structured planning.
   - Stable, well-defined scope favors Waterfall
   - Ambiguous or evolving requirements favor Agile
   - Mixed complexity favors Hybrid
2. **Regulatory Requirements:** Environments with strong audit, documentation, or safety requirements usually require more structure.
   - Waterfall or Hybrid works well for regulated industries such as finance, healthcare, and energy
3. **Stakeholder Engagement:** If stakeholders must provide frequent feedback, Agile or Hybrid may be a better fit.

4. **Timeline Predictability:** Fixed deadlines and hard cutover dates (for example, data center move events) are often better suited to predictive planning.
5. **Team Structure and** Culture.
    - Distributed teams with limited interaction may struggle with Agile
    - Teams used to documentation-heavy processes may need time to adapt to iterative delivery
    - Organizations with strong PMOs often adopt Hybrid or SAFe for consistency

Never force Agile on a project where the "Cost of Change" is high. You can refactor software code in an hour, but you cannot "refactor" a fiber optic trench or a generator pad once it is installed. Use Waterfall for physical infrastructure (where mistakes are expensive) and Agile for the software layer (where iteration is cheap).

Figure 14.5: Project Methodology Decision Tree Diagram

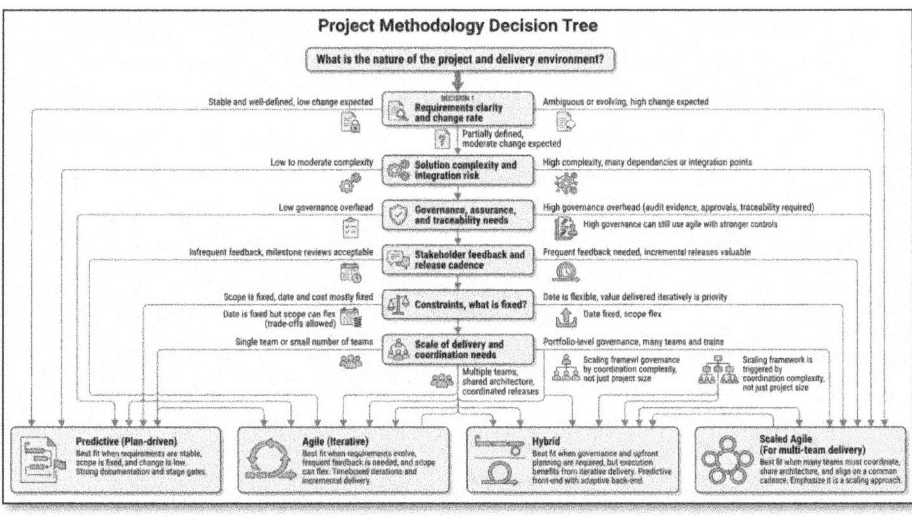

Example Methodology Guide

- Use **Waterfall** when scope is stable, requirements are clear, and compliance demands strict documentation
- Use **Agile** when requirements evolve, collaboration is intense, and rapid value delivery is essential
- Use **Hybrid** when regulatory oversight must coexist with iterative development
- Use **SAFe** when many teams must coordinate across large enterprise initiatives

This decision-making process helps organizations avoid two common methodology mismatches: applying Agile to projects where physical sequencing, safety requirements, or compliance documentation require strict phase control, and applying Waterfall to projects where requirements are expected to evolve and late-stage change becomes too costly. Both mistakes are common, and both lead to the same result, delivery friction, quality problems, and teams struggling against the framework instead of working effectively within it.

Common Implementation Challenges

Choosing a methodology can happen in a meeting. Implementing it usually takes months of behavioral change, process redesign, and difficult conversations about decision-making and authority. Most methodology failures are not failures of the framework itself. They are failures of adoption, teams falling back into familiar habits, governance structures that were never adjusted to fit the new model, or leaders who endorsed the methodology in theory but never changed how they managed in practice.

1. **Resistance to Change:** Teams accustomed to traditional structures may hesitate to adopt iterative methodologies. Without support and clear communication, employees may revert to old habits.

How to Address: Involve team members in the methodology design decision rather than announcing a process change from above. People are more likely to support what they helped shape than what was simply imposed on them. Start with a pilot team that volunteers, let that team demonstrate results, and use those results to build credibility with more skeptical groups. Provide structured training before the methodology goes live, not only after the first iteration exposes gaps.

2. **Governance Conflicts:** Many organizations attempt Agile transformations without adjusting their compliance processes. This creates friction between Agile speed and corporate control.

   How to Address: Map existing compliance requirements to the new methodology before rollout rather than trying to retrofit them afterward. Identify which controls require documentation, which require sign-offs, and which can be satisfied through sprint artifacts such as test evidence and acceptance criteria. Hybrid and SAFe models often make it possible to meet compliance requirements without forcing sequential phase gates onto all work. The governance team should be involved in methodology design from the beginning, not brought in only for review after the model is already in place.

Pro Tip

Most arguments about methodology are actually arguments about trust. Executives often push for Waterfall because they crave the *illusion* of certainty provided by fixed dates. You can bridge this gap by offering "fixed date, flexible scope" milestones. Promise a working demo on a specific date, but keep the exact feature set flexible. This gives leadership the predictability they need without handcuffing the engineering team.

3. **Skill Gaps:** New roles such as Scrum Master, Product Owner, or Release Train Engineer require training and experience. Without proper preparation, teams stumble and become frustrated.

How to Address: New roles like Scrum Master, Product Owner, and Release Train Engineer require both training and practical experience. Sending one person to a two-day certification class and expecting that alone to drive transformation is a predictable way to fail. Organizations need structured coaching, pairing with experienced practitioners, and protected time for new role holders to do the work before it is added on top of an already full workload.

4. **Misalignment with Organizational Culture:** If leadership does not support the chosen methodology, or if department priorities conflict, the approach breaks down.

   How to Address: Leadership behavior is the strongest cultural signal in a methodology transition. If executives ask Agile teams for fixed delivery dates, or require documentation artifacts the methodology does not naturally produce, teams will usually fall back into an informal hybrid model that satisfies neither approach well. Active sponsorship matters. Leadership needs to understand what the methodology requires from them, and the organization needs an honest assessment of cultural readiness before committing to full rollout.

What This Means in Practice

- Methodology selection is a constraint-matching exercise, not a philosophy debate. The most important inputs are requirement stability, the cost of mid-delivery errors, the regulatory environment, and the team's operational maturity
- Waterfall protects sequencing and auditability. It works best when scope is fixed, when mistakes are costly to correct, and when formal sign-offs between phases are required by contract, safety, or compliance
- Agile accelerates feedback and lowers the cost of course correction. It works best when requirements are expected to evolve, when user input shapes the final product, and when the team can sustain consistent iteration cycles
- Hybrid is not a fallback model. It is often the right approach for programs that must meet regulatory governance requirements while still allowing technical implementation to adapt as the project progresses
- SAFe is appropriate when multiple teams are working toward the same outcome and coordination failures cost more than coordination overhead. It is usually a poor fit for single-team efforts or projects where the ceremony burden outweighs the alignment benefit
- Implementation discipline determines whether any methodology delivers its intended value. A Waterfall project without enforced phase gates is not really Waterfall. An Agile team that does not inspect and adapt after each sprint is not functioning as Agile. A framework only works when the behaviors it requires are actually practiced

Figure 14.6: Summary Diagram - Comparative Overview of IT Project Methodologies

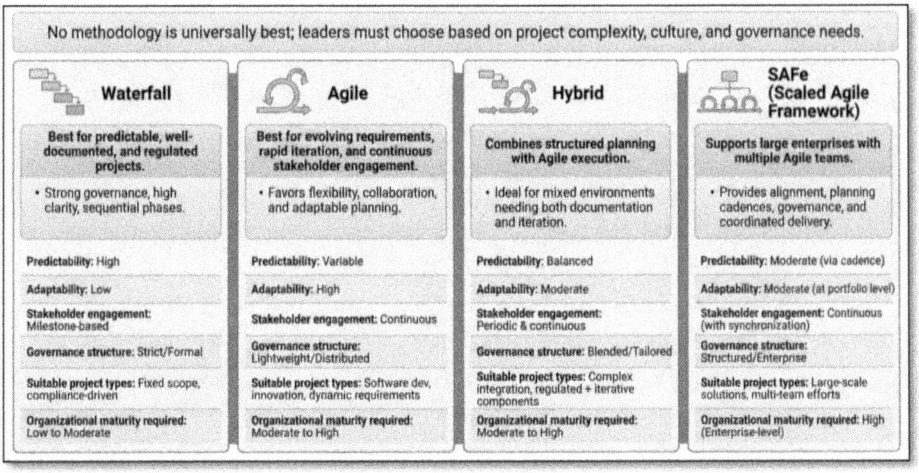

Chapter 15

PROJECT PLANNING AND INITIATION

Projects that fail often start failing during initiation, not execution. Scope is left vague, justification is assumed rather than documented, and stakeholder expectations are never formally aligned. Before technical work begins, the project manager's role is to turn a business request into a defined scope, a clear rationale, an identified stakeholder set, and a governance structure strong enough to let the project proceed with authority.

The cost of poor initiation shows up during execution. Projects without validated scope drift as stakeholders continue adding requirements. Projects without documented justification lose support when priorities change. Projects without clear governance stall whenever a decision requires authority that no one formally holds.

This chapter covers the initiation and planning disciplines that help prevent those outcomes: defining and validating scope, building a business case that holds up under executive review, developing a project charter that establishes clear authority, identifying and engaging stakeholders before they become blockers, estimating time and cost in ways that withstand scrutiny, and surfacing risks early enough to address them through design rather than reaction.

Figure 15.1: Project Lifecycle Context - Initiation and Planning as the Foundation of Execution

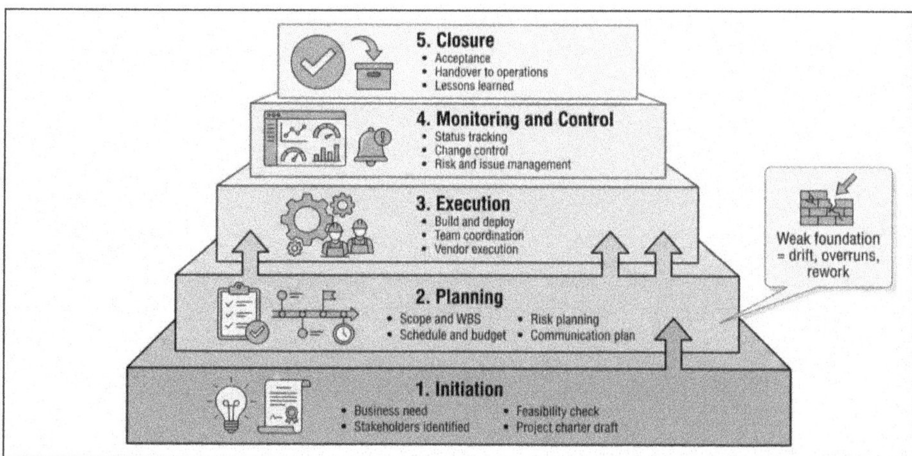

The Purpose of Project Initiation

Project initiation is the phase that turns a business request or strategic objective into an authorized, scoped, and resourced project. It produces the foundational decisions and documents the rest of the project depends on: the business case, charter, stakeholder map, preliminary budget and timeline, and the governance structure that gives the project manager authority to act.

Objectives of Project Initiation

1. Validate business justification and ensure strategic alignment.
2. Define preliminary scope and intended deliverables.
3. Identify stakeholders who will influence or be affected by the project.
4. Estimate high-level timeline, budget, and resource requirements.
5. Develop and approve the Project Charter, the primary output of the initiation phase.

Figure 15.2: Project Initiation Process

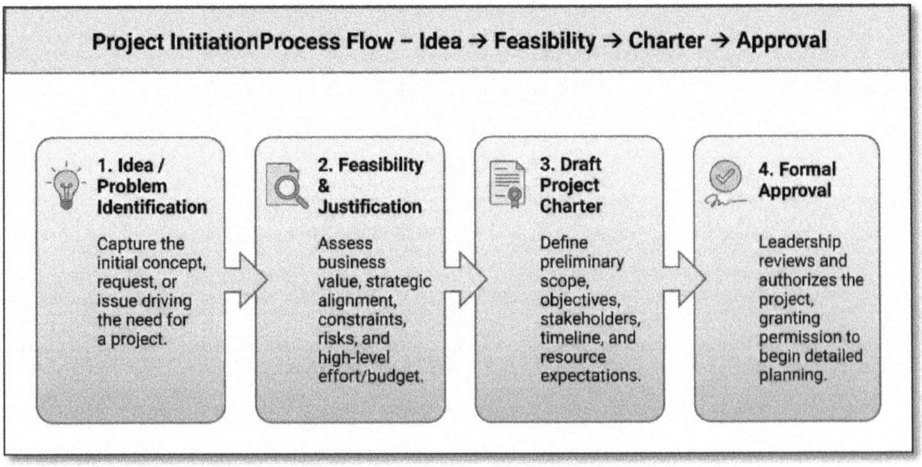

Example

A regional IT department recommended replacing aging firewalls. Through initiation, the team clarified scope, aligned the work with the organization's cybersecurity strategy, estimated costs, identified key roles, and received formal approval. Once completed, the project had clear direction, funding, and expectations before any technical tasks began.

How initiation secured approval and prevented scope drift (what the project owner actually did)
They wrote a short business justification tied to risk reduction and policy requirements, then translated it into a charter with clear boundaries, which sites were in scope, which were excluded, what "done" meant (cutover complete, rules migrated, validated failback), and what success would be measured against.

They brought Security, Network, and Finance into initiation early, confirmed required standards, documented assumptions and constraints (maintenance windows, vendor lead times, staffing), and produced a high-level cost and timeline estimate with a simple options view (minimum compliant refresh vs. full redesign). With stakeholders and roles named up front, leadership approved funding and the team started execution with clear expectations instead of debating scope mid-project.

Defining the Business Case

The business case is the document that helps leadership decide whether a project is worth funding and whether the recommended approach is the right one. A strong business case does not simply justify a predetermined solution. It frames the problem clearly, presents realistic options with their costs and tradeoffs, and recommends a path that leadership can evaluate, challenge, and approve with confidence.

Core Components of a Business Case

1. **Problem Statement:** Describes the operational or strategic challenge that needs resolution.
2. **Objectives:** Specific, measurable outcomes such as reducing downtime, lowering cost, or improving compliance.
3. **Options Analysis:** A comparison of alternatives, including the option of taking no action. This helps quantify opportunity cost.
4. **Cost–Benefit Analysis:** Shows estimated cost, projected value, return on investment, and payback period.
5. **Risk and Assumptions:** Lists key uncertainties and their potential impact.
6. **Recommendation:** Presents the preferred solution with reasoning and expected benefits.

Case Example

A logistics company evaluating WAN modernization compared traditional MPLS with SD-WAN and documented the difference in recurring annual spend. The business case showed the expected payback period, along with improvements in visibility and performance, giving executives the evidence they needed to approve the initiative.

How the business case was won (what the project owner actually did)

They started by framing the problem in business terms, peak-hour slowdowns, missed delivery SLAs, and the cost of outages at distribution sites. They pulled 90 days of circuit utilization, incident history, and carrier trouble ticket data to prove the pain was recurring, not anecdotal.

They presented three options with clear tradeoffs: do nothing, optimize MPLS, or move to a hybrid SD-WAN design. Costs were separated into one-time (edge devices, install, training) and recurring (circuits, licenses, support), and the savings model was tied to contracts that could actually be renegotiated. To reduce perceived risk, they proposed a pilot at a small set of high-impact sites, defined success metrics (SaaS latency, failover time, ticket volume), and included a rollback plan and governance gates before any broad rollout. That made approval feel controlled and reversible, not like a leap of faith.

Table: Sample Business Case Template - Problem, Benefit, Cost, Risk, Recommendation

Section	What to capture	Example (good level of detail)
Problem statement	What is failing, where, and business impact	"Branch WAN congestion causes POS slowdowns and missed SLA for order processing during peak hours."
Objectives	Measurable outcomes with targets and dates	"Reduce WAN spend by 25 percent in 12 months, improve SaaS latency by 30 percent, increase circuit resiliency to dual-path at all Tier 1 sites."
Options analysis	2 to 4 options including "do nothing," with tradeoffs	"Keep MPLS only, hybrid MPLS plus broadband, SD-WAN with broadband plus LTE backup, managed SD-WAN service."
Cost and effort	One-time and recurring costs, resourcing	"Year 1: hardware, licenses, install labor, carrier turn-ups. Run costs: circuits, support, monitoring. Internal hours by Network and Security."
Benefits and value	Financial and operational benefits	"Opex reduction, fewer outages from single-circuit failure, faster turn-ups, improved app experience, reduced troubleshooting time."
Risks and assumptions	Constraints, dependencies, what could go wrong	"Carrier lead times, site readiness, cutover window limits, training needs, security policy parity, assumed broadband quality."
Recommendation	Chosen option and why now	"Adopt hybrid SD-WAN, phase rollout by criticality, start with 10 pilot sites to validate app routing and security controls."

Creating the Project Charter

The Project Charter is the formal document that authorizes the project to proceed. It assigns the project manager, establishes scope and success criteria, documents known constraints and assumptions, and creates the reference point used to evaluate future scope change requests. A signed charter turns a business request into an authorized project with a named owner and agreed boundaries.

Typical Contents of a Charter

1. Project purpose and business objectives.
2. High-level scope and boundaries.
3. Major deliverables and expected outcomes.
4. Assumptions, constraints, and known risks.
5. Budget estimate and intended funding source.
6. Major milestones or preliminary timeline.
7. Key stakeholders and role assignments.
8. Success criteria and approval signatures.

Figure 15.3: Project Charter Outline Diagram

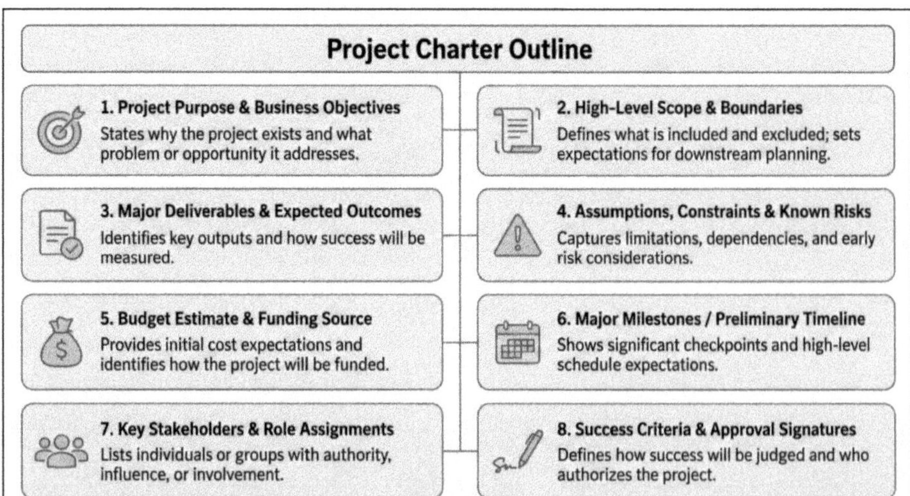

Charter Approval

- Reviewed by the Project Sponsor, PMO, and governance committees
- Approval grants the project manager authority to allocate resources and begin detailed planning
- Once signed, the charter becomes the baseline reference for scope and expectations

Example

An enterprise disaster recovery initiative defined a clear timeline, a documented budget, and an RTO target of 30 minutes for Tier-1 systems. With clear expectations and authority, infrastructure, application, and compliance teams aligned quickly around the project's goals.

How the charter created alignment fast (what the project owner actually did)
They made the charter unambiguous on scope: which Tier-1 systems were included, which were explicitly out, and what "RTO 30 minutes" meant in practice (measured from declaration to restored service, not "servers powered on"). They documented assumptions and constraints up front, replication method, required maintenance windows, and the minimum test cadence needed to accept the solution.

They also locked roles and decision rights early: who owned app runbooks, who approved network changes, who signed off on compliance evidence, and who could declare a DR event. The first milestone was a working pilot for one Tier-1 service with a timed failover drill, and the success criteria were tied to measurable outcomes (RTO met, data within RPO, validation checks completed, rollback proven). That let every team execute against the same definition of success instead of arguing later about what "ready" meant.

Stakeholder Identification and Analysis

Stakeholders are the individuals and groups whose decisions, input, or cooperation the project depends on, or who will be affected by what the project delivers. Identifying them early is not a formality. It helps the project avoid discovering critical dependencies in the middle of execution, such as a facilities team with scheduling constraints that were never considered, or a security review no one realized was required until the go-live date was already set.[9]

Stakeholder Analysis Steps

1. **Identify:** Compile a comprehensive list of internal and external stakeholders across technical and business units.
2. **Assess Influence and Interest:** Determine each stakeholder's level of authority and engagement needs.
3. **Develop Engagement Strategies:** Define communication frequency, channels, formats, and expectations.
4. **Document in a Stakeholder Register:** Maintain a living document updated throughout the lifecycle.

Table: Sample Stakeholder Analysis Matrix

Stakeholder	Role	Interest	Influence	Engagement Strategy
CIO	Executive Sponsor	High	High	Weekly updates
Network Team	Technical Execution	Medium	High	Daily stand-ups
Finance	Budget Oversight	Low	High	Monthly reports
End Users	Beneficiaries	High	Medium	Feedback sessions

[9] PMI defines stakeholders as individuals, groups, or organizations who may affect, be affected by, or perceive themselves to be affected by a project's decisions or outcomes. In IT projects, this typically includes technical teams, business owners, end users, security and compliance reviewers, vendors, and executive sponsors.

Example

During a data center migration, facilities management was not initially included as a stakeholder. Their late involvement caused delays due to scheduling and access issues. A revised stakeholder map corrected this gap and prevented further disruptions.

How the stakeholder gap was fixed (what the project owner actually did)

They updated the stakeholder map to add Facilities as a required approver for any work involving access, power, cooling, fire systems, or vendor entry. They then built Facilities dependencies directly into the project plan, badge requests, escort needs, hot work permits, change windows, and MEP support.

A single weekly coordination checkpoint was added with Facilities to confirm upcoming work, lock schedules, and clear constraints two weeks ahead. After that, access and scheduling stopped being last-minute blockers, and cutovers stayed on plan.

Figure 15.4: Stakeholder Influence vs. Interest Grid

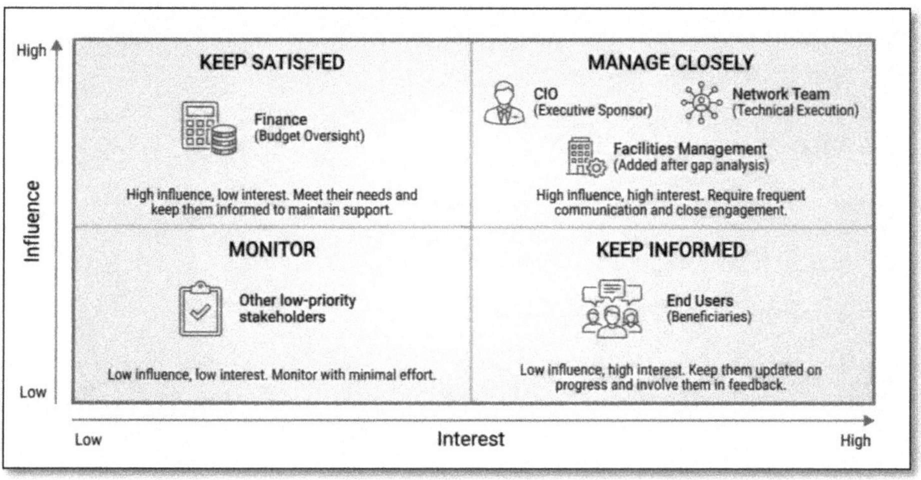

Scope Definition and Work Breakdown Structure (WBS)

Scope defines both what the project delivers and what it explicitly does not. The exclusions matter as much as the inclusions. When scope is vague, team members fill the gaps with assumptions, stakeholders interpret boundaries in their own favor, and the project absorbs work it was never resourced to deliver. Formal scope definition with explicit exclusions is the primary tool for preventing that pattern.

The Work Breakdown Structure (WBS) breaks major deliverables into manageable components, forming the backbone for estimation, scheduling, and resource planning.[10]

Steps to Define Scope

1. Identify major deliverables.
2. Break deliverables into smaller work packages.
3. Validate alignment with business case and objectives.
4. Obtain formal sponsor sign-off.

Example

A data center upgrade defined three major deliverables:

- Install new server racks
- Upgrade UPS and power cabling
- Redesign network core

Each deliverable was further decomposed into design, configuration, testing, and documentation tasks within the WBS.

---

[10] The Work Breakdown Structure (WBS), as defined in PMI's Practice Standard for Work Breakdown Structures, organizes the total scope of the project into manageable components by decomposing major deliverables into progressively smaller work packages. In IT projects, the WBS becomes the foundation for task estimation, resource assignment, schedule development, and scope change control.

How scope and the WBS prevented surprises (what the project owner actually did)

They wrote explicit in-scope and out-of-scope statements for each deliverable, including what would not be touched (no application refactoring, no storage redesign, no building automation changes). Each deliverable was decomposed into work packages that matched how the work would actually be executed: design approvals, procurement lead times, site readiness, install steps, testing criteria, rollback plan, and documentation updates.

They tied every work package to an owner and a measurable acceptance check (rack ready checklist signed, UPS cutover test passed under load, core failover validated, diagrams and CMDB updated). Sponsor sign-off was obtained on the WBS baseline, and any new request was treated as a change, not "extra work."

Scope Management Best Practices

Integrate the WBS with project scheduling tools. The WBS should serve as the source of truth for the schedule's task list. When WBS work packages are imported into or reflected in the scheduling tool, tasks stay connected to deliverables, and new scope creates a visible change to the plan instead of disappearing into an informal backlog. This connection also improves resource loading because effort is tied to specific deliverables rather than generic task categories.

Pro Tip

The most important heading in your Scope Statement is "Exclusions." It is easy to agree on what you *are* building; it is much harder to agree on what you are *not* doing. Explicitly list items like "historical data migration," "end-user training," or "hardware disposal" as out-of-scope. This prevents the painful "I assumed you were handling that" conversation during the final rollout.

Estimating Time, Cost, and Resources

Estimation during initiation establishes the financial and schedule baseline leadership uses to make a funding decision. An estimate that is too optimistic creates a project that is constantly over budget and behind schedule. An estimate that is too conservative may prevent a worthwhile initiative from being approved. Useful estimates are built from structured techniques, historical data, and clearly stated assumptions, not from rounded guesses or numbers reverse-engineered to fit a desired budget.

Estimating What Actually Matters

A usable estimate covers more than the build work. It should account for:

- **Delivery work** design, build, test, deploy, and rollback readiness
- **Governance work** CAB, security review, architecture review, procurement, approvals
- **Operational work** monitoring updates, runbooks, CMDB updates, training, hypercare
- **Dependencies** vendor lead times, maintenance windows, access approvals, change freezes

Estimation Techniques

Analogous Estimating [11]

Uses a similar past project as a reference point. This is best early, when scope is still high-level.

[11] The following estimation techniques are adapted from PMI's PMBOK Guide, where they are formally defined as standard project management practices. Organizations pursuing PMP certification should consult the current PMBOK Guide edition for the full definitions and application guidance

How to use it well:

- ✓ Choose a truly comparable project (scale, constraints, risk, compliance)
- ✓ Adjust for differences (site count, number of teams, tooling maturity, vendor involvement)
- ✓ Document what is assumed to be "the same" so reviewers can challenge it

Parametric Estimating

Uses measurable rates or formulas, which works well for repeatable work.
Examples:

- Hours per server migrated including validation and rollback readiness
- Days per rack install including burn-in and labeling
- Configuration time per site for SD-WAN plus test plan execution

How to use it well:

- ✓ Define the unit of work clearly so everyone measures the same thing
- ✓ Split into tiers (simple, moderate, complex) instead of using one average rate
- ✓ Include fixed overhead work separately (tooling setup, comms templates, governance)

Three-Point Estimating

Captures uncertainty by using three values and combining them into a weighted estimate. The optimistic value represents the best-case scenario, the pessimistic value reflects the worst case given identified risks, and the most likely value represents the realistic expected outcome. The standard weighted formula is: (Optimistic + 4 × Most Likely + Pessimistic) ÷ 6. This technique is most useful for high-uncertainty work packages where a single estimate would hide the real range of possible outcomes.

How to use it well:

- ✓ Apply it to the highest uncertainty areas, not every line item
- ✓ Tie the pessimistic number to specific risks (vendor delays, legacy dependencies)
- ✓ Keep the assumptions explicit so the estimate can be tightened later

Pro Tip

Never provide a single-point estimate during the Initiation phase. If you tell an executive "This will cost $50,000," they write it in stone. If you say "Between $45,000 and $60,000," they understand it is a forecast. Always present a range that reflects your current level of uncertainty. It protects your credibility when the final number inevitably lands somewhere in the middle.

Bottom-Up Estimating

Builds estimates from the WBS work-package level and rolls them up. This is the most accurate method, but it requires time and a stable scope baseline.

How to use it well:

- ✓ Estimate by role (engineer hours, PM hours, security hours) and by phase
- ✓ Include rework and testing cycles, not just the first execution
- ✓ Add explicit buffers for approvals, procurement, and change windows

Table: Estimation Techniques and Use Cases

Method	Accuracy	Use Case
Analogous	Low to Medium	Initiation stage, when scope is still broad
Parametric	Medium	Repeatable work with measurable units and stable rates
Three-Point	Medium to High	Work with high uncertainty or risk-driven variability
Bottom-Up	High	Detailed planning after scope and WBS are baselined

Example

A hybrid cloud migration required estimates for server migrations across multiple environments. The team used parametric estimating by defining a standard migration unit, including pre-checks, change ticket preparation, the move itself, validation, documentation, and rollback readiness. That gave the team a defensible hours-per-server rate. Historical data from prior migrations confirmed the estimate was within an acceptable variance range, which gave leadership confidence in the cost and schedule baseline.

How the estimate was built (what the project owner actually did)
They defined a standard "migration unit" (pre-checks, change ticket, move, validation, documentation, rollback readiness) so the six-hour rate meant the same thing for every team. They then segmented servers into tiers (simple, moderate, complex) and applied different rates per tier instead of averaging everything.

They validated rates using metrics from prior migrations, separated fixed overhead work (tooling, comms, governance checkpoints, hypercare staffing), and used three-point estimating for the riskiest subset (legacy and tightly coupled systems). Procurement and CAB lead times were modeled as schedule constraints, not hidden buffers, which made the cost range and timeline defensible during approval.

Risk Identification in the Initiation Phase

Risk identification begins during initiation, not after execution starts. Risks surfaced early can be mitigated through design decisions, procurement choices, resource planning, or schedule adjustments. Risks discovered during execution have to be managed reactively, which usually costs more, creates pressure, and leaves fewer options. The preliminary risk register created during initiation becomes the starting point for a risk process that continues throughout the project lifecycle.

Typical Early Risks

- Vendor lead time or supply chain delays
- Underestimated licensing or integration costs
- Insufficient resources or skill gaps
- Inaccurate scoping assumptions
- Delayed stakeholder engagement
- Regulatory or environmental constraints
- Data sensitivity considerations
- External dependencies such as contractors or facilities teams

Early risks should be documented in a preliminary risk register that evolves during planning and execution.

Pro Tip

Try a "Pre-Mortem" exercise to find hidden risks. Ask your team to imagine it is six months from now and the project has failed spectacularly. Then ask, "What went wrong?" This framing gives people permission to voice their deepest concerns—like vendor reliability or team capacity—without looking "negative" or unsupportive. You will uncover reality much faster this way.

Figure 15.5: Early Risk Register Template - Risk, Probability, Impact, Owner, Response

Early Risk Register Template (Initiation Phase)				
Risk	**Probability**	**Impact**	**Owner**	**Response / Mitigation**
Description of the threat or uncertainty.	Likelihood of occurrence (e.g., Low/Med/High).	Consequence to cost, timeline, or scope.	Person responsible for tracking or addressing the risk.	Action to reduce probability or impact.
(enter risk description)	(e.g., Low)	(e.g., High)	(enter owner name)	(enter action plan)
(enter risk description)	(e.g., Med)	(e.g., Med)	(enter owner name)	(enter action plan)
(enter risk description)	(e.g., High)	(e.g., Low)	(enter owner name)	(enter action plan)
(enter risk description)	(e.g., Low)	(e.g., Med)	(enter owner name)	(enter action plan)
(enter risk description)	(e.g., Med)	(e.g., High)	(enter owner name)	(enter action plan)

Project Governance and Approval

Project governance defines decision rights before the project needs to use them. Who can approve scope changes? Who can authorize additional budget? Who escalates when a vendor misses a commitment and the project timeline is at risk? Establishing those answers during initiation prevents the project from stalling every time a decision requires authority that was never formally assigned.

Governance Components

1. **Steering Committee:** Provides strategic guidance, resolves escalated issues, and ensures alignment with business goals.
2. **Project Sponsor:** Champions the initiative, secures funding, and provides directional decisions.
3. **Project Management Office (PMO):** Ensures standardization, documentation, methodology enforcement, and integration with portfolio management.
4. **Change Control Board (CCB):** Reviews scope, schedule, and resource changes that arise during planning and execution.

Figure 15.6: Project Governance Structure Diagram

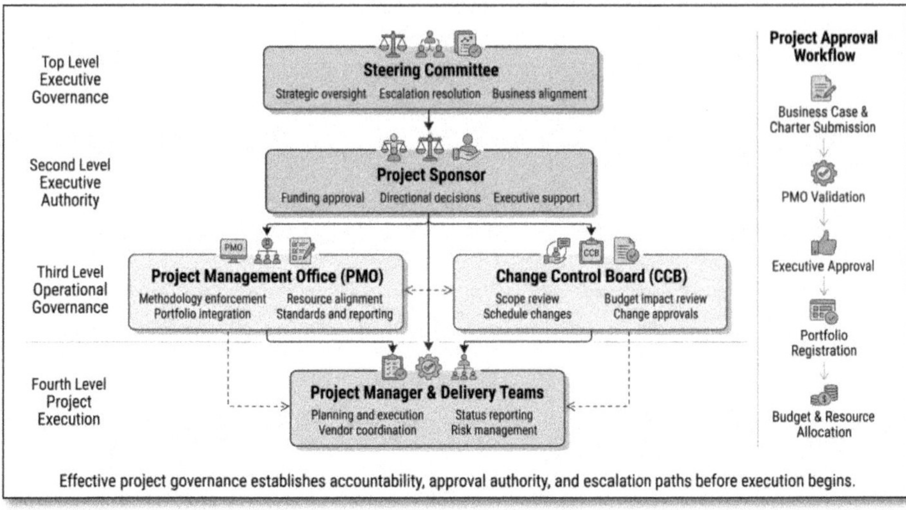

Approval Process

1. **Submit Business Case and Charter to the Project Sponsor:** The sponsor is the first reviewer because they hold funding authority and business accountability for the outcome. Their review confirms that the problem being solved is real, the proposed solution is reasonable, and the organization is prepared to commit to the project's requirements. Sponsor endorsement moves the proposal from an informal idea into a candidate for formal governance review.

2. **PMO Review and Validation:** The PMO validates methodology selection, resource feasibility, documentation completeness, and compliance with portfolio standards. If gaps are identified, the charter and business case are returned to the project owner for revision before the project advances to the governance board. This review cycle should be expected rather than treated as an exception. PMO review ensures proposals are complete, comparable across the portfolio, and ready for governance evaluation.

3. **Governance Board or Executive Approval:** Final approval is granted by the governance board or executive sponsor. The governance body evaluates the proposal against portfolio

priorities, available capacity, and strategic alignment. Approval at this stage authorizes the project to consume organizational resources and formally commits leadership support for execution. Conditional approvals, where additional funding depends on meeting defined milestones or review gates, are also handled here.

4. **Portfolio Registration:** Once approved, the project is entered into the organization's official portfolio record and becomes visible to portfolio management, finance, and governance functions. Portfolio visibility allows leadership to monitor delivery progress, manage cross-project dependencies, and identify capacity conflicts before they affect multiple initiatives.

5. **Formal Resource and Budget Allocation:** Approved funding is assigned to the project cost center, named resources receive documented allocation percentages, and procurement activity for hardware, software, or external services can begin. Formal allocation is what turns an approved project into one capable of execution. Without it, projects may have authorization on paper while still lacking the resources needed to begin work.

Tools and Templates for Initiation and Planning

Standardized templates reduce the variation that makes project documentation inconsistent across teams. When every project uses the same charter structure, stakeholder register format, and risk register format, reviews are faster, portfolio comparisons are easier, and audit evidence is simpler to compile. Mature PMOs maintain these assets and enforce their use as a form of quality control, not just convenience.

Common Tools

- Project Charter Template (Word, Confluence, or SharePoint). Establishes the formal authorization to begin work. It captures the project purpose, scope boundaries, sponsor and project manager authority, key objectives, known constraints and assumptions, and the signatures required before planning proceeds. A signed charter becomes the baseline reference for every scope dispute that follows

- Stakeholder Register (Excel, Smartsheet). Records each stakeholder's role, decision authority, communication preferences, and engagement requirements. Maintained as a living document throughout the project, it helps ensure no influencer or approver is missed before major milestones and provides the basis for the communication plan
- WBS and Gantt Scheduling (Microsoft Project, Primavera, Asana). Breaks project scope into manageable work packages and connects deliverables to timelines, dependencies, and resource assignments
- Risk Register (SharePoint, Jira, ServiceNow). Documents each identified risk with probability, impact rating, named owner, mitigation or contingency plan, and current escalation status. A live risk register is reviewed on a defined cadence, not filed after initiation and ignored
- Budget Tracker and Dashboard (Excel, connected project management platform, Power BI, Tableau, or native PMO reporting features). Provides real-time visibility into budget burn, forecast variance, and cost-to-complete
- Intake Forms (Microsoft Forms, SharePoint, ServiceNow, Jira, or PMO portal). Standardizes new project requests by requiring consistent inputs before a proposal enters the review queue: business problem, sponsor, expected value, urgency, rough scope, and initial resource needs. Intake forms prevent informal work from bypassing the portfolio process and give the PMO comparable data across all proposals

Automation Enhancements

- PMO dashboards to track proposals, approvals, and project health

- Automated workflow approvals for charters and business cases
- Integrations with ITSM platforms to streamline operational transition
- Notifications for governance deadlines and reporting requirements
- These tools help maintain consistency and allow organizations to scale project delivery without sacrificing control.

Figure 15.7: Example PMO Dashboard - Project Intake and Status Summary

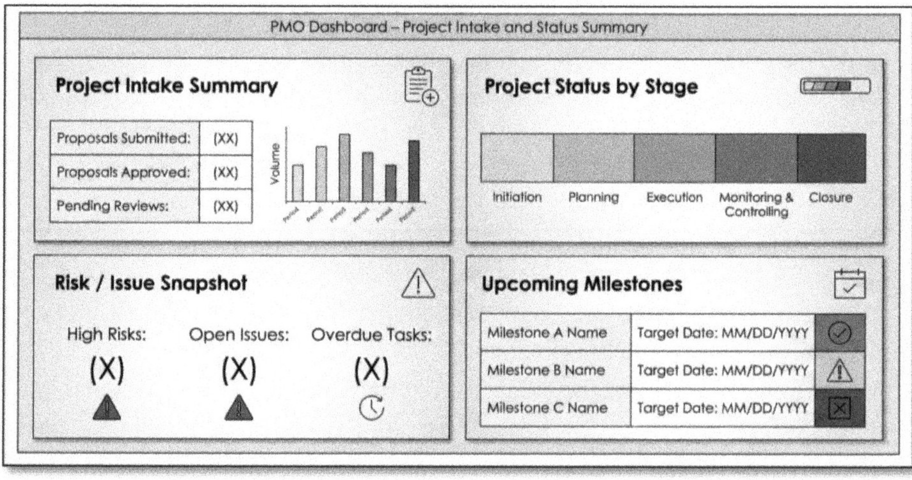

Transition to Detailed Planning

Once the charter is approved and governance has authorized the project, the initiative transitions from initiation to detailed planning. Planning refines initial assumptions, builds a complete execution roadmap, and ensures teams have the clarity needed to begin work.

Outputs of the Planning Phase

- A comprehensive project plan with task-level detail
- Resource assignments supported by capacity planning
- Procurement strategy and vendor onboarding timelines

- Risk mitigation plans and updated risk register
- Quality management strategies and acceptance criteria
- Stakeholder communication and reporting plan
- Project schedule with baselined milestones and dependencies

Case Example

After initiation, a cybersecurity program entered detailed planning by defining twelve major milestones, identifying sixteen technical dependencies, and securing vendor onboarding dates. The structured plan reduced surprises and synchronized activities across infrastructure, security, and application teams before any engineering tasks began.

How the transition was executed (what the program owner actually did)
They converted the charter into a planning backlog, then ran working sessions with each tower (identity, network, endpoint, logging, apps) to capture prerequisites, handoffs, and "cannot-start-until" items. Dependencies were documented in a single tracker and linked to milestones so teams could see upstream blockers early.

They locked the calendar before engineering began, maintenance windows, CAB submission dates, change freeze periods, and vendor lead times, then built the schedule around those constraints instead of hoping exceptions would be granted later. Owners were assigned to every milestone and dependency, and the risk register was updated with mitigations tied to specific tasks. Finally, they set a weekly checkpoint cadence (status, risks, decisions needed) so unresolved dependencies surfaced while there was still time to adjust.

What This Means in Practice

- Initiation is where the project either gets a strong foundation or inherits the problems that will surface later. Vague scope, unvalidated assumptions, and missing stakeholders during initiation become scope disputes, budget overruns, and blocked cutovers during execution
- The business case is a decision-support document, not a sales pitch. It should present options honestly, including the cost and risk of doing nothing, so leadership can make a real funding decision rather than approve an answer that was already chosen
- The project charter's value is in what it locks down: scope boundaries, success criteria, decision rights, and governance expectations. Once signed, it becomes the reference point for every scope change discussion that follows
- Stakeholders missed during initiation usually appear during execution, often just before a cutover, with constraints nobody planned for. The stakeholder map should be treated as a living control, not a one-time exercise
- Estimation improves when assumptions are explicit and structured techniques are applied consistently. Ranges with confidence levels are more useful than single-point estimates that create false precision
- Risk identification during initiation is not about building a comprehensive list. It is about surfacing exposures large enough to affect the design, timeline, scope, or authorization decision before the project is approved

Figure 15.8: Summary Diagram – IT Project Initiation Framework

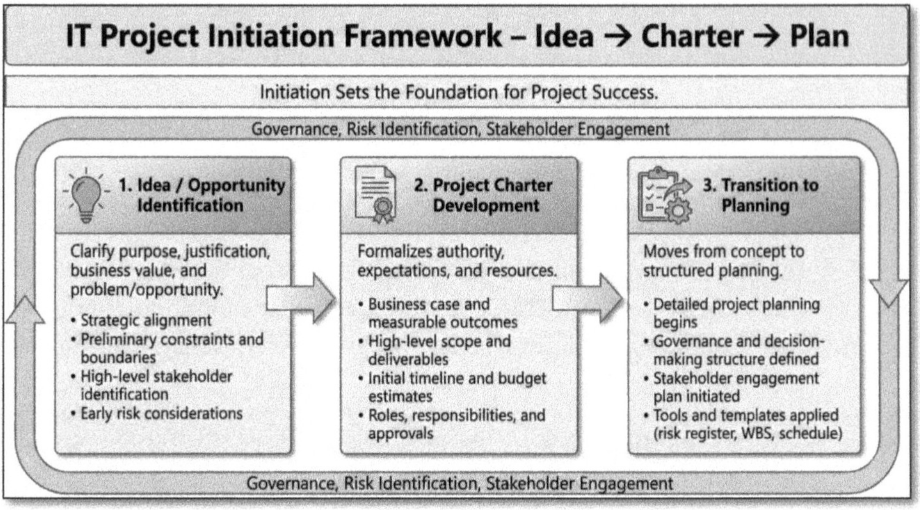

Chapter 16

DEFINING SCOPE, OBJECTIVES, AND BUSINESS CASES

Scope, objectives, and the business case determine whether a project is set up to succeed before execution begins. When scope is vague, teams interpret boundaries differently and absorb work they were never resourced to deliver. When objectives are not measurable, there is no shared definition of done. When the business case is weak or missing, the project loses funding and priority as soon as something more urgent appears.

Scope defines what the project will accomplish. Objectives describe how success will be measured. The business case provides justification, linking the project to strategic goals and demonstrating why the effort is worth funding. Together, these three elements anchor every downstream decision: what gets built, how success is measured, and why the organization should fund and prioritize the work.

This chapter explains how to create scope statements, define SMART objectives, build structured business cases, and ensure alignment between deliverables and business value.

Figure 16.1: Relationship Between Scope, Objectives, and Business Case

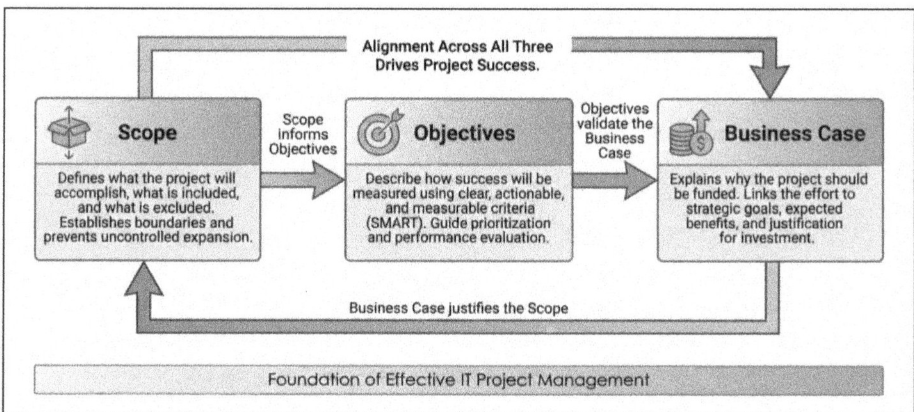

The Importance of Scope Definition

Scope establishes the operational boundaries of a project: what will be delivered, what will not, where the team's responsibility begins and ends, and what constraints govern the work. Without a formal scope statement, those boundaries exist only as individual assumptions, which means stakeholders may be operating from different versions of the project.

Benefits of Clear Scope

Clear scope definition delivers several operational benefits. It formally limits the project's work by establishing what is included, which is the primary defense against additions that were never planned, resourced, or budgeted. It also provides the basis for realistic cost, schedule, and resource estimates, because only explicitly defined work can be estimated with confidence. Scope definition establishes acceptance conditions that IT and business stakeholders can use to evaluate whether deliverables are complete. It aligns stakeholder groups around the same understanding of what the project will produce, reducing the misinterpretations that often surface during testing and go-live. Once baselined, the scope statement becomes the reference point for change requests, making it possible to evaluate additions on their merits rather than debating what was originally agreed.

Case Example

A cloud migration project initially assumed all systems would move to Azure. Once scope was clarified, legacy mainframe systems were intentionally excluded due to compliance restrictions. The decision saved considerable time and cost by avoiding unnecessary work and re-engineering.

How the scope was defined (what the project owner actually did)
The project owner built a system inventory and tagged each workload by data type, regulatory obligations, latency dependency, and integration complexity. They held a working session with compliance and application owners to identify workloads that could not leave the

current environment without redesign or approvals. The mainframe estate was then written into the scope as an explicit exclusion, documented with the compliance constraint and the decision owner. The scope statement was updated to "Azure for eligible workloads," with a separate track created for mainframe risk assessment and long-term options. That single scope decision prevented rework, removed unrealistic expectations, and kept the schedule and budget tied to what was actually feasible.

Table: Scope Definition Components

Component	What it captures	Example for the cloud migration scenario
Deliverables	What the project will produce and hand over	Azure landing zone set up, migrated Tier 1–3 eligible apps, identity integration, connectivity, runbooks, cutover plan, validation evidence
Exclusions	What is explicitly out of scope	Legacy mainframe systems excluded from migration due to compliance restrictions and required redesign, any refactoring of mainframe dependent apps beyond agreed interface changes
Boundaries	Where the project starts and stops, plus interfaces it will touch	Migration covers eligible workloads in specified data centers and subscriptions, includes network connectivity and IAM, stops at application deployment validation, upstream and downstream integrations remain owned by app teams unless listed in scope
Constraints	Hard limits that shape how work can be done	Compliance and data residency rules, approved regions only, maintenance windows, fixed budget ceiling, limited migration staff capacity, required security baselines and approval gates (CAB, security review)

Scope Statement and Deliverables

A scope statement provides the formal description of what the project will achieve, including its purpose, primary deliverables, acceptance criteria, exclusions, and constraints. It becomes the reference document for scope disputes during execution, especially when a stakeholder requests work that was never authorized and the project manager needs a documented basis for the decision.

Structure of a Scope Statement

1. **Project Purpose:** The business reason for undertaking the project.
2. **Objectives:** Expected outcomes that define success.
3. **Deliverables:** Tangible outputs such as systems, services, or documents.
4. **Acceptance Criteria:** Conditions that must be met to approve completion.
5. **Exclusions:** Items intentionally left out to avoid misunderstanding.
6. **Constraints and Assumptions:** Funding limits, resource availability, or technical restrictions.

A well-written scope statement does more than document intent. It improves the planning process by forcing the project team to define what is explicitly out of scope before work begins. Many projects run into difficulty not because the in-scope work was poorly defined, but because exclusions were vague or assumed to be understood. When a stakeholder later requests work that falls into that ambiguous space, the absence of a clear exclusion list leaves the project manager without a documented basis for pushback. Defining exclusions with the same level of detail applied to deliverables is one of the most practical habits a project manager can develop, especially during change control when pressure to absorb unplanned work is highest.

Figure 16.2: Example Scope Statement Template

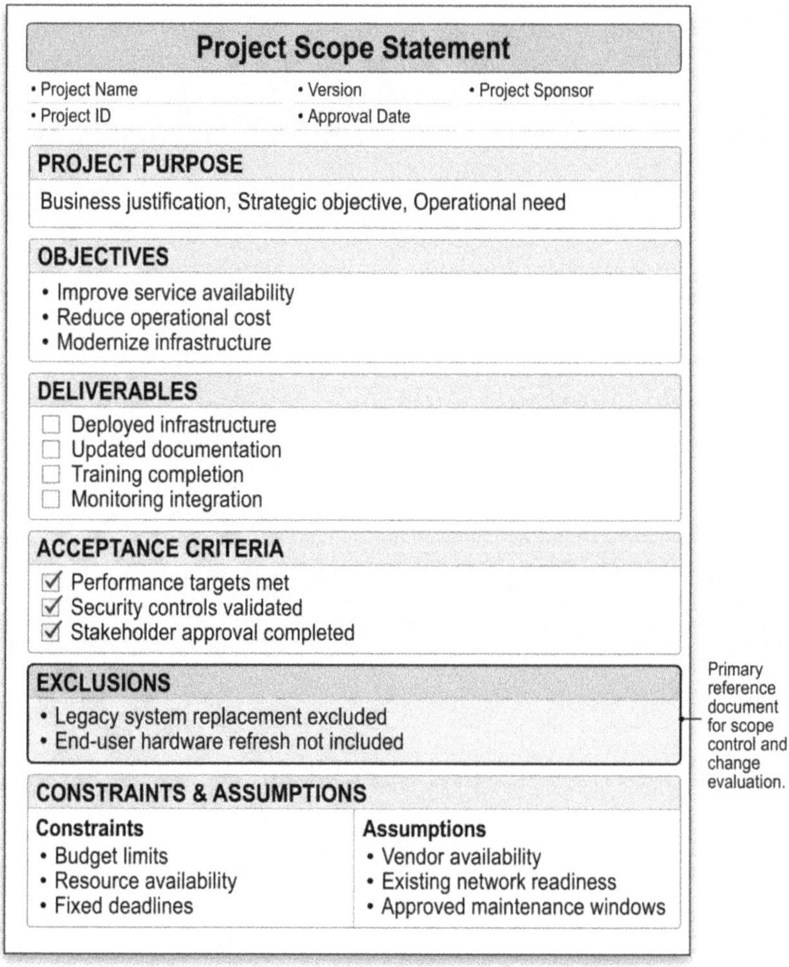

A clear scope statement defines project boundaries, aligns expectations, and supports controlled execution.

Example

Project Purpose: Modernize backup infrastructure to improve recovery times.

Deliverables:

- New Veeam environment
- Replication to DR site
- Retention compliance for 30 days
- **Exclusions:** Legacy tape system decommissioning
- **Constraints:** Ninety-day timeline, two hundred fifty thousand dollar budget, limited maintenance windows

Best Practices

✓ Review scope with all stakeholders before approval

✓ Require formal sign-off to prevent later disputes

✓ Integrate scope into the Work Breakdown Structure (WBS)

✓ Update scope only through formal change control

Establishing SMART Objectives[12]

Objectives convert the project's intent into measurable statements that can be tracked, reported, and used to determine whether the project delivered what it promised. Without measurable objectives, the team can complete all the technical work and still face disagreement about whether the project actually succeeded.

---

[12] The SMART objective framework, widely attributed to management literature dating to George Doran's 1981 work and adopted across project management, HR, and business strategy disciplines, provides a structure for ensuring objectives are clearly defined and trackable. The version used here reflects the common project management adaptation.

Table: SMART Objective Framework

Criterion	Description	Example
Specific	Focused and clearly defined	Migrate all Tier-1 applications to AWS
Measurable	Quantifiable and trackable	Achieve ninety-nine point nine percent uptime
Achievable	Realistic given constraints	Complete within nine months
Relevant	Supports business strategy	Enables rapid global expansion
Time-bound	Has a deadline	Go-live within nine months of charter approval

Figure 16.3: SMART Objective Model Diagram

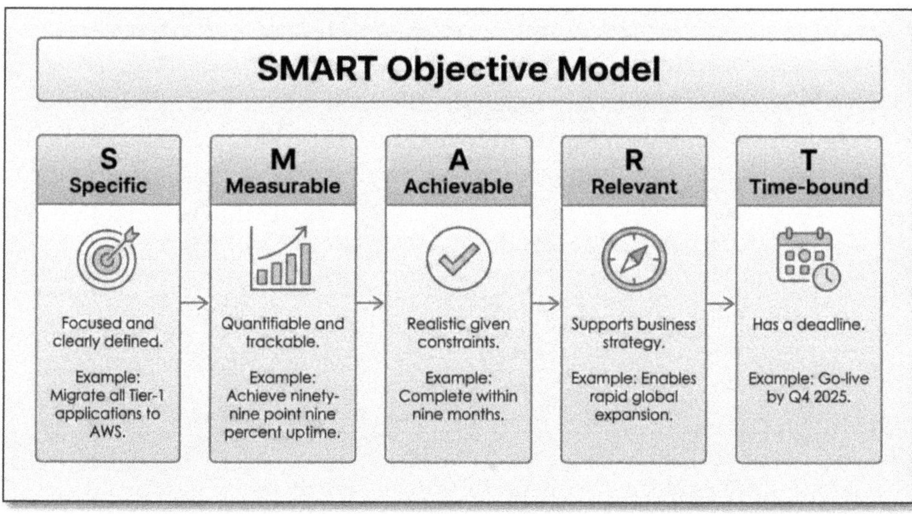

Example

Instead of "improve security," a SMART objective would be:

"Implement multifactor authentication for all VPN users by June 30, with at least ninety-five percent enrollment."

Tips for Defining Objectives

- Link directly to business priorities
- Limit to three to seven objectives to maintain focus
- Review progress throughout the project lifecycle
- Convert objectives into KPIs for dashboards and reporting

Don't confuse "outputs" with "outcomes." "Upgrading the email server" is an output (a technical task). "Reducing email delivery latency by 50%" is an outcome (a business result). When you write objectives, focus on the result the business gets, not the work the IT team does. This small shift makes your project harder to cut during budget reviews because you are selling value, not just hardware.

Managing Scope Creep

Scope creep occurs when additional work enters the project without formal review, approval, or adjustment to cost and schedule. It is one of the most common causes of budget overruns and missed delivery dates, and it often goes unnoticed until the project is already in trouble because each individual addition seems small and reasonable on its own.

Common Causes

- Ambiguous or incomplete scope definition
- Stakeholders requesting "small additions" without understanding impact
- Weak change-management processes
- Misaligned communication between IT and business teams

Prevention Strategies

- ✓ Maintain a formal Scope Management Plan
- ✓ Require all proposed changes to follow defined approval workflows
- ✓ Track cumulative impact of approved changes on cost and timeline
- ✓ Communicate trade-offs clearly when evaluating new requests
- ✓ Conduct periodic scope reviews with the sponsor

Use the "Zero-Sum" rule for late requests. When a stakeholder asks to add a feature mid-project, do not simply ask for more money or time. First, ask, "To fit this in, which existing feature would you like to drop?" This forces the stakeholder to value their own request against the agreed scope. Often, they will realize the new feature isn't important enough to sacrifice something else, and the request will disappear.

Figure 16.4: Scope Creep Prevention Workflow

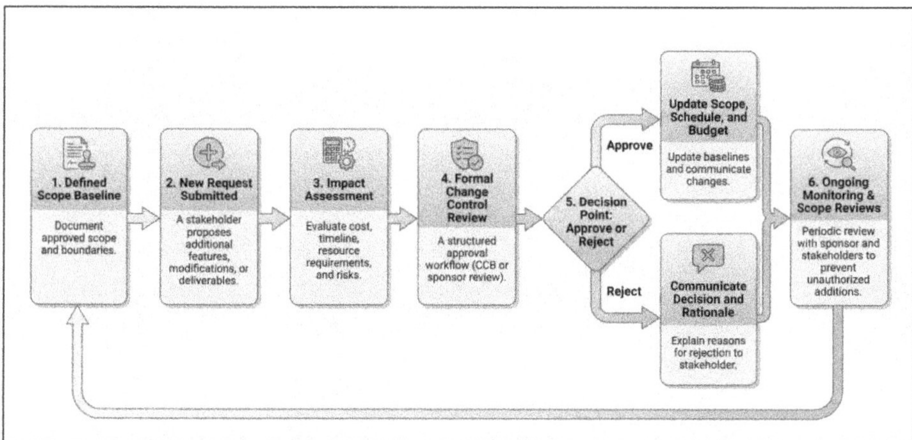

Example

During a software rollout, a business unit requested new dashboards after the design freeze. The project manager documented the request as a change, reviewed the impact, and re-baselined timelines. This avoided disputes later about missed deadlines or incomplete requirements.

How scope creep was controlled (what the project manager actually did)
The project manager stopped the request from entering the build queue informally. They wrote it as a change request with a clear definition of "done", data sources, access roles, and acceptance criteria. They pulled the core leads into a 30 minute impact review to estimate effort, testing, and release risk. Then they gave the sponsor a forced choice: approve a schedule change, approve added funding, or remove an equivalent scope item. The sponsor chose to defer the dashboards to Phase 2, and the team locked the baseline so the original go live date stayed intact.

Building a Strong Business Case

A strong business case connects the IT investment to organizational outcomes that leadership can evaluate against competing priorities. It answers three questions executives ask before approving significant spend: what problem does this solve, what will it cost, and what happens if we do not act? A business case that cannot answer all three clearly will struggle to survive a budget review.

Core Components of a Business Case

1. **Executive Summary:** A concise explanation of the project's purpose, recommended solution, and expected value.
2. **Problem or Opportunity Definition:** Describes current pain points, risks, inefficiencies, or opportunities for improvement.
3. **Proposed Solution:** Outlines the technical and operational approach, supported with high-level architecture or methodology.

4. **Cost–Benefit Analysis:** Quantifies the cost of implementation and the value of expected benefits.
5. **Risk Assessment:** Identifies threats and uncertainties, along with mitigation plans.
6. **Implementation Timeline:** Shows how and when value will be delivered.
7. **Recommendation:** Presents the preferred option with supporting rationale.

Table: Example Business Case

Category	Description	Financial Impact
Executive Summary	Briefly explains the project purpose, recommended solution, and expected business value.	Frames the investment in terms of return, risk reduction, or operational benefit.
Problem or Opportunity	Defines the current pain point, inefficiency, risk, or improvement opportunity.	Shows the cost of inaction, such as downtime, rework, lost productivity, or compliance exposure.
Proposed Solution	Describes the recommended technical and operational approach.	Connects the solution to measurable savings, avoided costs, or revenue protection.
Cost–Benefit Analysis	Compares implementation costs against expected benefits.	Quantifies CapEx, OpEx, savings, payback period, ROI, or total cost of ownership.
Risk Assessment	Identifies major risks, assumptions, dependencies, and mitigation plans.	Estimates potential financial exposure and the value of reducing or controlling that risk.
Implementation Timeline	Shows project phases, milestones, delivery dates, and when benefits begin.	Helps leadership understand cash flow timing, benefit realization, and schedule-related cost risk.
Recommendation	Presents the preferred option and explains why it is the best business decision.	Summarizes the expected financial return, strategic value, and cost of delaying action.

Pro Tip

Always calculate the "Cost of Inaction." Executives often view projects as optional spending, but they view risk as a mandatory fix. If your ROI looks thin, bolster your case by quantifying what happens if you *don't* do the project—fines, security breaches, or extended downtime. It is often easier to get funding to prevent a $100k loss than to generate a $100k gain.

Example

A company proposed a new backup solution and justified it with a simple business case:

- Capital cost: $200,000 for hardware and licensing
- Operational savings: $70,000 per year (reduced manual recovery effort, fewer emergency restores)
- Payback period: about 2.9 years ($200,000 / $70,000)
- Strategic benefit: improved recovery capability and stronger regulatory posture
- Cost of inaction: a single major restore event could create extended downtime and potential compliance exposure that would exceed the project cost

Best Practices

- ✓ Tie benefits directly to business outcomes (revenue protection, uptime, audit readiness), not just IT improvements
- ✓ Combine quantitative value (savings, avoided labor) with risk-based value (downtime avoided, audit findings avoided)
- ✓ Validate assumptions with Finance (rates, labor cost, depreciation model) before presenting
- ✓ Use sensitivity analysis: show best case, expected case, and worst case so leaders see the risk range

Performing Cost–Benefit and ROI Analysis

Cost-benefit analysis and ROI calculations give the business case quantitative credibility. Without them, the case rests on assertions. With them, it becomes a financial argument leadership can evaluate against other investment options, challenge with specific questions, and approve or reject based on evidence rather than preference. The numbers are only half the presentation. The other half is explaining what those numbers mean for operations, risk, and strategic capacity.

Common Financial Metrics

Return on Investment (ROI)

ROI = (Net Benefit / Total Cost) x100

In IT projects, Total Cost should include all implementation costs (CapEx, OpEx impacts, licensing, labor, and training) rather than hardware cost alone. Net Benefit should be limited to measurable, defensible savings or revenue contributions rather than aspirational projections that Finance will challenge.

Net Present Value (NPV)

Net Present Value (NPV) converts future benefits into today's dollars by discounting each year's projected savings or gains at an agreed rate. The result shows whether the investment creates more value than it costs, accounting for the time value of money. NPV is most useful when comparing two or more projects competing for the same budget, because it normalizes projects with different timelines and benefit profiles into a single comparable number.

- Use NPV when benefits extend multiple years and leadership compares projects competing for the same funding
- Pick a discount rate consistent with Finance practices so the analysis matches how the business evaluates investments

Payback Period

Payback is how long it takes for cumulative benefits to equal the upfront investment.

- Payback is easy for non-technical leaders to digest, but it should not be the only metric. A project can have a longer payback and still be worth it if it removes a major risk or supports critical growth

Figure 16.5: Example ROI and Payback Period Comparison Chart

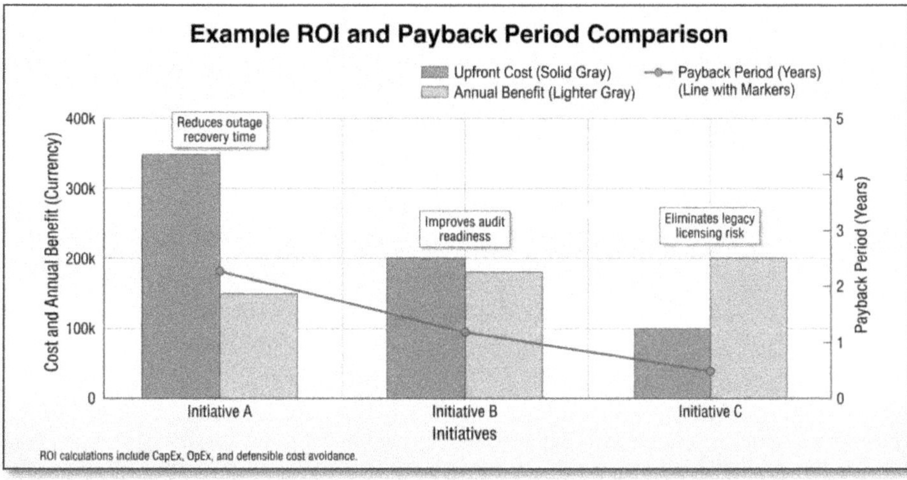

Example

A data center energy optimization effort required $500,000 upfront and produced $125,000 in annual savings.

- Payback: 4 years ($500,000 / $125,000)
- ROI (simple annual): 25 percent per year ($125,000 / $500,000 × 100)
- Long-term savings: Reduced operating expense after payback (savings continue annually)
- Non-financial benefits: Lower carbon footprint, improved sustainability reporting, and better capacity headroom due to reduced power and cooling pressure

Qualitative Benefits (Non-Financial)

Numbers do not capture everything. Many IT investments deliver value that is real but not fully expressed in dollars, especially when the primary driver is risk, reliability, or trust. Common qualitative benefits include:

- Reduced downtime and improved service reliability
- Lower security exposure and improved audit posture
- Faster delivery cycles and higher user satisfaction
- Improved support for strategic initiatives (new products, new markets, faster scaling)

Recommendation

Document both tangible and intangible benefits in the same business case. Many approvals are decided by a combined story: the financial return, the risk you reduce, and the strategic constraint you remove. When possible, tie qualitative benefits to a practical indicator leadership recognizes (audit findings, outage minutes, customer impact, delivery delays) so the discussion stays grounded.

Linking Scope and Business Value

Every project deliverable should be traceable to a measurable business outcome. When that connection is missing, projects are evaluated by whether tasks were completed rather than whether value was delivered. That framing makes IT look like a cost center because outputs are visible but outcomes are not. Linking scope to outcomes changes the conversation: instead of reporting what was built, the team reports what improved.

Example Mapping

The following mapping shows how deliverables can be tied to business outcomes. The improvement values are illustrative and will vary based on organization size, current baseline, and implementation quality. Actual targets should be validated with Finance and business owners during initiation.

Figure: Traceability Matrix – Requirements to Objectives to Outcomes

Deliverable	Business Outcome
Migrate ERP to Azure	Reduce data center costs (typically 15 to 25 percent depending on consolidation scope)
Implement MFA	Lower probability of security breach by seventy percent
Deploy SD-WAN	Improve global latency by forty percent
Automate server builds	Reduce provisioning time from five days to two hours

Case Example

A manufacturing company was funding multiple IT workstreams, but executive updates kept stalling because progress was reported as tasks completed, not outcomes delivered. The program owner rebuilt the plan so every deliverable had a named KPI owner, a baseline, and a target.

How scope was linked to business value (what the program owner actually did)

- Pulled the top business KPIs from Operations and Finance (production uptime, order cycle time, operating margin), then picked a small set of KPIs (typically six to eight) that leadership already reviewed monthly.
- For each project deliverable, wrote a one-line "value statement" and matched it to exactly one primary KPI and, if needed, one secondary KPI to avoid diluted ownership

- Established baselines from the last 90 days (for example, downtime minutes per line, average response time to production tickets), then set target ranges and the measurement window
- Updated the scope document so work that did not move a KPI was either removed, deferred, or rewritten as a prerequisite deliverable with clear dependency labeling
- Built a simple traceability view for reporting: Deliverable, KPI, Baseline, Target, KPI Owner, Expected impact date
- Ran monthly reviews where IT reported progress in KPI movement first, then technical completion second, which made executive reporting clearer and improved accountability across both IT and the plant operations teams

Scope and Objective Validation

Before execution begins, the project team should confirm that scope and objectives have been reviewed and accepted by every group affected by or contributing to the project. Validation is not a sign-off formality. It is the mechanism that surfaces assumptions that were never shared, constraints that were never documented, and dependencies that were never discussed before they become problems during execution.

Validation Checklist

- Are deliverables aligned with organizational strategy?
- Are success criteria objectively measurable?
- Are exclusions and assumptions clearly documented?
- Have all affected departments reviewed and approved the scope?
- Has the sponsor formally approved the business case and charter?

Case Example

A major network refresh project slipped early because scope validation only included IT, Procurement, and the vendor. HR and Facilities were treated as "notify later," which backfired once the work required contractor onboarding, badging, escort rules, and after-hours access.

How scope and objectives were validated (what the project owner actually did)
The project owner rebuilt the stakeholder list and made HR and Facilities required approvers for any work involving physical access, shift impacts, or contractor onboarding. They ran a formal scope validation review where deliverables, success criteria, exclusions, and assumptions were reviewed line by line, and each department's constraints were captured as written requirements. Facilities inputs were converted into schedule dependencies such as power work windows, escort availability, and safety restrictions, while HR inputs were converted into onboarding lead times for background checks, badge issuance, and required training. The owner then updated the schedule with confirmed access windows and added a governance gate so no site work could begin until HR onboarding and Facilities access approvals were complete. Finally, they documented ownership in the scope statement (who approves access, who provides escorts, who owns outage communications) and obtained sign-off, preventing later disputes about responsibilities or "surprise" constraints.

Common Pitfalls in Scope and Business Case Definition

Even experienced teams can fall into common traps during early project definition. Recognizing these pitfalls early helps avoid downstream issues.

Frequent Pitfalls

1. **Overly Broad Objectives:** Objectives such as "improve system performance" lack measurable detail.
2. **Ignoring Dependencies:** Failing to consider vendor, compliance, or facilities constraints leads to unrealistic timelines.
3. **Underestimating Costs:** Teams often overlook licensing, support contracts, integration work, or migration complexity.
4. **Unclear Ownership:** Unassigned deliverables lead to confusion, misalignment, and accountability issues.
5. **Weak Executive Sponsorship:** Projects without strong business backing struggle to maintain momentum or secure resources.

Mitigation Techniques

1. Conduct peer reviews of scope and business case documents.
2. Use lessons learned and templates from previous similar projects.
3. Engage Finance, Security, and Compliance early.
4. Apply version control for all scope modifications.
5. Validate assumptions with subject matter experts.

What This Means in Practice

- Scope is a control, not just a description. A scope statement that defines inclusions without explicitly listing exclusions is incomplete. Exclusions are what prevent the project from absorbing work it was never resourced to deliver
- SMART objectives bridge the business problem and the project plan. Without them, the team may deliver technically while leadership still questions whether the investment worked
- A business case that cannot answer "what happens if we do not act?" is missing one of its strongest elements. Cost of inaction is often more compelling than ROI for initiatives that reduce risk or prevent compliance exposure
- The WBS converts deliverables into executable work. Its value is not the hierarchy itself, but the discipline it enforces: every work package has an owner, prerequisites, and defined acceptance conditions before the project can claim completion
- Scope validation turns implicit assumptions into explicit requirements. Groups missed during validation often appear during execution with constraints that stall work, force schedule changes, and damage trust between IT and the business
- Business value mapping keeps IT reporting connected to what leadership measures. Projects that report only task completion lose the audience. Projects that report KPI movement earn support for the next initiative

Figure 16.6: Summary Diagram - From Scope Definition to Business Justification Flow

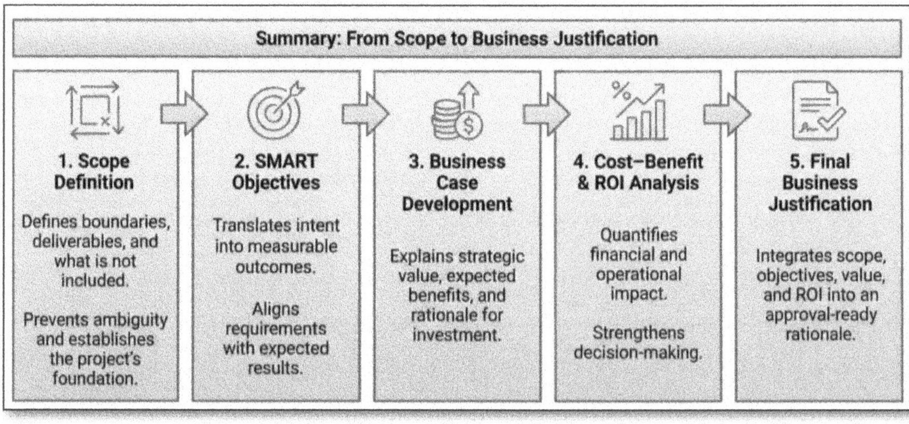

Chapter 17

BUILDING THE FOUNDATION: WHERE THIS BOOK ENDS AND WHAT COMES NEXT

Most IT management books end where the real work begins. They describe frameworks, list best practices, and present models that look clean on paper, then leave the reader to figure out how to use any of it when the environment is messy, the team is short-staffed, and leadership wants answers by Friday.

This book was written differently. The goal was not to give you a catalog of concepts but to give you the operational vocabulary, judgment frameworks, and leadership habits that make the difference between an IT manager who reacts to problems and one who builds an environment stable enough to prevent most of them.

Chapter by chapter, the book moved from leadership and governance through infrastructure, security, cloud, networking, data center operations, monitoring, service management, continuity planning, and project delivery. That sequence was not arbitrary. Each layer builds on the one before it. You cannot govern what you do not understand. You cannot improve what you do not measure. You cannot lead what you have not structured. The chapters were ordered to reflect how operational maturity actually develops, not how a textbook would organize topics.

This closing chapter does three things. It synthesizes the arc of the book so the connections between chapters are explicit. It gives you a practical starting point for applying what you have read. And it describes what this book does not cover, which is the honest setup for the second volume in this series.

How the Chapters Connect

The book is organized in four layers that build on each other. Understanding how they fit together helps you apply any individual chapter more effectively.

Layer one: Leadership and organizational foundation (Chapters 1 through 4)

The first four chapters established the non-negotiable foundation. Chapter 1 defined what modern IT management actually requires: not technical execution, but leadership, strategic alignment, and the ability to translate technology decisions into business outcomes. Chapter 2 extended that into alignment, showing how IT strategy connects to business objectives and why misalignment is the most common reason technology investments underdeliver. Chapter 3 addressed the team itself, how high-performing IT teams are built, led, and sustained, and why the people layer determines the ceiling on everything else. Chapter 4 closed the foundation with governance, the decision structure that keeps the organization consistent, accountable, and audit-ready as it scales.

These four chapters are the ones most often skipped in technical handbooks. They are also the ones that most directly determine whether the technical content in the rest of the book actually works in practice. Technology that is governed well, led well, and aligned to the business creates compounding returns. Technology that is not creates compounding debt.

Layer two: Infrastructure and operational disciplines (Chapters 5 through 9)

Chapters 5 through 9 covered the physical and logical infrastructure that IT runs on: servers, storage, networking, data centers, cloud and virtualization, and monitoring. These chapters were written for IT managers who need enough architectural and operational literacy to govern and lead technical teams, evaluate vendor claims, make sound tradeoff decisions, and hold engineers accountable for the environments they build and maintain.

The thread connecting these chapters is operational discipline. Architecture diagrams describe intent. Monitoring, documentation, change control, capacity planning, and performance optimization are what keep that intent aligned with reality as the environment grows and changes. Chapter 9, which covered monitoring and performance management, is the chapter that ties the operational layer together. Without measurement, everything else in layers one and two is managed by assumption.

Layer three: Security, continuity, and governance (Chapters 10 and 12)

Chapter 10 addressed security, compliance, and risk management as an integrated operational discipline, not a separate function. Chapter 12 extended that into business continuity and disaster recovery, covering how organizations maintain operational capability when infrastructure fails, attackers succeed, or external events disrupt normal operations.

The connection between these chapters and the rest of the book is intentional. Security and continuity are not add-ons to a well-run IT environment. They are properties of one. An environment with strong change control, well-documented architecture, tested runbooks, and clear ownership is also an environment that responds faster to incidents, contains breaches more effectively, and recovers from disruptions with less chaos. The chapters in layer two create the conditions that make layer three achievable.

Layer four: Service management and project delivery (Chapters 11, 13, 14, 15, and 16)

The final layer addressed how work gets delivered and managed across its lifecycle. Chapter 11 covered ITSM: incident, problem, and change management as the operational processes that keep services stable and improving. Chapters 13 through 16 covered IT project management: the lifecycle, methodology selection, planning, initiation, scope definition, and business case development.

This layer is where the management disciplines from layers one through three are applied to specific delivery contexts. A project manager who understands governance, infrastructure, security, and service management makes better decisions at every stage of delivery than one who knows only project management methodology. The chapters in this layer were written with that integration in mind.

What You Should Do First

Reading this book cover to cover gives you the full picture. Applying it requires prioritization, because no organization improves everything at once, and attempting to do so is one of the most reliable ways to improve nothing.

The most practical starting point is an honest assessment of where your current environment sits across the four layers described above. The following questions are not a formal audit instrument. They are the questions that experienced IT leaders ask when they take over a new environment or step back to evaluate one they have been running for a while.

On leadership and governance:

- Does your team understand how the work they do connects to business outcomes, or do they measure themselves by uptime and ticket counts?
- Are decision rights clear: who approves spend, who accepts risk, who can override priorities, and who owns each service end to end?
- Is governance producing decisions and reducing repeated debates, or is it producing reports and creating overhead?

On infrastructure and operations:

- Can any qualified engineer on your team execute a standard change, recover a service, and operate the environment during an incident without needing a specific expert online?
- Is your documentation current enough to be used under pressure, or does it describe a state of the environment that no longer exists?
- Are your monitoring thresholds tied to service-level outcomes, or to hardware metrics that may show green while users are experiencing problems?

On security and continuity:

- Does your risk register reflect the current environment and get reviewed on a defined cadence, or was it built during a compliance exercise and not touched since?
- Have your recovery plans been tested under conditions that resemble a real event, or have they only been reviewed in tabletop exercises where everyone knows the answers in advance?
- Do your vendors have documented, tested, and contractually required continuity capabilities, or are you assuming their resilience without evidence?

On service management and project delivery:

- Are incidents being reviewed for root cause and producing corrective actions that close, or are post-incident reviews producing documentation that nobody acts on?
- Are your projects starting with validated scope, approved business cases, and named decision authority, or are they starting with enthusiasm and good intentions?
- Is your change process protecting the environment from self-inflicted outages, or has it become either a rubber stamp or a bottleneck that teams route around?

The gaps that produce the most discomfort in answering these questions are the right places to start. Address the foundation first. A governance or leadership gap in layer one will limit the return from every investment in layers two through four. An infrastructure or monitoring gap in layer two will make security and continuity in layer three significantly harder to achieve. The layers are not independent.

Using This Book as an Ongoing Reference

This book was designed to be read once and returned to often. Each chapter is self-contained enough to serve as a reference for a specific topic, and the case examples and

GLOSSARY

Key Terms in IT Management, Infrastructure, Security, and Project Delivery

A note on this glossary

Terms are listed alphabetically. Where a term has a specific meaning in a particular framework (ITIL, NIST, PMI, ISO), that context is noted. Definitions are written for operational clarity, not academic completeness. Cross-references to related terms are included where the distinction between two terms matters in practice.

A

Agile A family of iterative software and project delivery frameworks built on the principles of the Agile Manifesto (2001). Agile approaches prioritize working output, continuous feedback, and adaptation over comprehensive upfront planning. Common Agile frameworks include Scrum, Kanban, and Extreme Programming. See also: *Scrum, SAFe, Hybrid methodology.*

AIOps (Artificial Intelligence for IT Operations) The application of machine learning and data analytics to IT operations data, including logs, metrics, events, and traces, to automate anomaly detection, correlate alerts, predict failures, and reduce the volume of actionable incidents requiring human triage. AIOps platforms are not a substitute for well-designed monitoring; they require accurate, structured telemetry to function effectively.

Ansible An open-source automation platform that uses agent-free, YAML-based playbooks to automate configuration management, application deployment, and infrastructure provisioning across servers and network devices. Commonly used for repeatable, version-controlled infrastructure changes.

Asynchronous replication A data replication method where writes are committed to the primary system first and transferred to the secondary system with a defined delay. Suitable for long-distance replication where latency and bandwidth constraints make synchronous replication impractical. Introduces a replication lag, meaning the secondary copy may not reflect the most recent writes at the time of a failure. See also: *Synchronous replication, Replication.*

Automatic Transfer Switch (ATS) An electrical device that automatically switches a load between two power sources, typically utility power and generator power, without interrupting the downstream equipment. A critical component in data center power redundancy design. ATS performance under load is one of the most important and most commonly untested elements of a power redundancy validation program.

Availability The proportion of time a system or service is operational and accessible to users, typically expressed as a percentage. Availability is a function of both reliability (how often failures occur) and recoverability (how quickly service is restored after a failure). Common targets include 99.9% (approximately 8.7 hours of downtime per year) and 99.99% (approximately 52 minutes per year).

B

Balanced Scorecard A performance management framework that tracks organizational objectives across multiple dimensions, typically financial, customer, internal process, and learning and growth. In IT management, balanced scorecards are used to present IT performance in terms that connect technical metrics to business outcomes rather than reporting on infrastructure health alone.

Bare-metal hypervisor A Type 1 hypervisor that runs directly on physical hardware without a host operating system. Examples include VMware ESXi, Microsoft Hyper-V, and KVM. Bare-metal hypervisors offer better performance and isolation than hosted hypervisors and are the standard for enterprise virtualization platforms. See also: *Hypervisor.*

Bastion host A hardened server positioned at the boundary between a trusted internal network and an untrusted external network, used as the single entry point for administrative access to internal systems. Bastion hosts reduce attack surface by concentrating and logging privileged access through a controlled, auditable path.

BIA (Business Impact Analysis) A structured assessment that identifies an organization's critical business functions, quantifies the operational and financial impact of disruptions to those functions, and defines recovery objectives including Maximum Tolerable Downtime (MTD), Recovery Time Objective (RTO), and Recovery Point Objective (RPO). The BIA is the foundational input to business continuity and disaster recovery planning. See also: *RTO, RPO, MTD.*

Blast radius The scope of impact from a failure, security incident, or misconfiguration. A key design principle in resilient architecture and security is to minimize blast radius by isolating components, segmenting networks, and limiting the lateral reach of any single failure or breach. Used informally across infrastructure, security, and incident management contexts.

Budget variance The difference between planned and actual spend at a point in time. Positive variance means spending is below plan; negative variance means spending exceeds plan. Budget variance tracking is a standard component of project financial governance and portfolio management reporting.

Business case A structured document that justifies a project or investment by connecting it to measurable organizational value. A strong business case includes a problem statement, options analysis, cost-benefit analysis, risk assessment, and a recommendation. It supports objective executive decision-making rather than advocacy for a predetermined solution. See also: *ROI, NPV, Payback period.*

Business continuity (BC) The organizational capability to continue delivering critical business functions during and after a disruptive event. Business continuity planning addresses people, processes, facilities, and technology, and is broader in scope than disaster recovery, which focuses specifically on IT system restoration. See also: *Disaster recovery, BIA.*

C

CAB (Change Advisory Board) A governance body responsible for reviewing, evaluating, and approving or deferring changes to IT production systems. The CAB assesses risk, evaluates implementation readiness, and coordinates scheduling to minimize service disruption. Not all changes require full CAB review; standard pre-approved changes typically bypass this process. See also: *Change management, Standard change, Emergency change.*

Capacity planning The discipline of forecasting future resource requirements across compute, storage, and network to ensure systems can meet anticipated demand without over-provisioning. Effective capacity planning combines historical utilization data, growth trend analysis, and business roadmap inputs to identify saturation points and procurement decision dates before they become emergencies.

CapEx (Capital Expenditure) Spending on long-lived physical or intangible assets that are capitalized on the balance sheet and depreciated over time. In IT, CapEx typically includes hardware purchases, software licenses, and data center construction. Contrasted with OpEx. See also: *OpEx.*

Change management (ITSM) The ITSM process that governs how additions, modifications, and removals to IT systems are planned, reviewed, approved, implemented, and verified. Change management exists to prevent uncontrolled modifications from introducing service instability. In ITIL, change types are categorized as standard, normal, and emergency. See also: *CAB, ITIL, Standard change, Emergency change.*

Change management (organizational) The discipline of planning and managing the human side of organizational transitions, including technology rollouts, process changes, and structural reorganization. Distinct from ITSM change management, which governs technical modifications. Organizational change management addresses adoption, communication, training, and resistance.

CMDB (Configuration Management Database) A repository that stores records of IT assets (configuration items) and their relationships to each other and to business services. The CMDB supports incident management, change impact assessment, problem investigation, and asset lifecycle tracking. Its value depends on the accuracy and currency of its records, which degrade without disciplined maintenance processes.

COBIT (Control Objectives for Information and Related Technology) An IT governance and management framework developed by ISACA. COBIT provides a structured approach to aligning IT with business goals, managing risk, and ensuring regulatory compliance. It separates governance (evaluate, direct, monitor) from management (plan, build, deliver, operate) and is widely used in regulated industries and audit-intensive environments.

Cold site A disaster recovery facility that provides basic physical infrastructure (power, space, connectivity) but no pre-installed IT equipment. Recovery at a cold site requires procuring, installing, and configuring systems after a disaster declaration, resulting in the longest recovery times of the standard DR site models. See also: *Warm site, Hot site, Cloud DR.*

Compliance The state of meeting the requirements defined by applicable laws, regulations, contractual obligations, or internal policies. IT compliance involves implementing and evidencing controls that satisfy those requirements. Compliance is necessary but not sufficient for security; an organization can be compliant and still be vulnerable if controls are designed around audit evidence rather than actual risk reduction.

Configuration drift The gradual divergence of a system's actual configuration from its approved baseline, typically caused by manual changes, failed updates, or undocumented modifications. Configuration drift creates unpredictable behavior, complicates troubleshooting, and introduces security exposure. Automated configuration compliance scanning and Infrastructure as Code practices are the primary tools for detecting and preventing drift.

Container A lightweight, portable runtime unit that packages an application and its dependencies together so it behaves consistently across development, test, and production environments. Containers share the host operating system kernel, unlike virtual machines which each run a full guest OS. This makes containers faster to start and more resource-efficient, but requires disciplined image management, runtime security, and orchestration. See also: *Docker, Kubernetes.*

Continuous improvement An ongoing operational discipline of regularly reviewing processes, metrics, and outcomes to identify and implement incremental improvements. In ITSM, continuous improvement is formalized as Continual Service Improvement (CSI). In broader IT management, it involves scheduled retrospectives, metric-driven reviews, and structured improvement backlogs that are tracked to completion rather than discussed and forgotten.

CRAC (Computer Room Air Conditioning) Traditional perimeter cooling units used in data centers to supply chilled air, typically through raised floors. CRAC units provide broad room-level cooling and are common in legacy data center environments. In high-density deployments, CRAC-only cooling is often insufficient and is supplemented or replaced by in-row cooling or liquid cooling approaches.

CVSS (Common Vulnerability Scoring System) A standardized framework maintained by FIRST (Forum of Incident Response and Security Teams) for rating the severity of security vulnerabilities. CVSS scores range from 0 to 10 and incorporate factors including attack vector, complexity, privileges required, user interaction, and potential impact. Scores are used to prioritize remediation but should be combined with exposure and asset criticality assessments rather than used as the sole prioritization criterion.

D

Data classification The process of categorizing data based on its sensitivity, regulatory requirements, and business value, and applying appropriate controls to each category. Common classification tiers include public, internal, confidential, and restricted. Data classification is a prerequisite for storage governance, access control design, and data loss prevention.

Deduplication A storage optimization method that identifies and eliminates duplicate data blocks or files so identical data is stored only once. References replace duplicate copies, significantly reducing storage consumption in environments with repetitive datasets such as backup repositories, virtual machine infrastructure, and file-sharing systems. The tradeoff is processing overhead during data ingestion. See also: *Tiering*, *Snapshots*.

Defense in depth A security architecture principle that layers multiple independent controls so the failure of any single control does not result in a complete compromise. Controls span perimeter security, network segmentation, endpoint protection, identity and access management, data encryption, and monitoring. The goal is to increase the cost and complexity of a successful attack and limit the blast radius of any breach.

DevOps A set of cultural practices and technical disciplines that integrate software development and IT operations to shorten delivery cycles, improve deployment frequency, and increase the reliability of releases. Core DevOps practices include continuous integration, continuous delivery, infrastructure as code, automated testing, and blameless post-incident review. DevOps is as much an organizational model as a technical approach.

Disaster recovery (DR) The IT-specific discipline of restoring systems, applications, and data after a disruptive event. DR planning defines recovery objectives (RTO and RPO), selects infrastructure models (hot, warm, cold, cloud), and documents the procedures for failing over and recovering. DR is a component of the broader business continuity program. See also: *Business continuity*, *RTO*, *RPO*, *Hot site*.

Docker An open-source platform for building, packaging, and running containers. Docker standardized the container image format and tooling, making containers widely accessible for development and deployment workflows. In enterprise environments, container runtime has increasingly moved to alternatives such as containerd and Podman, but Docker remains the dominant tool for image building. See also: *Container, Kubernetes.*

E

EDR (Endpoint Detection and Response) Security software deployed on endpoint devices (laptops, servers, workstations) that monitors behavior in real time, detects suspicious activity, and supports investigation and response. EDR goes beyond traditional antivirus by providing visibility into process execution, file changes, network connections, and lateral movement indicators. EDR coverage and health is a standard security KPI in mature organizations.

Emergency change A change to an IT system that is required urgently to resolve a critical failure or prevent imminent service impact. Emergency changes bypass standard approval timelines but must be reviewed and documented retrospectively to maintain governance integrity. Overuse of the emergency change category is a common governance failure that signals inadequate planning discipline rather than genuine emergencies.

Escalation The process of raising an issue to a higher level of authority or expertise when the current responder cannot resolve it within defined time or capability thresholds. Effective escalation paths are defined in advance, tested during drills and exercises, and embedded in incident runbooks and on-call procedures. Unclear escalation paths are one of the most common causes of extended incident duration.

F

Failover The process of switching workloads, traffic, or services from a failed or degraded primary system to a secondary system. Failover may be automatic (triggered by health check failure) or manual (triggered by an operator decision). Failover testing, not just failover design, is what validates whether a recovery architecture actually works under real conditions.

Fault tolerance The ability of a system to continue operating correctly in the presence of one or more component failures. Fault-tolerant systems are designed so that no single failure interrupts service, typically through full redundancy of all critical components. Distinguished from high availability, which may tolerate brief interruptions during failover. See also: *High availability, Redundancy.*

Firewall A network security control that monitors and filters traffic between network segments based on defined rules. Firewalls may be hardware-based, software-based, or cloud-delivered, and range from simple packet filters to next-generation platforms with application awareness, intrusion prevention, and encrypted traffic inspection. Firewall rule management is a common area of configuration drift and audit finding.

Forward Schedule of Changes (FSC) A calendar maintained by the change management process that shows all approved and planned changes, their implementation windows, and their potential service impact. The FSC is used to identify conflicts between changes, protect critical business periods, and coordinate cross-team dependencies before changes are executed.

G

GDPR (General Data Protection Regulation) A European Union regulation governing the collection, processing, storage, and transfer of personal data belonging to EU residents. GDPR applies to any organization handling EU resident data regardless of geographic location and establishes strong individual rights including consent, erasure, and data portability. Non-compliance carries significant financial penalties. See also: *HIPAA, PCI DSS, Compliance.*

Governance The structure of policies, decision rights, oversight mechanisms, and accountability frameworks that guide how an organization plans, prioritizes, and controls its technology investments and operations. IT governance connects strategy to execution, ensures decisions are made with appropriate authority, and provides the transparency needed for audit and regulatory compliance. See also: *COBIT, IT Steering Committee.*

GRC (Governance, Risk, and Compliance) A consolidated approach to managing governance structures, risk programs, and compliance obligations within a single integrated framework or platform. GRC platforms centralize policy management, control evidence, risk registers, audit workflows, and reporting to reduce duplication and improve visibility across all three disciplines.

H

High availability (HA) An infrastructure design approach that minimizes service downtime by eliminating or reducing the impact of individual component failures. High availability typically involves redundant hardware, clustering, load balancing, and automated failover. Availability targets are expressed as a percentage of uptime and should be tied to defined SLA commitments. See also: *Fault tolerance, Redundancy, SLA.*

HIPAA (Health Insurance Portability and Accountability Act) A US federal regulation governing how healthcare organizations and their business associates protect, access, transmit, and audit protected health information (PHI). The HIPAA Security Rule defines technical safeguards for electronic PHI. The Privacy Rule governs how PHI may be used and disclosed. See also: *GDPR, PCI DSS, Compliance.*

Hot aisle / Cold aisle containment A data center airflow management design that physically separates server intake air (cold aisles) from exhaust air (hot aisles) to improve cooling efficiency, reduce hotspots, and enable higher rack densities. Containment prevents hot and cold air from mixing, reducing the volume of air that cooling systems must condition and improving Power Usage Effectiveness (PUE). See also: *PUE, CRAC.*

Hot site A fully operational disaster recovery facility with live infrastructure, current data replication, and automated failover capability. Hot sites support the shortest recovery time objectives and are appropriate for Tier-1 services with minimal tolerable downtime. The highest-cost DR infrastructure model. See also: *Warm site, Cold site, Cloud DR.*

Hybrid cloud An IT deployment model that combines on-premises infrastructure with public cloud resources, connected through network links and managed through a common governance framework. Hybrid cloud allows organizations to place workloads based on performance, compliance, cost, and data sovereignty requirements. Effective hybrid cloud management requires consistent identity, monitoring, and security policies across both environments.

Hybrid methodology A project delivery approach that combines elements of predictive (Waterfall) and adaptive (Agile) methods. Typically, requirements, architecture, and governance follow a structured predictive model, while development or configuration work executes in iterative cycles. Hybrid is well-suited to regulated environments that require formal documentation and approvals alongside iterative delivery. See also: *Waterfall, Agile, SAFe*.

Hypervisor Software that enables multiple virtual machines to run on a single physical host by managing the allocation of CPU, memory, storage, and network resources among them. Type 1 (bare-metal) hypervisors run directly on hardware; Type 2 (hosted) hypervisors run on top of a host operating system. Examples include VMware ESXi (Type 1), Microsoft Hyper-V (Type 1), and VirtualBox (Type 2). See also: *Virtual machine, Virtualization*.

I

IaC (Infrastructure as Code) The practice of defining and provisioning infrastructure through machine-readable configuration files rather than manual processes or interactive tools. IaC enables repeatable, version-controlled infrastructure deployments that reduce configuration drift and improve auditability. Common tools include Terraform, Ansible, Chef, Puppet, and PowerShell DSC. See also: *Configuration drift, Ansible, Terraform*.

IAM (Identity and Access Management) The set of policies, processes, and technologies used to manage digital identities and control access to systems, applications, and data. IAM encompasses authentication (verifying who a user is), authorization (determining what they can access), privileged access management, and periodic access reviews. Weak IAM is one of the most common root causes of security incidents.

Incident An unplanned interruption or degradation that affects an IT service's ability to deliver its expected performance. Incidents are managed through the Incident Management process, which prioritizes rapid service restoration over root cause investigation. Distinguished from a problem, which is the underlying cause of one or more incidents. See also: *Incident management, Problem, MTTR.*

Incident management The ITSM process responsible for detecting, logging, classifying, prioritizing, investigating, resolving, and closing incidents. The primary objective of incident management is to restore normal service operation as quickly as possible while minimizing business impact. See also: *ITIL, Problem management, Change management.*

ISO 22301 The international standard for business continuity management systems, published by the International Organization for Standardization. ISO 22301 defines requirements for planning, establishing, implementing, operating, monitoring, reviewing, and improving a documented BC management system. Certification requires independent audit and verification.

ISO/IEC 27001 The international standard for information security management systems (ISMS), published by ISO and IEC. ISO 27001 defines requirements for establishing, implementing, maintaining, and improving an ISMS using a risk-based approach. Controls are selected based on assessed risk rather than applied uniformly. Widely adopted across industries as a baseline for security governance. See also: *NIST SP 800-53, SOC 2.*

ITIL (Information Technology Infrastructure Library) A framework of best practices for IT service management, currently maintained by Axelos in its fourth major version (ITIL 4). ITIL provides a common vocabulary, defined process roles, and structured workflows for managing services across their lifecycle. Core ITIL processes covered in this book include incident management, problem management, change management, and continual service improvement. See also: *ITSM, CAB, Problem management.*

ITSM (IT Service Management) The discipline of designing, delivering, supporting, and improving IT services to meet defined business outcomes. ITSM frames technology as a set of services rather than a collection of technical components, and uses structured processes, defined roles, and measurable SLAs to create consistent and accountable service delivery. See also: *ITIL, Service desk, SLA.*

K

Kanban An Agile workflow management method that uses a visual board to represent work in progress and applies work-in-progress (WIP) limits to improve flow efficiency. Unlike Scrum, Kanban does not use fixed-length sprints; work is pulled as capacity allows. Particularly suited to operational teams managing continuous demand rather than time-boxed delivery cycles. See also: *Agile, Scrum.*

KEDB (Known Error Database) A repository maintained by the Problem Management process that documents identified problems, their root causes, known workarounds, and resolution status. The KEDB allows service desk and resolver teams to apply known workarounds quickly during incidents while permanent fixes are in progress, reducing resolution time for recurring issues. See also: *Problem management.*

KPI (Key Performance Indicator) A measurable value that demonstrates how effectively an organization or team is achieving a defined objective. In IT management, KPIs connect technical operational metrics (MTTR, patch compliance, change success rate) to business outcomes (service availability, customer impact, cost efficiency). Effective KPIs are specific, measurable, and reviewed on a consistent cadence.

Kubernetes An open-source container orchestration platform that automates the scheduling, scaling, deployment, and management of containerized applications. Kubernetes manages how containers are distributed across nodes, how services discover each other, how deployments are rolled out and rolled back, and how the cluster maintains desired state when individual components fail. The dominant platform for running containers in production at scale. See also: *Container, Docker.*

L

LACP (Link Aggregation Control Protocol) A network protocol that combines multiple physical network links between two devices into a single logical link to increase bandwidth and provide redundancy. LACP is commonly used in data center switching to improve both throughput and fault tolerance at the access and distribution layers.

Landing zone A pre-configured cloud environment that establishes baseline governance, security, networking, and identity controls before workloads are deployed. Landing zones provide guardrails that ensure new deployments conform to organizational standards without requiring manual review of every provisioning request. Common in enterprise cloud adoption programs.

Lateral movement A technique used by attackers to progressively move through a network after an initial compromise, accessing additional systems and escalating privileges. Limiting lateral movement is a core objective of network segmentation, zero trust architecture, and endpoint detection capabilities. See also: *Zero Trust, Micro-segmentation.*

Lean Portfolio Management A SAFe (Scaled Agile Framework) practice that aligns work selection and funding decisions to business priorities using lightweight governance. Lean Portfolio Management connects strategy to execution by maintaining a portfolio backlog, applying value-based prioritization, and funding value streams rather than individual projects. See also: *SAFe.*

M

Micro-segmentation A security architecture approach that divides a network into very small, isolated segments with granular access controls between them. Unlike traditional perimeter-based segmentation, micro-segmentation limits lateral movement inside the network, so a compromised endpoint cannot easily reach other systems. Implemented through software-defined networking, next-generation firewalls, or host-based controls. See also: *Lateral movement, Zero Trust.*

MPLS (Multiprotocol Label Switching) A WAN technology that routes network traffic using short path labels rather than long network addresses. MPLS provides strong reliability, traffic prioritization, and consistent performance, making it well-suited for enterprise WAN environments. Higher cost and lower flexibility compared to SD-WAN and broadband alternatives make it less common in modern, cloud-first architectures. See also: *SD-WAN.*

MTBF (Mean Time Between Failures) A reliability metric representing the average time a system or component operates between failures. Used in infrastructure and data center contexts to assess the reliability of hardware components and plan preventive maintenance schedules.

MTD (Maximum Tolerable Downtime) The longest period a business function can be unavailable before the impact reaches an unacceptable level for the organization. MTD is determined by business owners, not IT, and sets the upper boundary that any RTO target must stay within. An RTO greater than or equal to the MTD means the recovery plan cannot meet the business requirement. See also: *RTO, RPO, BIA.*

MTTR (Mean Time to Repair or Restore) A metric measuring the average time from incident detection to service restoration. MTTR is a primary indicator of incident management effectiveness and is used to track improvement trends over time. Lower MTTR reflects faster detection, better runbooks, clearer ownership, and more effective escalation paths. See also: *Incident management, KPI.*

Multi-cloud A deployment model in which an organization uses services from more than one public cloud provider simultaneously. Multi-cloud may be adopted to access provider-specific capabilities, reduce dependency on a single vendor, meet regional availability requirements, or optimize cost. It adds governance complexity and requires consistent identity, monitoring, and security controls across providers. See also: *Hybrid cloud.*

N

NaaS (Network as a Service) A cloud-based consumption model for networking capabilities in which organizations subscribe to networking functions rather than owning and managing physical network hardware. NaaS suits distributed branch environments, temporary deployments, or organizations with limited staff for hardware management. Requires careful evaluation of performance guarantees, data sovereignty, and exit flexibility.

NAC (Network Access Control) A security mechanism that evaluates the compliance and identity posture of devices before granting them access to the network. NAC checks may include OS version, patch level, endpoint protection status, and certificate posture. Non-compliant devices are typically redirected to a quarantine network where remediation is possible without exposing internal resources. See also: *Zero Trust.*

NIST SP 800-34 A NIST publication providing contingency planning guidance for federal information systems. Its risk-tiered approach to recovery planning is widely adapted by regulated industries and private sector organizations as a structured methodology for developing and maintaining IT disaster recovery and business continuity plans.

NIST SP 800-53 A comprehensive catalog of security and privacy controls published by the National Institute of Standards and Technology, used by federal agencies and widely adopted in regulated industries. Controls are organized into families covering access control, incident response, system integrity, risk assessment, and more than a dozen other domains. See also: *ISO/IEC 27001, SOC 2.*

NPV (Net Present Value) A financial metric that calculates the value of a future stream of benefits in today's dollars by discounting each period's projected benefit at an agreed rate and subtracting the initial investment. NPV is used to compare projects with different timelines and benefit profiles on a consistent basis. A positive NPV indicates the investment is expected to create more value than it costs. See also: *ROI, Payback period, Business case.*

O

Observability The capacity to understand what is happening inside a system by analyzing the signals it produces externally, including metrics, logs, and traces. Observability goes beyond traditional monitoring by enabling teams to diagnose novel failure modes without requiring prior knowledge of what specifically to look for. Often described through the three pillars of metrics, logs, and distributed traces.

On-call rotation A schedule that assigns responsibility for responding to alerts and incidents outside normal working hours to team members in a defined sequence. Effective on-call rotations distribute load fairly, include primary and backup coverage, define clear escalation paths, and are reviewed regularly to prevent burnout from concentrated load on specific individuals.

OpEx (Operating Expenditure) Ongoing costs for running IT systems and services, including cloud consumption, software subscriptions, support contracts, and staff. OpEx is expensed in the period it is incurred rather than capitalized. Cloud adoption often shifts spending from CapEx (hardware) to OpEx (consumption), which has financial reporting implications that should be validated with Finance before major architectural decisions. See also: *CapEx.*

P

Patch management The operational discipline of identifying, evaluating, testing, and applying software updates to operating systems, applications, firmware, and network devices to address known vulnerabilities. Effective patch management requires defined severity-based SLAs, automated compliance tracking, exception management with time-bounded risk acceptance, and integration with change management processes.

Payback period The time required for cumulative project benefits to equal the initial investment. Payback period is a straightforward financial metric accessible to non-technical stakeholders, but should not be the sole evaluation criterion. A longer payback period may still represent a sound investment if the project removes significant risk or enables critical strategic capability. See also: *ROI, NPV, Business case.*

PCI DSS (Payment Card Industry Data Security Standard) A security standard developed by the PCI Security Standards Council governing how organizations that handle payment card data must protect cardholder information. PCI DSS mandates specific technical controls including network segmentation, encryption, access restriction, and continuous monitoring of cardholder data environments. See also: *HIPAA, GDPR, Compliance.*

PDCA (Plan-Do-Check-Act) A four-stage iterative management cycle, adapted from W. Edwards Deming's quality management principles, used to drive continuous improvement. Plan: identify the objective and design the change. Do: implement on a small scale. Check: evaluate results against expectations. Act: standardize the improvement or adjust and repeat. Widely applied in IT operations and quality management programs.

PDU (Power Distribution Unit) A device used in data centers to distribute electrical power from a circuit to multiple IT equipment loads. Intelligent PDUs provide real-time monitoring of power consumption at the outlet level, enabling load balancing, capacity planning, and early detection of overload conditions. See also: *UPS, ATS.*

PI Planning (Program Increment Planning) A SAFe ceremony in which all teams on an Agile Release Train (ART) come together for two days to plan the next program increment, typically eight to twelve weeks of work. PI Planning aligns teams around shared objectives, surfaces dependencies, identifies risks, and produces a set of team PI Objectives that connect execution to business outcomes. See also: *SAFe, ART.*

PMO (Project Management Office) An organizational function that standardizes project management practices, maintains project portfolio visibility, ensures governance compliance, and supports project managers with templates, tools, and methodology guidance. PMO models range from supportive (advisory) to directive (controlling all project delivery) depending on organizational maturity and structure.

Post-incident review (PIR) A structured review conducted after a significant incident to document what happened, analyze root causes, evaluate the effectiveness of the response, and define corrective actions to prevent recurrence. Also called a blameless postmortem in DevOps and SRE contexts. The value of a PIR is in the corrective actions it produces, not the document it generates.

Problem In ITSM, the underlying root cause of one or more incidents. Problem management focuses on identifying, documenting, and permanently resolving problems to prevent incident recurrence, distinct from incident management which focuses on rapid service restoration. See also: *Incident, Problem management, KEDB.*

Problem management The ITSM process responsible for identifying the root causes of incidents, managing known errors, and implementing permanent fixes to prevent recurrence. Problem management operates on a longer timescale than incident management and is measured by reduction in recurring incidents rather than speed of resolution. See also: *ITIL, KEDB, RCA.*

PUE (Power Usage Effectiveness) A data center efficiency metric developed by The Green Grid, calculated as total facility energy divided by IT equipment energy. A PUE of 1.0 represents perfect efficiency. Modern facilities typically target a PUE between 1.2 and 1.4. PUE trending over time identifies waste in cooling, power distribution, or lighting that can be addressed through operational or infrastructure improvements. See also: *Hot aisle / Cold aisle containment.*

R

RACI matrix A responsibility assignment framework that maps four roles to tasks or decisions: Responsible (does the work), Accountable (owns the outcome), Consulted (provides input before the decision), and Informed (receives updates on outcomes). RACI is used in IT project management and ITSM to eliminate ownership ambiguity and clarify decision authority across multi-team initiatives.

RAID (Redundant Array of Independent Disks) A disk configuration approach that spreads data, redundancy information, or both across multiple drives so a single drive failure does not immediately cause data loss. Protection level depends on the RAID type: some configurations mirror data, while others use parity for reconstruction. The tradeoff is typically among write performance, storage efficiency, and fault tolerance.

RCA (Root Cause Analysis) A structured investigation technique used in problem management to identify the underlying cause of an incident or recurring failure rather than addressing symptoms alone. Common RCA techniques include the 5 Whys (associated with the Toyota Production System), Fishbone diagrams (developed by Kaoru Ishikawa), and Fault Tree Analysis. Effective RCA aims for clarity and preventive action, not blame assignment. See also: *Problem management, KEDB.*

Redundancy The duplication of critical components or systems so that a single failure does not interrupt service. Redundancy must be evaluated end to end across compute, storage, network, power, and control plane dependencies. A redundant design is only as reliable as its least-redundant dependency. See also: *Fault tolerance, High availability.*

Replication The process of copying data from one system or location to another to support availability, resilience, and disaster recovery. Replication may be synchronous (writes committed to both locations simultaneously) or asynchronous (updates transferred with a delay). Replication supports fast recovery from hardware and site failures but does not protect against logical corruption or ransomware that propagates to the secondary before detection. See also: *Synchronous replication*, *Asynchronous replication*, *Snapshots*.

Risk register A living document that catalogs identified risks across a project or operational environment, including their probability, potential impact, named owner, mitigation or contingency plan, and current status. Effective risk registers are reviewed on a defined cadence, updated as conditions change, and used to drive decisions rather than filed as compliance artifacts.

ROI (Return on Investment) A financial metric calculated as (Net Benefit / Total Cost) × 100, expressing the return on an investment as a percentage of its cost. In IT business cases, Total Cost should include all implementation and ongoing operational costs, and Net Benefit should be limited to defensible, measurable savings or value rather than aspirational projections. See also: *NPV*, *Payback period*, *Business case*.

RPO (Recovery Point Objective) The maximum age of data that an organization can recover to without unacceptable business impact following a disruption. An RPO of 15 minutes means the organization must be able to restore to a state no older than 15 minutes before the event. RPO drives replication frequency and backup cadence decisions. See also: *RTO*, *MTD*, *BIA*.

RTO (Recovery Time Objective) The maximum duration the organization can tolerate before a disrupted service must be restored to operational status. RTO drives the technical design of recovery solutions; tighter RTOs require more expensive infrastructure such as hot sites and synchronous replication. RTO must be set within the bounds of the Maximum Tolerable Downtime determined by the business. See also: *RPO*, *MTD*, *BIA*.

Runbook A documented procedure that provides step-by-step instructions for executing a specific operational task, responding to a known incident type, or recovering a service. Effective runbooks include trigger conditions, prerequisites, decision points, validation checks, rollback steps, and escalation triggers. A runbook that cannot be followed by a qualified engineer who did not write it has not been completed. See also: *SOP*, *KEDB*.

S

SAFe (Scaled Agile Framework) A proprietary framework developed by Scaled Agile, Inc. for coordinating multiple Agile teams working toward the same product, platform, or business outcome. SAFe organizes delivery across team, program, and portfolio layers, with Agile Release Trains (ARTs) as the primary coordination structure. Suited for large enterprises with heavy cross-team dependencies and a need for portfolio-level governance. See also: *Agile, ART, PI Planning*.

SAN (Storage Area Network) A high-speed dedicated network that connects servers to shared storage arrays using protocols such as Fibre Channel or iSCSI. SANs provide block-level storage access with low latency and high throughput, making them suitable for mission-critical databases and performance-sensitive workloads. See also: *NAS, DAS.*

SD-WAN (Software-Defined Wide Area Network) A WAN architecture that uses a centralized controller to manage routing policies, security settings, and traffic steering across multiple transport links (MPLS, broadband, cellular). SD-WAN enables application-aware routing, dynamic path selection based on real-time link conditions, and centralized policy management without site-by-site configuration. See also: *MPLS, WAN.*

Scrum An Agile framework, defined in the Scrum Guide by Ken Schwaber and Jeff Sutherland, that organizes delivery into fixed-length sprints (typically two to four weeks). Scrum includes defined ceremonies (sprint planning, daily stand-up, sprint review, sprint retrospective) and roles (Product Owner, Scrum Master, Development Team). See also: *Agile, Kanban, SAFe.*

SIEM (Security Information and Event Management) A platform that aggregates, correlates, and analyzes security event data from across the IT environment to detect threats, support investigations, and maintain audit trails. SIEM platforms collect data from firewalls, identity systems, endpoints, servers, and applications, and apply rules, behavioral analytics, and threat intelligence to surface actionable alerts.

SLA (Service Level Agreement) A formal commitment between a service provider and a consumer that defines the expected level of service performance, including availability targets, response times, and resolution timelines. SLAs in IT are used both externally (with customers or vendors) and internally (between IT and business units). Breach of SLA typically triggers defined consequences such as service credits or escalation. See also: *SLO, KPI.*

SLO (Service Level Objective) An internal performance target used to measure and manage service quality, typically set more conservatively than the external SLA to provide a buffer for detection and response before an SLA breach occurs. SLOs are used in SRE practices to define the acceptable error budget for a service. See also: *SLA.*

Snapshot A point-in-time copy that preserves the state of a system, volume, or dataset at a specific moment. Snapshots are used for rapid recovery from accidental deletion, corruption, or ransomware events. Most modern platforms implement snapshots incrementally, storing only changed data blocks after the initial capture. Snapshots reside on the same storage platform as the source data and are not a substitute for independent backups. See also: *Replication, Deduplication.*

SOC 2 Type II An attestation standard developed by the American Institute of Certified Public Accountants (AICPA) that evaluates whether a service organization's security, availability, processing integrity, confidentiality, and privacy controls are consistently applied over a defined audit period, typically six to twelve months. SOC 2 Type II is commonly required by enterprise customers evaluating vendors who handle their data. See also: *ISO/IEC 27001, Compliance.*

SOP (Standard Operating Procedure) A documented, step-by-step procedure for performing a routine or repeatable task consistently. SOPs reduce dependence on individual knowledge, support training, and provide the evidence basis for operational consistency and audit readiness. An SOP that cannot be followed by a qualified person who did not write it has not been completed. See also: *Runbook.*

Standardization The practice of establishing and enforcing consistent designs, configurations, processes, and documentation formats across an IT environment. Standardization reduces operational variability, simplifies support, improves monitoring coverage, and enables automation. Environments with low standardization tend to accumulate configuration drift, tribal knowledge dependencies, and audit risk.

STP (Spanning Tree Protocol) A Layer 2 network protocol that prevents switching loops by logically blocking redundant paths between network switches. Loops in switched networks cause broadcast storms and network instability. Rapid STP (RSTP) is the modern implementation, providing faster convergence than the original protocol.

Synchronous replication A data replication method where writes are committed to both primary and secondary systems before the write is acknowledged as complete. Synchronous replication ensures data consistency between sites but requires low-latency, high-bandwidth connectivity to avoid degrading write performance. Used where RPO of near-zero is required and the sites are geographically close. See also: *Asynchronous replication, Replication.*

T

Terraform An open-source Infrastructure as Code tool developed by HashiCorp that defines and provisions infrastructure through declarative configuration files. Terraform manages infrastructure state, plans changes before applying them, and supports multiple cloud providers and on-premises systems through a provider plugin model. See also: *IaC, Ansible.*

Tiering (storage) A storage management approach that places data on different classes of storage based on access frequency, performance requirements, and cost. High-performance storage (NVMe-based SSDs) holds frequently accessed data; lower-cost tiers (HDD, object storage, cloud archive) hold infrequently accessed or archival data. Automated tiering systems monitor access patterns and relocate data without manual intervention. See also: *Deduplication, Snapshots*.

Tier classification (data center) A framework published by the Uptime Institute that defines four levels of data center infrastructure reliability and redundancy. Tier I provides a single path for power and cooling with no redundancy. Tier II adds redundant capacity components. Tier III is designed for concurrent maintainability, allowing maintenance without service interruption. Tier IV is fully fault-tolerant with redundancy across all critical systems. See also: *Uptime Institute*.

U

UPS (Uninterruptible Power Supply) A battery-backed power device that provides temporary power during utility outages and conditions power to protect sensitive electronics from voltage sags and spikes. In data centers, the UPS bridges the gap between utility failure and generator startup. UPS runtime, load capacity, and transfer behavior must be validated under real load conditions, not just on paper. See also: *ATS, PDU, Generator*.

Uptime Institute An independent organization that developed and maintains the Tier Standard for data center infrastructure reliability. The Tier Standard defines four levels of site infrastructure capability (Tier I through Tier IV) based on redundancy, concurrent maintainability, and fault tolerance. Tier certification requires independent assessment by the Uptime Institute. See also: *Tier classification*.

V

Virtual machine (VM) A software-based emulation of a physical computer that runs on a hypervisor and shares the underlying hardware resources of the host. Virtual machines provide isolation between workloads, enable rapid provisioning and migration, and support disaster recovery through snapshots and live migration capabilities. See also: *Hypervisor, Virtualization, Container.*

Virtualization The abstraction of physical hardware resources (compute, storage, network) into software-defined entities that can be provisioned, moved, and scaled independently of the underlying hardware. Virtualization is the foundational technology beneath private cloud, public cloud, and hybrid infrastructure. See also: *Hypervisor, Virtual machine, Container.*

VLAN (Virtual Local Area Network) A logical network segment created within a physical switched network that isolates traffic between groups of devices without requiring separate physical infrastructure. VLANs improve security by separating traffic between departments or device types, reduce broadcast domain size, and support network policy enforcement at the access layer. See also: *Segmentation, Micro-segmentation.*

Vulnerability management The operational discipline of continuously identifying, prioritizing, remediating, and verifying security weaknesses across IT systems. Effective vulnerability management defines severity-based response SLAs, tracks remediation to closure, manages exceptions with time-bounded risk acceptance, and reports outcomes to leadership in terms of exposure reduction rather than scan volume. See also: *CVSS, Patch management.*

W

WAN (Wide Area Network) A network that connects geographically distributed sites, data centers, or cloud environments. Traditional WAN technologies include MPLS and leased lines. Modern WAN architectures increasingly use SD-WAN to combine multiple transport types with centralized policy management. WAN performance directly affects the user experience for cloud applications and remote work tools. See also: *SD-WAN, MPLS.*

Warm site A disaster recovery facility with some infrastructure pre-deployed and data replication established, requiring configuration completion and application validation before becoming fully operational. Warm sites balance cost and recovery speed, typically supporting RTOs measured in hours. See also: *Hot site, Cold site, Cloud DR.*

Waterfall A linear, sequential project delivery methodology in which each phase must be completed and formally approved before the next begins. Waterfall is well-suited to projects with stable, well-defined requirements, regulated documentation requirements, and sequential engineering dependencies. Less suitable for projects where requirements evolve or where late-stage changes are expensive. See also: *Agile, Hybrid methodology.*

WBS (Work Breakdown Structure) A hierarchical decomposition of project scope into progressively smaller work packages that can be owned, estimated, and tracked. The WBS is the foundational structure for schedule development, cost estimation, resource assignment, and scope change control. Defined in PMI's Practice Standard for Work Breakdown Structures. See also: *Project charter, Scope statement.*

Z

Zero Trust A security architecture principle that treats no device, user, or network location as inherently trustworthy. Every access request is evaluated based on identity, device posture, context, and least-privilege authorization, regardless of whether the request originates inside or outside the corporate network. Zero Trust reduces lateral movement risk and limits the blast radius of compromised credentials or endpoints. The concept was formalized in NIST SP 800-207. See also: *NAC, IAM, Micro-segmentation, Lateral movement.*

Terms in this glossary reflect usage as defined or applied in this book. Where frameworks are referenced (ITIL, NIST, PMI, ISO, SAFe, Uptime Institute, The Green Grid), readers should consult the current published editions of those standards for authoritative definitions.

INDEX

Page numbers refer to printed pages. Topics defined in the Glossary may also appear in chapter discussions listed below.

W

Z

Trademark Disclaimer

All product names, trademarks, registered trademarks, service marks, company names, brand names, and logos referenced in this publication are the property of their respective owners. Use of these names, marks, and brands does not imply endorsement, affiliation, sponsorship, or recommendation by the respective trademark holders. The author and publisher acknowledge the proprietary rights of all trademark owners referenced throughout this book.

The following trademarks and registered trademarks are referenced within this publication and are acknowledged as the property of their respective owners:

Active Directory® - Microsoft Corporation
Agile® - Agile Alliance®
Amazon CloudWatch® - Amazon Web Services, Inc.
Amazon EC2® - Amazon Web Services, Inc.
Amazon Web Services® (AWS®) - Amazon Web Services, Inc.
Ansible® - Red Hat, Inc.
AppDynamics® - Cisco Systems, Inc.
Asana® - Asana, Inc.
AWS CloudFormation - Amazon Web Services, Inc.
AWS Config - Amazon Web Services, Inc.
AWS Organizations - Amazon Web Services, Inc.
AXELOS® - AXELOS Limited
Azure® - Microsoft Corporation
Azure Active Directory® - Microsoft Corporation
Azure DevOps® - Microsoft Corporation
Azure Monitor - Microsoft Corporation
Azure Network Watcher - Microsoft Corporation
Azure Policy - Microsoft Corporation
Azure Site Recovery® - Microsoft Corporation
BMC Helix - BMC Software, Inc.
BMC Remedy® - BMC Software, Inc.
Chef® - Progress Software Corporation
Cisco® - Cisco Systems, Inc.
Cisco DNA Center® - Cisco Systems, Inc.
Cisco ThousandEyes® - Cisco Systems, Inc.
Cisco Umbrella® - Cisco Systems, Inc.
COBIT® - ISACA®
Confluence® - Atlassian Corporation Plc
CrowdStrike® - CrowdStrike Holdings, Inc.
Datadog® - Datadog, Inc.
Docker® - Docker, Inc.
Dynatrace® - Dynatrace LLC
FFIEC - Federal Financial Institutions Examination Council
GDPR - European Union
GitHub® - GitHub, Inc.
Google Cloud® - Google LLC

Grafana® – Grafana Labs
Green Grid® / PUE™ – The Green Grid Association
HIPAA – United States Department of Health and Human Services
Hyper-V® – Microsoft Corporation
ISO/IEC 27001 / ISO 22301 – International Organization for Standardization
ITIL® – PeopleCert Group
Jenkins® – LF Charities Inc.
Jira® – Atlassian Corporation Plc
Juniper Apstra® – Juniper Networks, Inc.
Kanban® – Kanban University® / associated trademark holders
Kubernetes® – The Linux Foundation®
KVM® – Red Hat, Inc.
Linux® – Linus Torvalds
Microsoft® – Microsoft Corporation
Microsoft 365® – Microsoft Corporation
Microsoft Defender® – Microsoft Corporation
Microsoft Entra ID® – Microsoft Corporation
Microsoft Excel® – Microsoft Corporation
Microsoft Forms – Microsoft Corporation
Microsoft Power BI® – Microsoft Corporation
Microsoft Project® – Microsoft Corporation
Microsoft Sentinel® – Microsoft Corporation
Microsoft SharePoint® – Microsoft Corporation
Microsoft Teams® – Microsoft Corporation
Microsoft Word® – Microsoft Corporation
Nagios® – Nagios Enterprises, LLC
New Relic® – New Relic, Inc.
NIST – National Institute of Standards and Technology
Office 365® – Microsoft Corporation
Okta® – Okta, Inc.
OpenShift® – Red Hat, Inc.
Outlook® – Microsoft Corporation
PCI DSS® – PCI Security Standards Council
PMBOK® Guide – Project Management Institute, Inc.
PMI® – Project Management Institute, Inc.
PMP® – Project Management Institute, Inc.
Podman® – Red Hat, Inc.
PowerShell® – Microsoft Corporation
Primavera® – Oracle Corporation
PRINCE2® – AXELOS Limited
Prometheus® – The Linux Foundation®
PRTG Network Monitor® – Paessler AG
Puppet® – Perforce Software, Inc.
Qualys® – Qualys, Inc.
Rapid7® – Rapid7, Inc.
Red Hat® – Red Hat, Inc.
SAFe® – Scaled Agile, Inc.
Salesforce® – Salesforce, Inc.
Scrum® – Scrum Alliance®, Inc.
ServiceNow® – ServiceNow, Inc.
Slack® – Slack Technologies, LLC
Smartsheet® – Smartsheet Inc.

SOC 2® – American Institute of Certified Public Accountants (AICPA)
SolarWinds® – SolarWinds Worldwide, LLC
Splunk® – Cisco Systems, Inc.
Tableau® – Salesforce, Inc.
Tenable® – Tenable, Inc.
Terraform® – HashiCorp, Inc.
Ubuntu® – Canonical Ltd.
Uptime Institute® Tier Standard – Uptime Institute, LLC
Veeam® – Veeam Software Group GmbH
VirtualBox® – Oracle Corporation
VMware® – VMware, Inc.
VMware ESXi™ – VMware, Inc.
VMware vCenter™ – VMware, Inc.
VMware Workstation™ – VMware, Inc.
WhatsApp® – WhatsApp LLC
Windows Server® – Microsoft Corporation
Workday® – Workday, Inc.
XenServer® – Citrix Systems, Inc.
Zabbix® – Zabbix LLC

www.ingramcontent.com/pod-product-compliance
Lightning Source LLC
LaVergne TN
LVHW050906210926
848482LV00012B/360
* 9 7 9 8 9 9 2 2 7 9 5 5 9 *